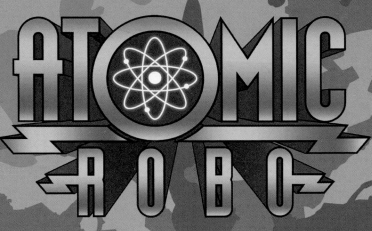

# ATOMIC ROBO

## VOLUME TWO

★ ★ ★

## ATOMIC ROBO AND THE DOGS OF WAR

D0475107

Publishers
PAUL ENS and SCOTT CHITWOOD

Graphic Design
JEFF POWELL

ATOMIC ROBO VOLUME TWO: ATOMIC ROBO and the DOGS OF WAR

Copyright © 2008, 2009. All rights reserved. Atomic Robo, the Atomic Robo logo, and all
characters, likeness and situations featured herein are trademarks and/or registered
trademarks of Brian Clevinger and Scott Wegener. Except for review purposes, no portion
of this publication may be reproduced or transmitted, in any form or by any means,
without the express written permission of Red 5 Comics, Ltd.  All names, characters,
locations and events in this publication are fictional. Any resemblance to actual persons
(living or dead), events, institutions, or locales, without satiric intent, is coincidental.

This volume collects ATOMIC ROBO: DOGS OF WAR #1 through #5 of the comic-book series
originally printed by Red 5 Comics.

Published by
RED 5 COMICS
298 Tuscany Vista Rd NW, Calgary, Alberta, Canada, T3L 3B4

www.red5comics.com

To find a comics shop in your area, call the Comic Shop Locator Service toll-free
at 1-888-266-4226

First edition:
ISBN-13: 978-0-9809302-2-1

Printed in Canada.

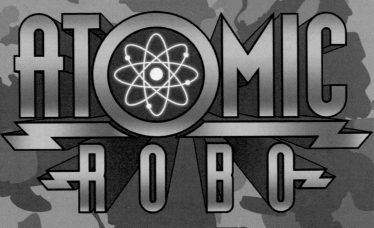

# VOLUME TWO

★ ★ ★

# ATOMIC ROBO AND THE DOGS OF WAR

**WORDS**
**BRIAN CLEVINGER**

★ ★ ★

**ART**
**SCOTT WEGENER**

★ ★ ★

**COLORS**
**RONDA PATTISON**

★ ★ ★

**LETTERS**
**JEFF POWELL**

www.red5comics.com // www.atomic-robo.com

"Why World War II?" We got asked that a lot. And then Brian and I would stare blankly at each other through the Internet and wonder, "How can we not?" It was then that we had to remind ourselves that most people are not the huge history nerds that we are. So I'll tell you why.

The events of the 1930's and 40's radically altered our world. Not a country, not a region, The World. Over 60 million people lost their lives. For perspective, that's the entire population of the UK in 2007. Judaism was almost annihilated, and an isolated second-rate player on the national stage became the sole superpower to survive into the 21st century.

My mother is from Scotland, and her parents lived through that war. My Gran once told me about watching the blitz on London from the rooftop of the hospital where she worked; my grandfather told me about hiding in a ruined French barn while panzers rolled past outside. After an eye-injury forced him out of the Army, Grandpa became a merchant sailor and survived the Battle of the Atlantic. To this day, one of my most prizes possessions is a small newspaper clipping describing how his ship was torpedoed but he and three others returned safely home.

As a kid on Staten Island, my grandparents were everything to me. I worshiped them. They talked funny, took tea at 4 o'clock, called oatmeal porridge, and watched football on the Spanish channels because American's were too dumb to broadcast "the Beautiful Game". My grandfather more than anyone shaped the man I am today, and in everything I do I am constantly comparing my actions to what I think he would have done. Because he and my Gran spoke so little about the war, it made me want to know more, as a way of better understanding who they were.

So that, more than anything else for me, is why we had to do an Atomic Robo Weird War II book.

This is for my Grandpa. James "Scottie" Milligan.

-Scott Wegener

When my grandfather died in April of 2006, I had the horrible realization that I never got to know him as well as I'd have liked. Partly it was that I never seriously believed there could be a time when he wouldn't be there. He always had an energy to him. It's the kind of thing would make you say he had a "youthful" quality, but that's not really it. He was a force of nature. He was as inevitable as gravity.

I mean, the man fought to get into Vietnam. Fought! He was forty-two at the time and he gave up his rank in one branch of the military to join another so he could get into the war. Why would anyone do that? Well, if you asked him, he'd have said something about how he couldn't stand the idea of someone else's son going to that war, maybe to die, when he could do the same job.

You hear a thing like that growing up, it makes an impression on you.

You can find a lot of my grandfather in Robo. I didn't mean for it to turn out that way, but I suppose it was inevitable that I would invent a short, wise-cracking, unstoppable old hero given that I'd grown up around one. Their lives even mirror one another. They were both born in the .20s. They were both the sons of immigrants. They both owed a great deal to the military, and served proudly, but neither was defined by it or afraid to speak against it when the cause was not just. And they both do what they do so a stranger's son doesn't have to put his life on the line to do it.

But, it's the little things too.

Grandpa had a thing about science fiction. There was this one time we watched the Star Wars films with him, probably a Thanksgiving Day marathon on television ages ago. He spent the entire time complaining about the gross military inaccuracies. AT-ATs, for instance, offended him because, he said, any society technologically advanced enough to trivialize interstellar travel would have long since abandoned lumbering walker-type tanks in favor of faster hovering tanks that a plucky resistance can't ever trip.

I think that moment is more responsible for the world of Atomic Robo than anything else.

I wish he had lived to see this comic book. I think he'd have appreciated that our ridiculous science fiction makes some kind of sense. Like hovering tanks.

This book is for Michael J. Novosel.

-Brian Clevinger

## Introduction:

Okay -- I have to tell my Scott Wegener story before I do anything else, because any time Scott has come up, or ATOMIC ROBO has come up, in the last year or so, I tell this story regardless of anything. It's a way to, uh, purge my guilty conscience or something, I dunno. I figure putting it into the intro for this second ATOMIC ROBO collection ought to burn off a lot of guilt in one go. So, okay, Wegener:

My son was born about three weeks early. Not early-early, not trouble-early, just early enough to knock my schedule out of whack. Wah wah, I know. I had one script I wanted to have done before the little guy showed up and I didn't get it done. Before we're out of the hospital I had to start noodling around on the thing. Scott's gonna draw it. And I have to get it to him in pieces, or at least I sent it to editorial in pieces, because, well, new baby. I'd be up a couple days, crank out a few pages before sleeping a couple hours, send it in, get back to the baby for another day and a half, repeat. In short, it's a thing that's being written in a state of blind exhaustion. I had an outline to follow, so the heavy lifting was done (for me, that part is the heavy lifting); I just had to, y'know, follow the damn thing.

Right. Okay. So as Scott starts drawing it, he'd send in these polite notes -- things like, "Hey guys, on page 4, he's leaving a room with a lead pipe and a shotgun, then on page 5, you've got him coming into a new room with a chainsaw, seventeen rabid dogs, and clown shoes. I'll just stick with the lead pipe, okay?"

And again. And again. And AGAIN. I'd written this script in a fugue state of baby-daddy exhaustion, blowing continuity in-between page-flips and scenes. Amateur mistake 101. I felt so embarrassed, so sloppy, so... giftless. What a scam. What a hack.

But Scott -- Scott just politely pointed out where I blew it, fixed it like a pro, and never once sneered or mocked me. And, man, I'm telling you, I totally deserved sneering and mockery. The script I was sending in was not fit for human consumption, dear readers. Our man Wegener took the high road AND produced amazing pages; for that, he is hereby known throughout the land as a good egg and is entitled to all the honors and benefits occurring thereto.

So now then: ATOMIC ROBO.

Scott introduced me to the book while we were working together as he'd detected that maybe it would be my thing. A minor underestimation on his point -- my life (in fact all life on Earth) is much better with ATOMIC ROBO in it.

The book had me at the words "Atomic" and "Robo," to tell the truth. The Tesla-invented action-scientist Robo (Brought to you by Tesladyne! If that word, that glorious... what is that, a portmanteau? Sure. If that glorious portmanteau doesn't make you skip to the end of my rigmarole and get to the guts of the story then nothing will, my friends, and you should maybe browse elsewhere) has an rival in the great Professor Stephen Hawking, for god's sake. Even the little details -- Robo wearing a helmet -- intoxicate me. The stuff that pours out of Brian Clevinger's head is my kind of stuff, y'know? The mashing of time periods, the mixing and remixing of genres, the absolute wealth of ideas -- and that's just the guts of the thing. Brian writes as big and as fun as he thinks, if that makes sense, and in Scott Wegener, that prince amongst princes, he's got himself the perfect partner in crime. Together they're making a universe full of charm and wit and the kinds of berserk flights of absolute imagination that drew us all to comics in the first place.

Whenever I get asked "why comics," and I tend to get asked it a fair bit I suppose, I don't exactly lie, but I never exactly tell the whole truth. Here's what I hold back: when I was a kid, making comics gave me the best feeling ever. The blast of building an entire world in my head, the charge that came along with completely unfettering your imagination and just going with it was -- and I don't know if I've ever used this word before to describe anything -- thrilling. There's no other word for it, I suppose. And when I really get going on something, I feel that same thrill I felt then, making comics with crayons or colored pencils, when I write today.

Thing is, I think I can recognize it in other people's work, y'know? You can recognize that energy in the work of someone that feels the infinite possibilities awaiting them. A reader can feel it when a creator feels it and it makes the whole thing that much better.

ATOMIC ROBO is one of those books. Thanks for making it, guys.

Matt Fraction
Kansas City
05 Jan 09

PS: Ronda Pattison will be spoken of one day in the same reverent and celebrated tones as Matt Hollingsworth, Dave Stewart, Val Staples, and Laura Martin. If you don't believe me, just flip the page...

# OPERATION HUSKY

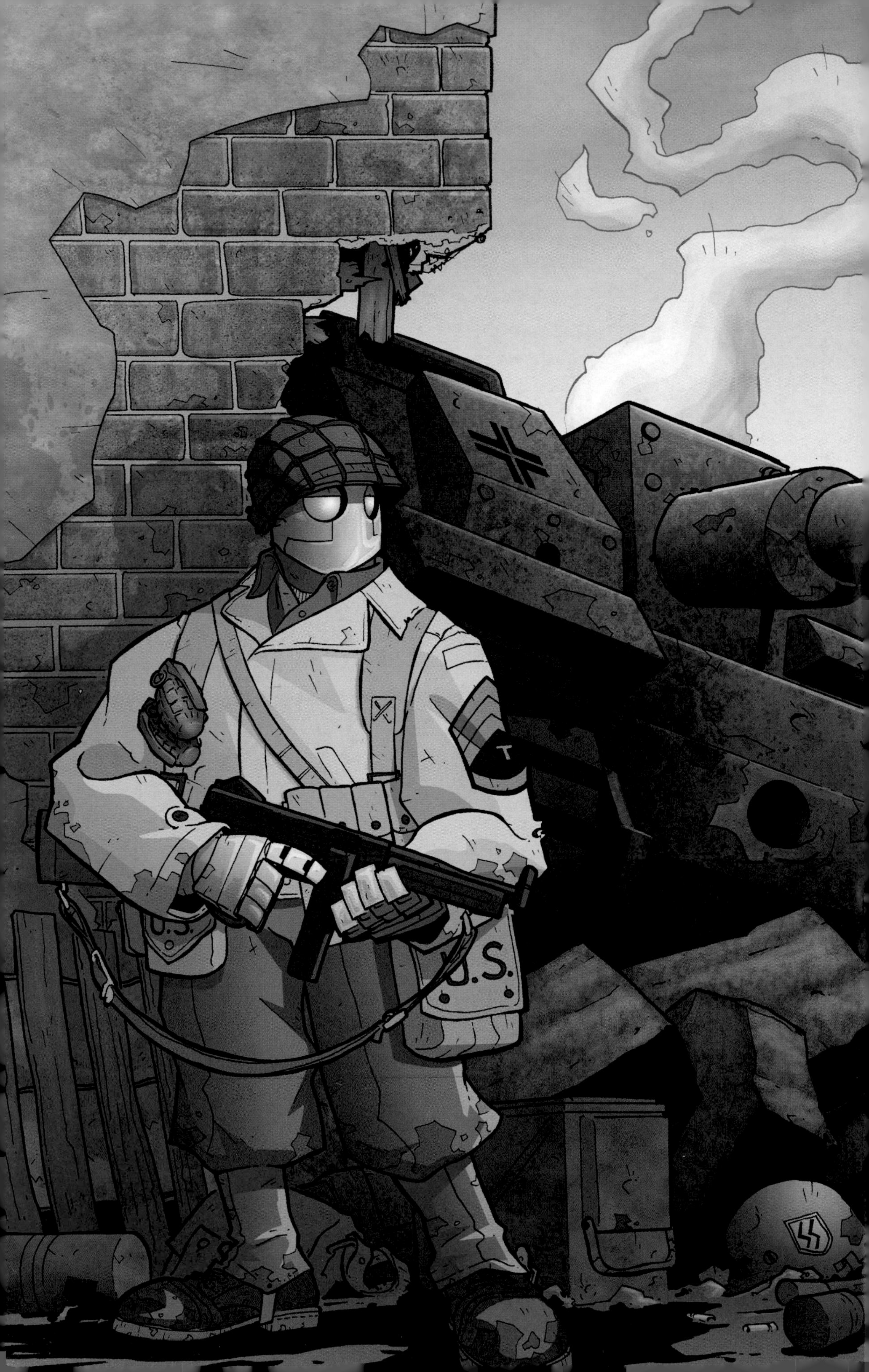
U.S.
U.S.

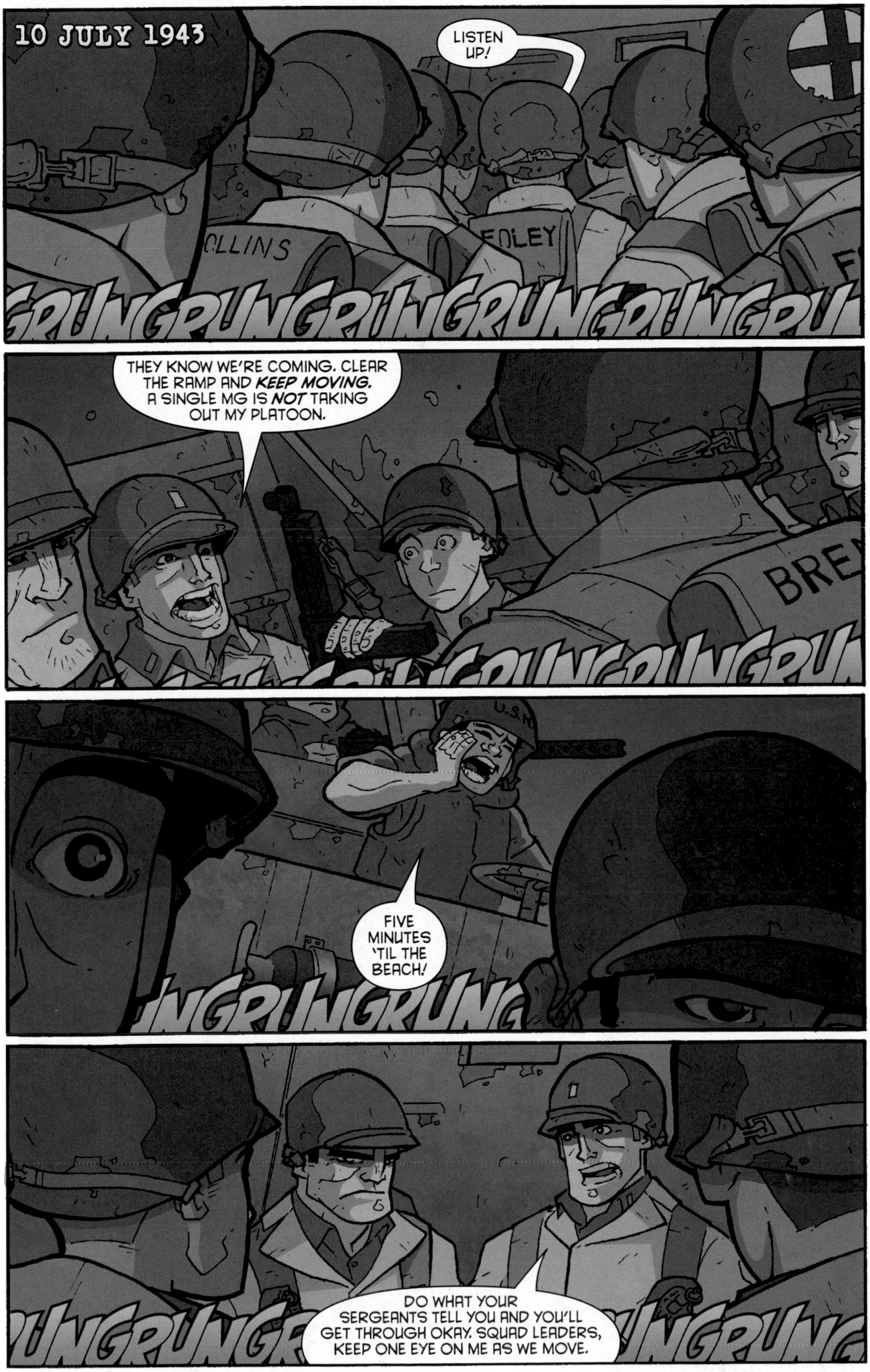
10 JULY 1943
LISTEN UP!
COLLINS
FOLEY
GRUNGRUNGRUNGRUNGRUNGRUNGRU
THEY KNOW WE'RE COMING. CLEAR THE RAMP AND *KEEP MOVING.* A SINGLE MG IS *NOT* TAKING OUT MY PLATOON.
BREN
GRUNGRUNGRUN
FIVE MINUTES 'TIL THE BEACH!
NGRUNGRUNG
DO WHAT YOUR SERGEANTS TELL YOU AND YOU'LL GET THROUGH OKAY. SQUAD LEADERS, KEEP ONE EYE ON ME AS WE MOVE.

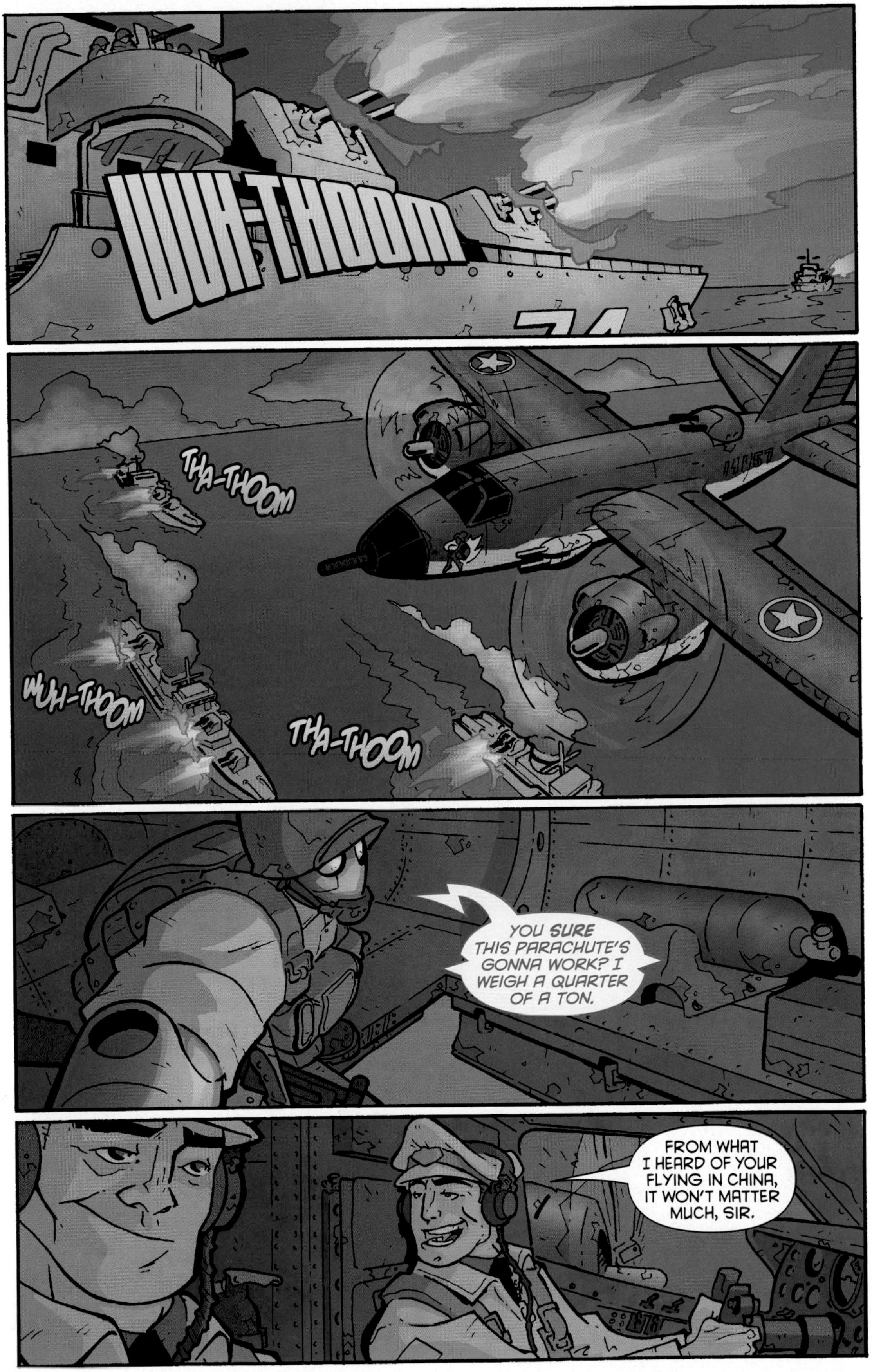
WUH-THOOM
74
THA-THOOM
WUH-THOOM
THA-THOOM
YOU SURE THIS PARACHUTE'S GONNA WORK? I WEIGH A QUARTER OF A TON.
FROM WHAT I HEARD OF YOUR FLYING IN CHINA, IT WON'T MATTER MUCH, SIR.

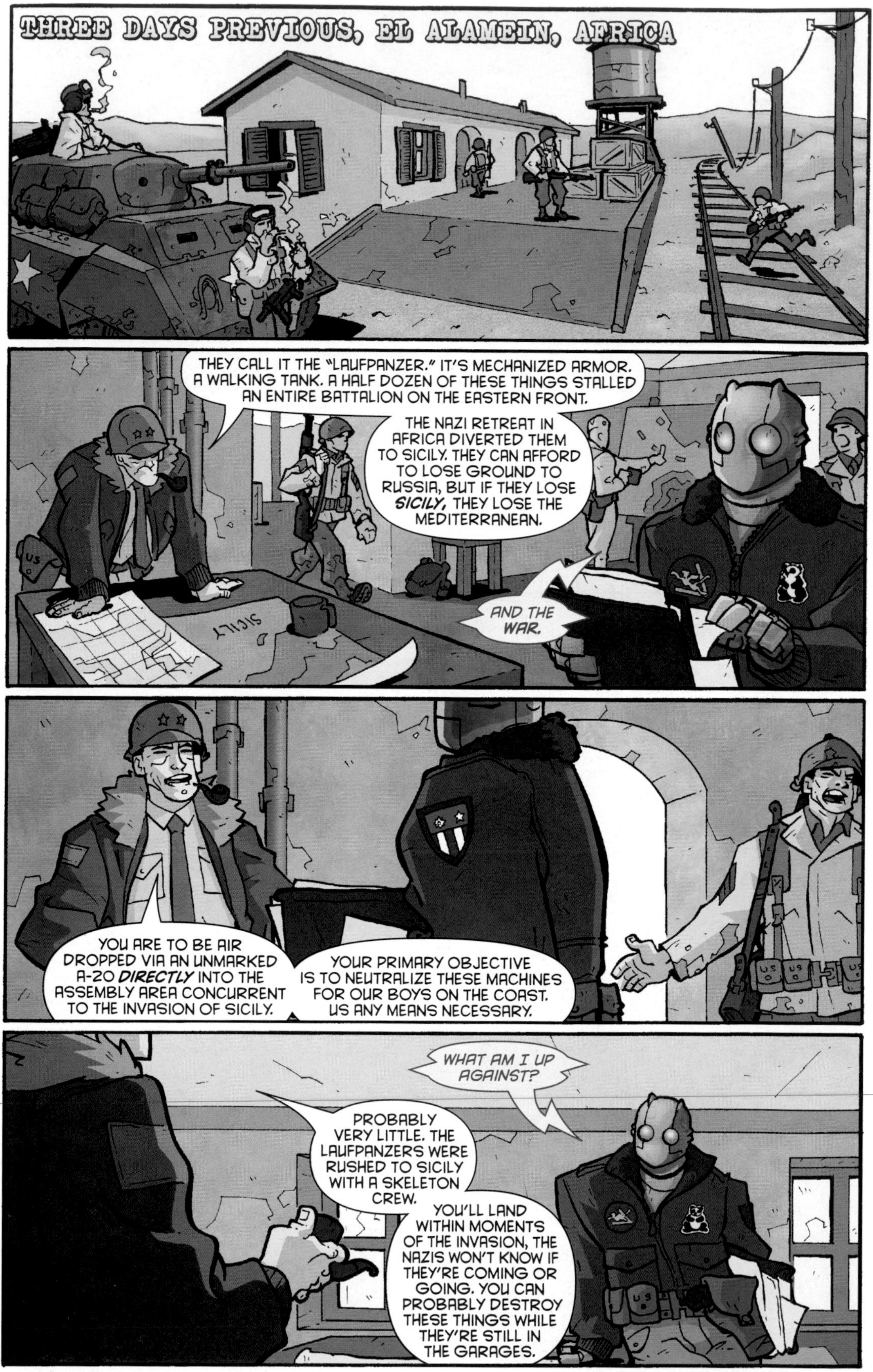
THREE DAYS PREVIOUS, EL ALAMEIN, AFRICA
THEY CALL IT THE "LAUFPANZER." IT'S MECHANIZED ARMOR. A WALKING TANK. A HALF DOZEN OF THESE THINGS STALLED AN ENTIRE BATTALION ON THE EASTERN FRONT.
THE NAZI RETREAT IN AFRICA DIVERTED THEM TO SICILY. THEY CAN AFFORD TO LOSE GROUND TO RUSSIA, BUT IF THEY LOSE SICILY, THEY LOSE THE MEDITERRANEAN.
AND THE WAR.
SICILY
YOU ARE TO BE AIR DROPPED VIA AN UNMARKED A-20 DIRECTLY INTO THE ASSEMBLY AREA CONCURRENT TO THE INVASION OF SICILY.
YOUR PRIMARY OBJECTIVE IS TO NEUTRALIZE THESE MACHINES FOR OUR BOYS ON THE COAST. US ANY MEANS NECESSARY.
WHAT AM I UP AGAINST?
PROBABLY VERY LITTLE. THE LAUFPANZERS WERE RUSHED TO SICILY WITH A SKELETON CREW.
YOU'LL LAND WITHIN MOMENTS OF THE INVASION, THE NAZIS WON'T KNOW IF THEY'RE COMING OR GOING. YOU CAN PROBABLY DESTROY THESE THINGS WHILE THEY'RE STILL IN THE GARAGES.

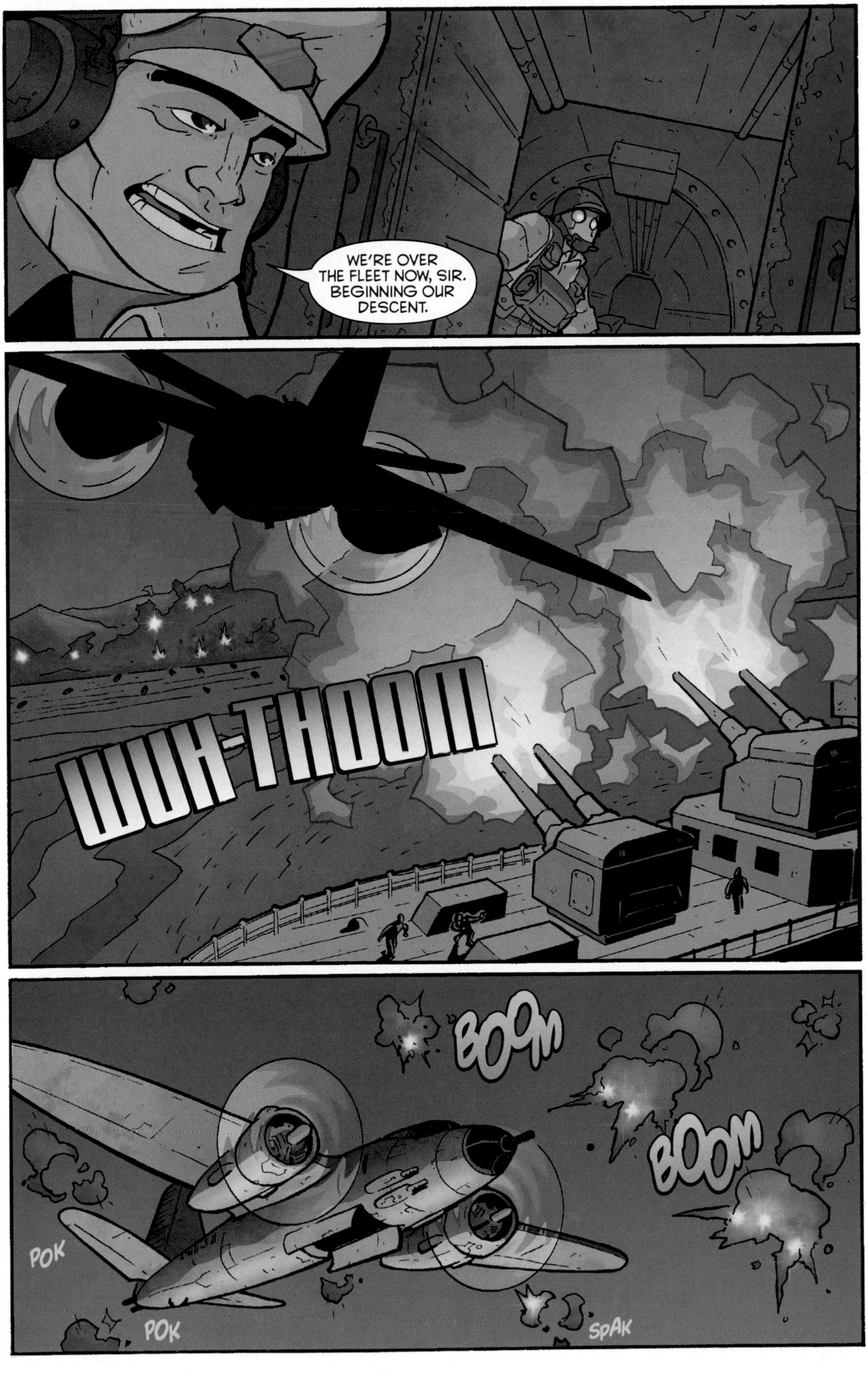
WE'RE OVER THE FLEET NOW, SIR. BEGINNING OUR DESCENT.
WUH-THOOM
BOOM
BOOM
POK
POK
SPAK

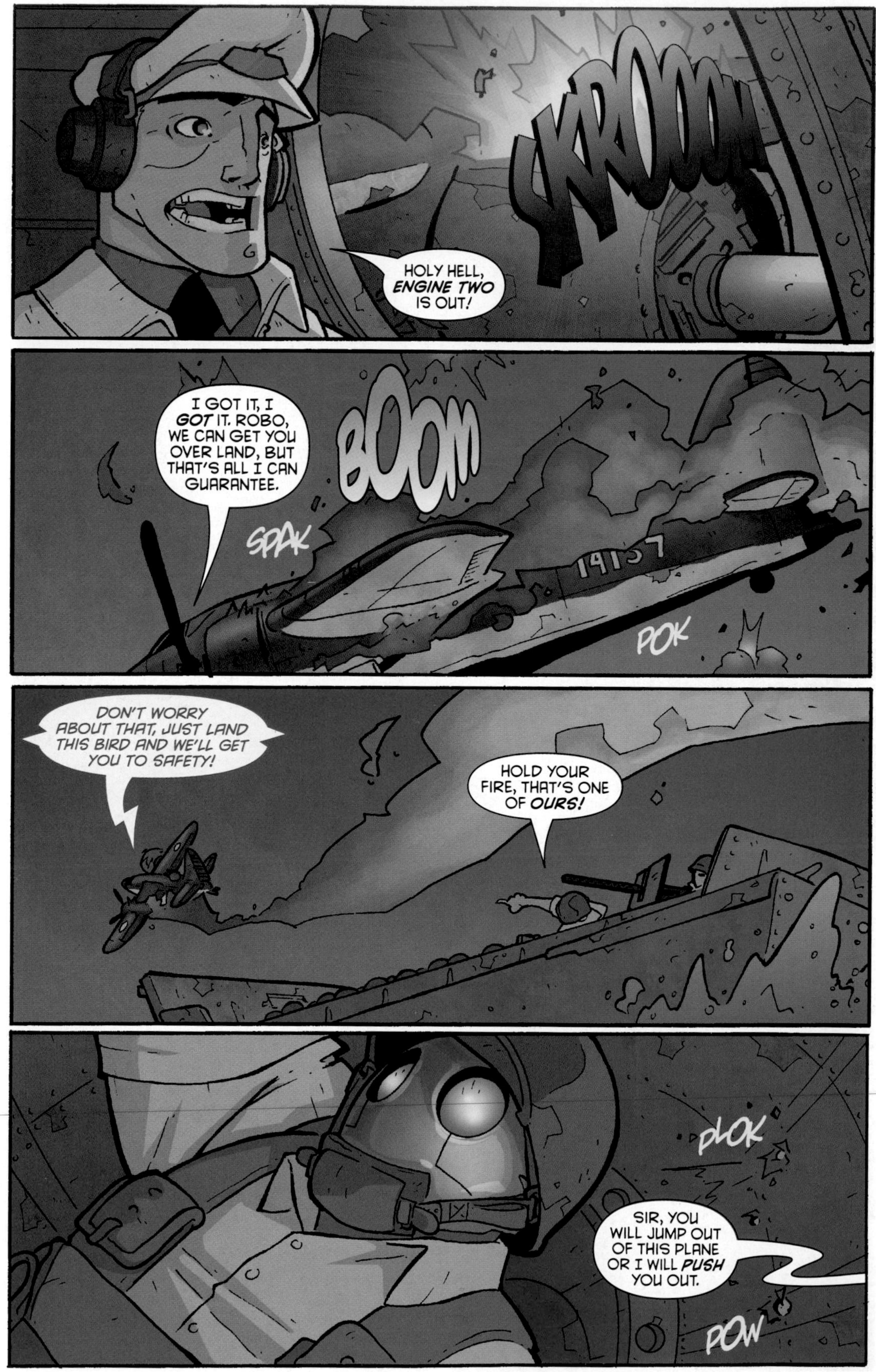
SKROOOM
HOLY HELL, ENGINE TWO IS OUT!
I GOT IT, I GOT IT. ROBO, WE CAN GET YOU OVER LAND, BUT THAT'S ALL I CAN GUARANTEE.
BOOM
SPAK
POK
DON'T WORRY ABOUT THAT, JUST LAND THIS BIRD AND WE'LL GET YOU TO SAFETY!
HOLD YOUR FIRE, THAT'S ONE OF OURS!
PLOK
SIR, YOU WILL JUMP OUT OF THIS PLANE OR I WILL PUSH YOU OUT.
POW

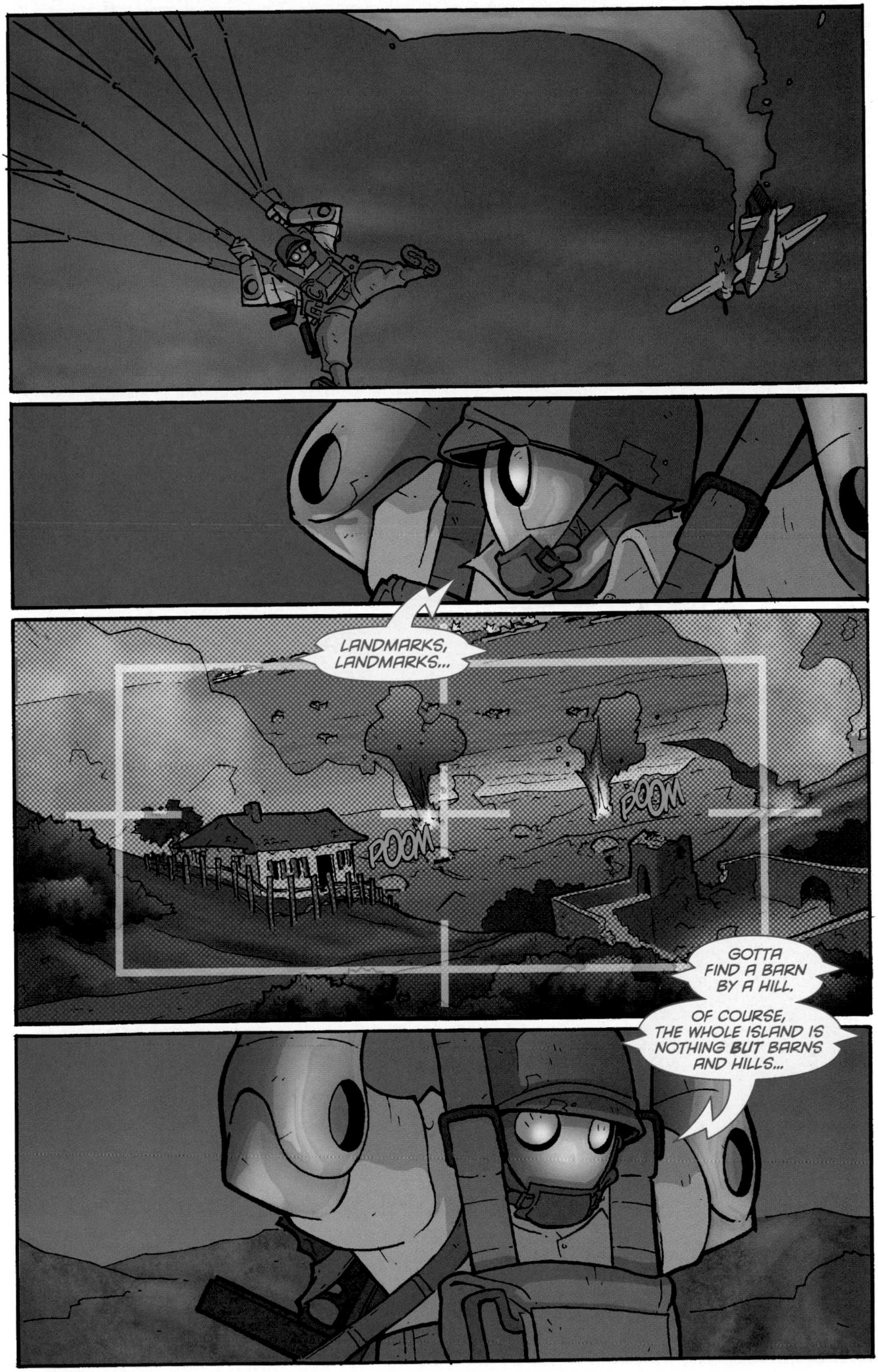
LANDMARKS, LANDMARKS...
POOM
POOM
GOTTA FIND A BARN BY A HILL.
OF COURSE, THE WHOLE ISLAND IS NOTHING BUT BARNS AND HILLS...

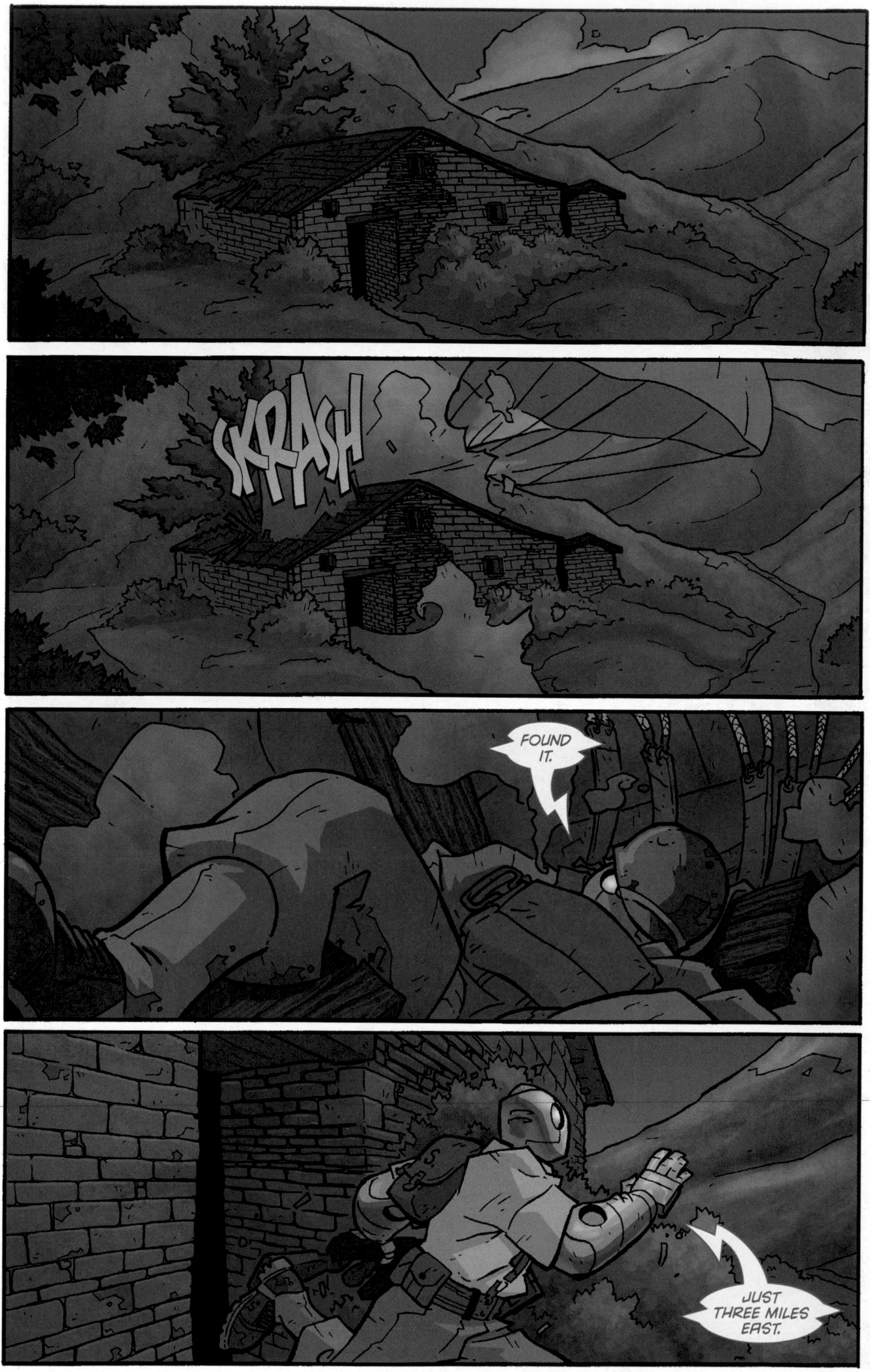
SKRASH
FOUND IT.
JUST THREE MILES EAST.

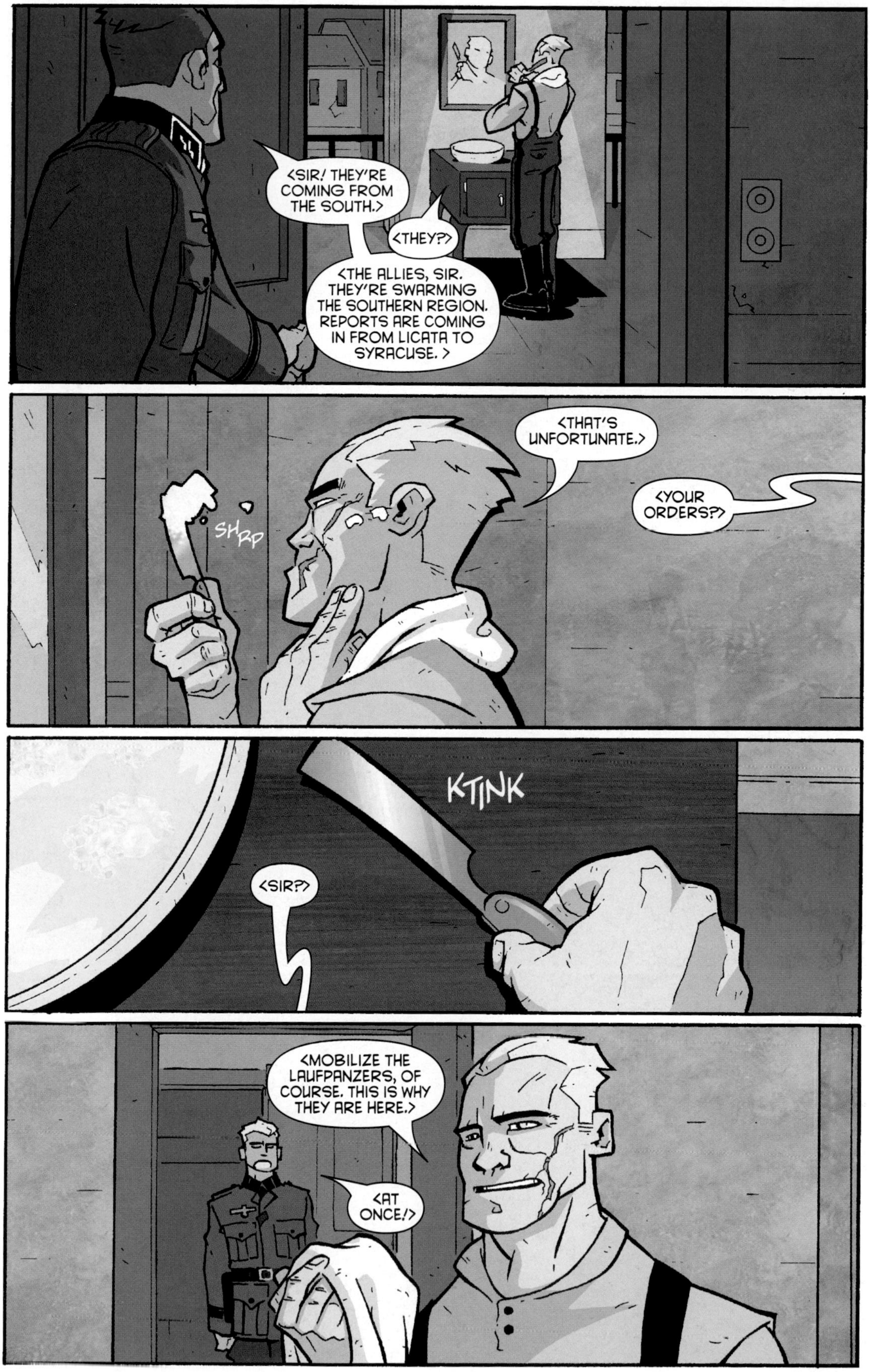
<SIR! THEY'RE COMING FROM THE SOUTH.>
<THEY?>
<THE ALLIES, SIR. THEY'RE SWARMING THE SOUTHERN REGION. REPORTS ARE COMING IN FROM LICATA TO SYRACUSE. >
SHRP
<THAT'S UNFORTUNATE.>
<YOUR ORDERS?>
KTINK
<SIR?>
<MOBILIZE THE LAUFPANZERS, OF COURSE. THIS IS WHY THEY ARE HERE.>
<AT ONCE!>

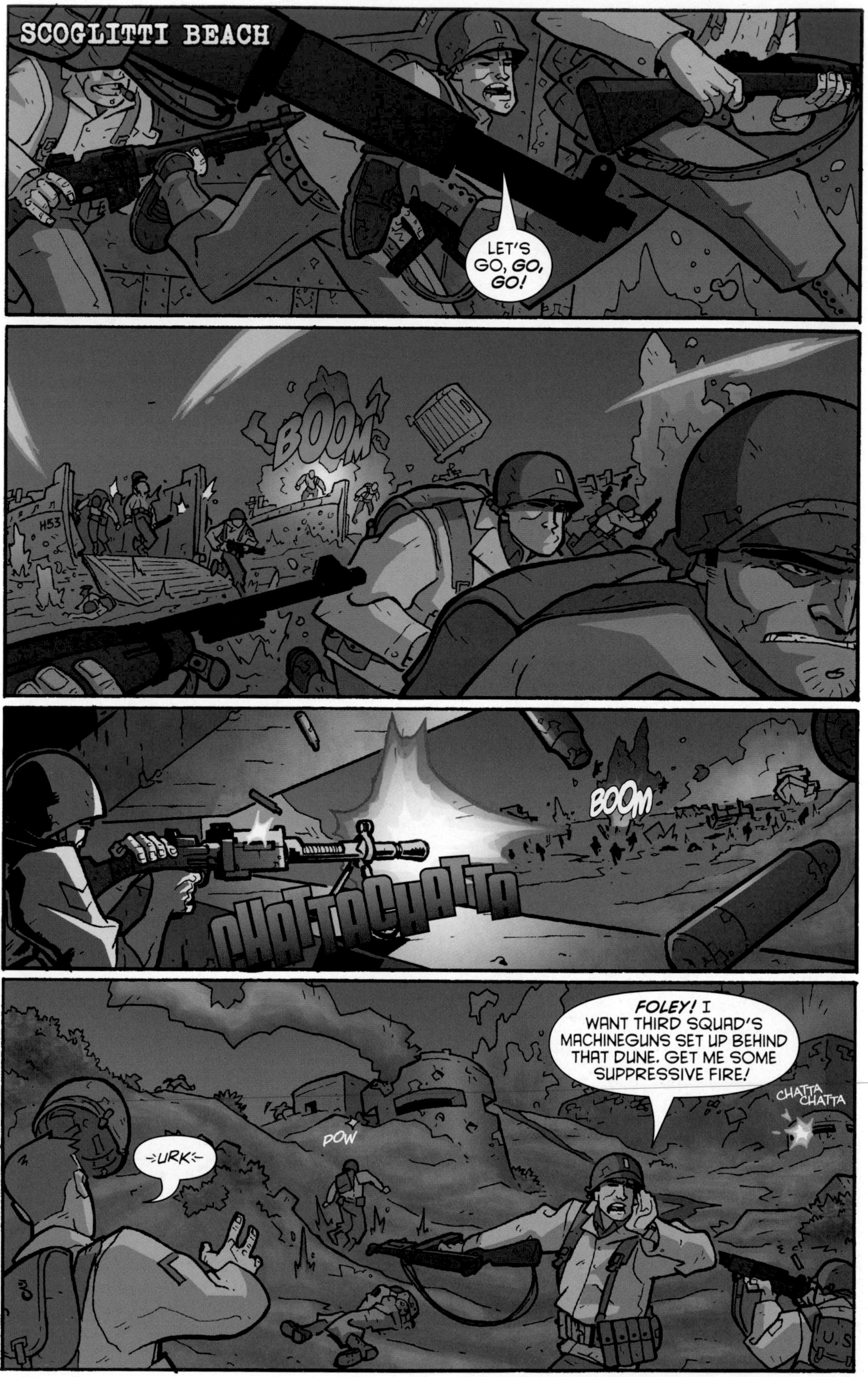
SCOGLITTI BEACH
LET'S GO, GO, GO!
BOOM
BOOM
CHATTACHATTA
FOLEY! I WANT THIRD SQUAD'S MACHINEGUNS SET UP BEHIND THAT DUNE. GET ME SOME SUPPRESSIVE FIRE!
CHATTA CHATTA
POW
URK

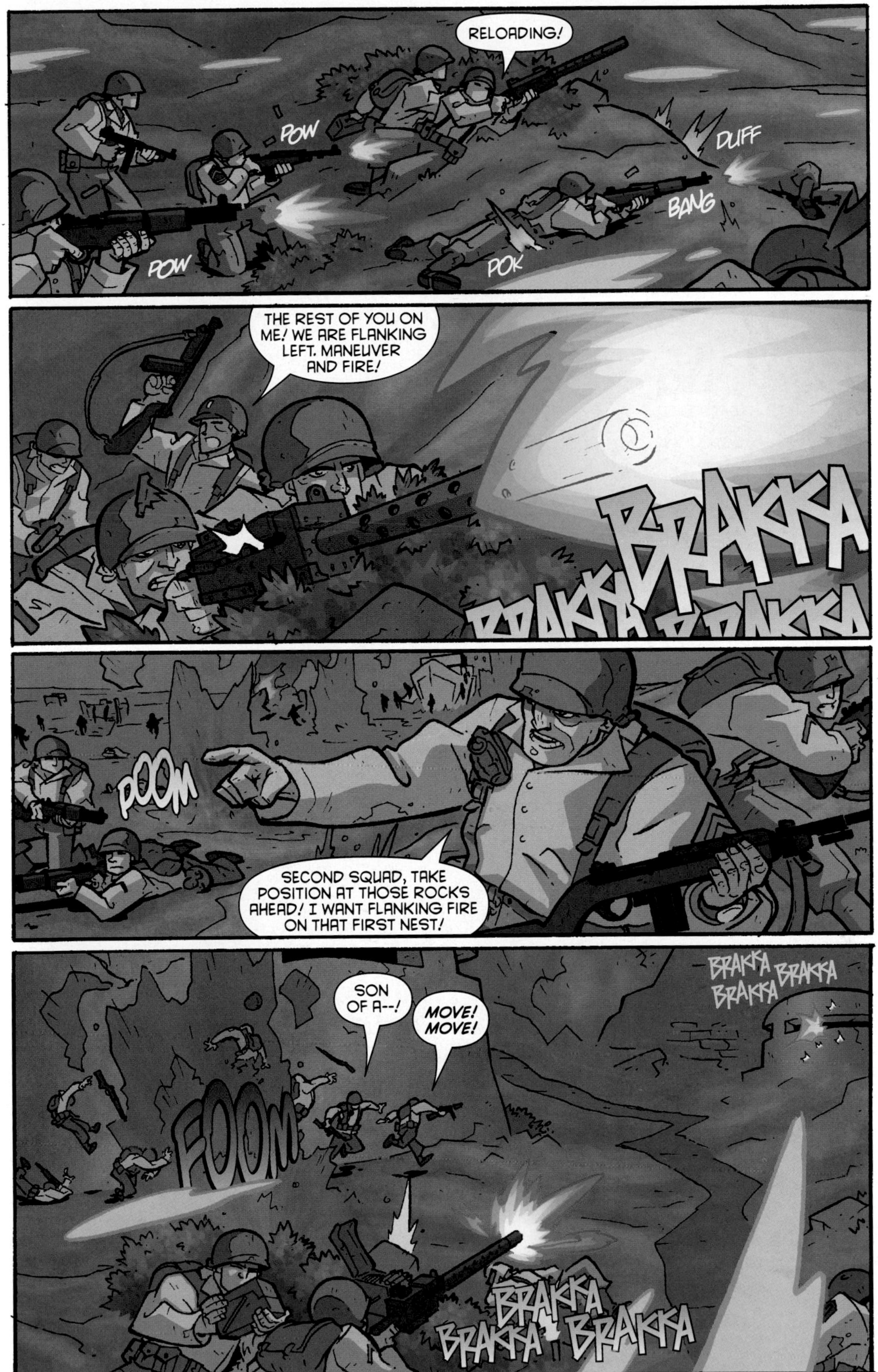
RELOADING!
POW
DUFF
BANG
POW
POK
THE REST OF YOU ON ME! WE ARE FLANKING LEFT. MANEUVER AND FIRE!
BRAKKA
POOM
SECOND SQUAD, TAKE POSITION AT THOSE ROCKS AHEAD! I WANT FLANKING FIRE ON THAT FIRST NEST!
BRAKKA BRAKKA BRAKKA
SON OF A--!
MOVE! MOVE!
FOOM
BRAKKA BRAKKA BRAKKA

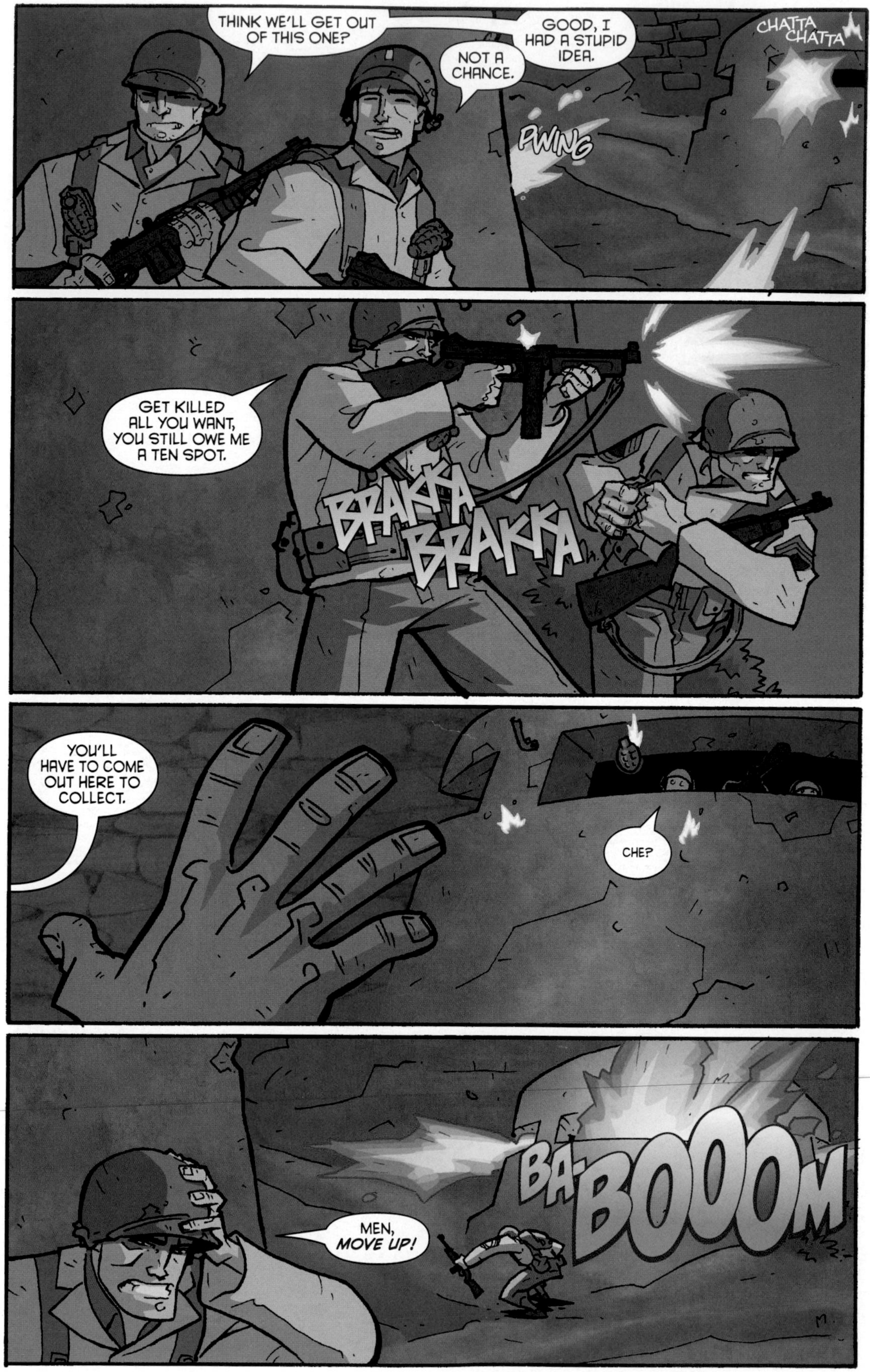
THINK WE'LL GET OUT OF THIS ONE?
NOT A CHANCE.
GOOD, I HAD A STUPID IDEA.
CHATTA CHATTA
PWING
GET KILLED ALL YOU WANT, YOU STILL OWE ME A TEN SPOT.
BRAKKA BRAKKA
YOU'LL HAVE TO COME OUT HERE TO COLLECT.
CHE?
BA-BOOOM
MEN, *MOVE UP!*

&lt;AS SOON AS THIS SHIFT IS OVER, I'M GOING TO SLEEP FOR A *WEEK*.&gt;

&lt;I WOULD *PAY* TO SEE YOU TELL SKORZENY THAT.&gt;

&lt;WHAT HE DOESN'T FIND OUT WON'T GET ME KILLED.&gt;

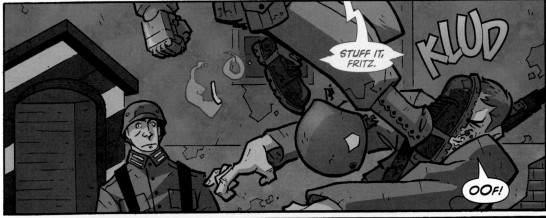

*STUFF IT, FRITZ.*

KLUD

*OOF!*

&lt;STOP, OR I'LL--&gt;

U.S.

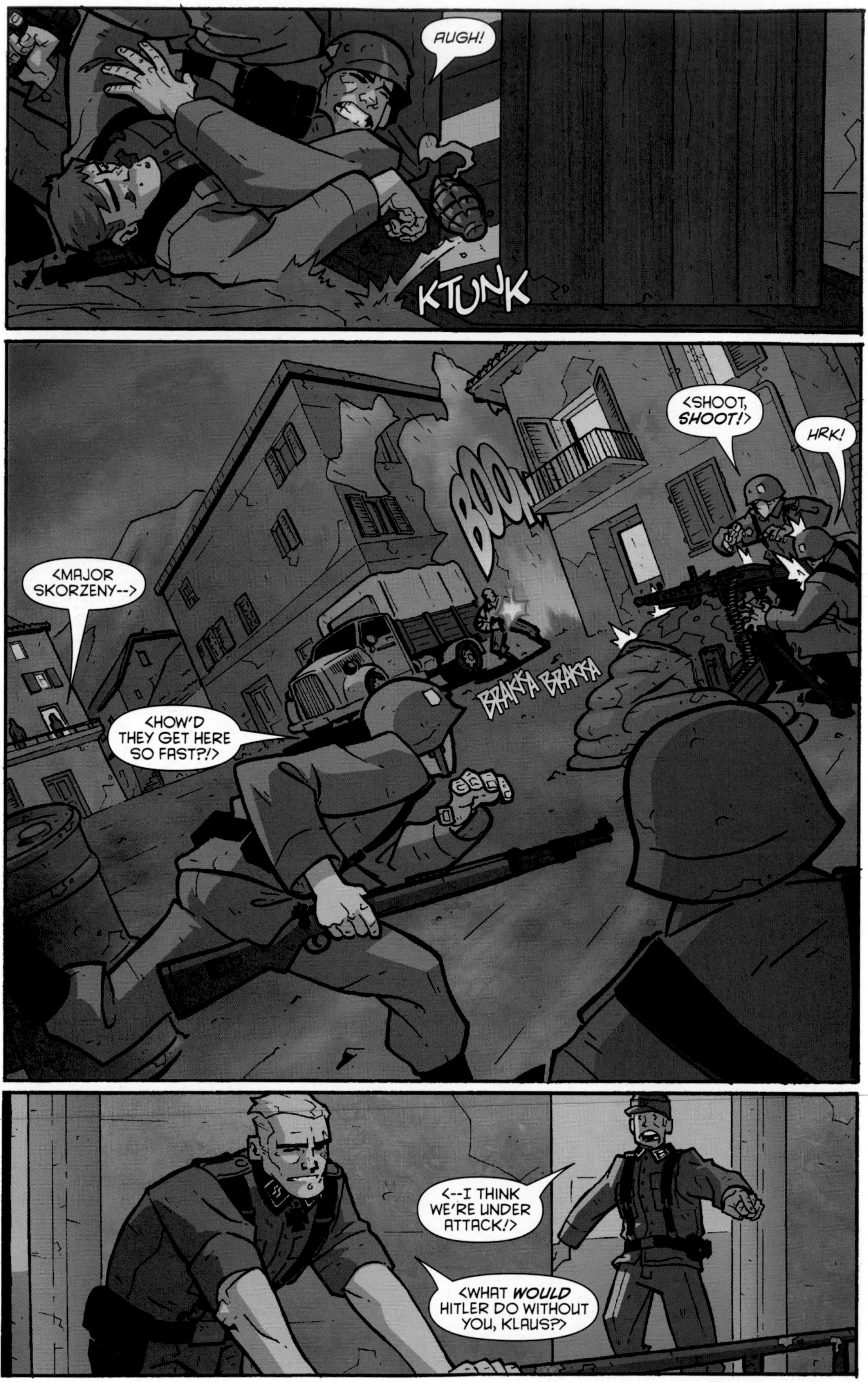
AUGH!
KTUNK
<MAJOR SKORZENY-->
BOO
<SHOOT, *SHOOT!*>
HRK!
BRAKKA BRAKKA
<HOW'D THEY GET HERE SO FAST?!>
<--I THINK WE'RE UNDER ATTACK!>
<WHAT *WOULD* HITLER DO WITHOUT YOU, KLAUS?>

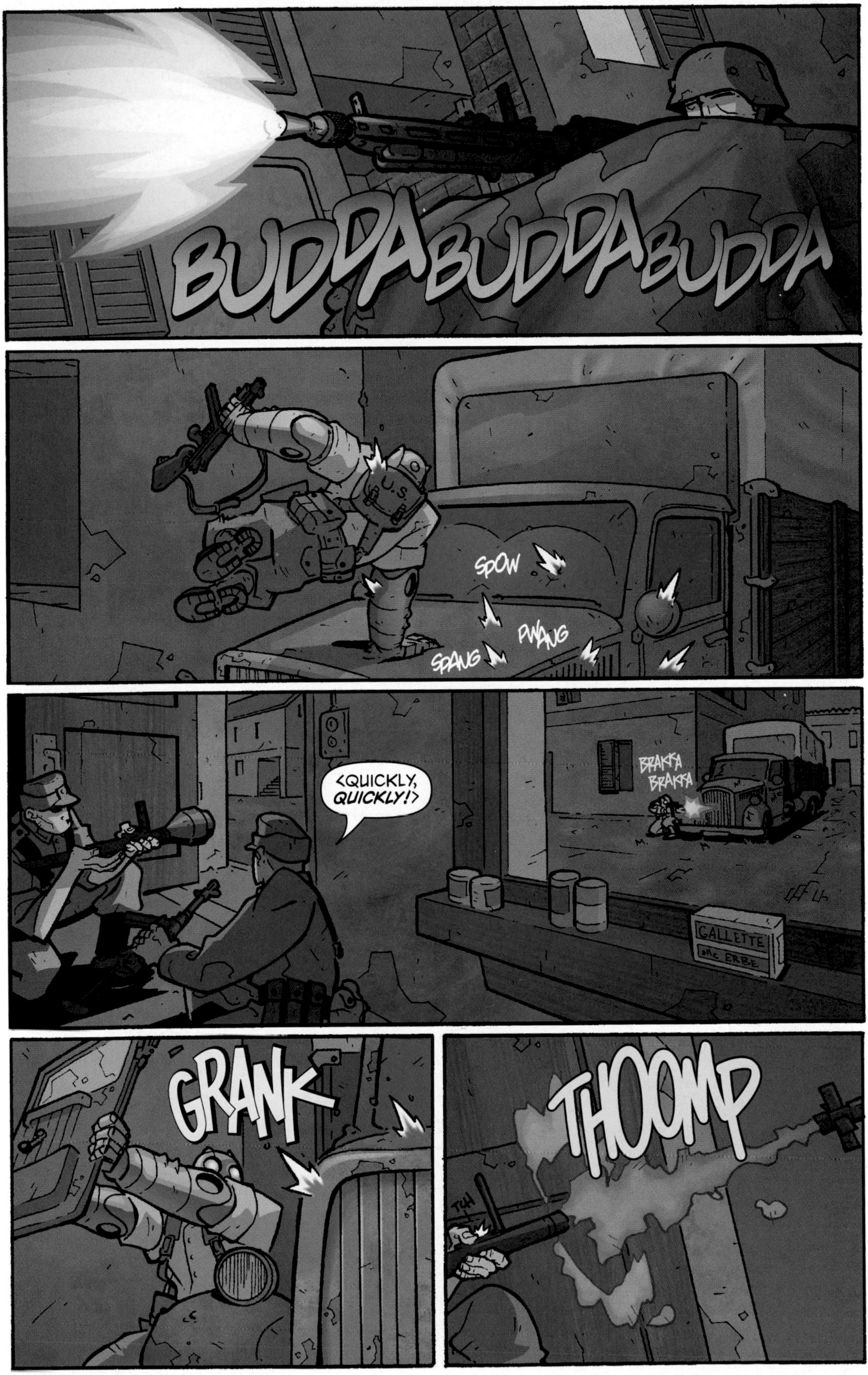
BUDDA BUDDA BUDDA
SPOW
PWANG
SPANG
BRAKKA
BRAKKA
<QUICKLY, QUICKLY!>
GALLETTE
ERBE
GRANK
THOOMP
TCH

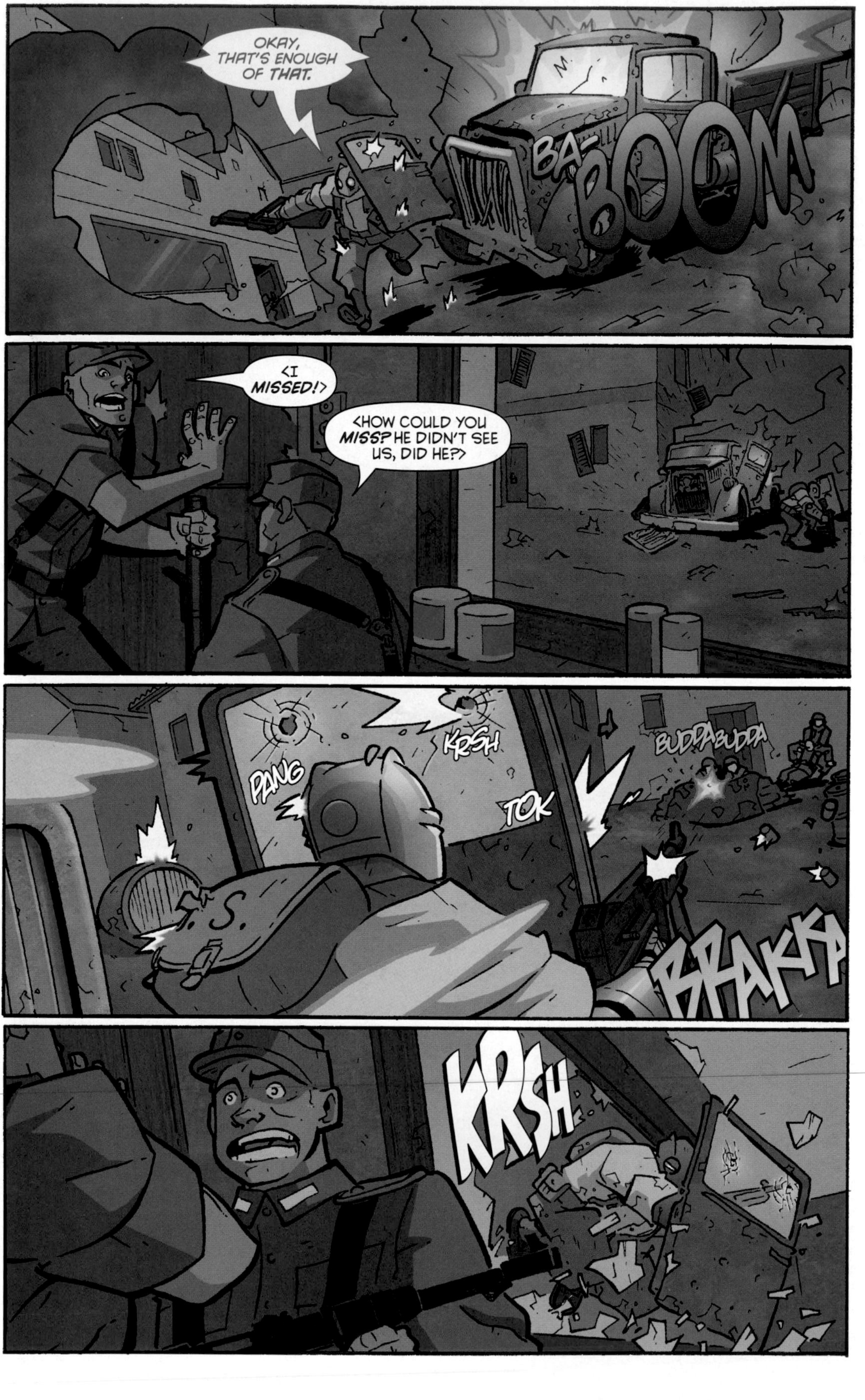

OKAY, THAT'S ENOUGH OF THAT.
BA-BOOM
<I MISSED!>
<HOW COULD YOU MISS? HE DIDN'T SEE US, DID HE?>
KRSH
BUDDABUDDA
PANG
TOK
BRAKKA
KRSH

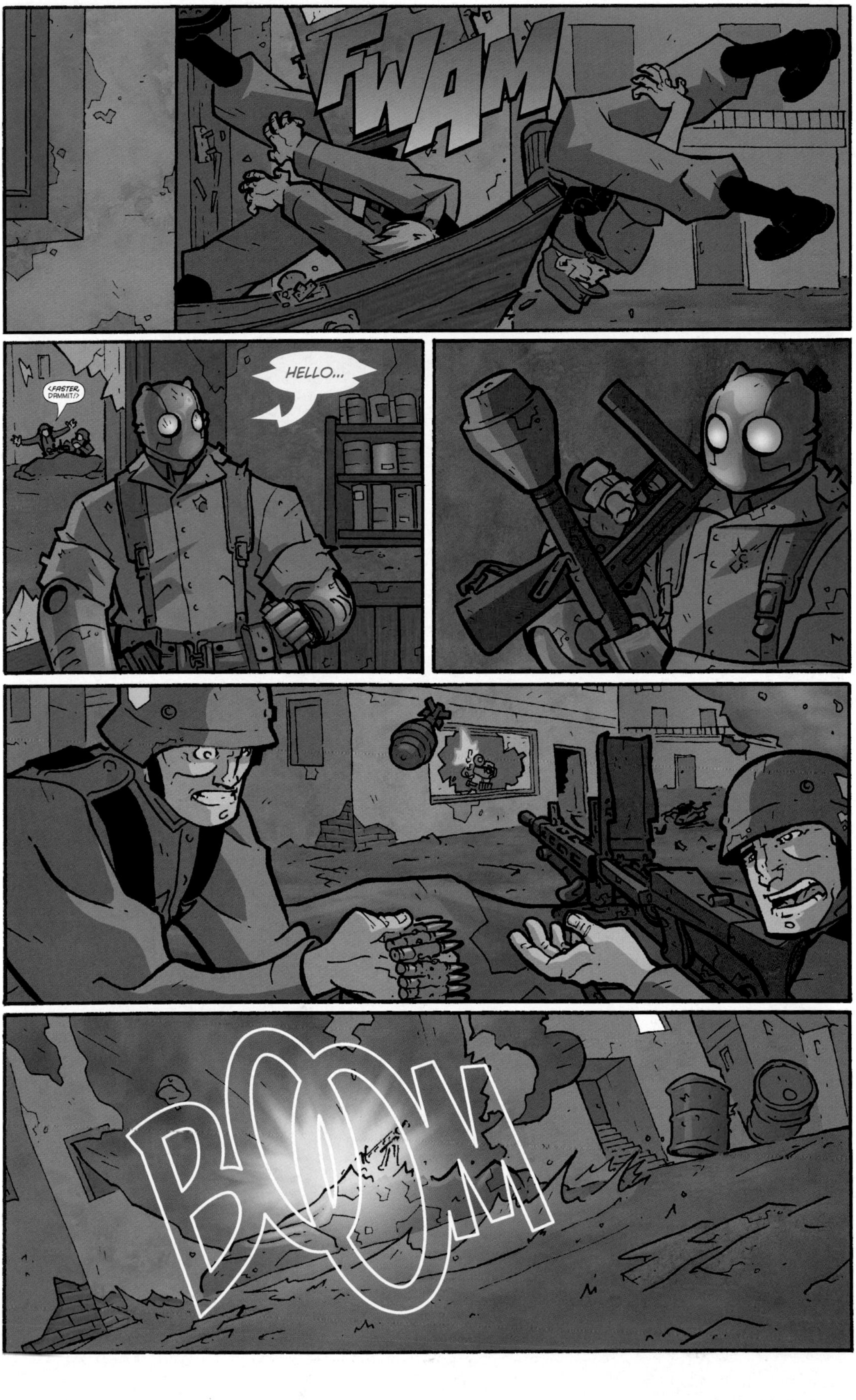
FWAM
<FASTER, DAMMIT!>
HELLO...
BOOM

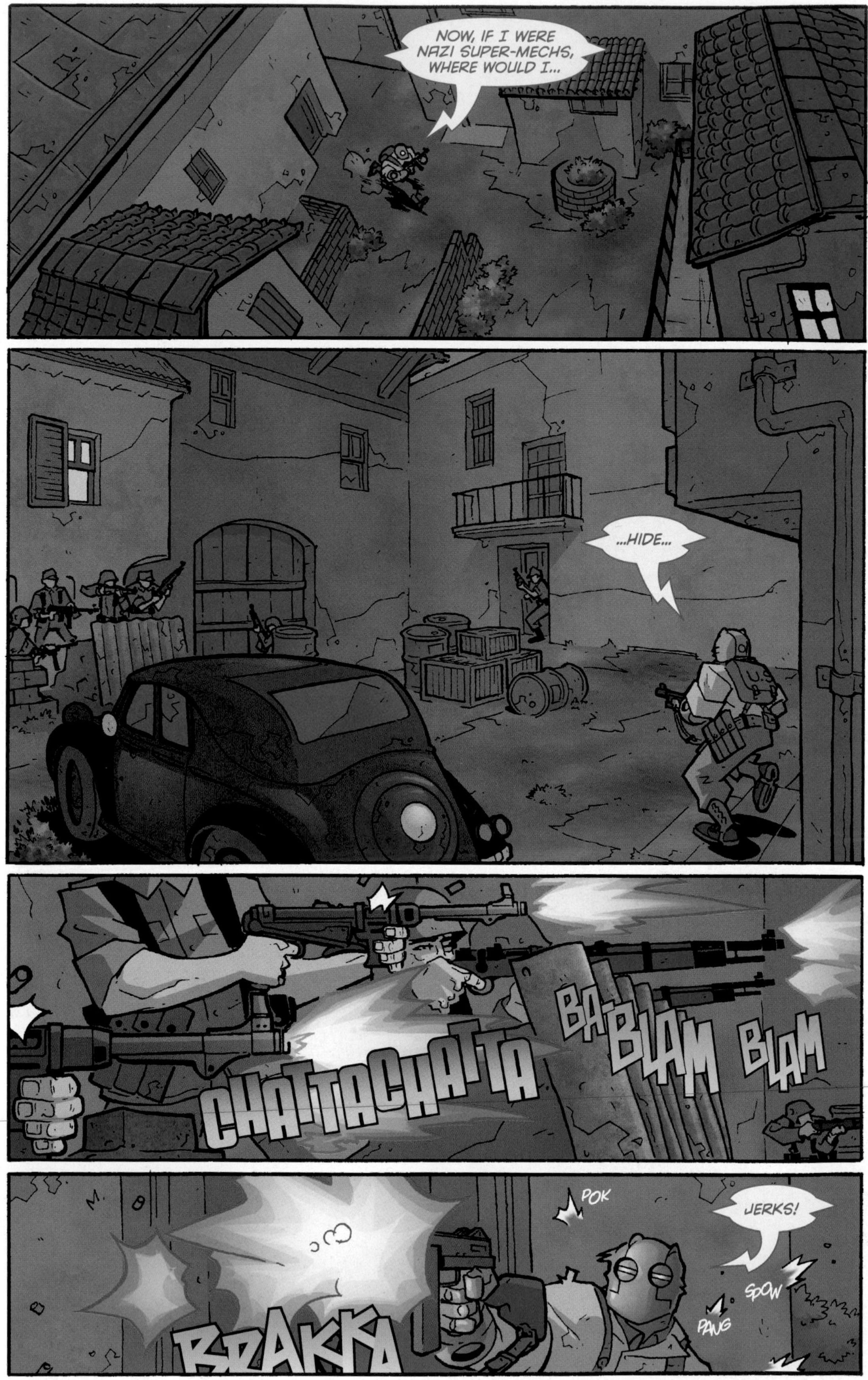
NOW, IF I WERE NAZI SUPER-MECHS, WHERE WOULD I...
...HIDE...
CHATTACHATTA
BA-BLAM BLAM
POK
JERKS!
SPOW
PANG
BRAKKA

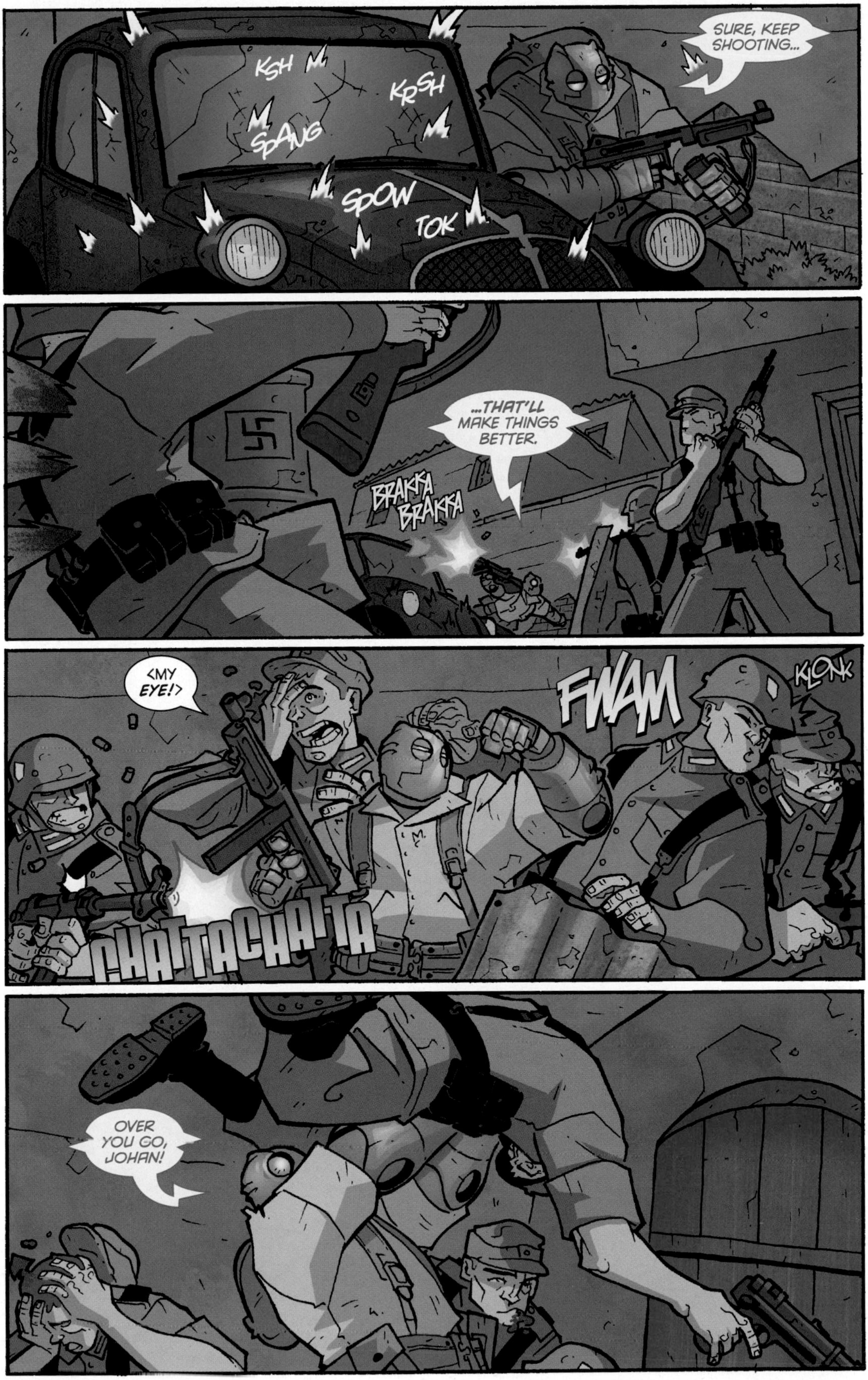
KSH
KRSH
SPANG
SPOW
TOK
SURE, KEEP SHOOTING...
...THAT'LL MAKE THINGS BETTER.
BRAKKA BRAKKA
<MY EYE!>
FWAM
KLONK
CHATTACHATTA
OVER YOU GO, JOHAN!

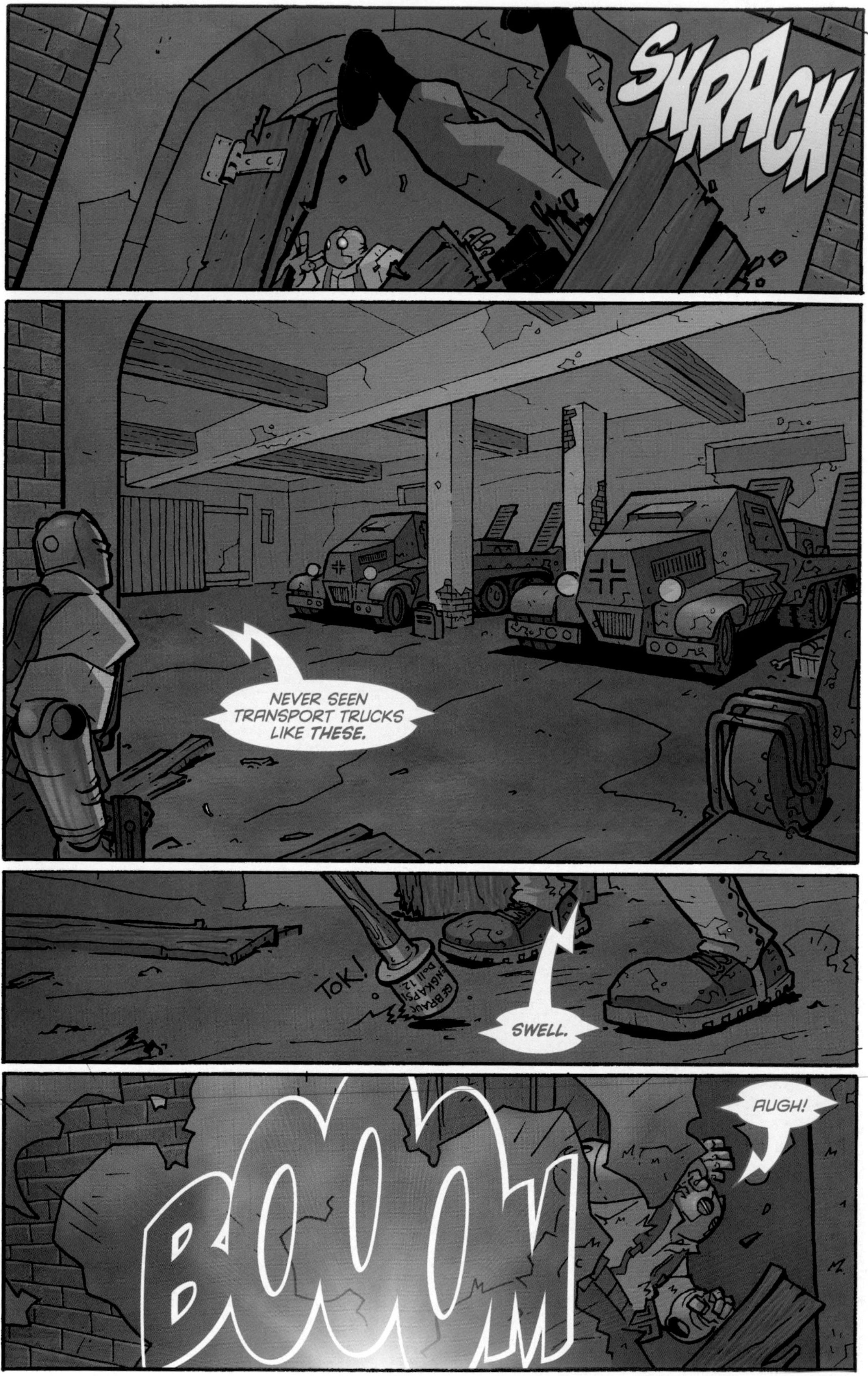
SKRACK
NEVER SEEN TRANSPORT TRUCKS LIKE THESE.
TOK!
SWELL.
BOOOM
AUGH!

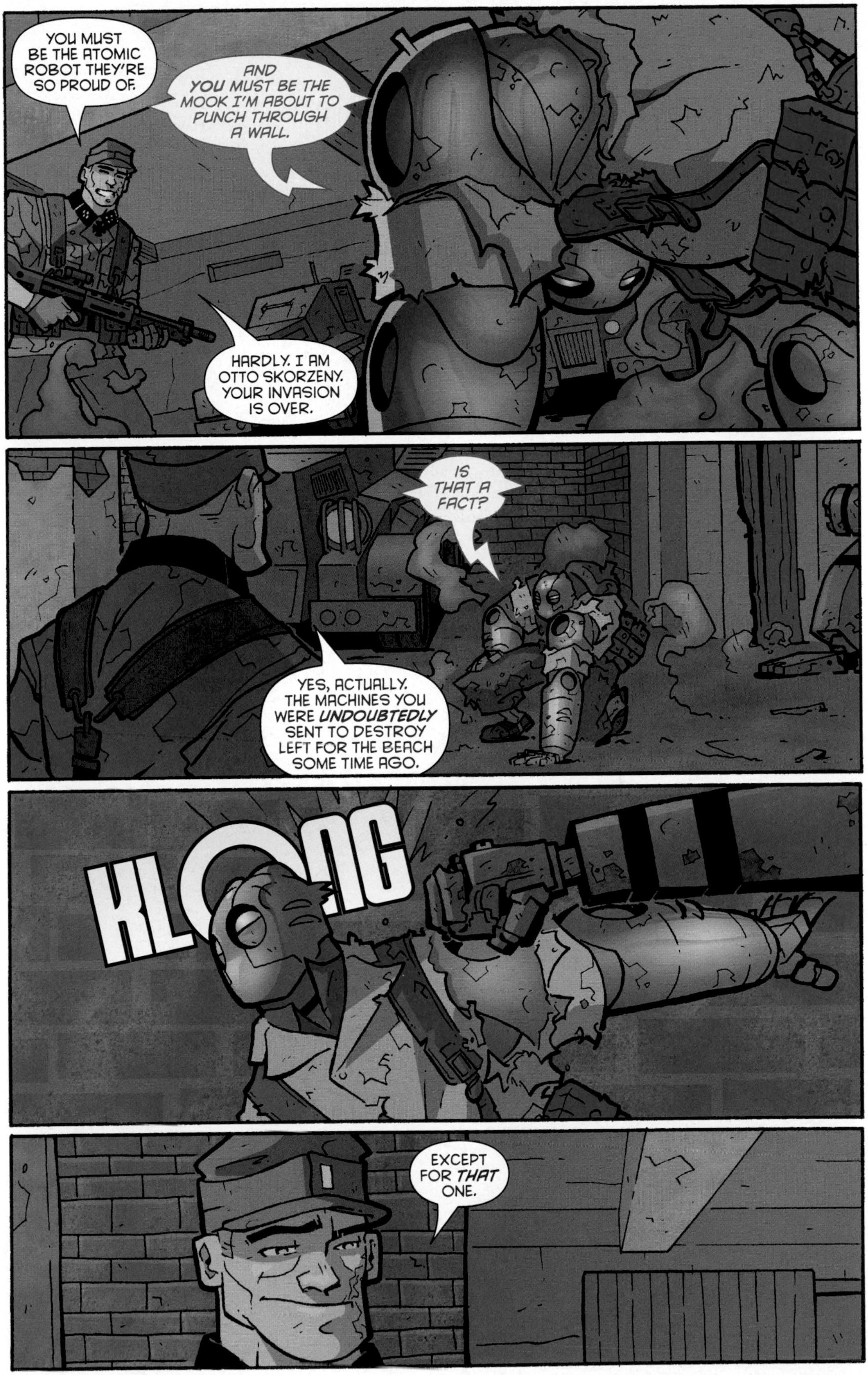

YOU MUST BE THE ATOMIC ROBOT THEY'RE SO PROUD OF.
AND YOU MUST BE THE MOOK I'M ABOUT TO PUNCH THROUGH A WALL.
HARDLY. I AM OTTO SKORZENY. YOUR INVASION IS OVER.
IS THAT A FACT?
YES, ACTUALLY. THE MACHINES YOU WERE UNDOUBTEDLY SENT TO DESTROY LEFT FOR THE BEACH SOME TIME AGO.
KLONG
EXCEPT FOR THAT ONE.

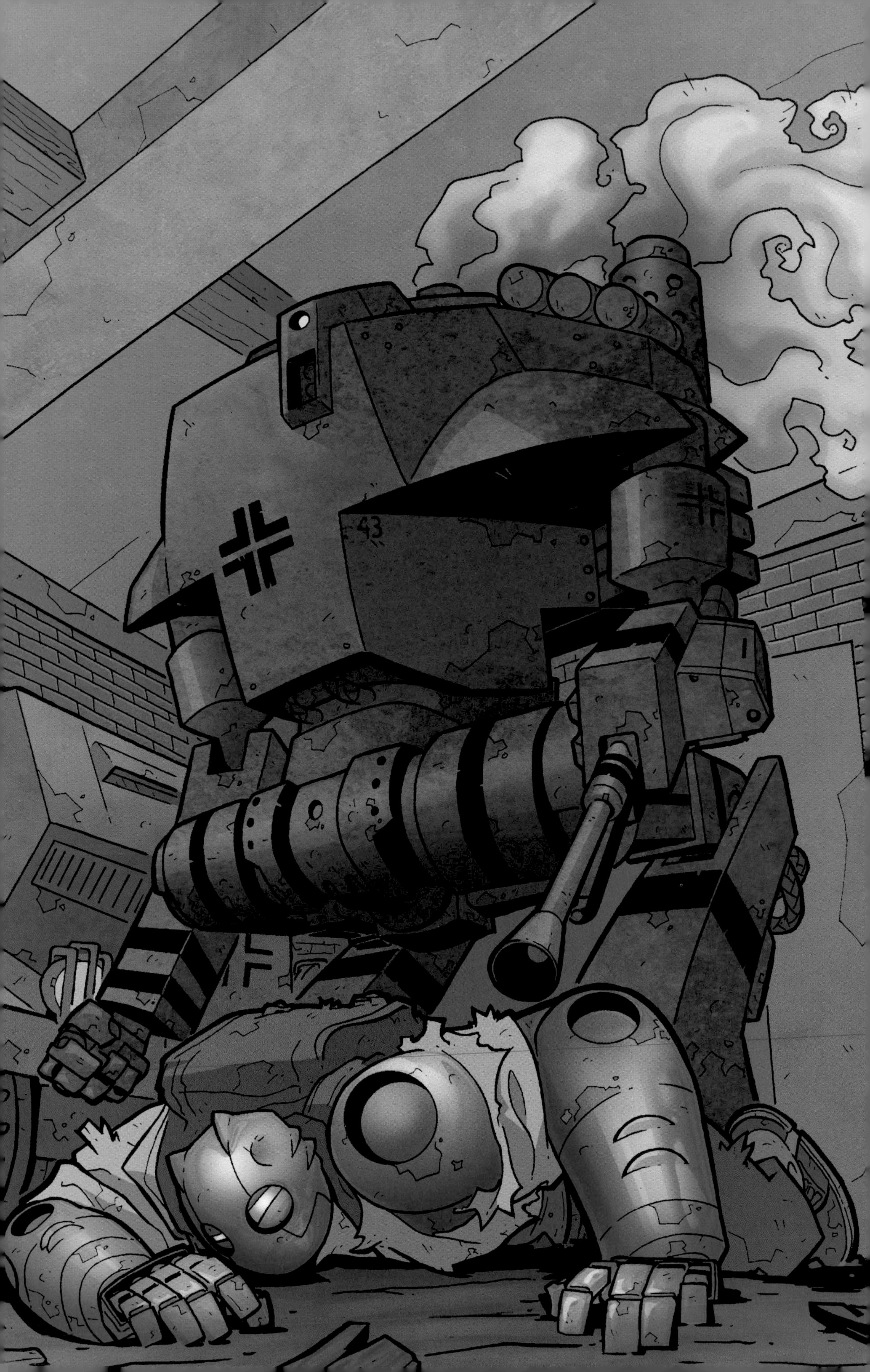
43

# AND THEN THERE'S THE ROBOTS

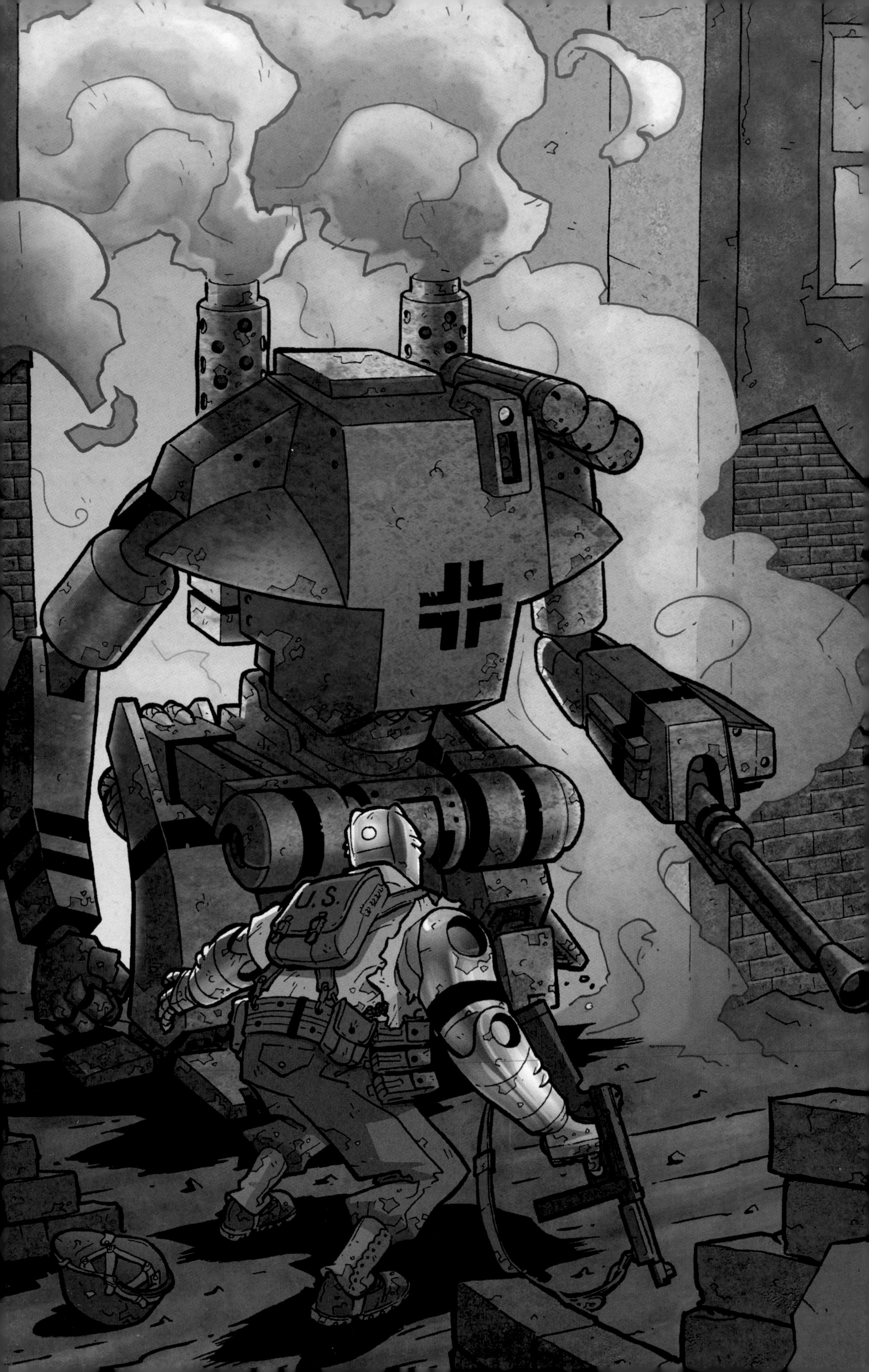
U.S.

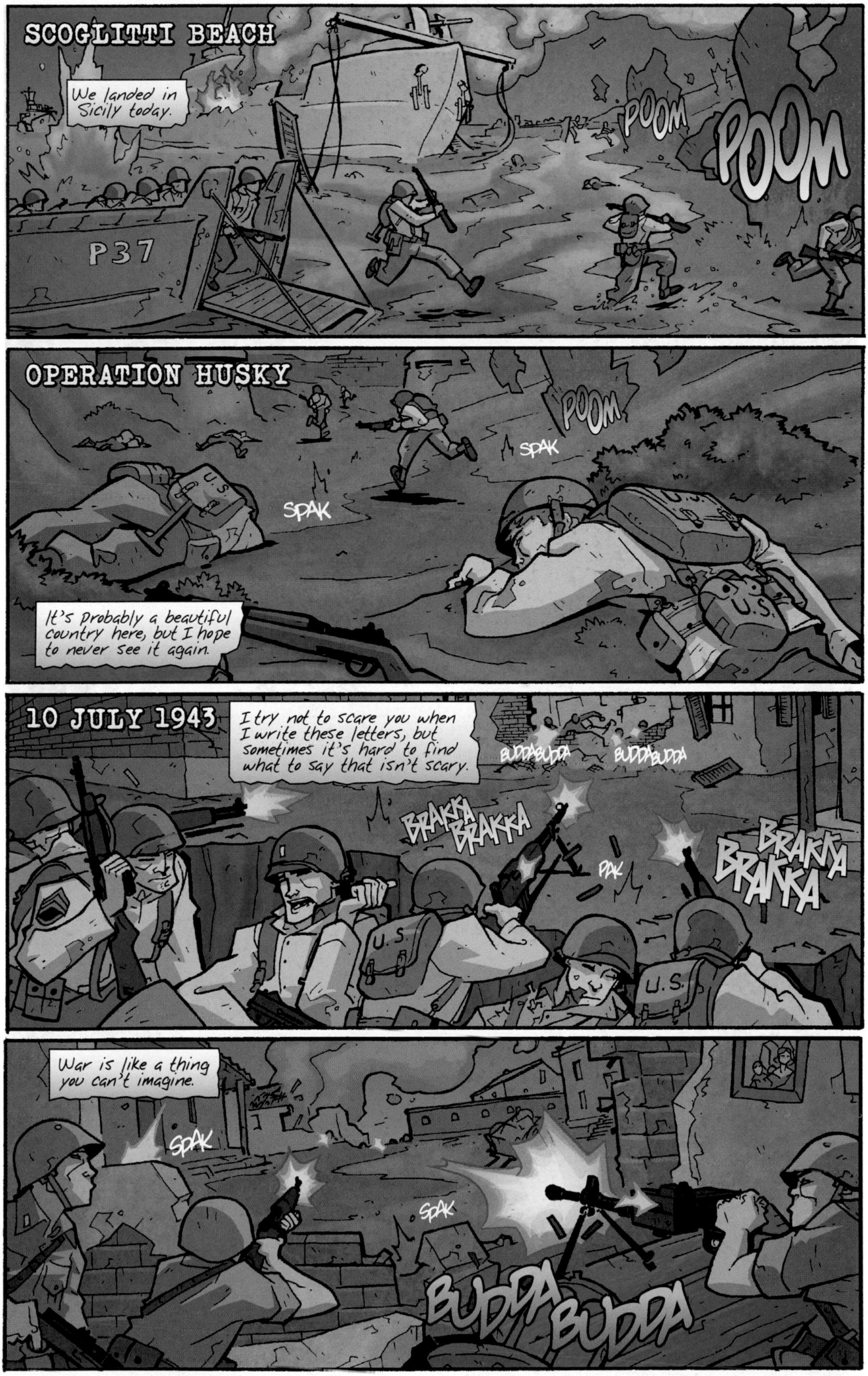
SCOGLITTI BEACH
We landed in Sicily today.
P37
POOM
POOM
OPERATION HUSKY
POOM
SPAK
SPAK
It's probably a beautiful country here, but I hope to never see it again.
10 JULY 1943
I try not to scare you when I write these letters, but sometimes it's hard to find what to say that isn't scary.
BUDDABUDDA
BUDDABUDDA
BRAKKA BRAKKA
PAK
BRAKKA BRAKKA
U.S.
War is like a thing you can't imagine.
SPAK
SPAK
BUDDA BUDDA

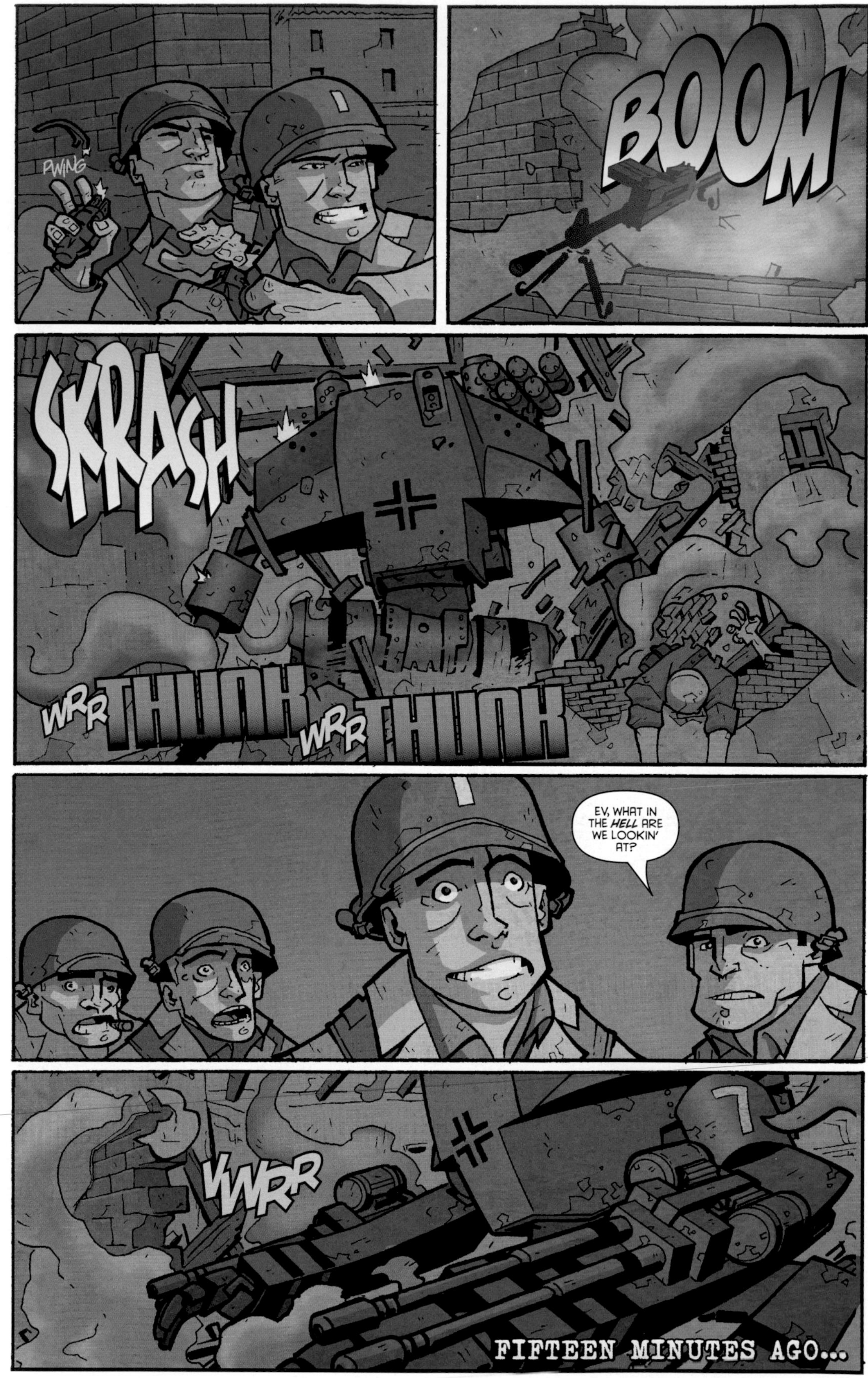
PWING
BOOM
SKRASH
WRR THUNK WRR THUNK
EV, WHAT IN THE HELL ARE WE LOOKIN' AT?
VWRR
FIFTEEN MINUTES AGO...

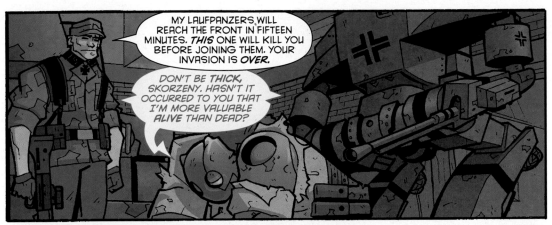

MY LAUFPANZERS WILL REACH THE FRONT IN FIFTEEN MINUTES. *THIS* ONE WILL KILL YOU BEFORE JOINING THEM. YOUR INVASION IS *OVER*.

DON'T BE *THICK*, SKORZENY. HASN'T IT OCCURRED TO YOU THAT I'M MORE VALUABLE *ALIVE* THAN DEAD?

NO, I QUITE DOUBT THAT.

DO YOU THINK THEY'D SEND ME HERE WITHOUT GIVING ME THE *BIG PICTURE?* HELL, I'M HERE AT FDR'S *PERSONAL* REQUEST. YOU COULD WIN THE WAR IN A *MONTH* USING WHAT I KNOW.

WENN ER NUR DIE *GERINGSTE* BEWEGUNG IN MEINE RICHTUNG MACHT, FEUERN SIE AUF IHN. HÖREN SIE *NICHT* AUF ZU FEUERN, BIS ICH DEN BEFEHL DAZU GEBE.

JAWOHL, OBERST!

I HAVE INSTRUCTED HIM TO DESTROY YOU IF YOU SO MUCH AS *THINK* ABOUT MOVING TOWARD ME.

NOW, WHAT DO YOU KNOW?

FAIR ENOUGH.

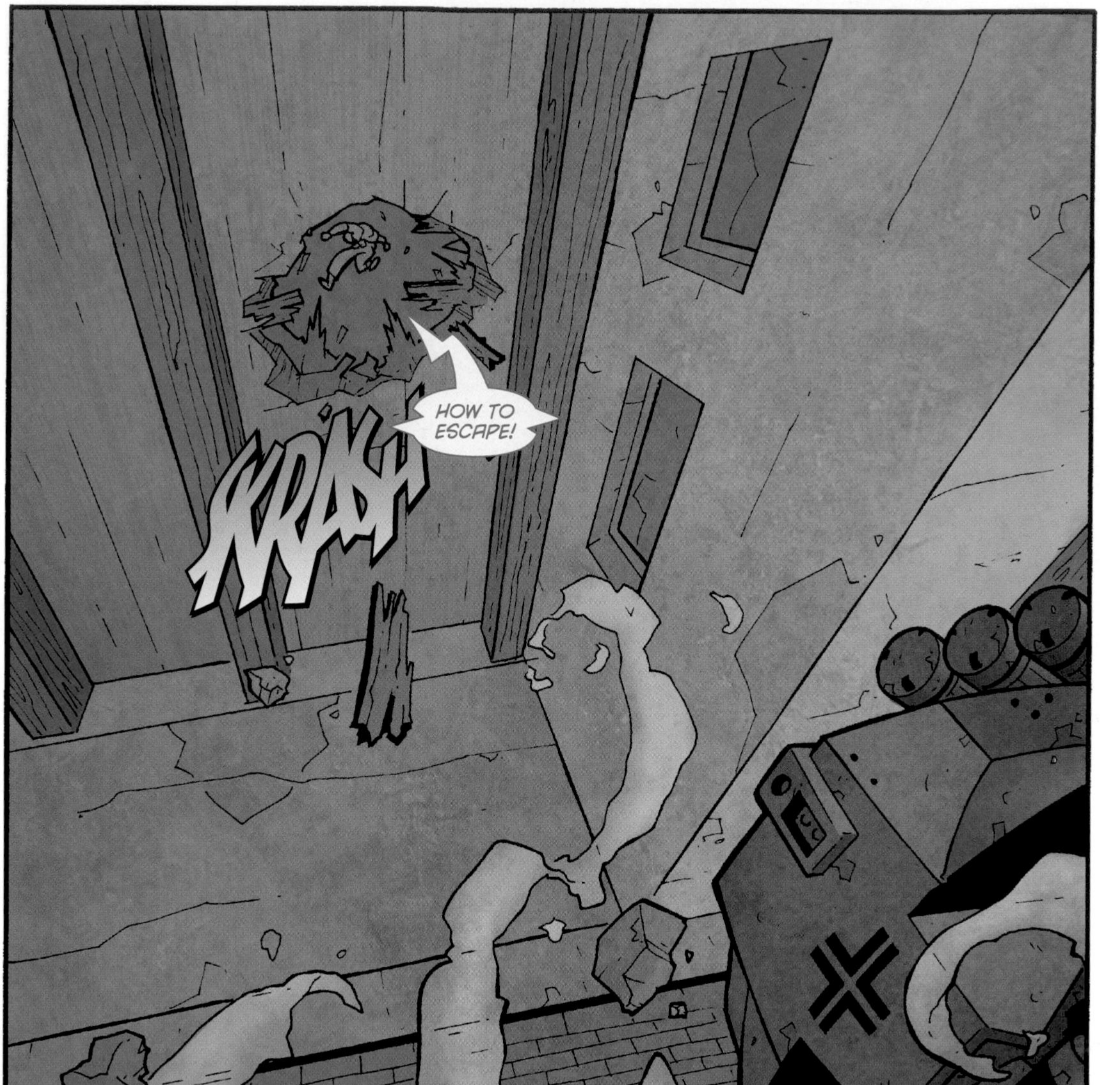
KRASH
HOW TO ESCAPE!

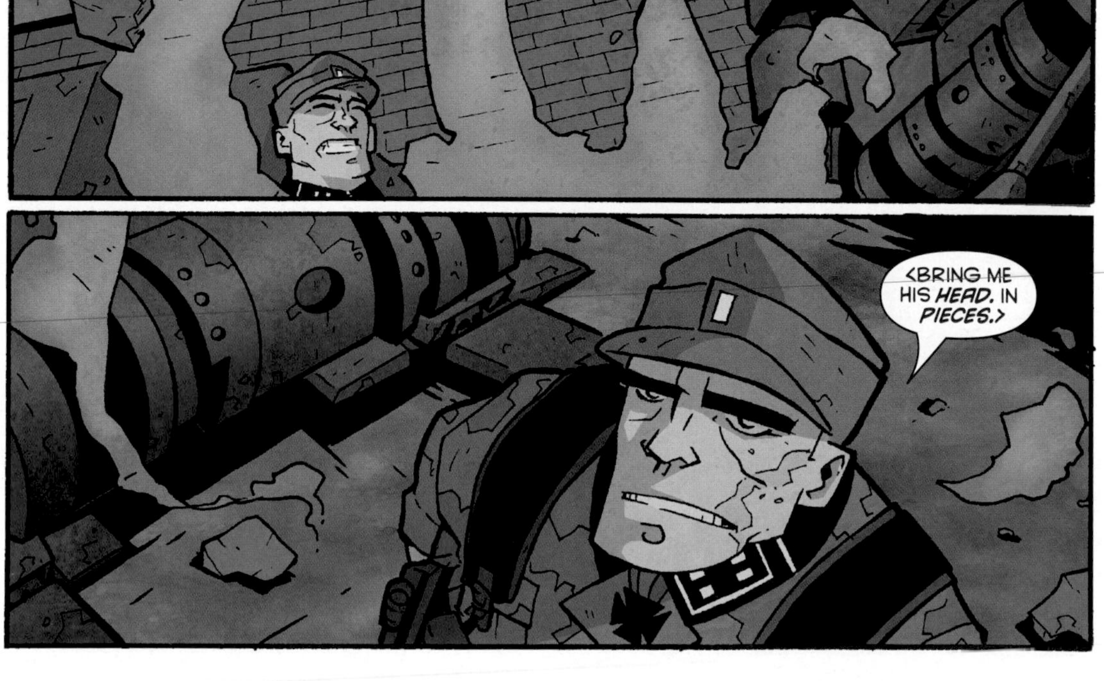
<BRING ME HIS HEAD. IN PIECES.>

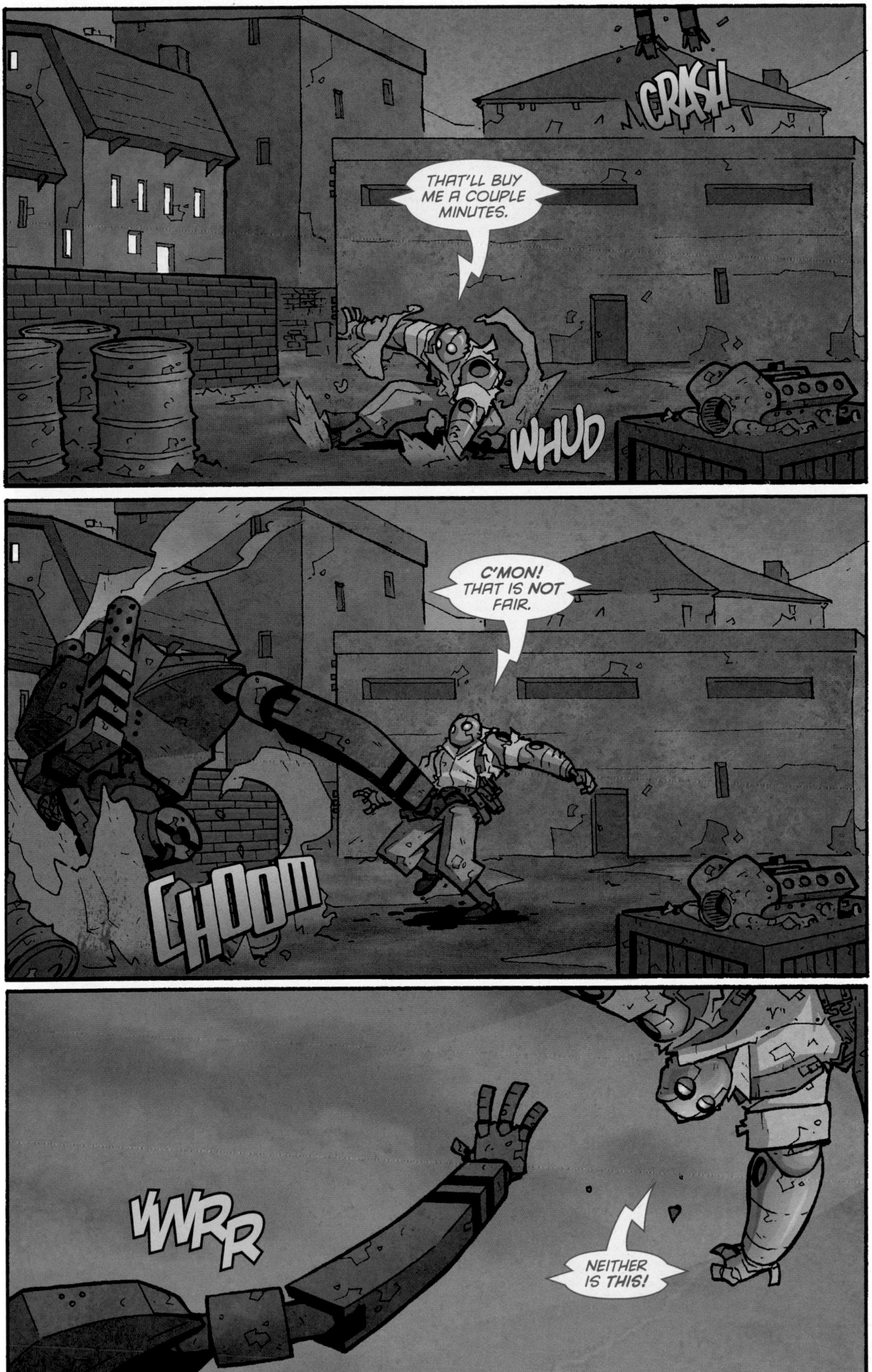
CRASH
THAT'LL BUY ME A COUPLE MINUTES.
WHUD
C'MON! THAT IS NOT FAIR.
CHOOM
VWRR
NEITHER IS THIS!

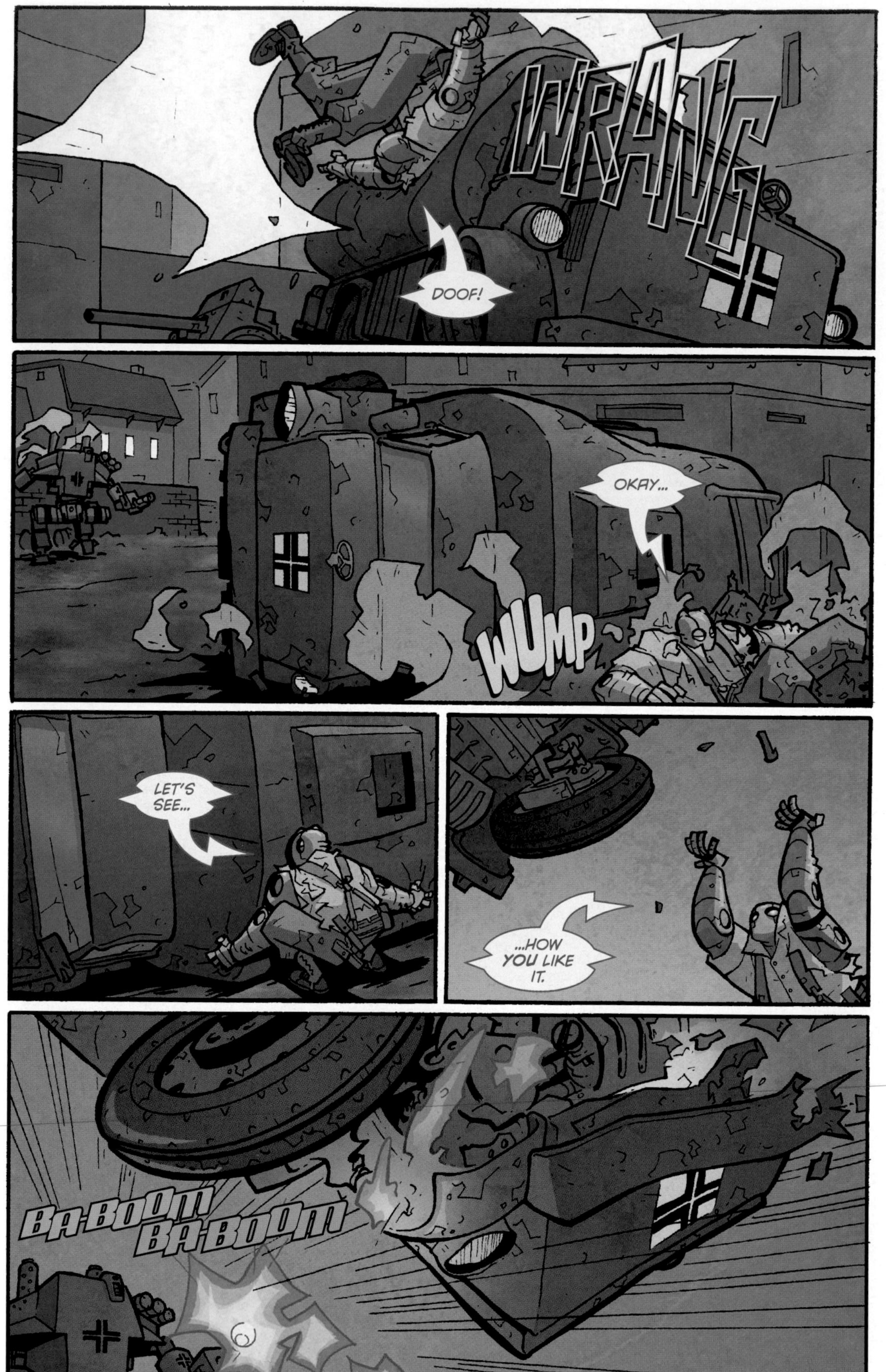
WRANG
DOOF!
OKAY...
WUMP
LET'S SEE...
...HOW YOU LIKE IT.
BA-BOOM
BA-BOOM

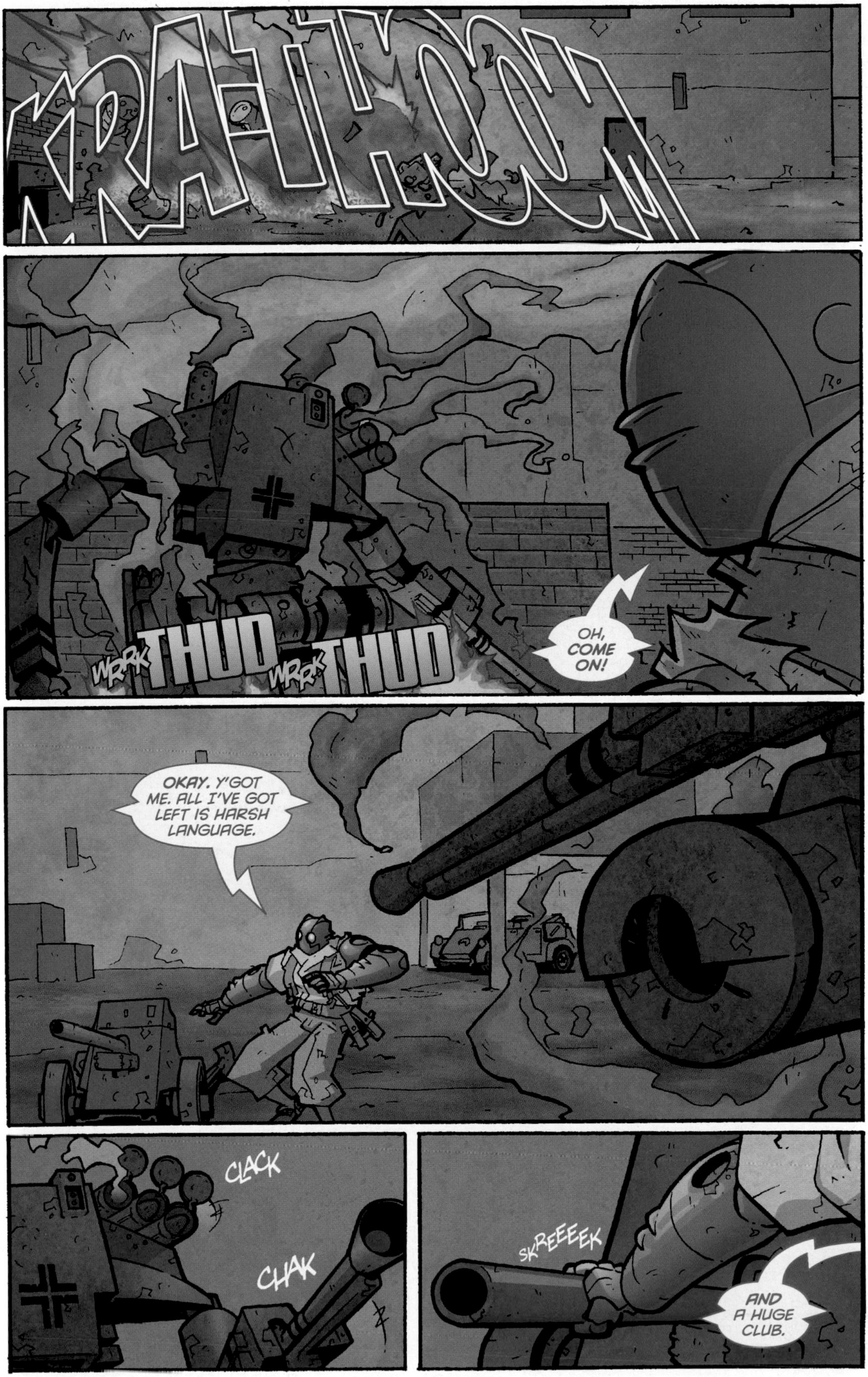
KRA-THOOM
WRRK THUD WRRK THUD
OH, COME ON!
OKAY. Y'GOT ME. ALL I'VE GOT LEFT IS HARSH LANGUAGE.
CLACK
CHAK
SKREEEEEK
AND A HUGE CLUB.

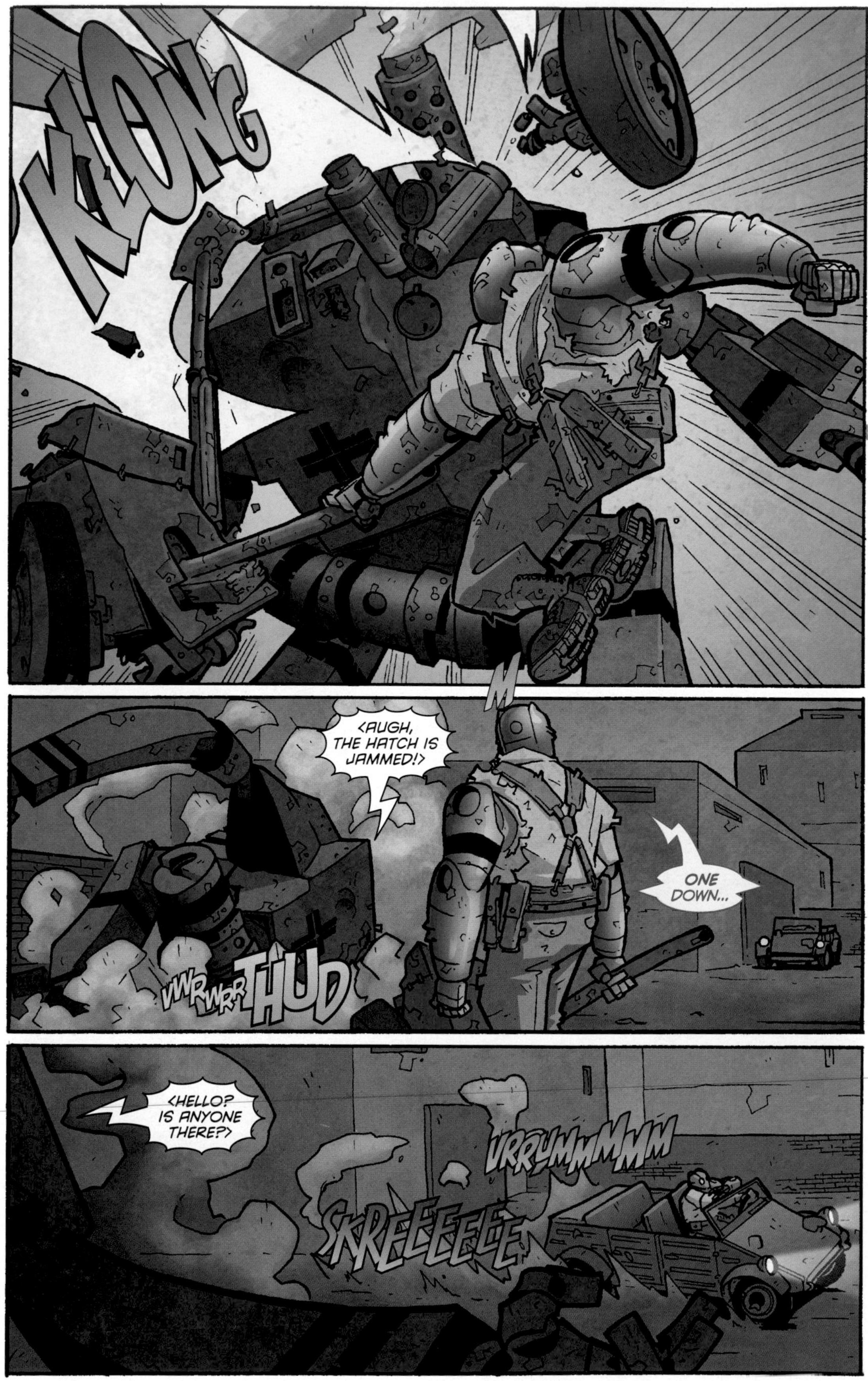
KLONG
M
<AUGH, THE HATCH IS JAMMED!>
ONE DOWN...
VWRWRR THUD
<HELLO? IS ANYONE THERE?>
URRUMMMMM
SKREEEEELE

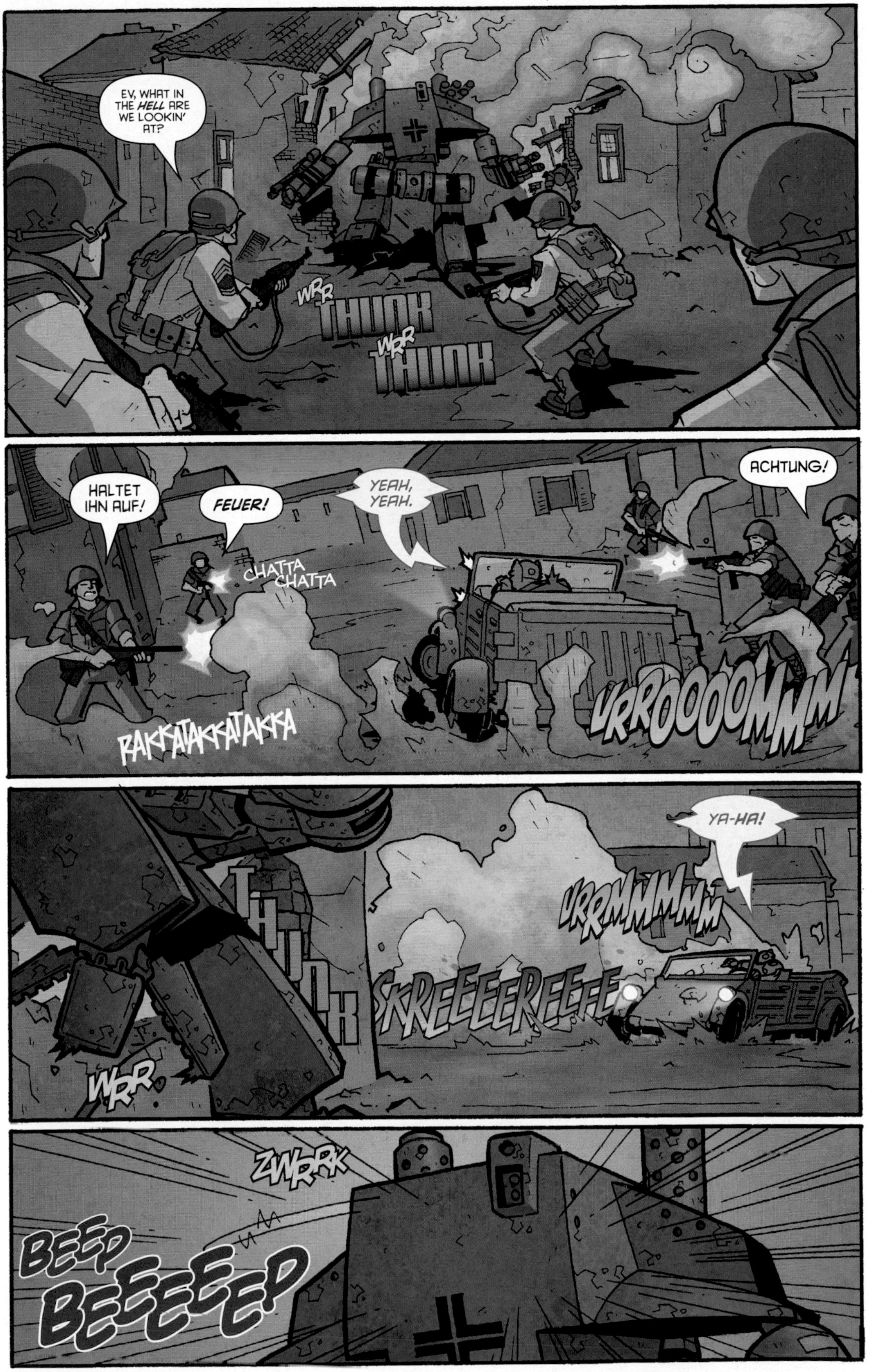
EV, WHAT IN THE HELL ARE WE LOOKIN' AT?
WRR
THUNK
WRR
THUNK
HALTET IHN AUF!
FEUER!
YEAH, YEAH.
ACHTUNG!
CHATTA CHATTA
RAKKATAKKATAKKA
URROOOOOMMM
YA-HA!
THUNK
URRMMMMMM
SKREEEEREEEE
WRR
ZWRRK
BEEP
BEEEEEEP

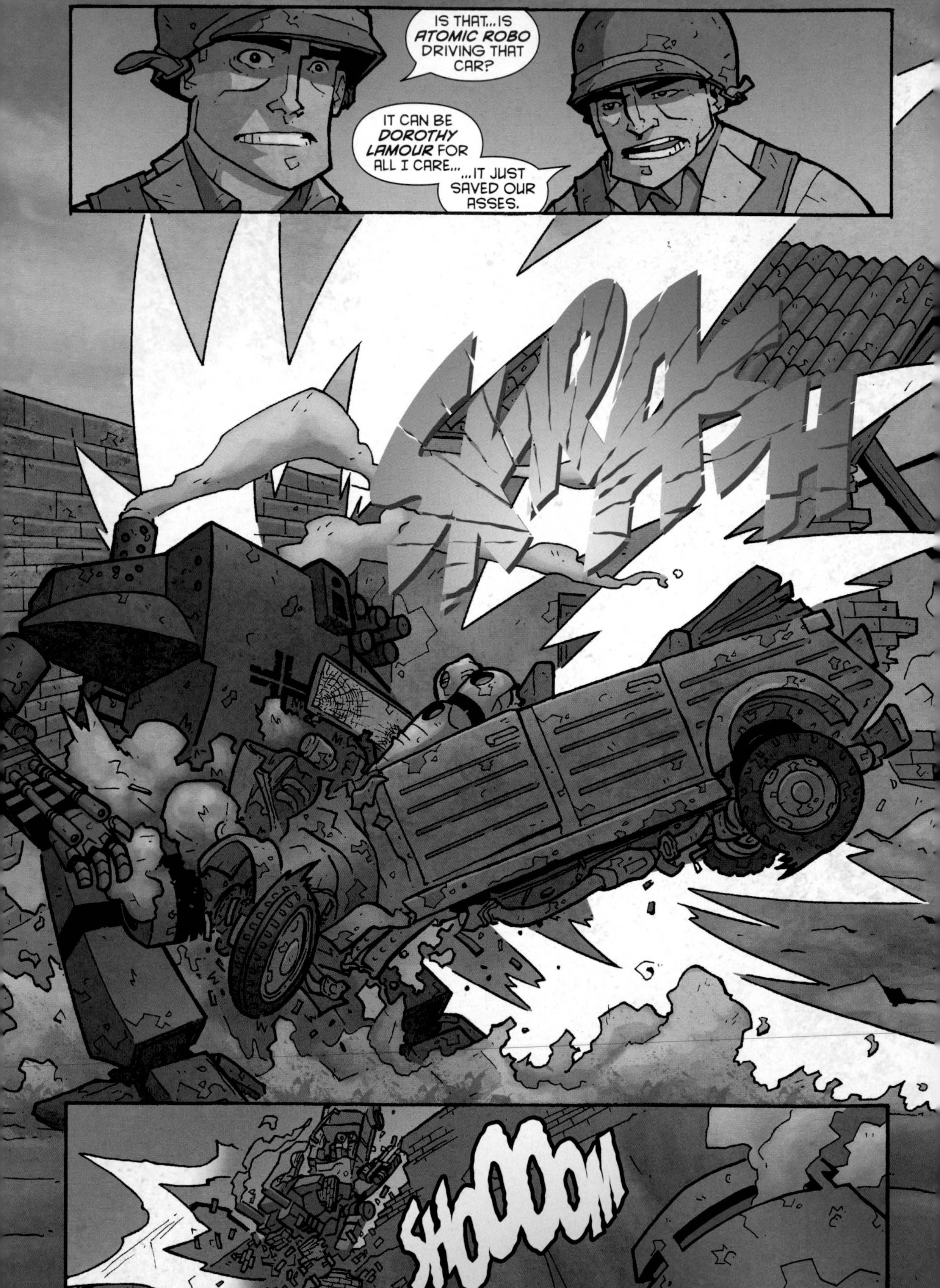
IS THAT...IS ATOMIC ROBO DRIVING THAT CAR?
IT CAN BE DOROTHY LAMOUR FOR ALL I CARE...
...IT JUST SAVED OUR ASSES.
SHOOOOM

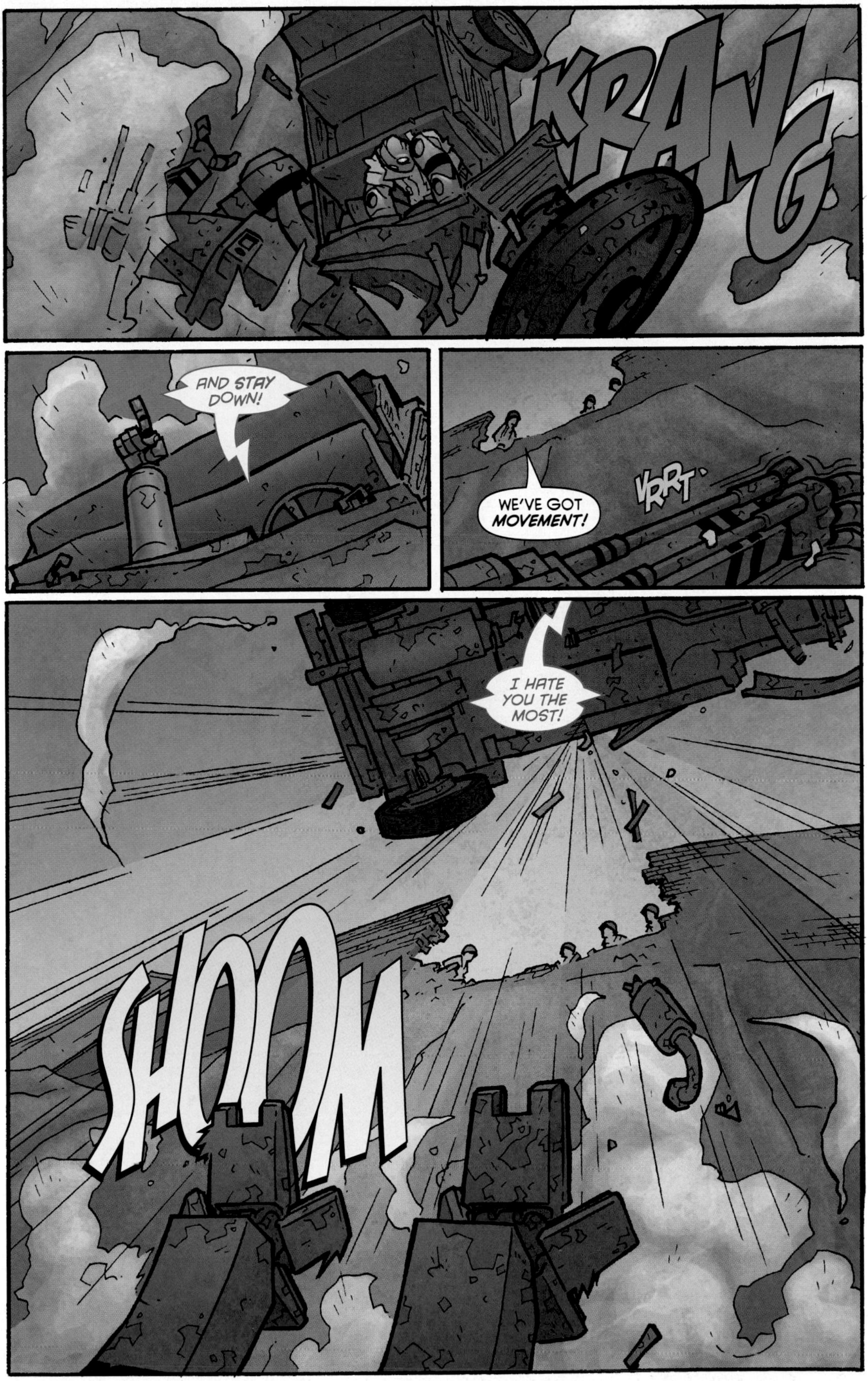
KRANG
AND STAY DOWN!
WE'VE GOT MOVEMENT!
VRRT
I HATE YOU THE MOST!
SHOOM

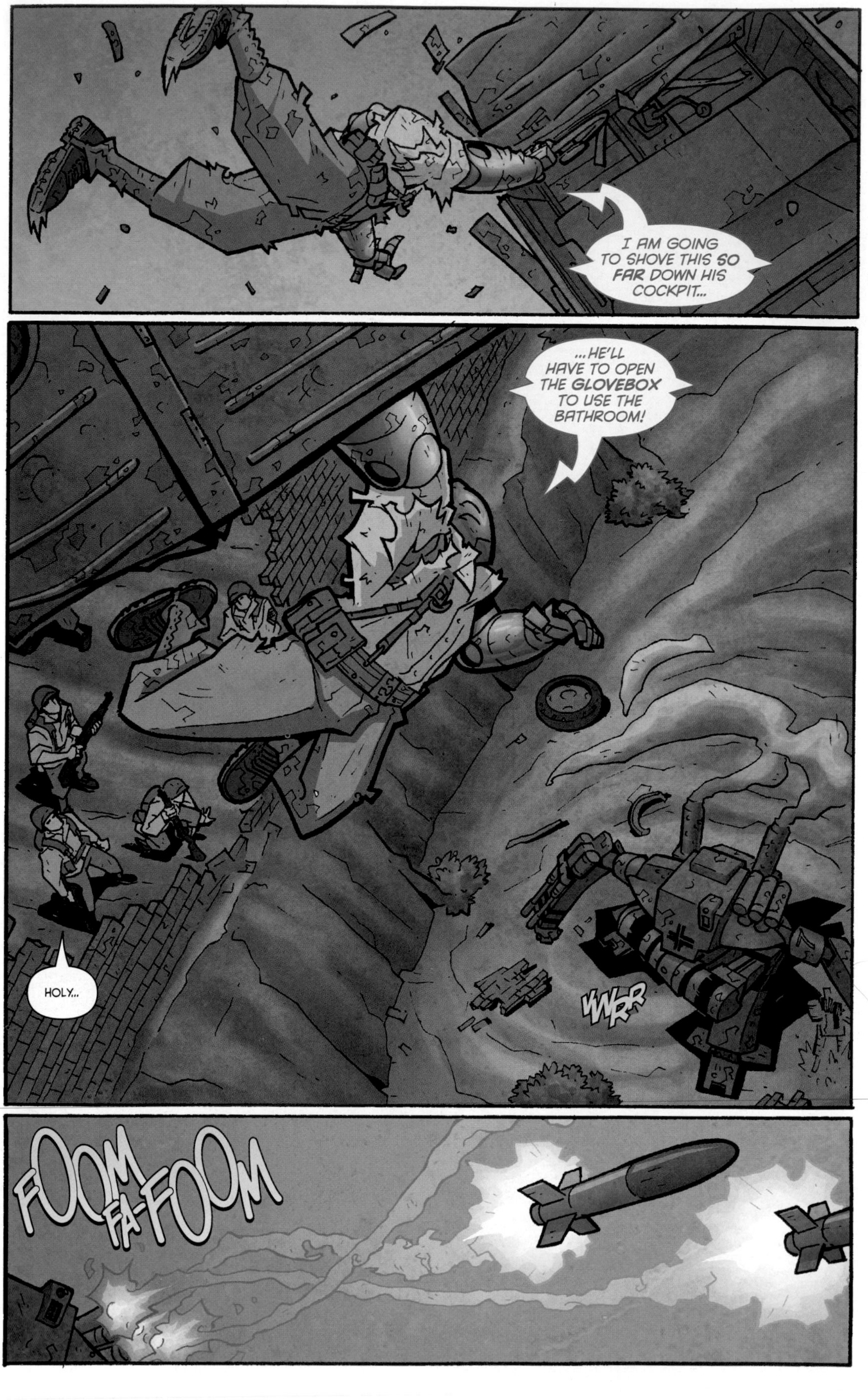
I AM GOING TO SHOVE THIS SO FAR DOWN HIS COCKPIT...
...HE'LL HAVE TO OPEN THE GLOVEBOX TO USE THE BATHROOM!
HOLY...
VVRR
FOOM FA-FOOM

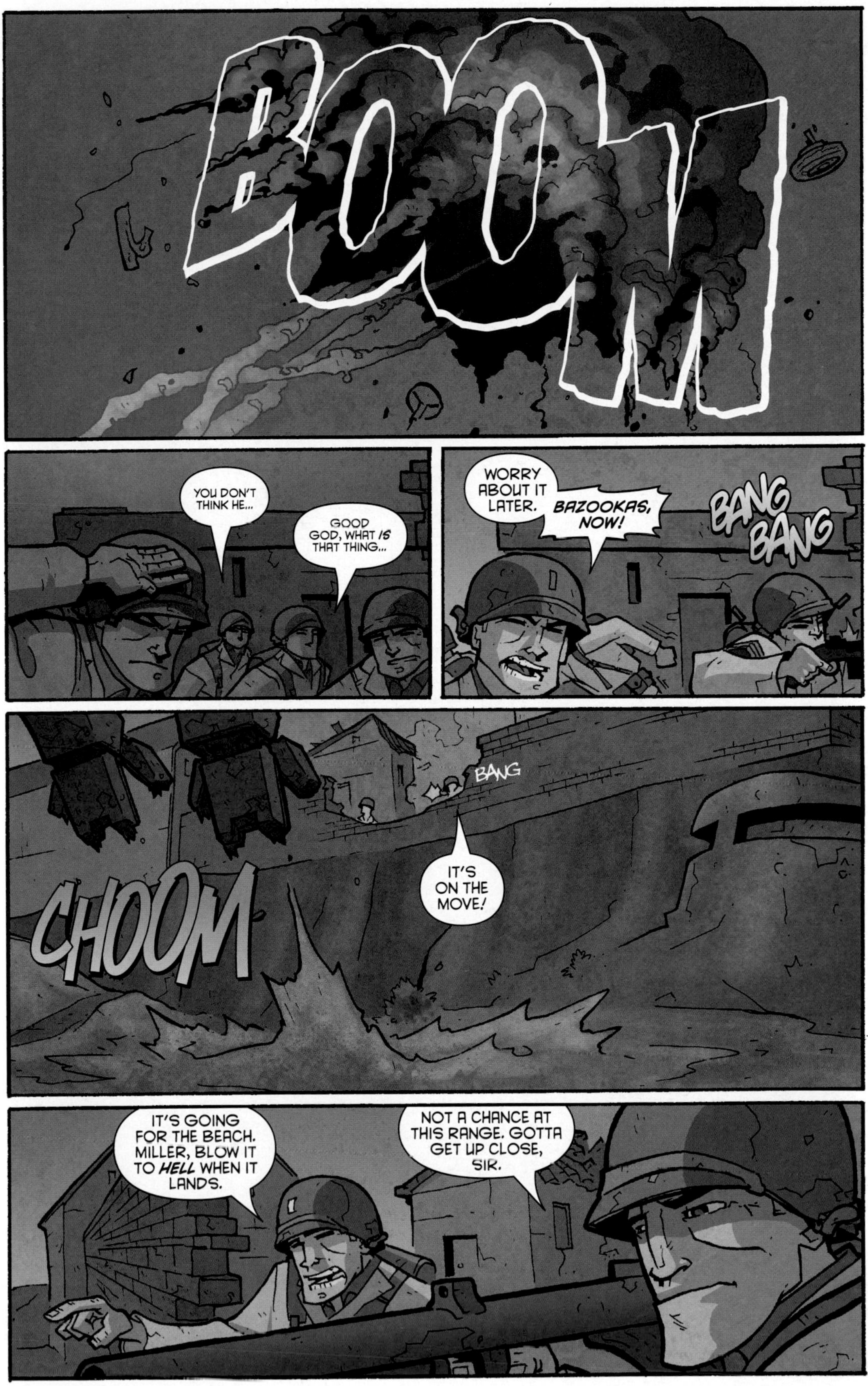
BOOM
YOU DON'T THINK HE...
GOOD GOD, WHAT IS THAT THING...
WORRY ABOUT IT LATER.
BAZOOKAS, NOW!
BANG BANG
BANG
IT'S ON THE MOVE!
CHOOM
IT'S GOING FOR THE BEACH. MILLER, BLOW IT TO HELL WHEN IT LANDS.
NOT A CHANCE AT THIS RANGE. GOTTA GET UP CLOSE, SIR.

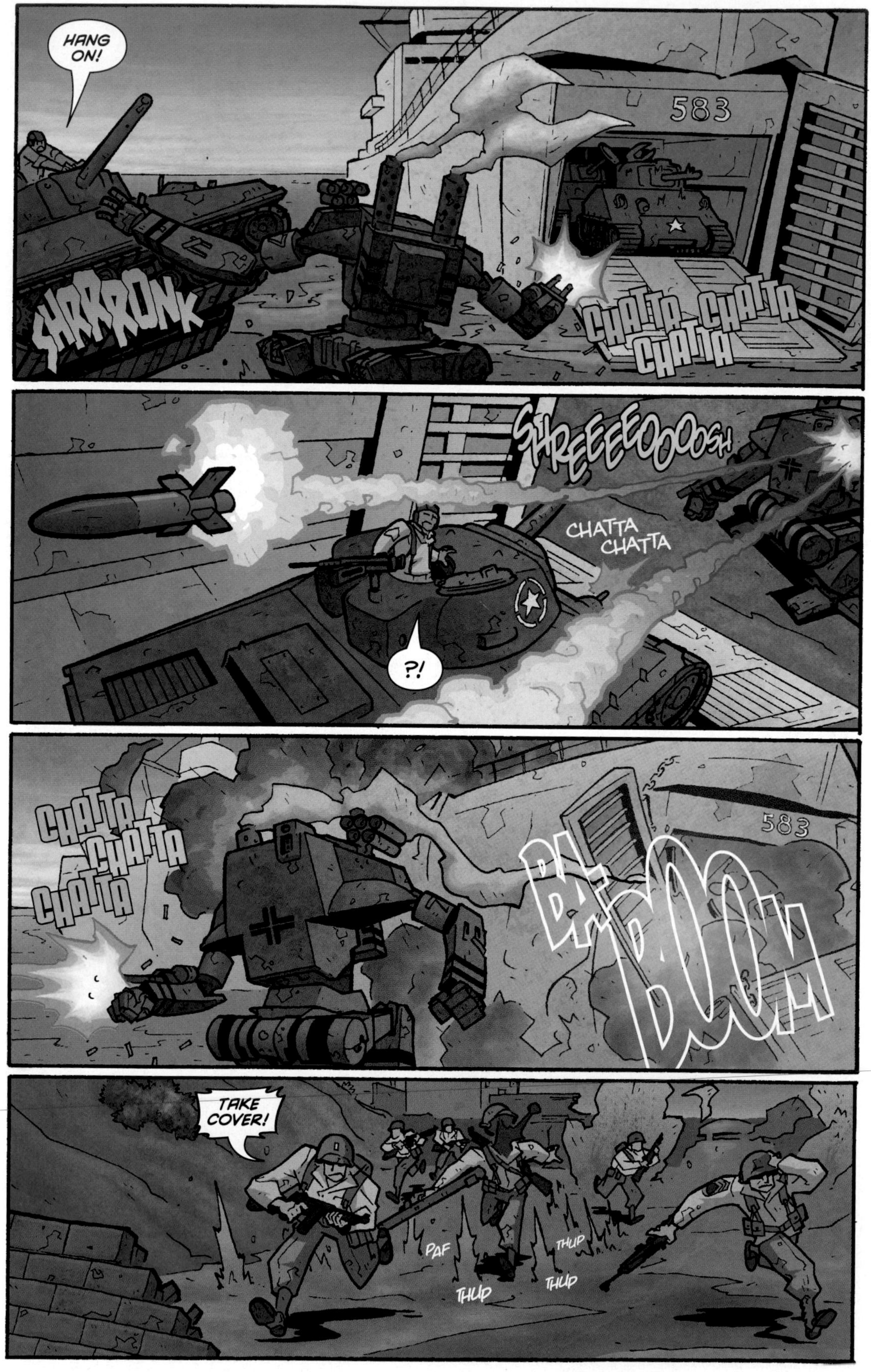
HANG ON!
583
SHRRONK
CHATTA CHATTA CHATTA
SHREEEEOOOOSH
CHATTA CHATTA
?!
CHATTA CHATTA CHATTA
583
BA-BOOM
TAKE COVER!
PAF
THUP
THUP
THUP

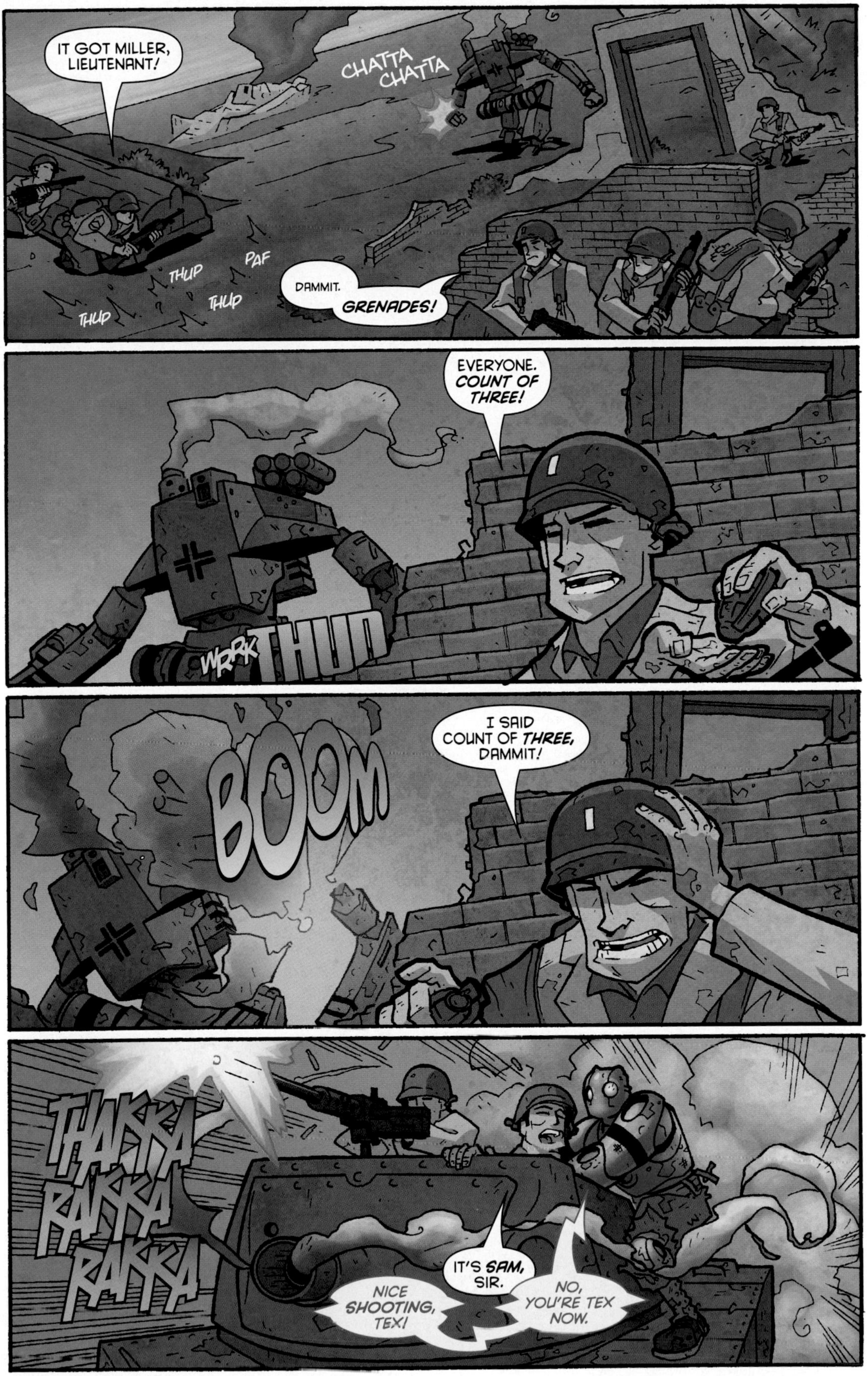
IT GOT MILLER, LIEUTENANT!
CHATTA CHATTA
THUP
PAF
THUP
THUP
DAMMIT. GRENADES!
EVERYONE. COUNT OF THREE!
WRRK THUD
BOOM
I SAID COUNT OF THREE, DAMMIT!
THAKKA RAKKA RAKKA
NICE SHOOTING, TEX!
IT'S SAM, SIR.
NO, YOU'RE TEX NOW.

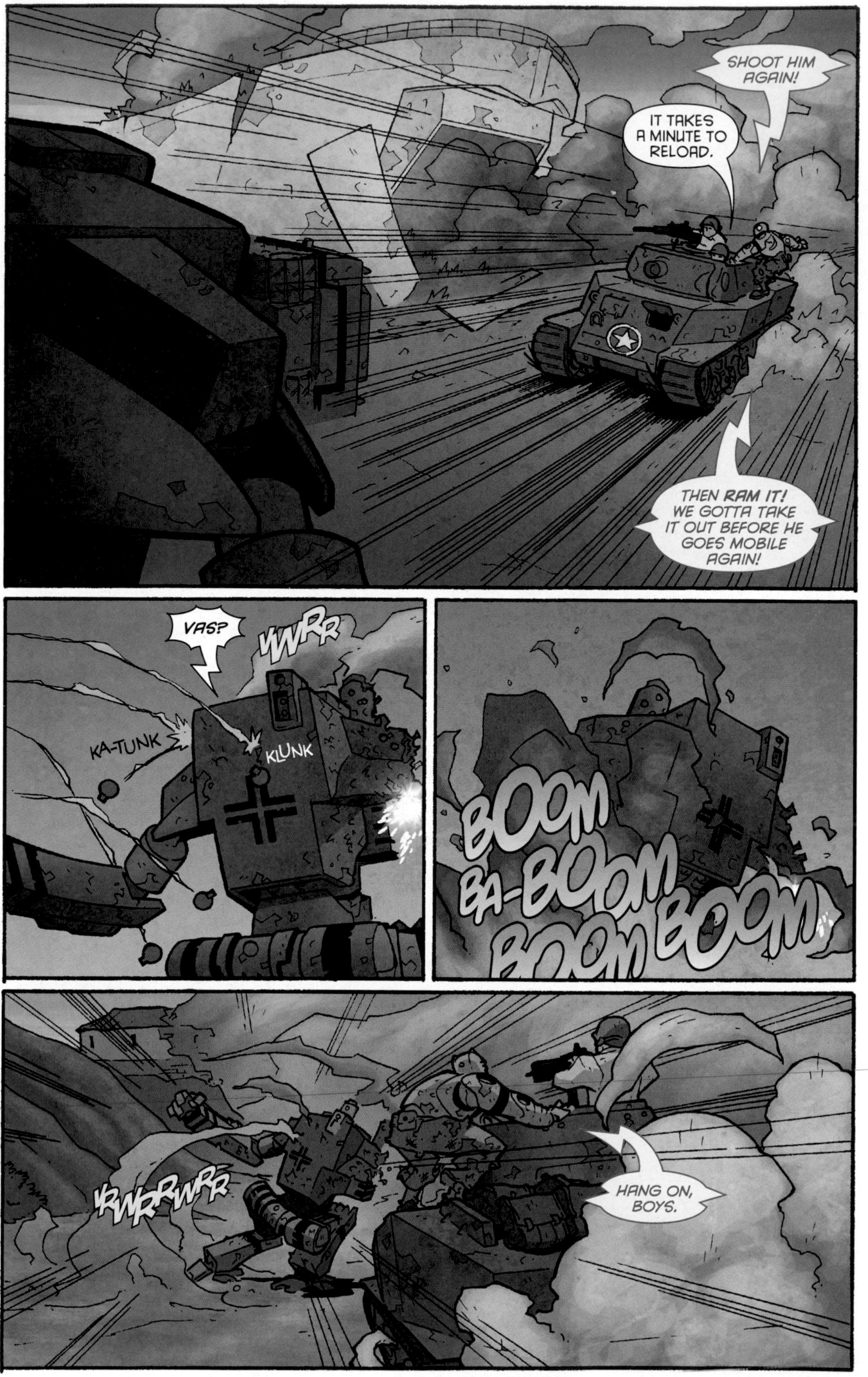
SHOOT HIM AGAIN!
IT TAKES A MINUTE TO RELOAD.
THEN RAM IT! WE GOTTA TAKE IT OUT BEFORE HE GOES MOBILE AGAIN!
VAS?
WWRR
KA-TUNK
KLUNK
BOOM BA-BOOM BOOM BOOM
VRWRRWRR
HANG ON, BOYS.

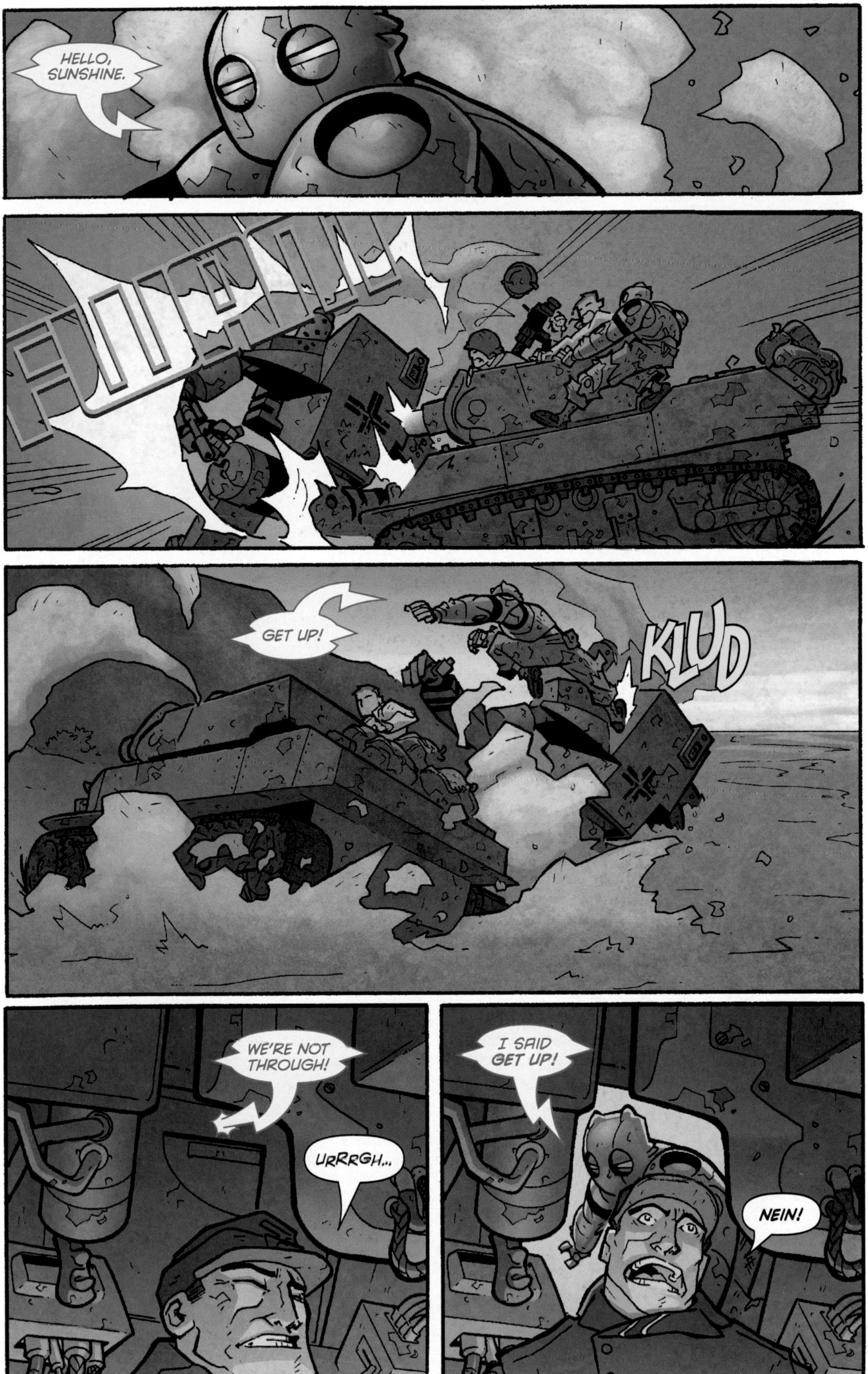
HELLO, SUNSHINE.
GET UP!
KLUD
WE'RE NOT THROUGH!
URRRGH...
I SAID GET UP!
NEIN!

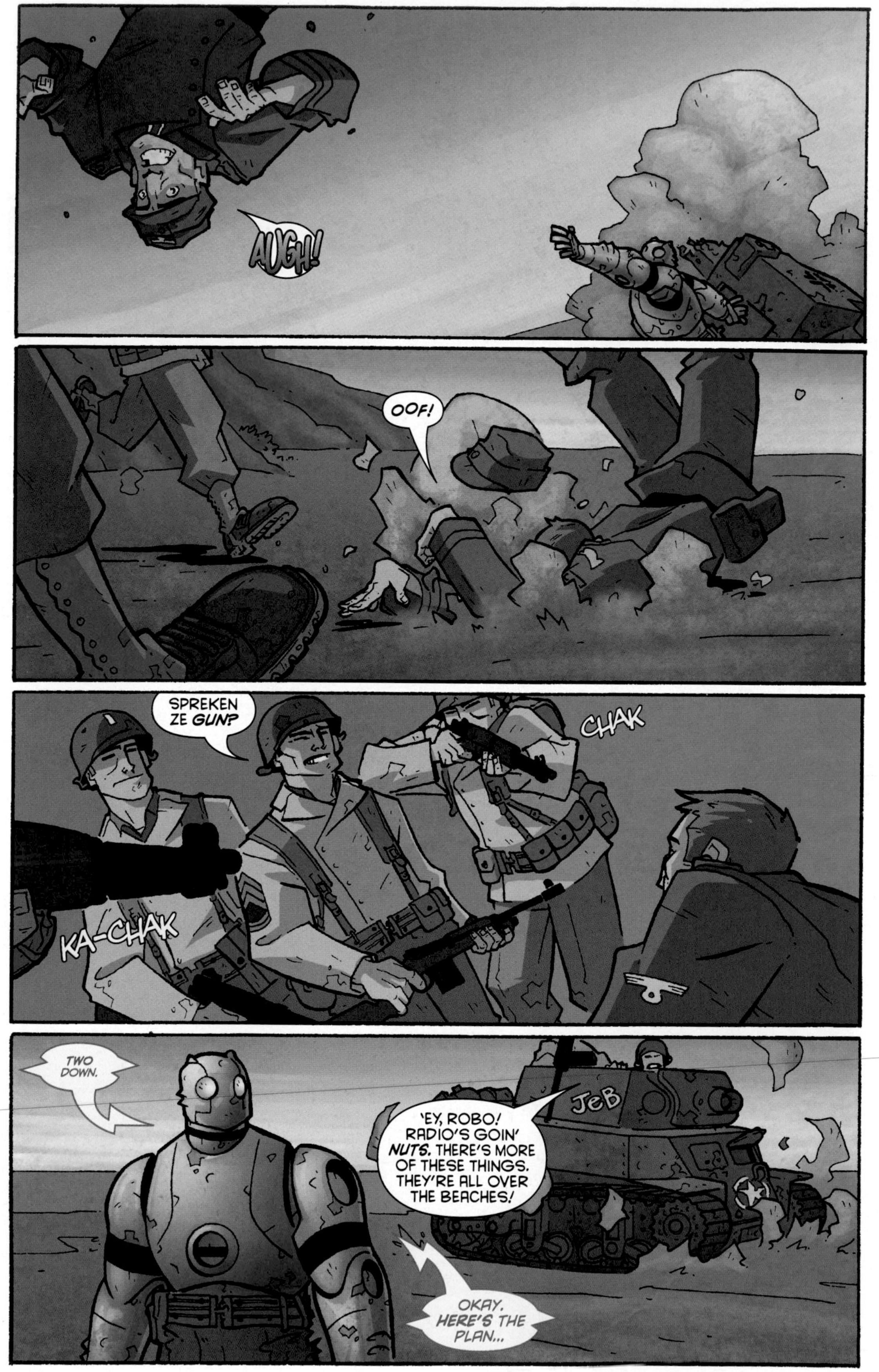
AUGH!
OOF!
SPREKEN ZE GUN?
CHAK
KA-CHAK
TWO DOWN.
'EY, ROBO! RADIO'S GOIN' NUTS. THERE'S MORE OF THESE THINGS. THEY'RE ALL OVER THE BEACHES!
JeB
OKAY. HERE'S THE PLAN...

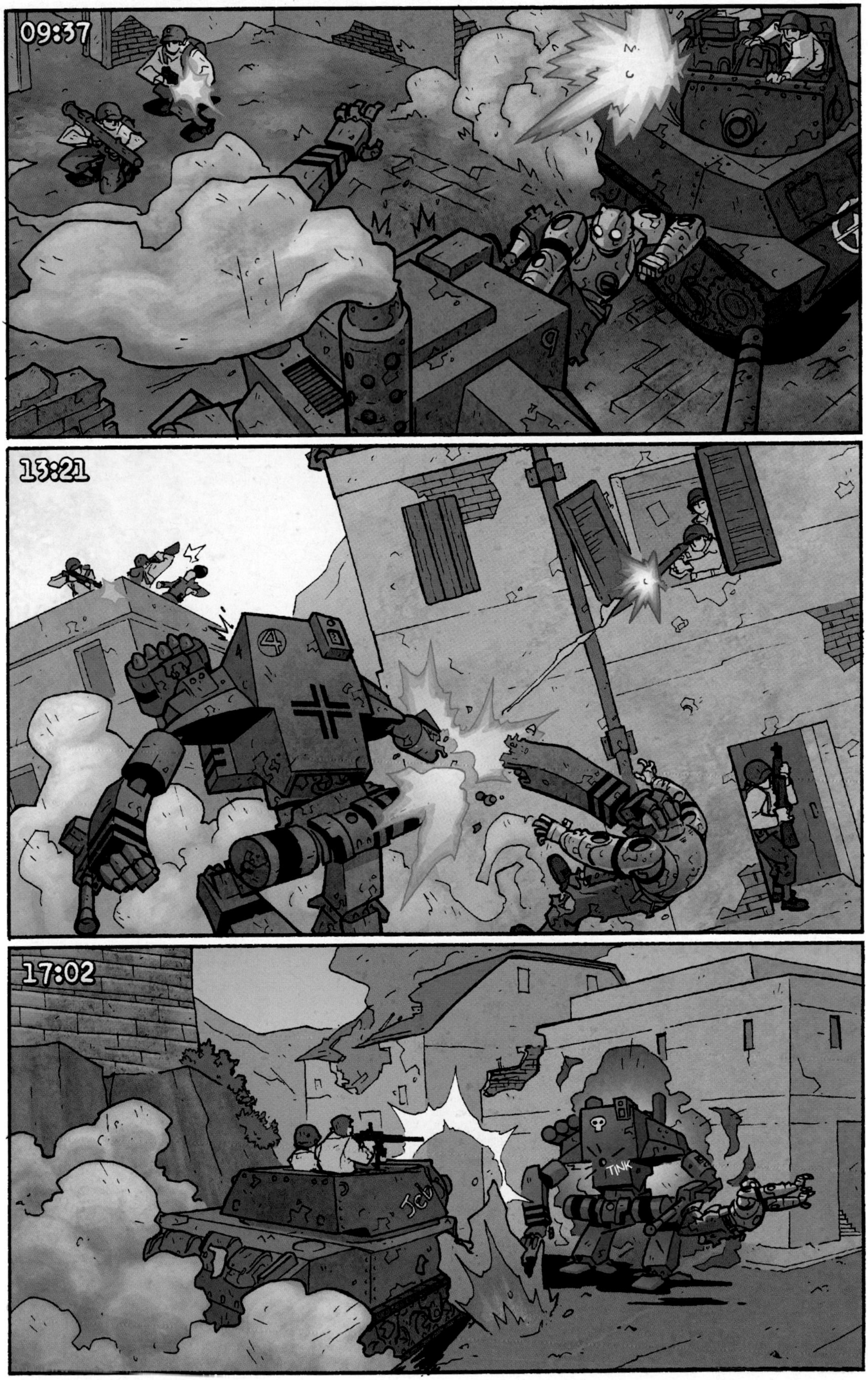
09:37
13:21
17:02
TINK

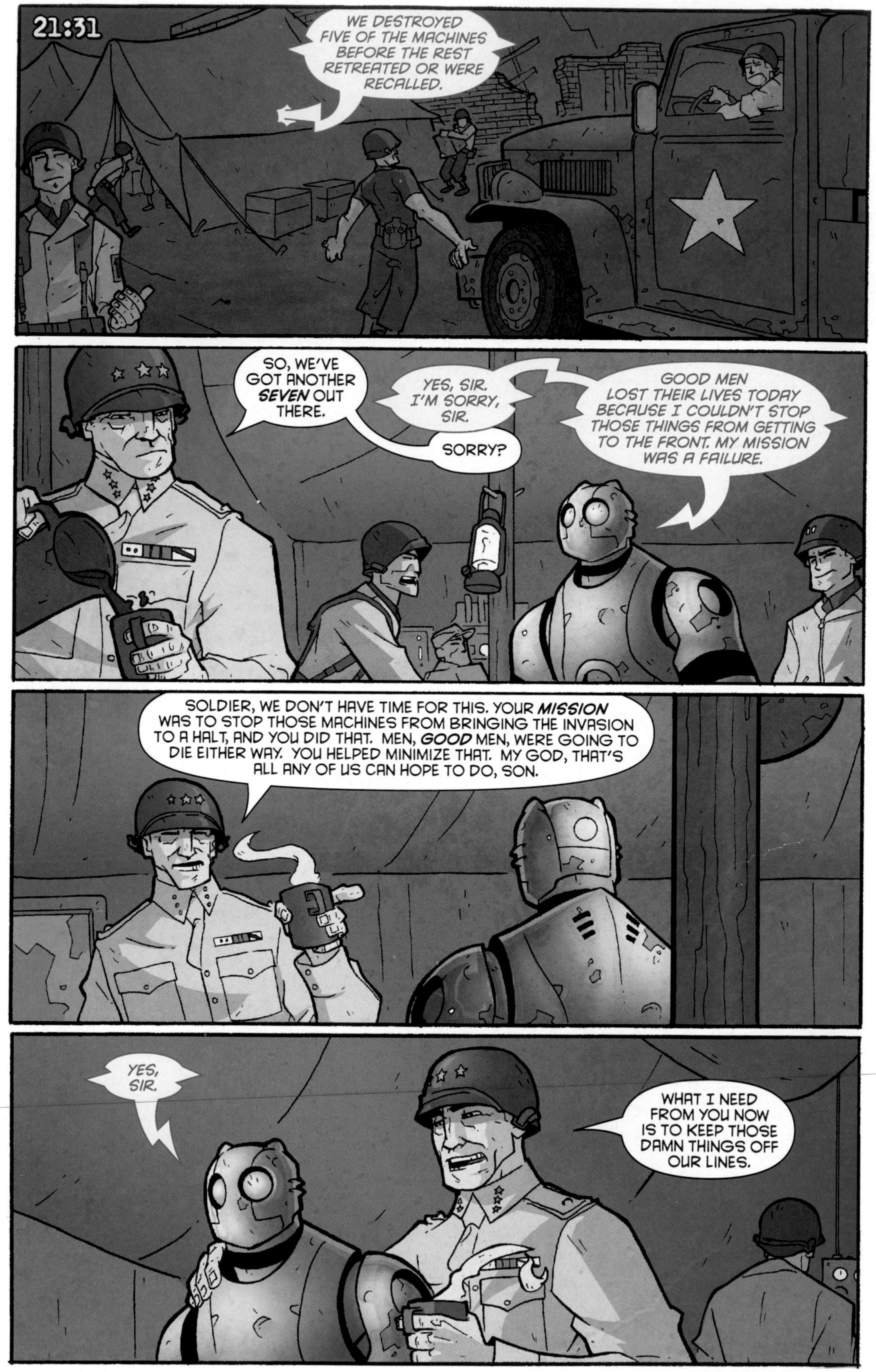
21:31
WE DESTROYED FIVE OF THE MACHINES BEFORE THE REST RETREATED OR WERE RECALLED.
SO, WE'VE GOT ANOTHER SEVEN OUT THERE.
YES, SIR. I'M SORRY, SIR.
SORRY?
GOOD MEN LOST THEIR LIVES TODAY BECAUSE I COULDN'T STOP THOSE THINGS FROM GETTING TO THE FRONT. MY MISSION WAS A FAILURE.
SOLDIER, WE DON'T HAVE TIME FOR THIS. YOUR MISSION WAS TO STOP THOSE MACHINES FROM BRINGING THE INVASION TO A HALT, AND YOU DID THAT. MEN, GOOD MEN, WERE GOING TO DIE EITHER WAY. YOU HELPED MINIMIZE THAT. MY GOD, THAT'S ALL ANY OF US CAN HOPE TO DO, SON.
YES, SIR.
WHAT I NEED FROM YOU NOW IS TO KEEP THOSE DAMN THINGS OFF OUR LINES.

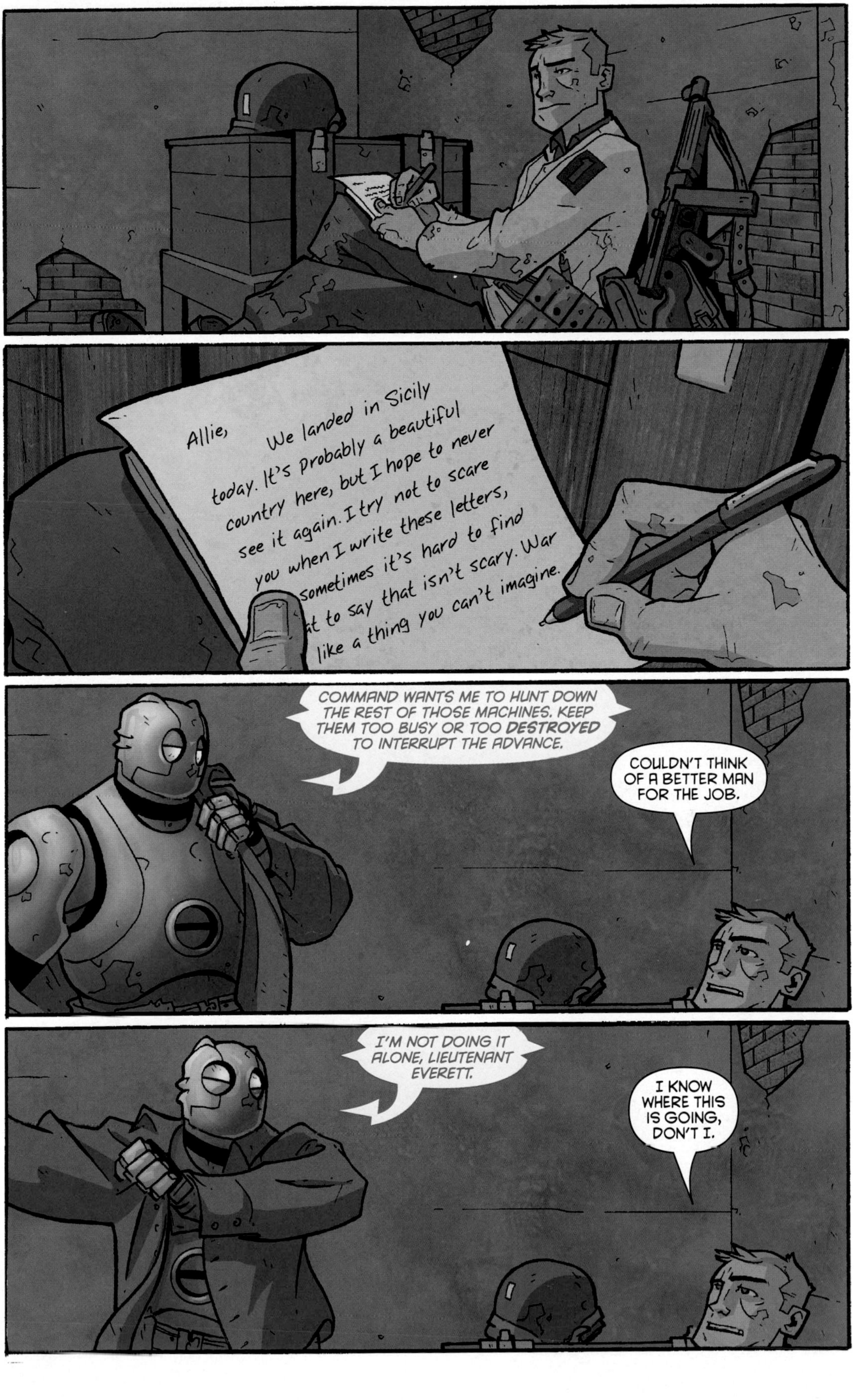
Allie,
We landed in Sicily
today. It's probably a beautiful
country here, but I hope to never
see it again. I try not to scare
you when I write these letters,
sometimes it's hard to find
at to say that isn't scary. War
like a thing you can't imagine.
COMMAND WANTS ME TO HUNT DOWN THE REST OF THOSE MACHINES. KEEP THEM TOO BUSY OR TOO DESTROYED TO INTERRUPT THE ADVANCE.
COULDN'T THINK OF A BETTER MAN FOR THE JOB.
I'M NOT DOING IT ALONE, LIEUTENANT EVERETT.
I KNOW WHERE THIS IS GOING, DON'T I.

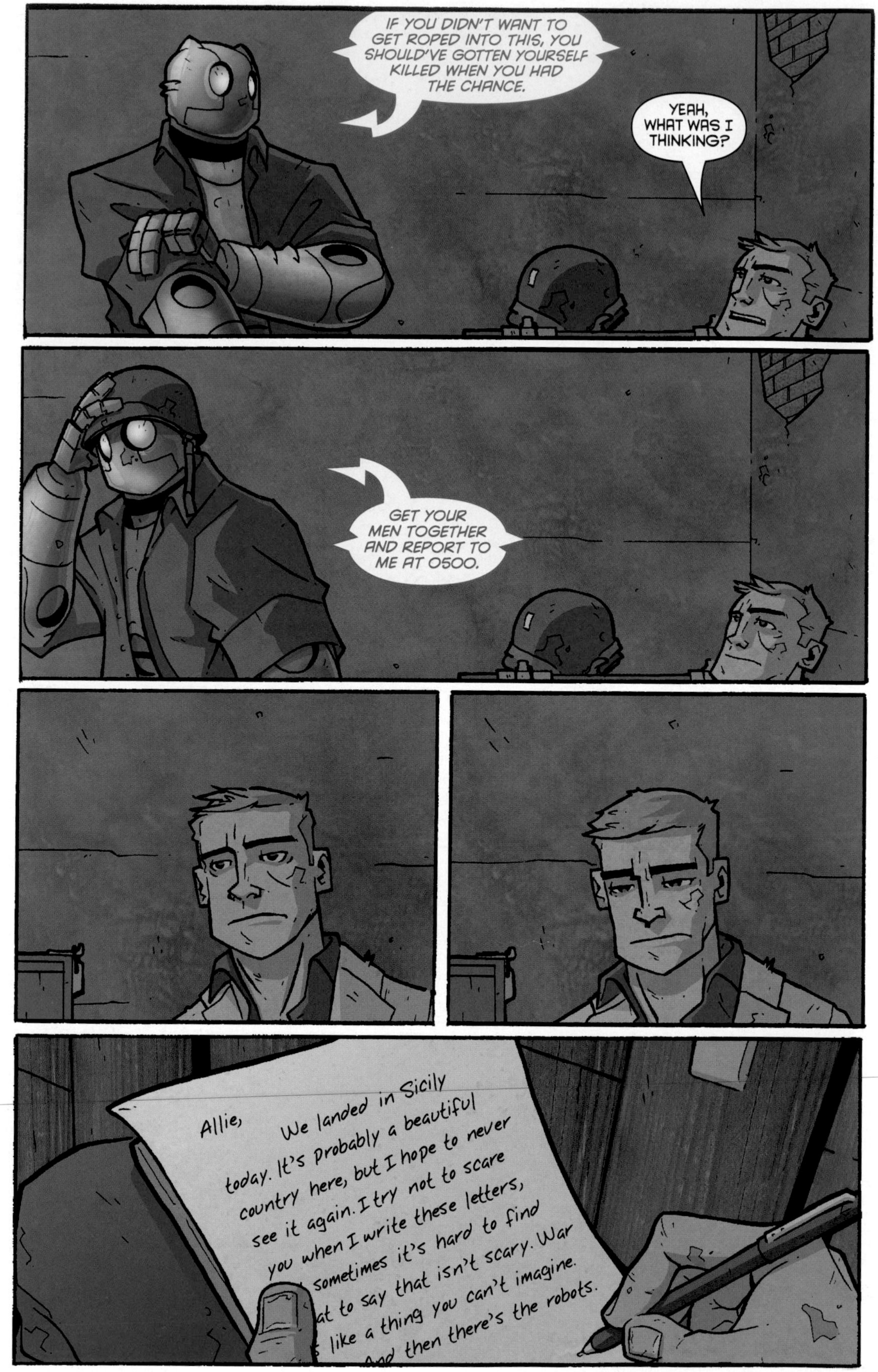
IF YOU DIDN'T WANT TO GET ROPED INTO THIS, YOU SHOULD'VE GOTTEN YOURSELF KILLED WHEN YOU HAD THE CHANCE.
YEAH, WHAT WAS I THINKING?
GET YOUR MEN TOGETHER AND REPORT TO ME AT 0500.
Allie,
We landed in Sicily today. It's probably a beautiful country here, but I hope to never see it again. I try not to scare you when I write these letters, sometimes it's hard to find at to say that isn't scary. War like a thing you can't imagine. And then there's the robots.

# GOING OFF TRACK

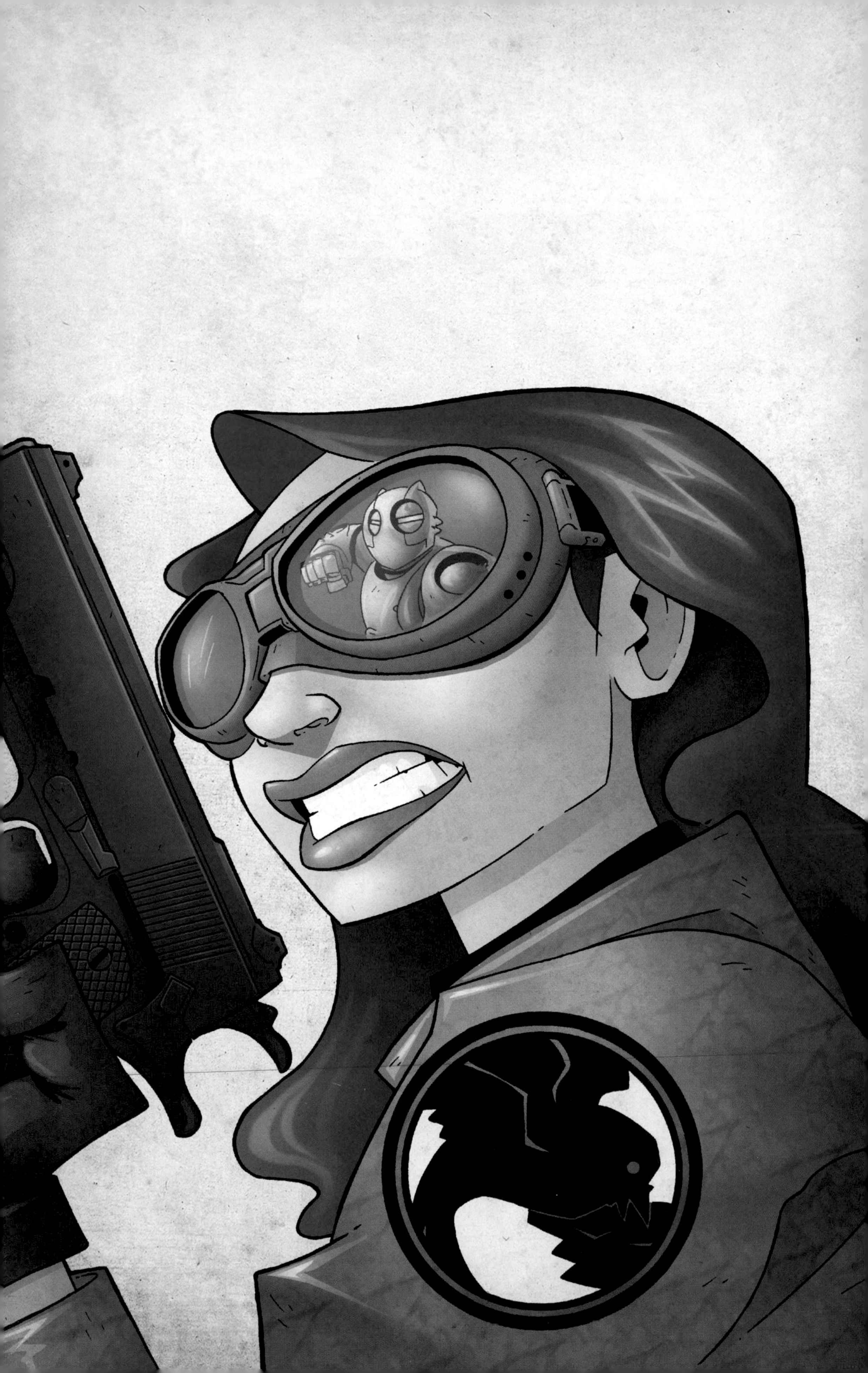

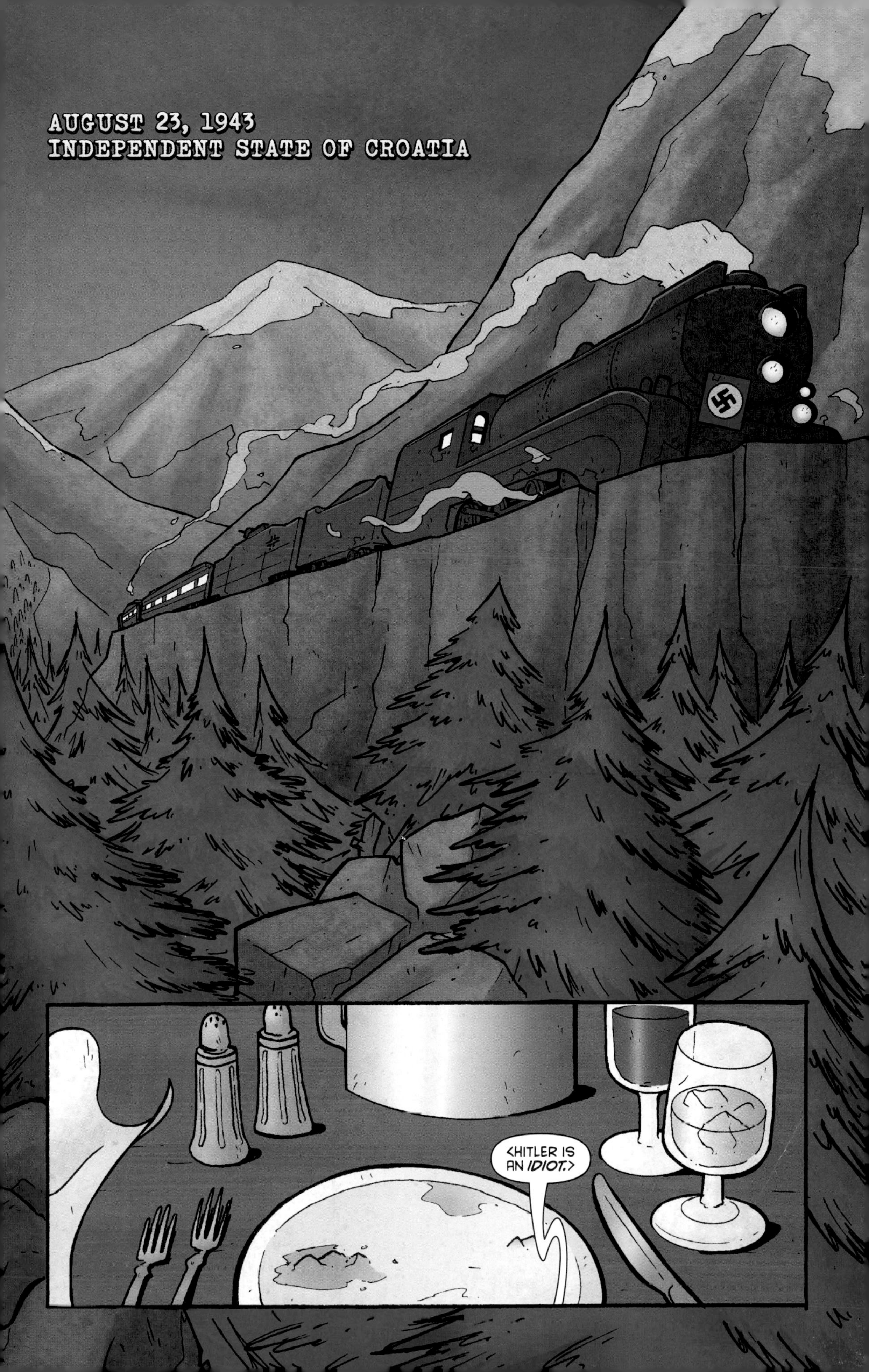
AUGUST 23, 1943
INDEPENDENT STATE OF CROATIA
<HITLER IS AN *IDIOT.*>

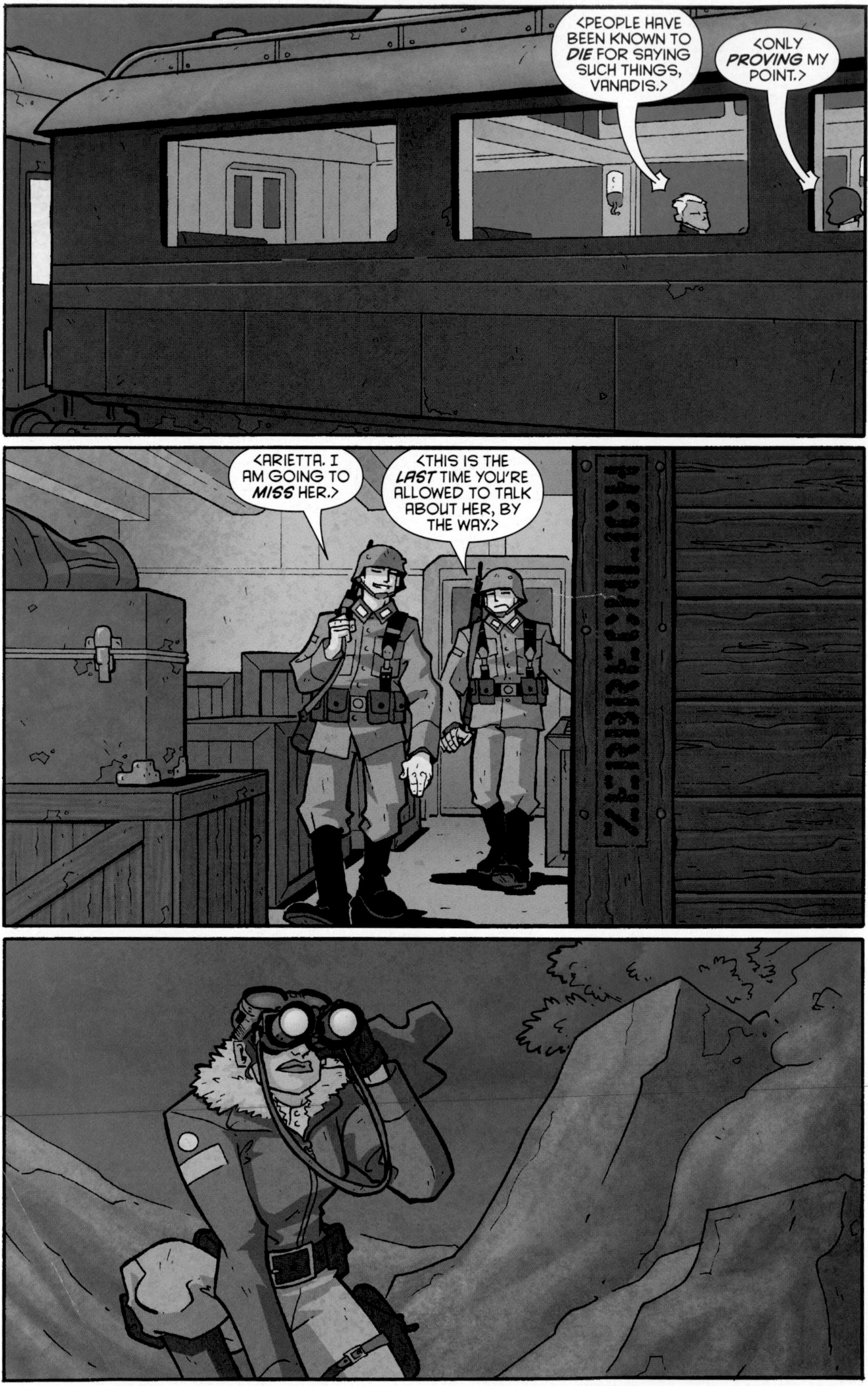
<PEOPLE HAVE BEEN KNOWN TO DIE FOR SAYING SUCH THINGS, VANADIS.>
<ONLY PROVING MY POINT.>
<ARIETTA. I AM GOING TO MISS HER.>
<THIS IS THE LAST TIME YOU'RE ALLOWED TO TALK ABOUT HER, BY THE WAY.>

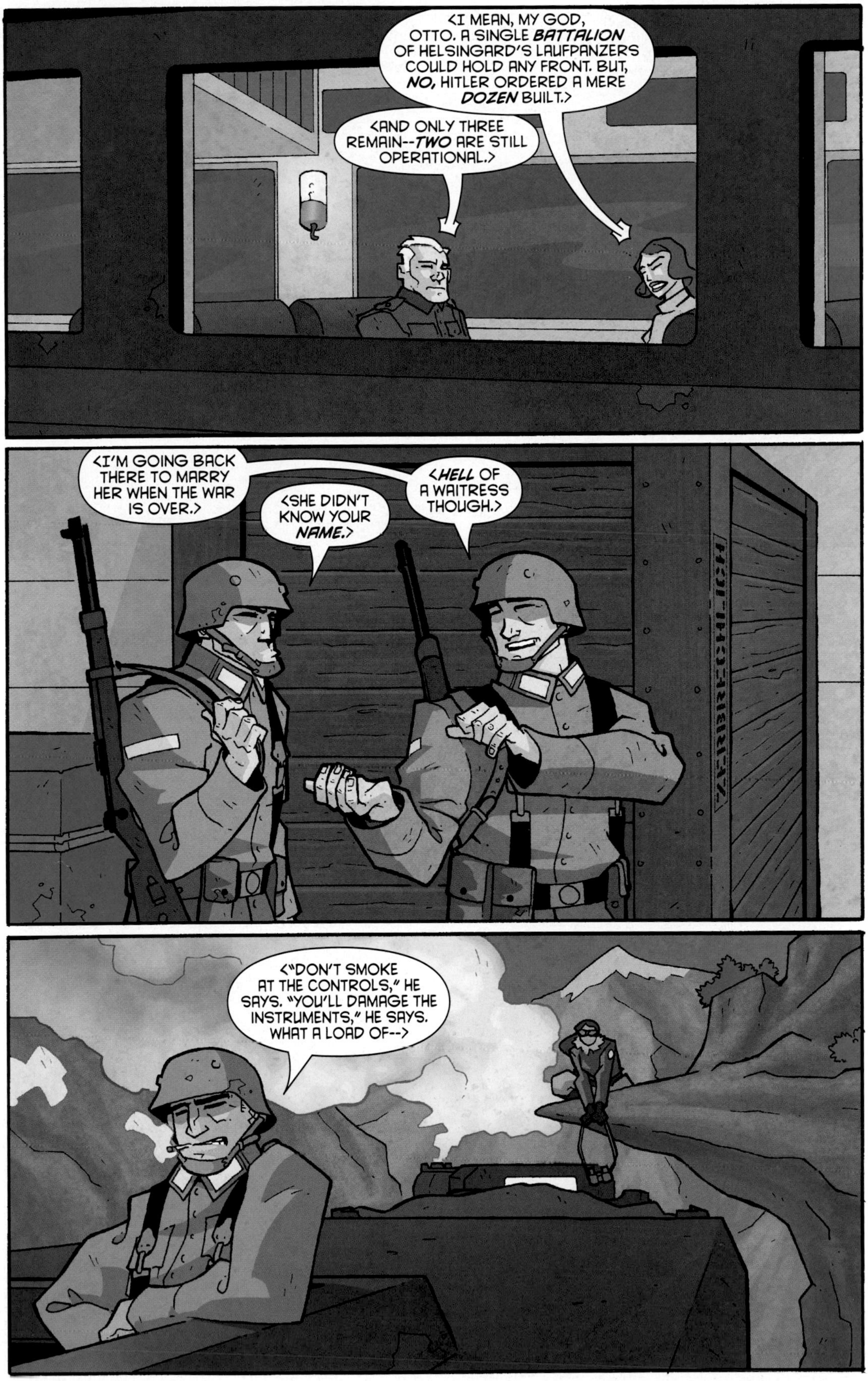
<I MEAN, MY GOD, OTTO. A SINGLE BATTALION OF HELSINGARD'S LAUFPANZERS COULD HOLD ANY FRONT. BUT, NO, HITLER ORDERED A MERE DOZEN BUILT.>
<AND ONLY THREE REMAIN--TWO ARE STILL OPERATIONAL.>
<I'M GOING BACK THERE TO MARRY HER WHEN THE WAR IS OVER.>
<SHE DIDN'T KNOW YOUR NAME.>
<HELL OF A WAITRESS THOUGH.>
<"DON'T SMOKE AT THE CONTROLS," HE SAYS. "YOU'LL DAMAGE THE INSTRUMENTS," HE SAYS. WHAT A LOAD OF-->

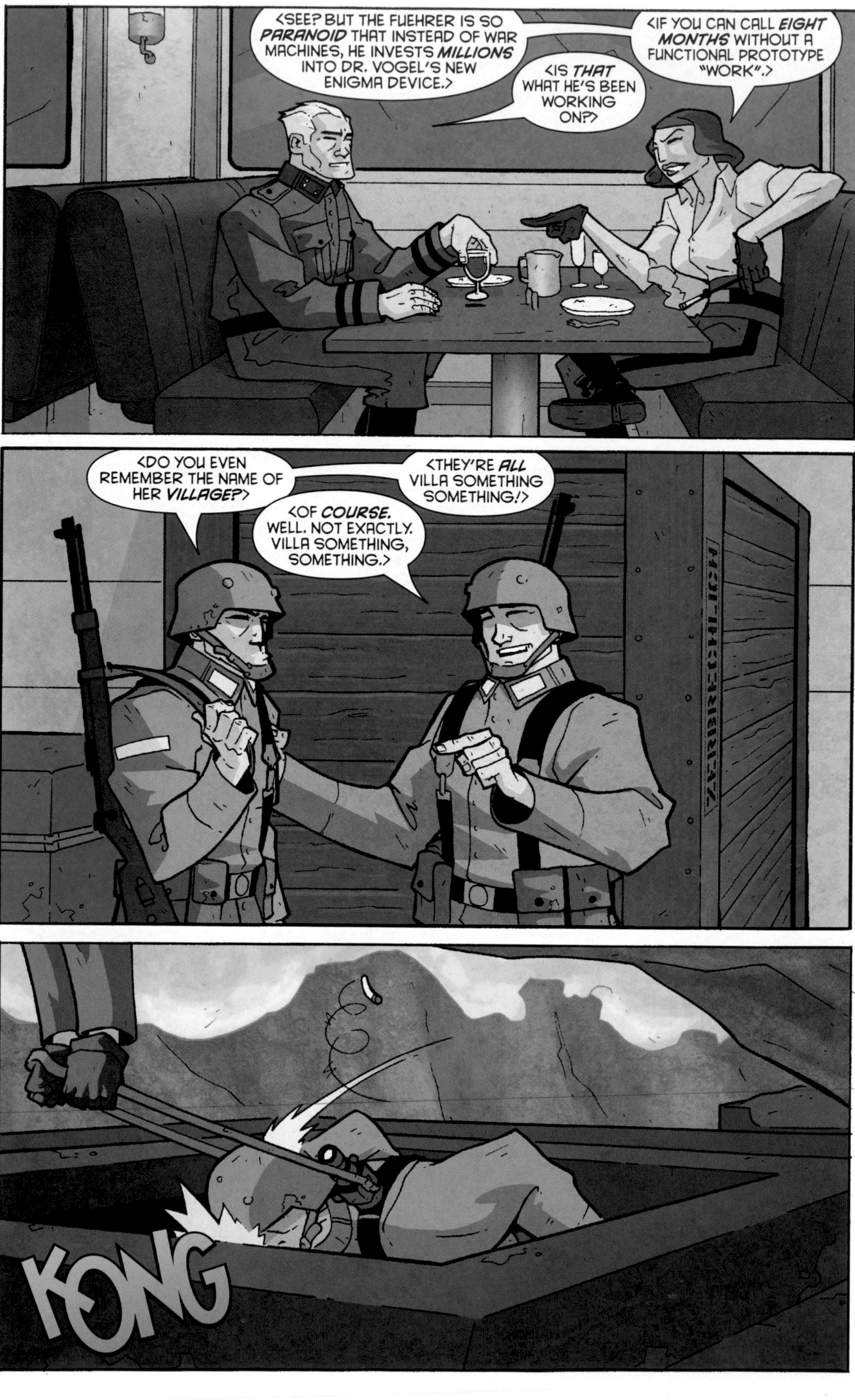
<SEE? BUT THE FUEHRER IS SO PARANOID THAT INSTEAD OF WAR MACHINES, HE INVESTS MILLIONS INTO DR. VOGEL'S NEW ENIGMA DEVICE.>
<IS THAT WHAT HE'S BEEN WORKING ON?>
<IF YOU CAN CALL EIGHT MONTHS WITHOUT A FUNCTIONAL PROTOTYPE "WORK".>
<DO YOU EVEN REMEMBER THE NAME OF HER VILLAGE?>
<OF COURSE. WELL. NOT EXACTLY. VILLA SOMETHING, SOMETHING.>
<THEY'RE ALL VILLA SOMETHING SOMETHING!>
KONG

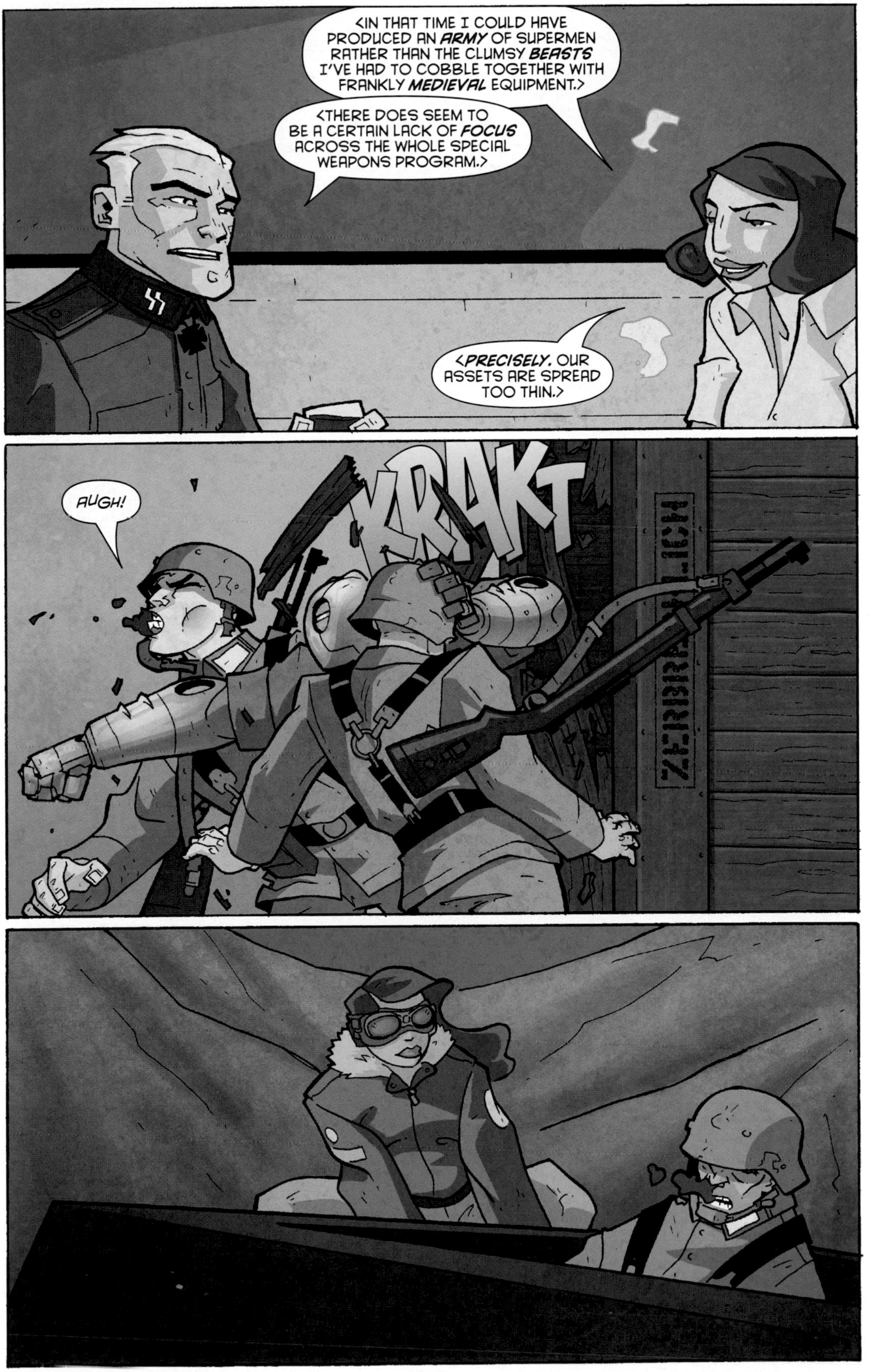
<IN THAT TIME I COULD HAVE PRODUCED AN *ARMY* OF SUPERMEN RATHER THAN THE CLUMSY *BEASTS* I'VE HAD TO COBBLE TOGETHER WITH FRANKLY *MEDIEVAL* EQUIPMENT.>
<THERE DOES SEEM TO BE A CERTAIN LACK OF *FOCUS* ACROSS THE WHOLE SPECIAL WEAPONS PROGRAM.>
<*PRECISELY.* OUR ASSETS ARE SPREAD TOO THIN.>
AUGH!
KRAKT

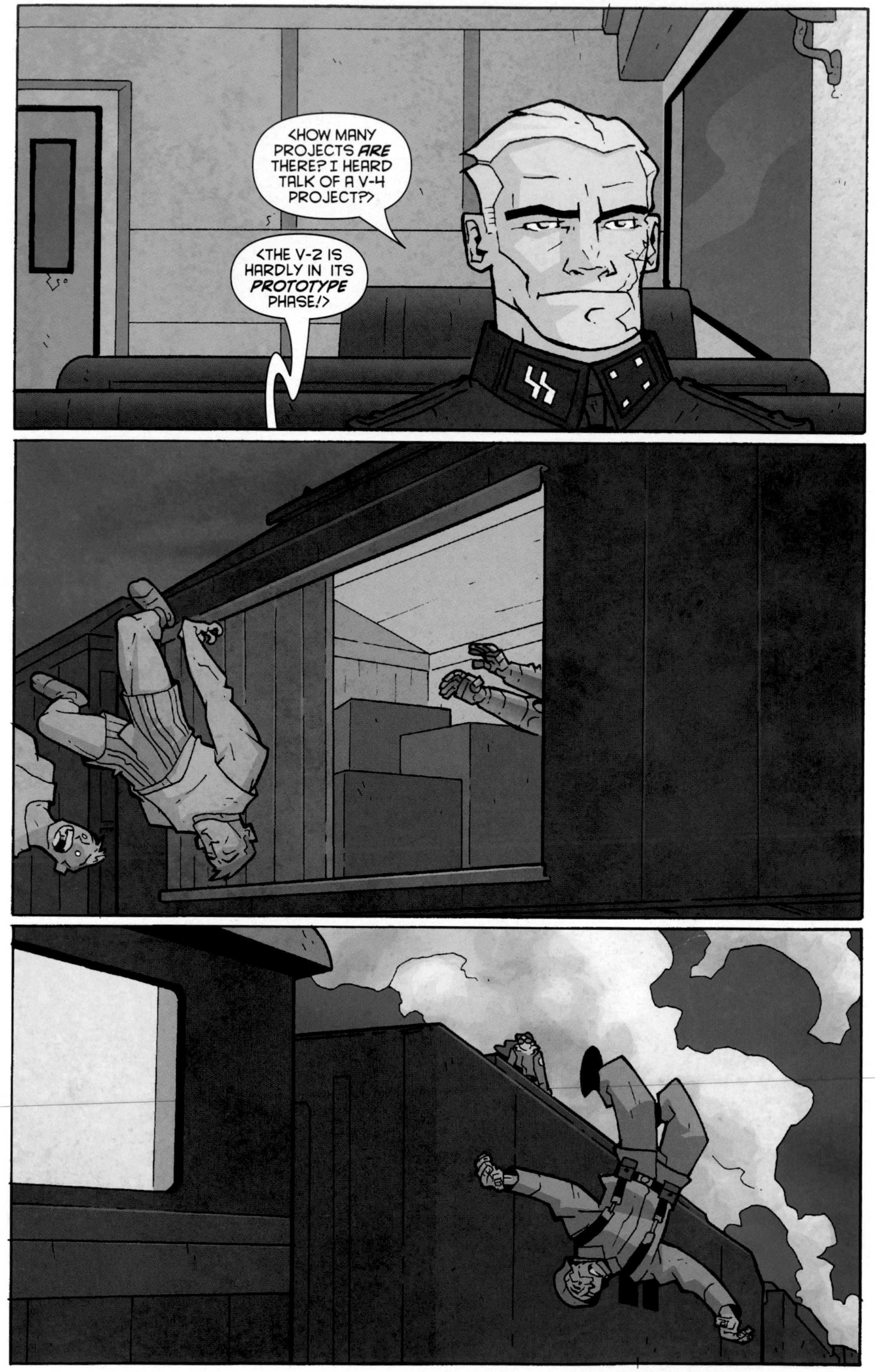
<HOW MANY PROJECTS ARE THERE? I HEARD TALK OF A V-4 PROJECT?>
<THE V-2 IS HARDLY IN ITS PROTOTYPE PHASE!>

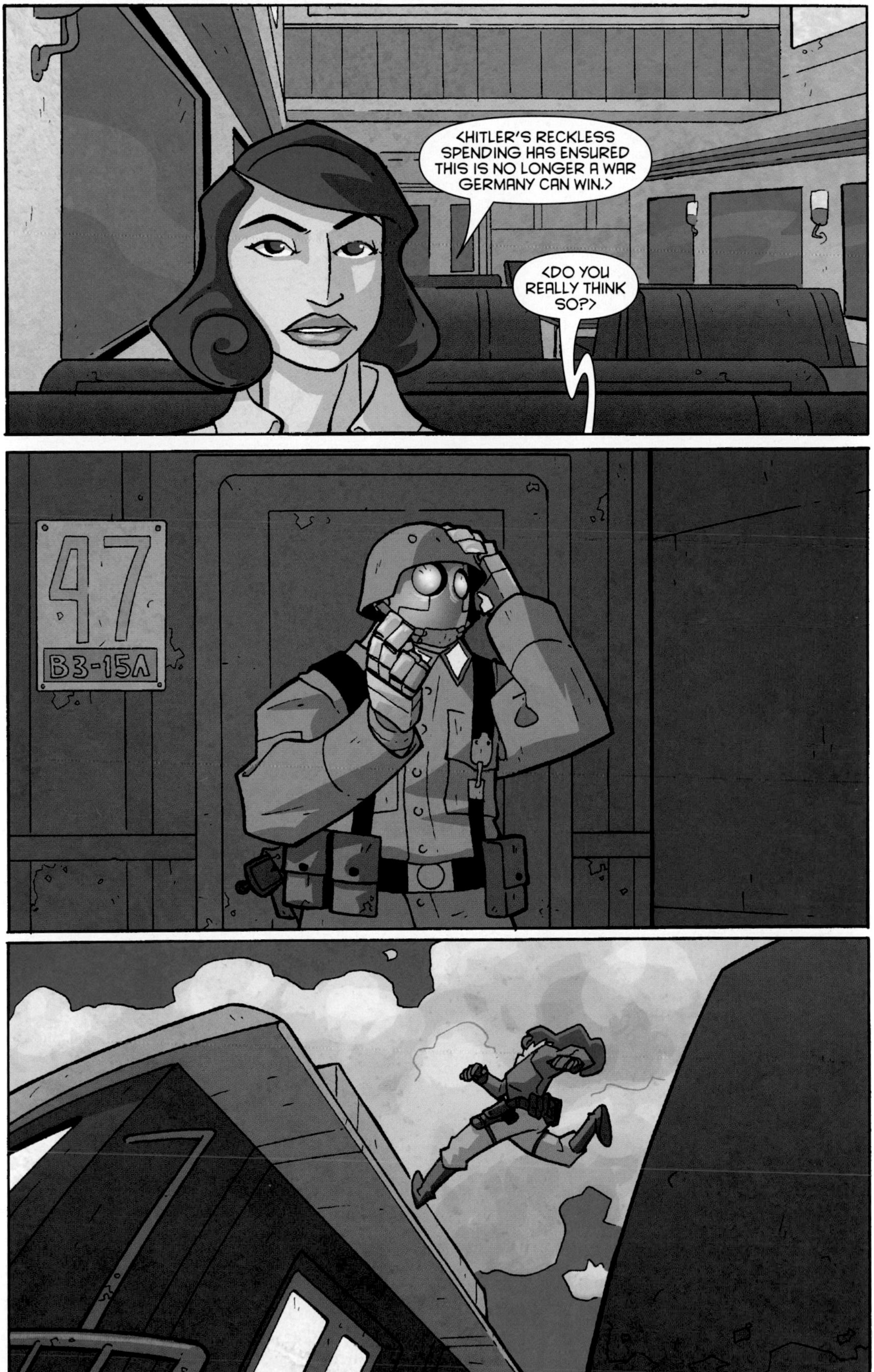
<HITLER'S RECKLESS SPENDING HAS ENSURED THIS IS NO LONGER A WAR GERMANY CAN WIN.>
<DO YOU REALLY THINK SO?>
47
B3-15A

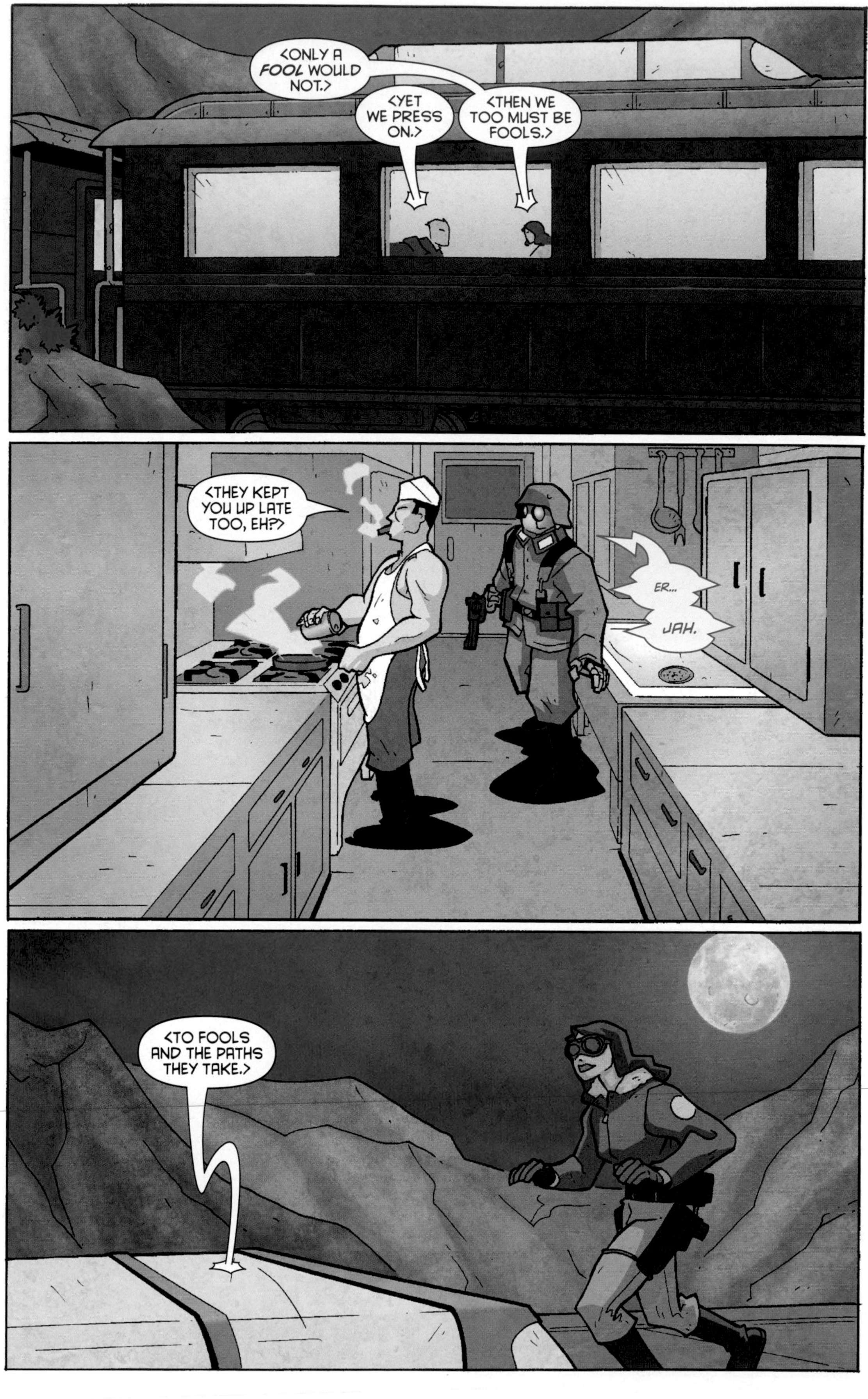

<ONLY A *FOOL* WOULD NOT.>
<YET WE PRESS ON.>
<THEN WE TOO MUST BE FOOLS.>
<THEY KEPT YOU UP LATE TOO, EH?>
ER...
JAH.
<TO FOOLS AND THE PATHS THEY TAKE.>

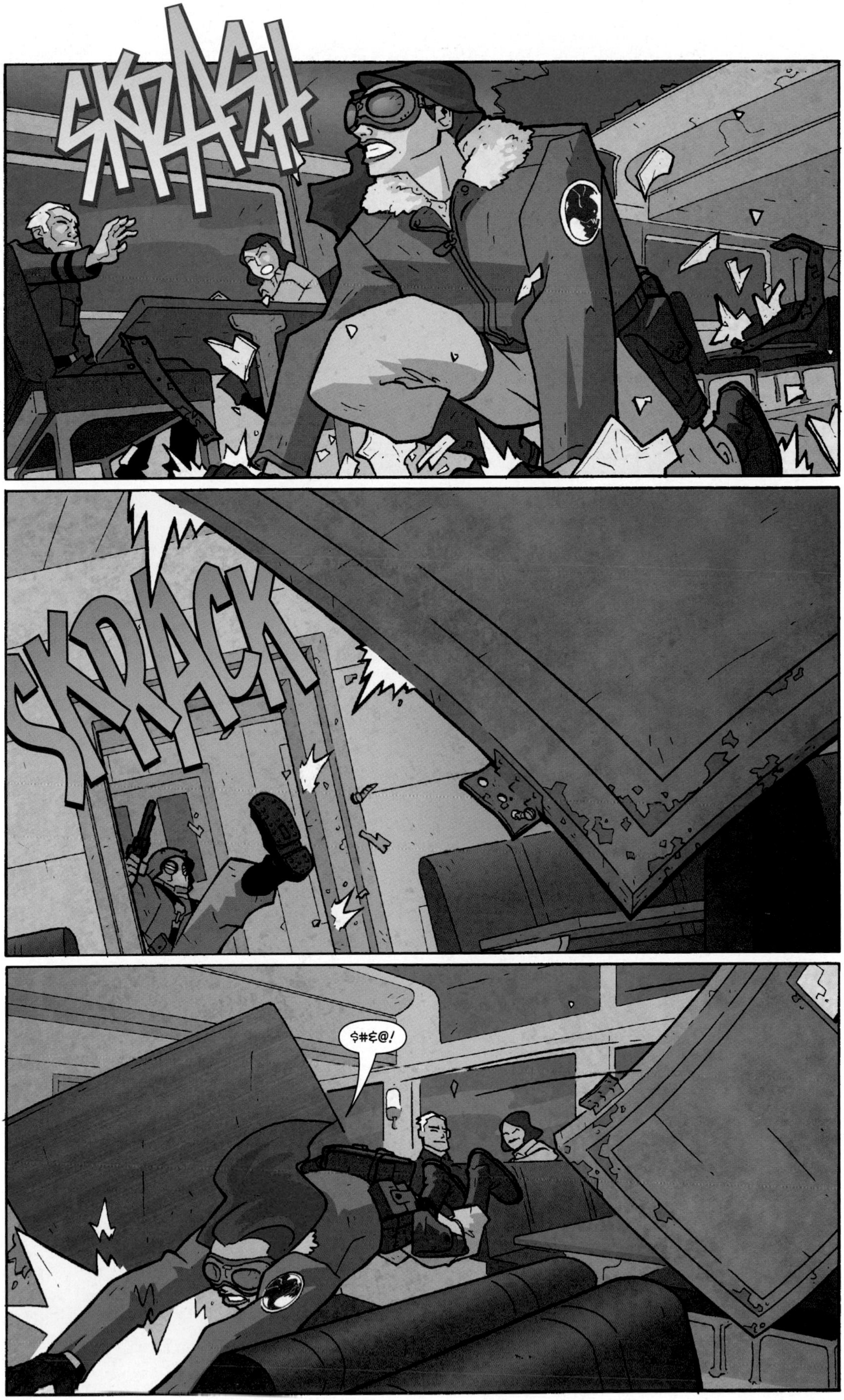
SKRASH
SKRACK
$#&@!

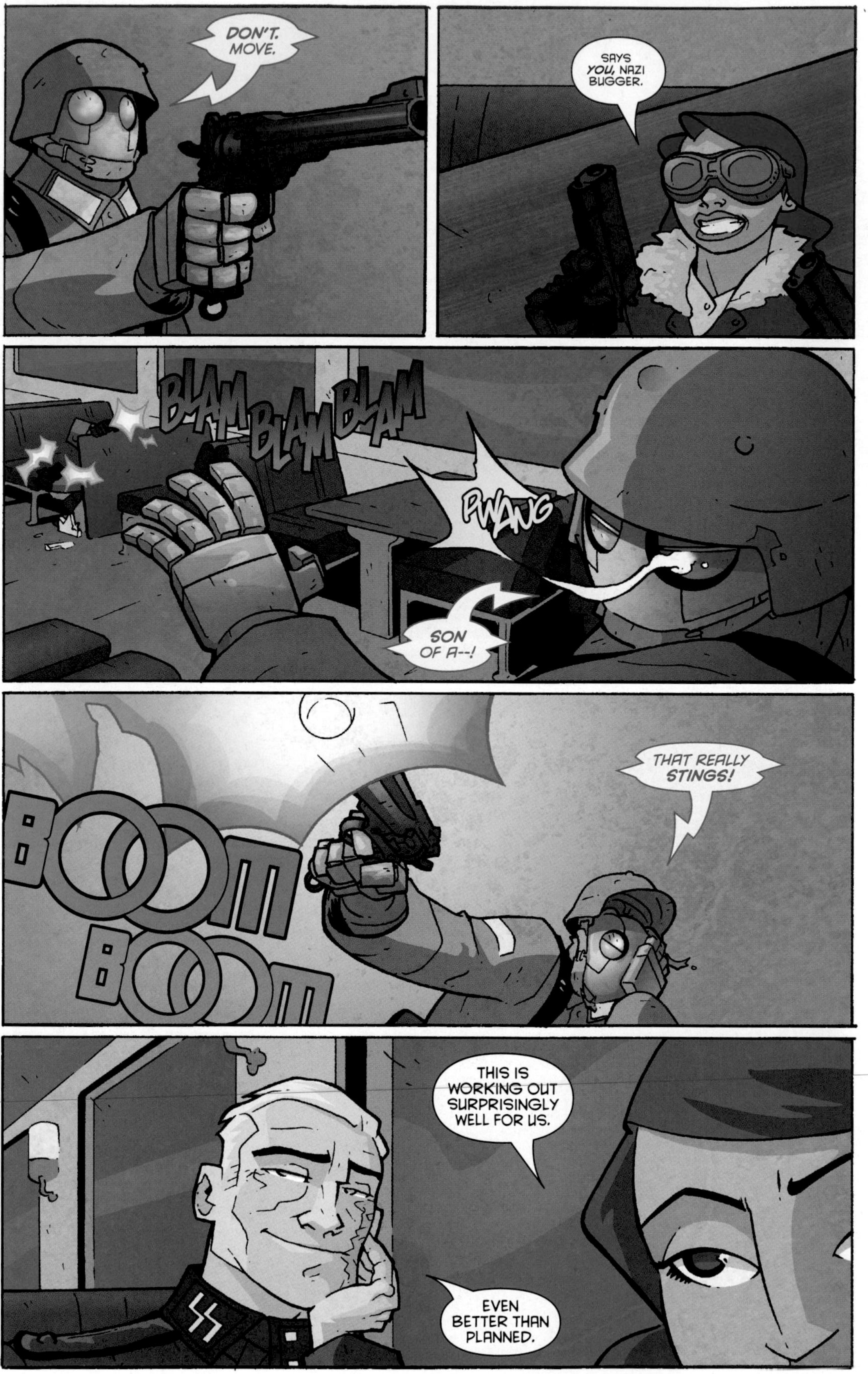
DON'T. MOVE.
SAYS YOU, NAZI BUGGER.
BLAM BLAM BLAM
PWANG
SON OF A--!
THAT REALLY STINGS!
BOOM BOOM
THIS IS WORKING OUT SURPRISINGLY WELL FOR US.
EVEN BETTER THAN PLANNED.

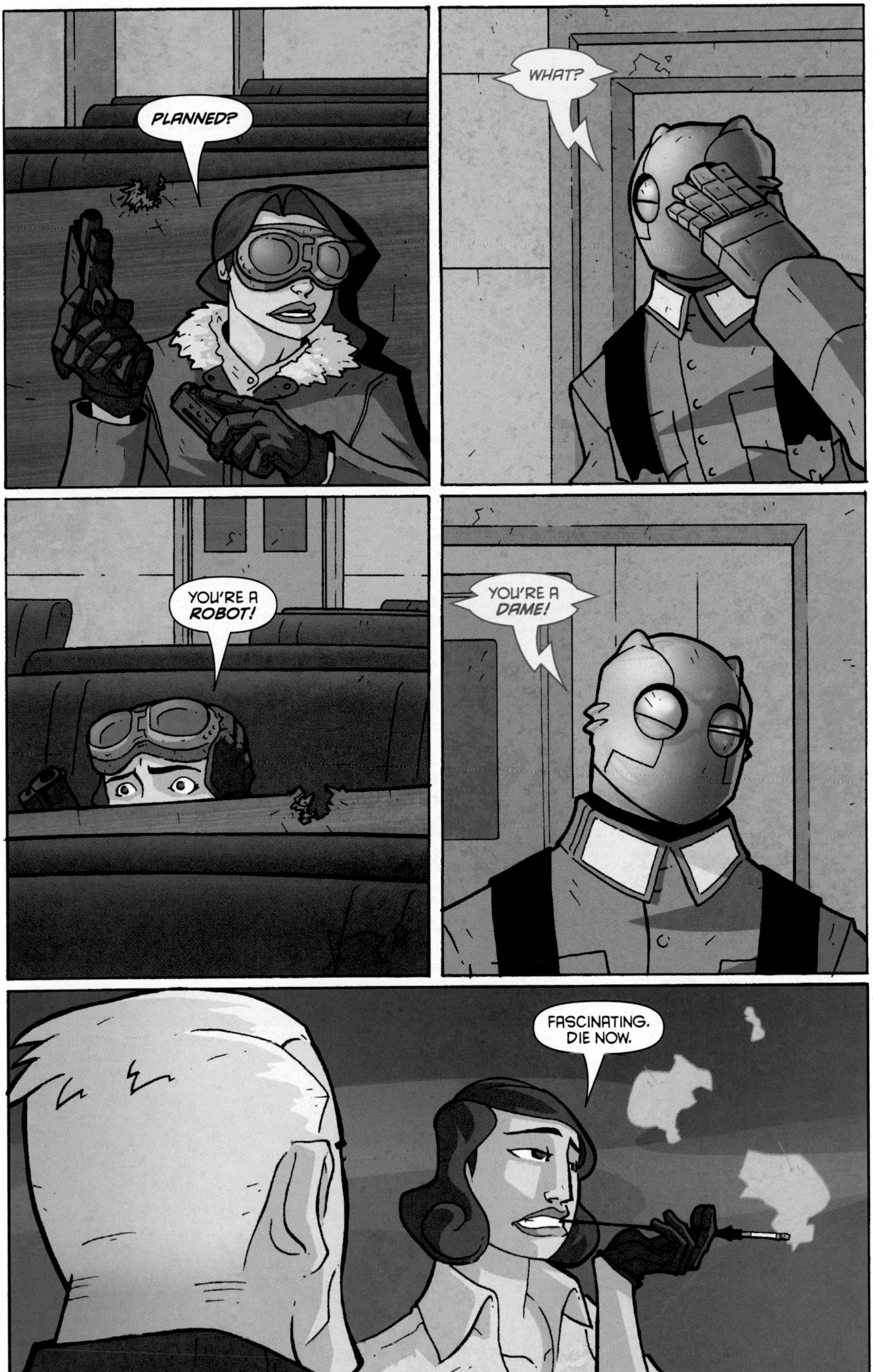
PLANNED?
WHAT?
YOU'RE A ROBOT!
YOU'RE A DAME!
FASCINATING. DIE NOW.

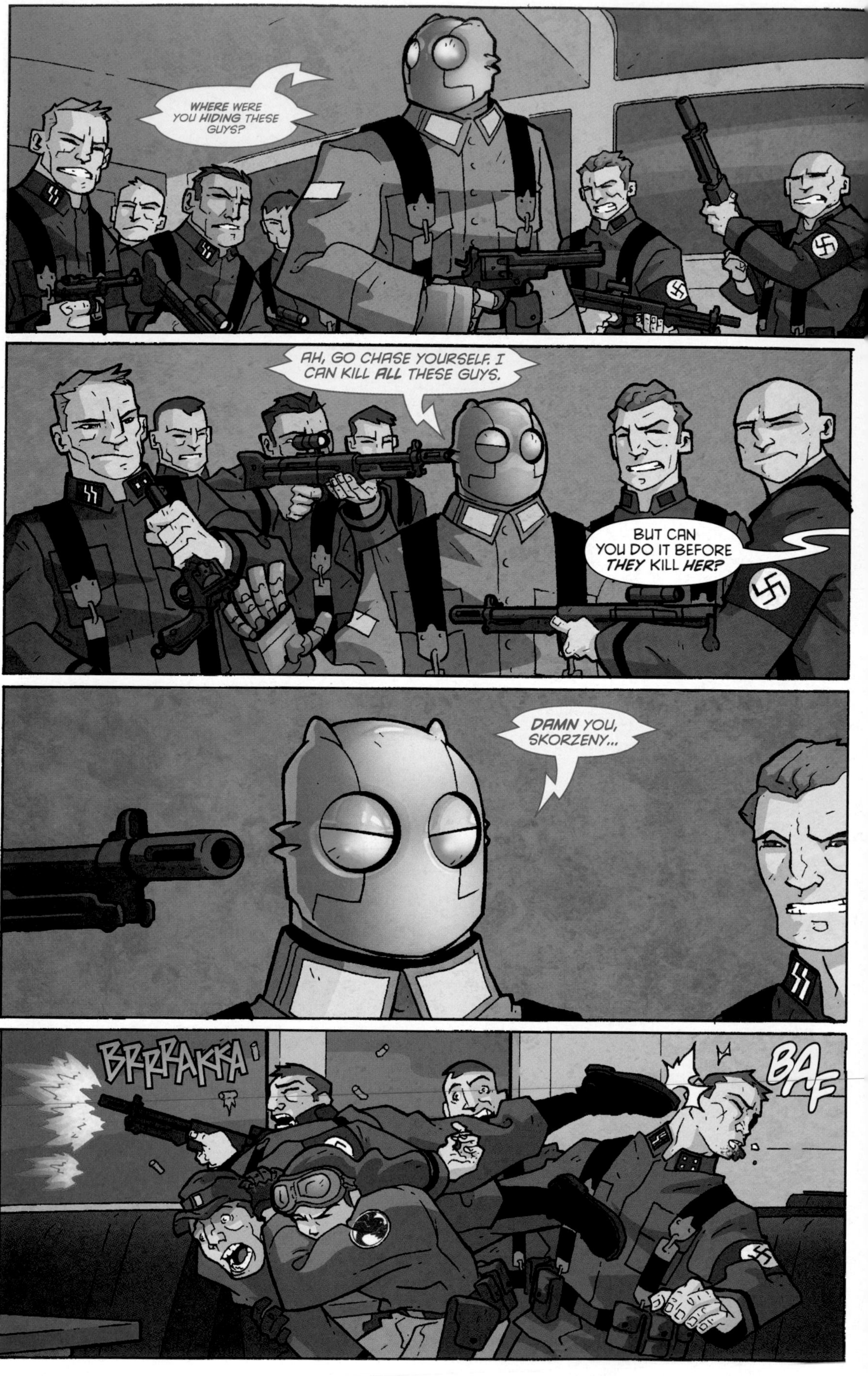
WHERE WERE YOU HIDING THESE GUYS?
AH, GO CHASE YOURSELF. I CAN KILL ALL THESE GUYS.
BUT CAN YOU DO IT BEFORE THEY KILL HER?
DAMN YOU, SKORZENY...
BRRRAKKA
BAF

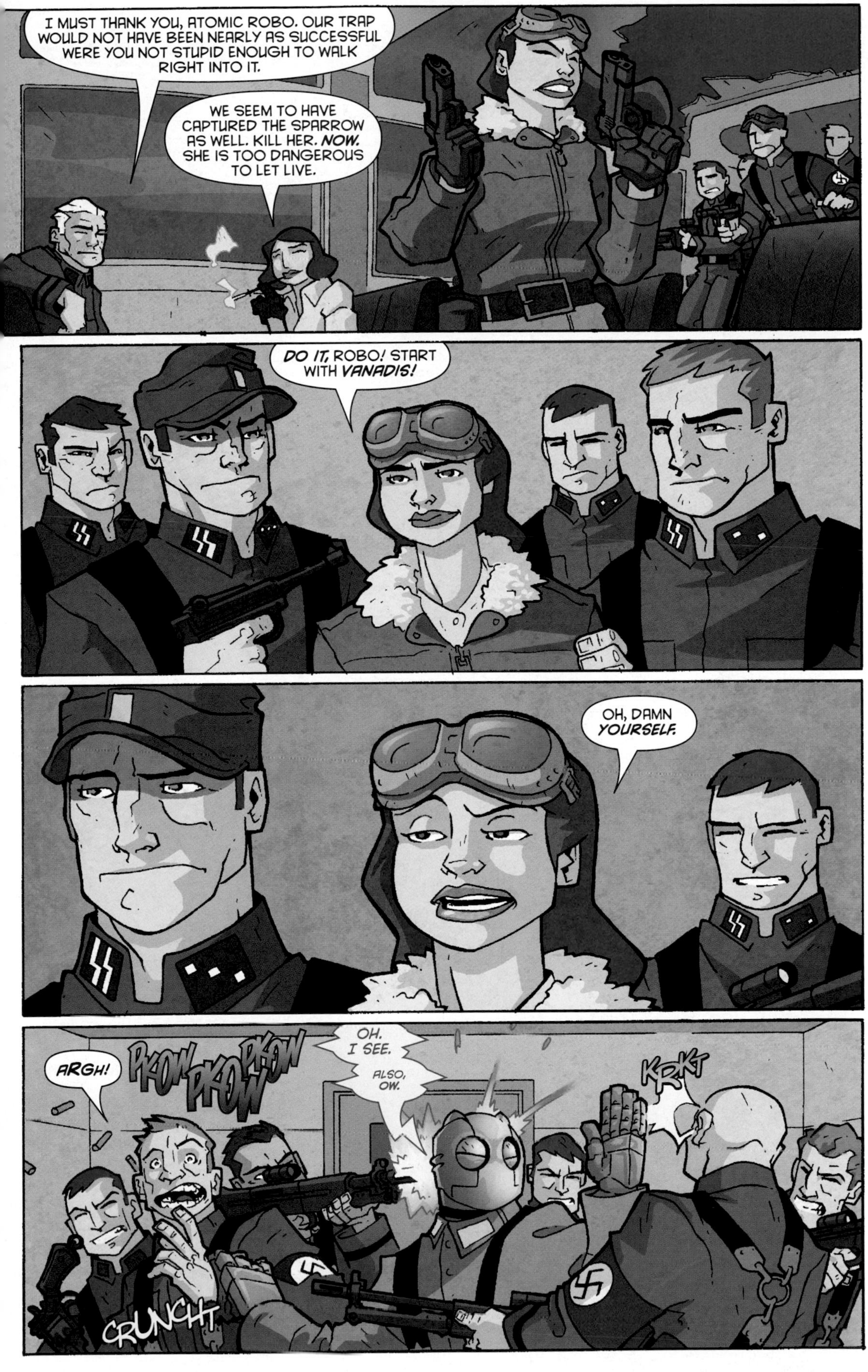
I MUST THANK YOU, ATOMIC ROBO. OUR TRAP WOULD NOT HAVE BEEN NEARLY AS SUCCESSFUL WERE YOU NOT STUPID ENOUGH TO WALK RIGHT INTO IT.
WE SEEM TO HAVE CAPTURED THE SPARROW AS WELL. KILL HER. NOW. SHE IS TOO DANGEROUS TO LET LIVE.
DO IT, ROBO! START WITH VANADIS!
OH, DAMN YOURSELF.
ARGH!
PKOW PKOW PKOW PKOW
OH. I SEE.
ALSO, OW.
KRKT
CRUNCHT

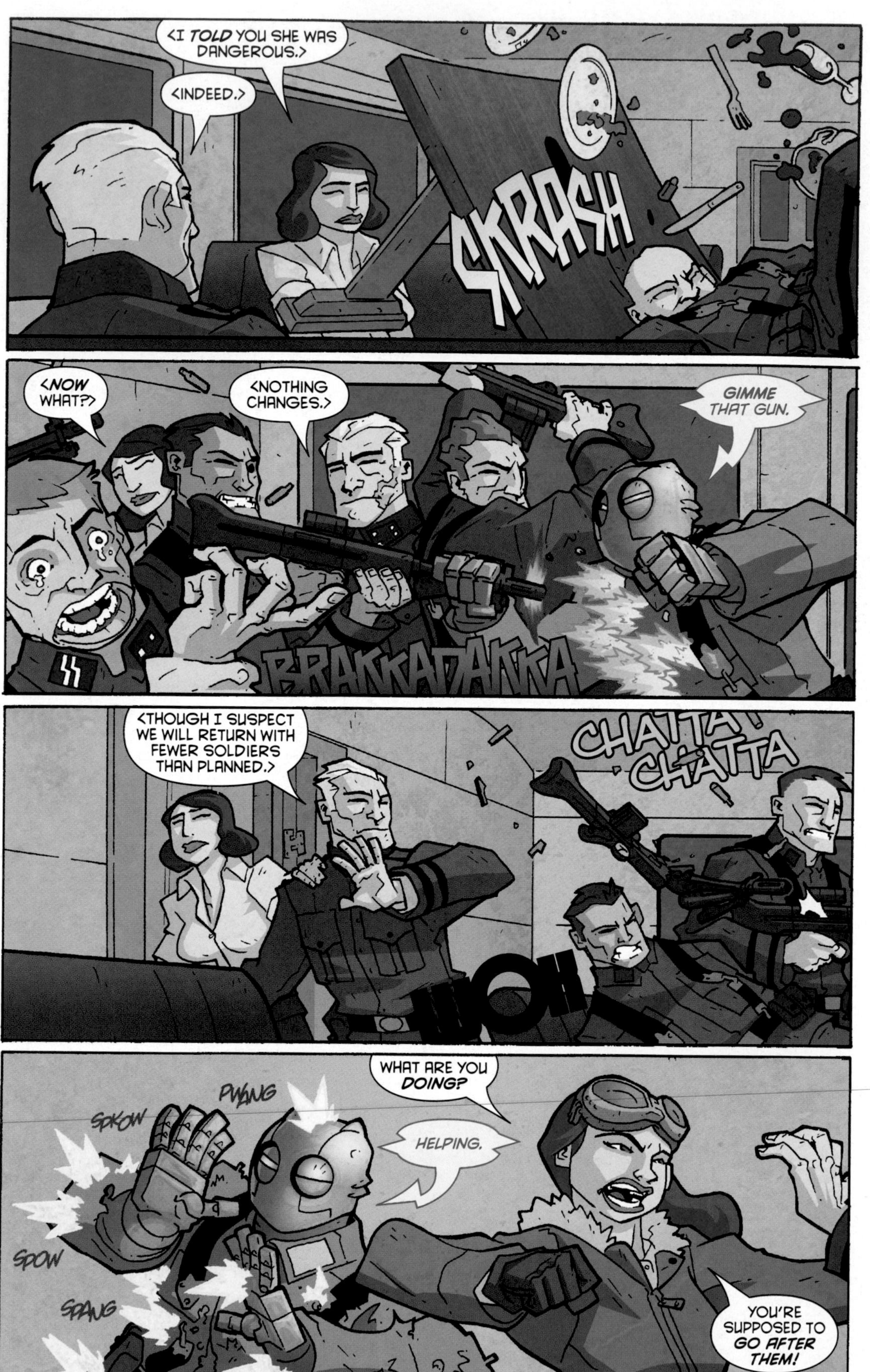
<I TOLD YOU SHE WAS DANGEROUS.>
<INDEED.>
SKRASH
<NOW WHAT?>
<NOTHING CHANGES.>
GIMME THAT GUN.
BRAKKADAKKA
<THOUGH I SUSPECT WE WILL RETURN WITH FEWER SOLDIERS THAN PLANNED.>
CHATTA CHATTA
PWANG
SPKOW
WHAT ARE YOU DOING?
HELPING.
SPOW
SPANG
YOU'RE SUPPOSED TO GO AFTER THEM!

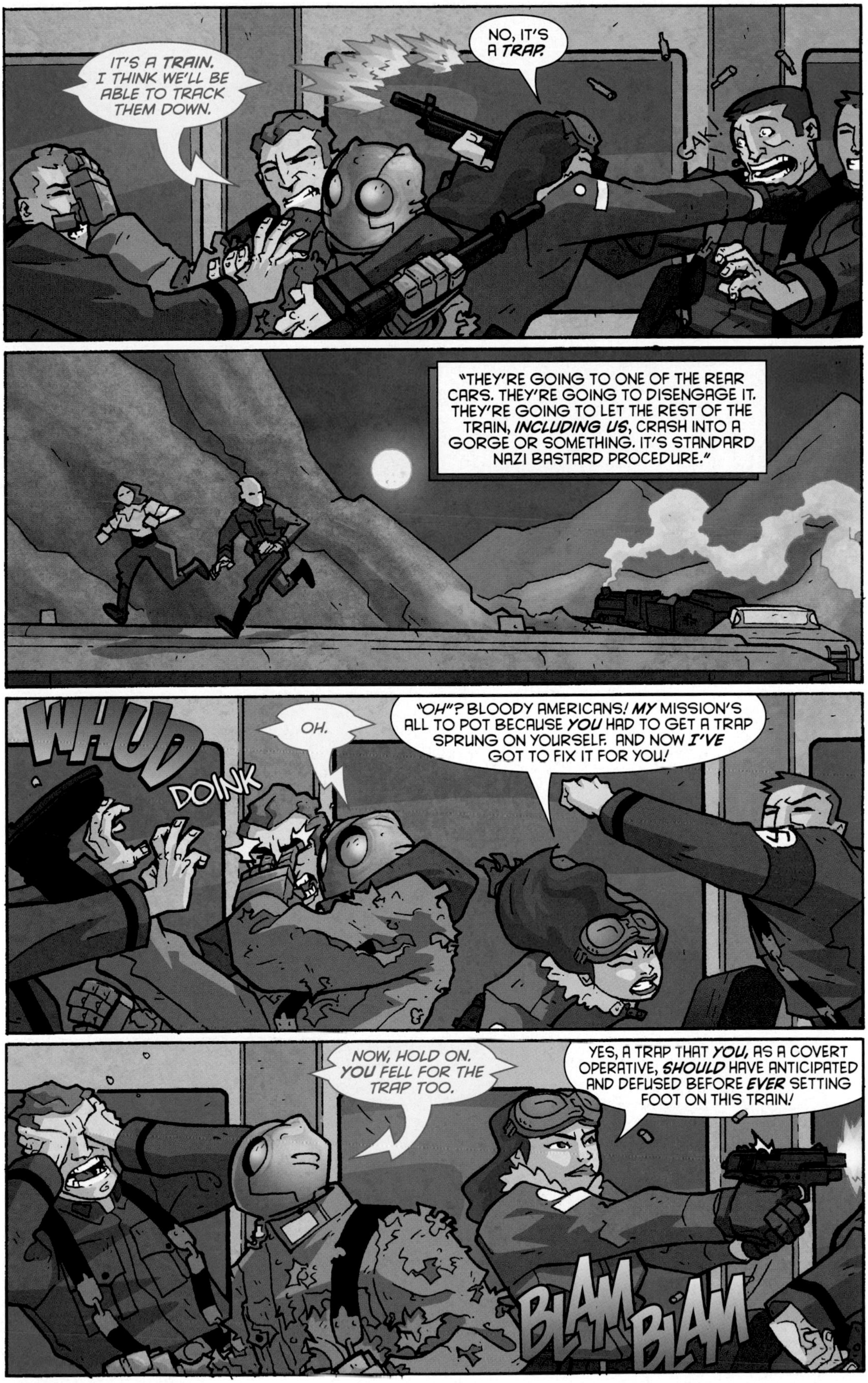

IT'S A TRAIN. I THINK WE'LL BE ABLE TO TRACK THEM DOWN.
NO, IT'S A TRAP.
GAK!
"THEY'RE GOING TO ONE OF THE REAR CARS. THEY'RE GOING TO DISENGAGE IT. THEY'RE GOING TO LET THE REST OF THE TRAIN, INCLUDING US, CRASH INTO A GORGE OR SOMETHING. IT'S STANDARD NAZI BASTARD PROCEDURE."
WHUD
DOINK
OH.
"OH"? BLOODY AMERICANS! MY MISSION'S ALL TO POT BECAUSE YOU HAD TO GET A TRAP SPRUNG ON YOURSELF. AND NOW I'VE GOT TO FIX IT FOR YOU!
NOW, HOLD ON. YOU FELL FOR THE TRAP TOO.
YES, A TRAP THAT YOU, AS A COVERT OPERATIVE, SHOULD HAVE ANTICIPATED AND DEFUSED BEFORE EVER SETTING FOOT ON THIS TRAIN!
BLAM
BLAM

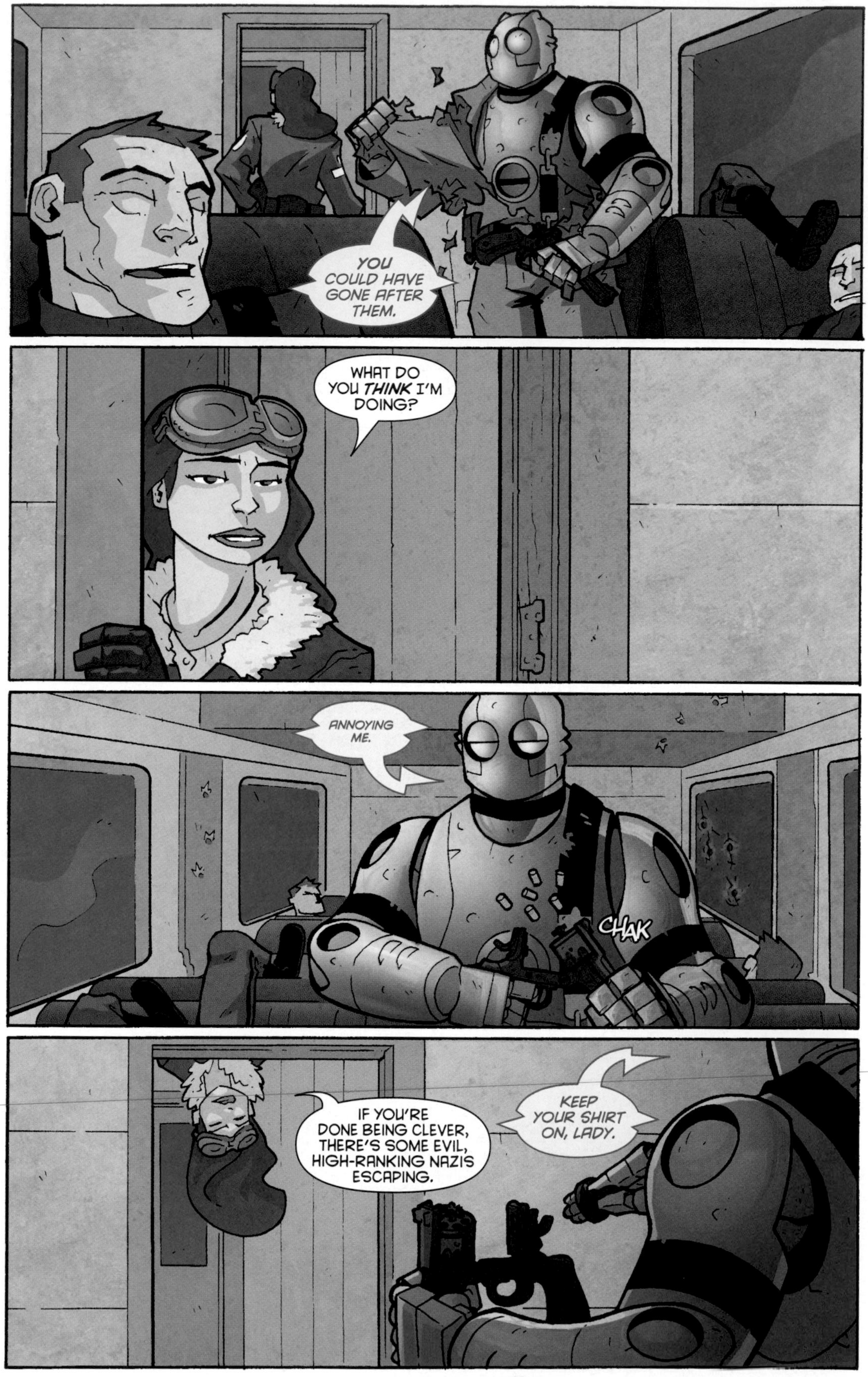
YOU COULD HAVE GONE AFTER THEM.
WHAT DO YOU THINK I'M DOING?
ANNOYING ME.
CHAK
IF YOU'RE DONE BEING CLEVER, THERE'S SOME EVIL, HIGH-RANKING NAZIS ESCAPING.
KEEP YOUR SHIRT ON, LADY.

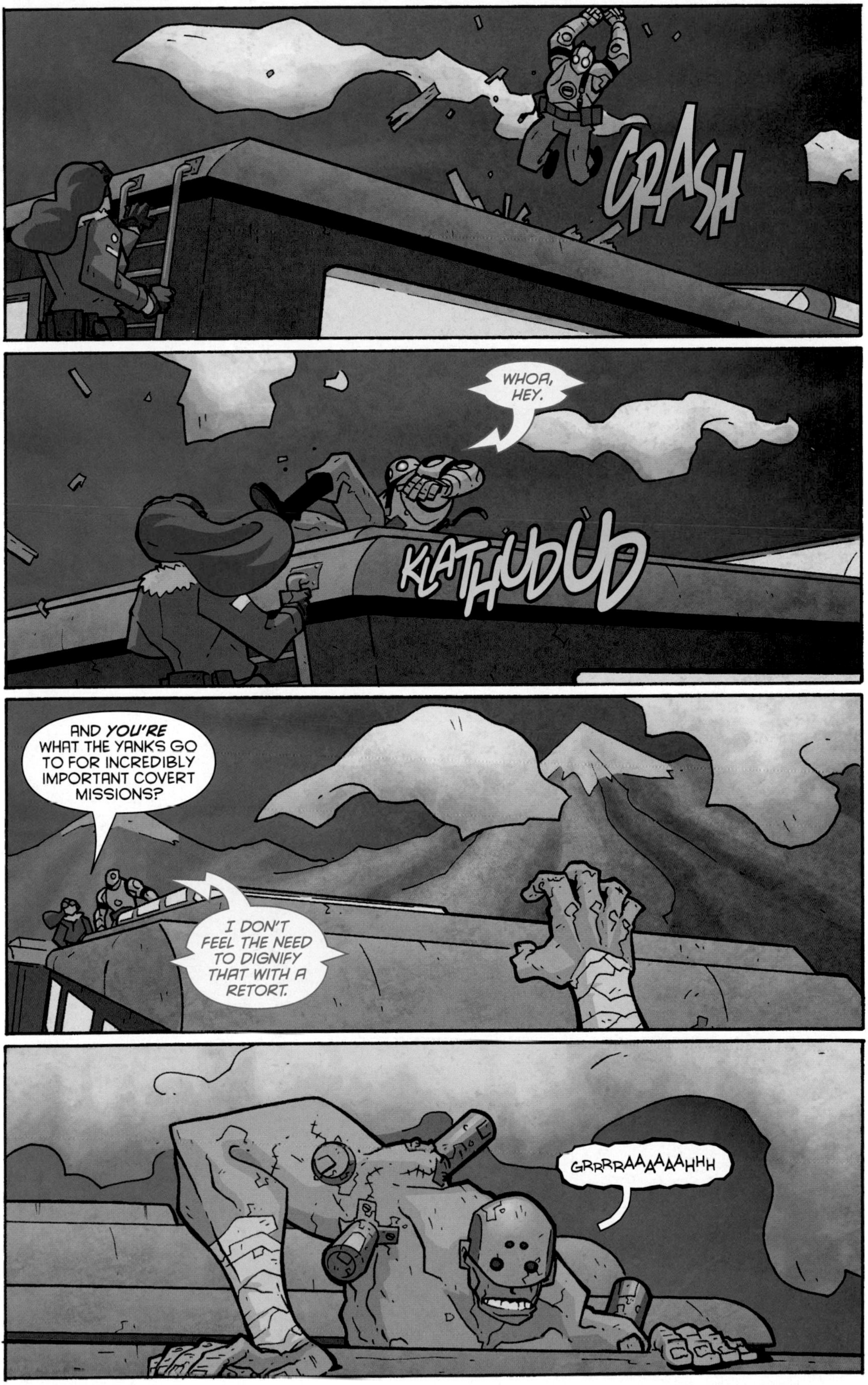
CRASH
WHOA, HEY.
KLATHUDUD
AND YOU'RE WHAT THE YANKS GO TO FOR INCREDIBLY IMPORTANT COVERT MISSIONS?
I DON'T FEEL THE NEED TO DIGNIFY THAT WITH A RETORT.
GRRRRAAAAAAHHH

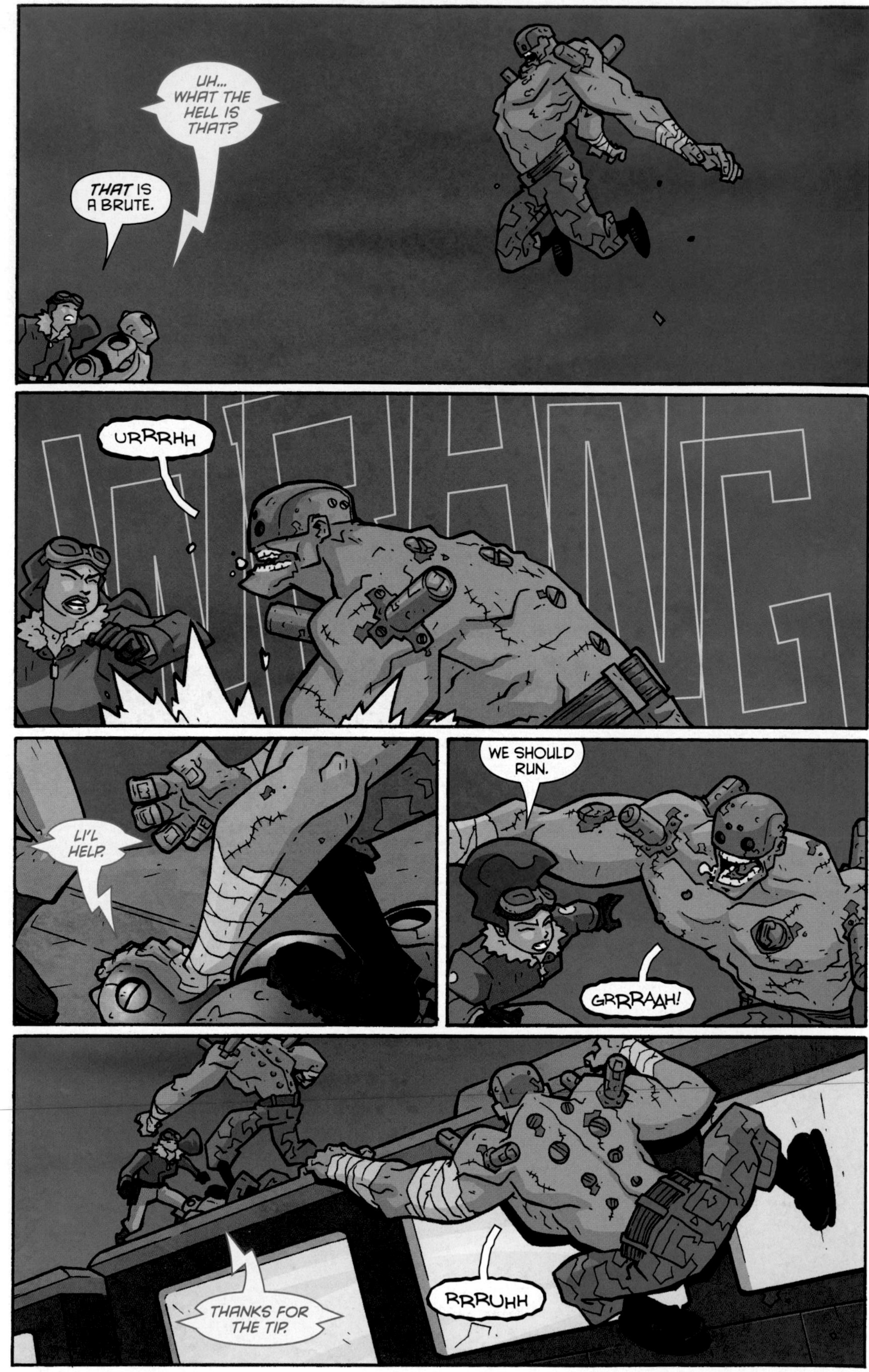
UH... WHAT THE HELL IS THAT?
THAT IS A BRUTE.
URRRHH
LI'L HELP.
WE SHOULD RUN.
GRRRAAH!
THANKS FOR THE TIP.
RRRUHH

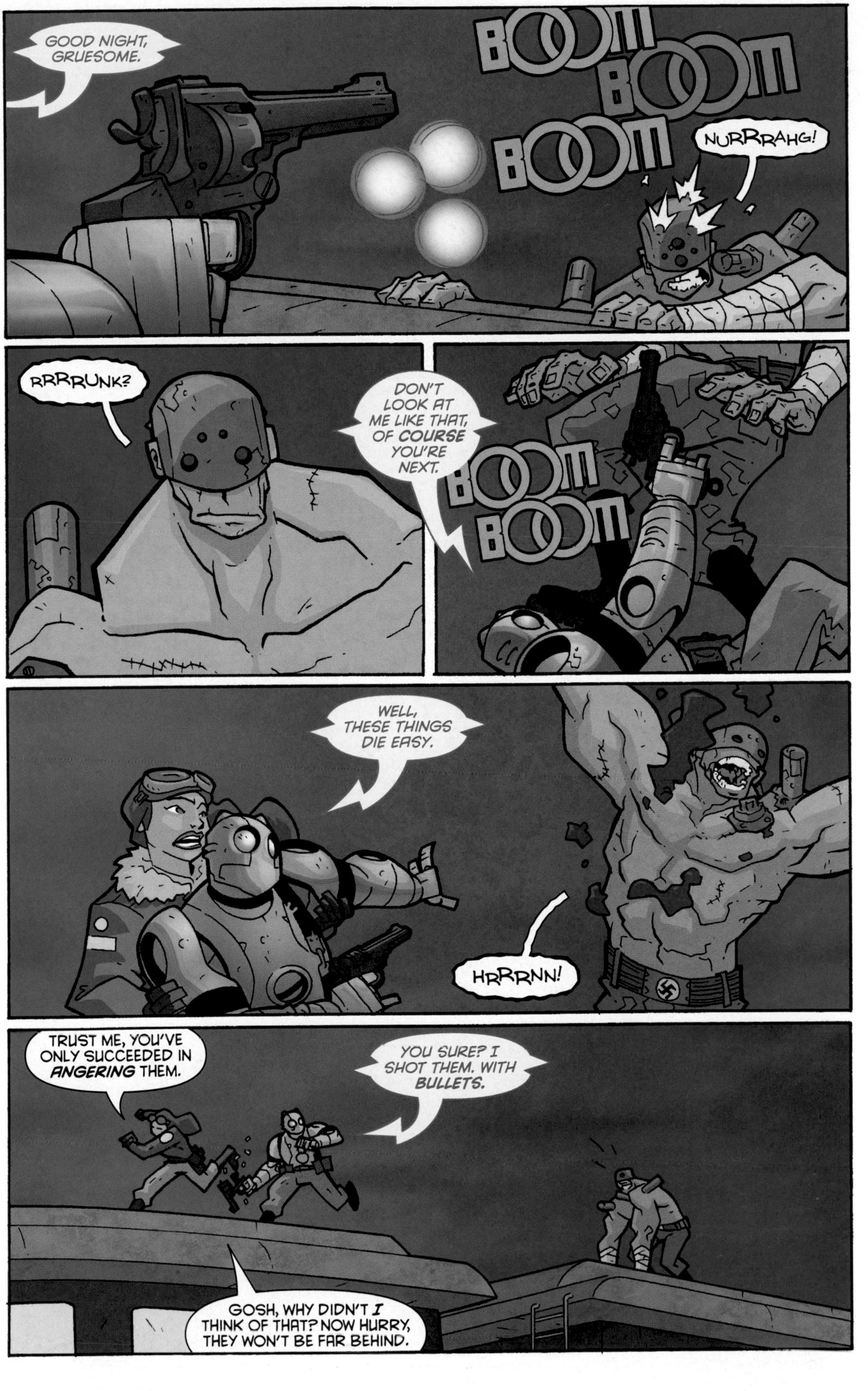
GOOD NIGHT, GRUESOME.
BOOM BOOM BOOM
NURRRAHG!
RRRRUNK?
DON'T LOOK AT ME LIKE THAT, OF COURSE YOU'RE NEXT.
BOOM BOOM
WELL, THESE THINGS DIE EASY.
HRRRNN!
TRUST ME, YOU'VE ONLY SUCCEEDED IN ANGERING THEM.
YOU SURE? I SHOT THEM. WITH BULLETS.
GOSH, WHY DIDN'T I THINK OF THAT? NOW HURRY, THEY WON'T BE FAR BEHIND.

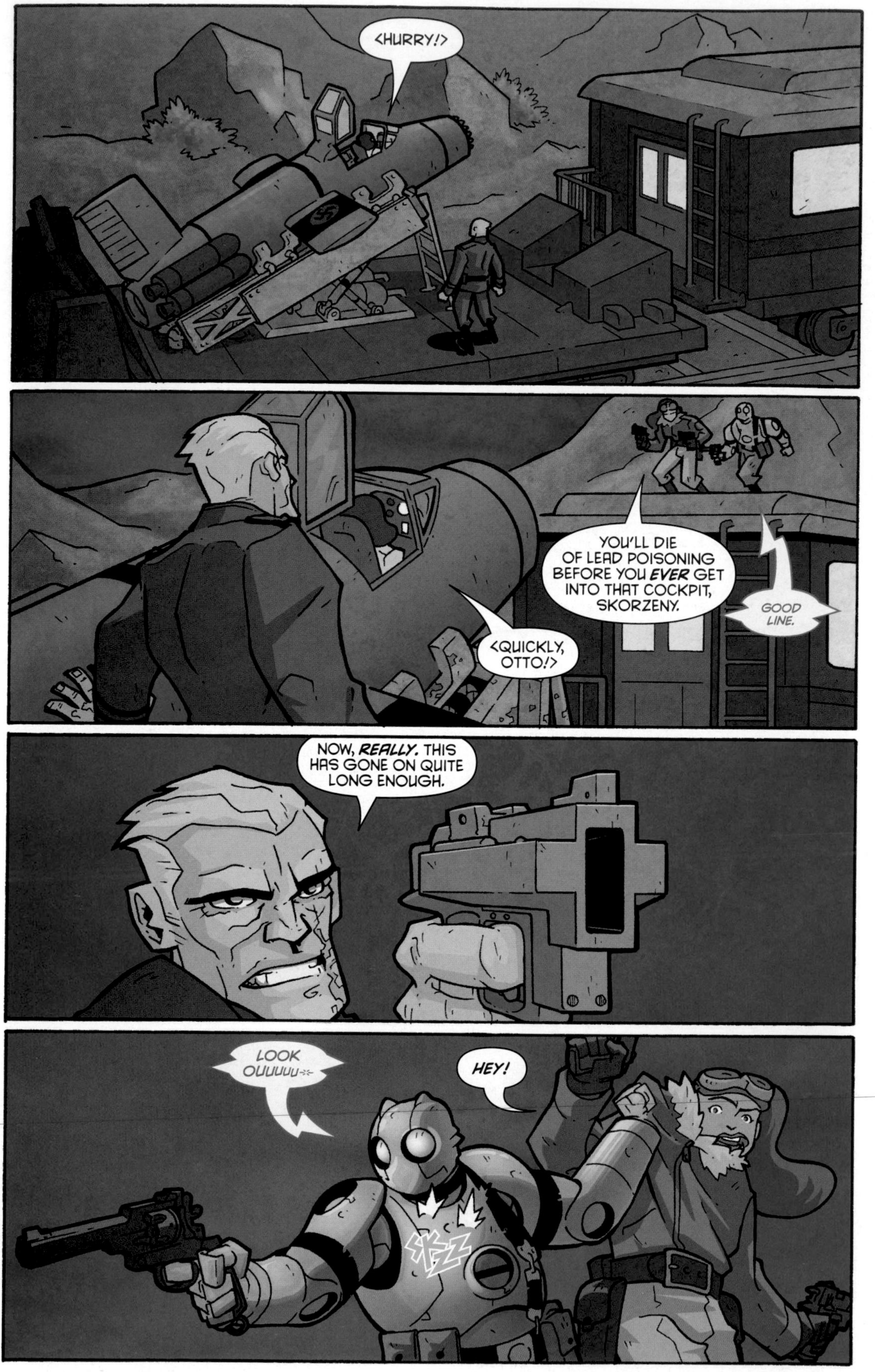
<HURRY!>
YOU'LL DIE OF LEAD POISONING BEFORE YOU EVER GET INTO THAT COCKPIT, SKORZENY.
GOOD LINE.
<QUICKLY, OTTO!>
NOW, REALLY. THIS HAS GONE ON QUITE LONG ENOUGH.
LOOK OUUUUU—
HEY!
SKZZ

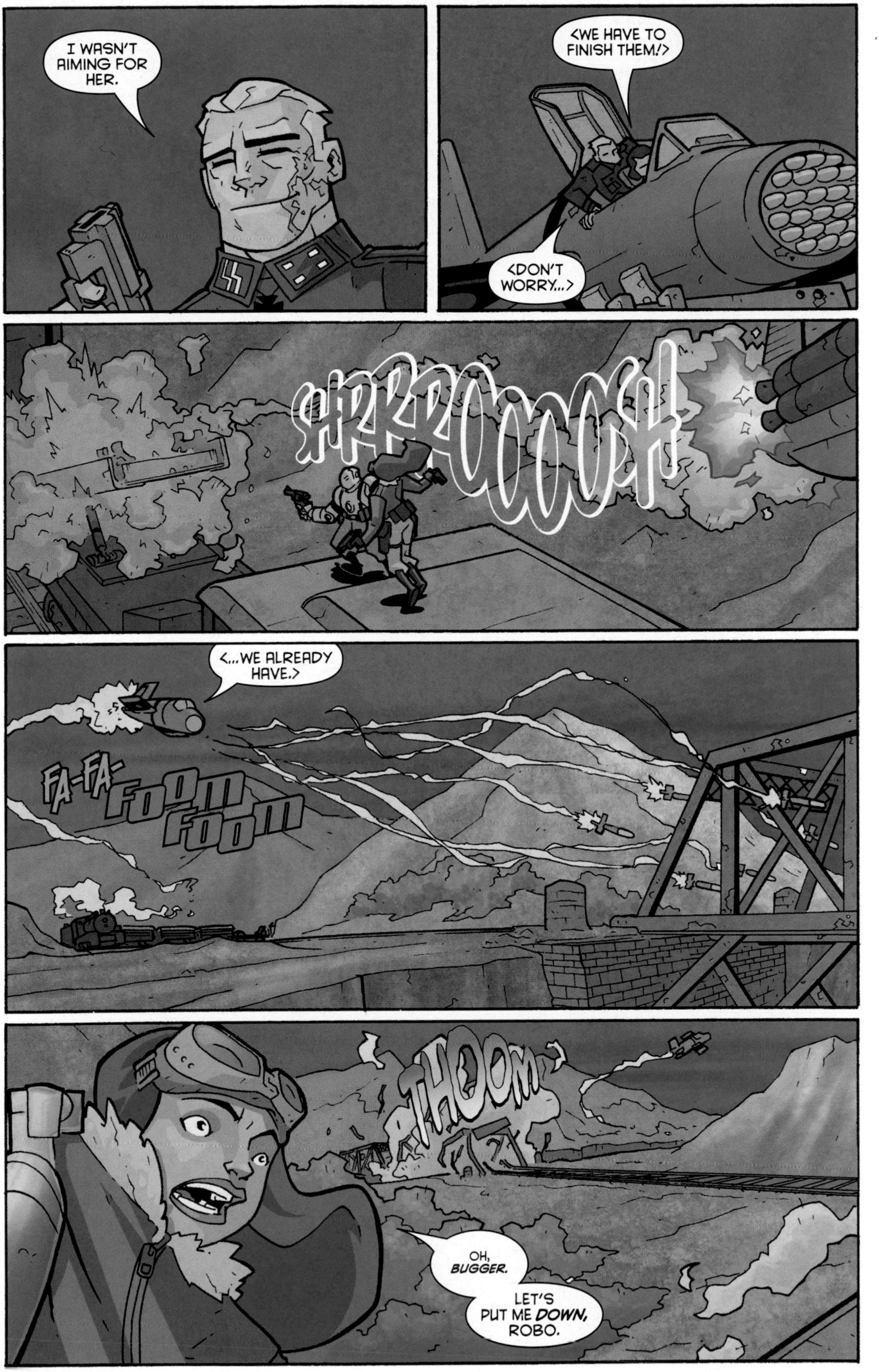
I WASN'T AIMING FOR HER.
<WE HAVE TO FINISH THEM!>
<DON'T WORRY...>
SHRRROOOOOSH
<...WE ALREADY HAVE.>
FA-FA-FOOM FOOM
THOOM
OH, *BUGGER.*
LET'S PUT ME *DOWN,* ROBO.

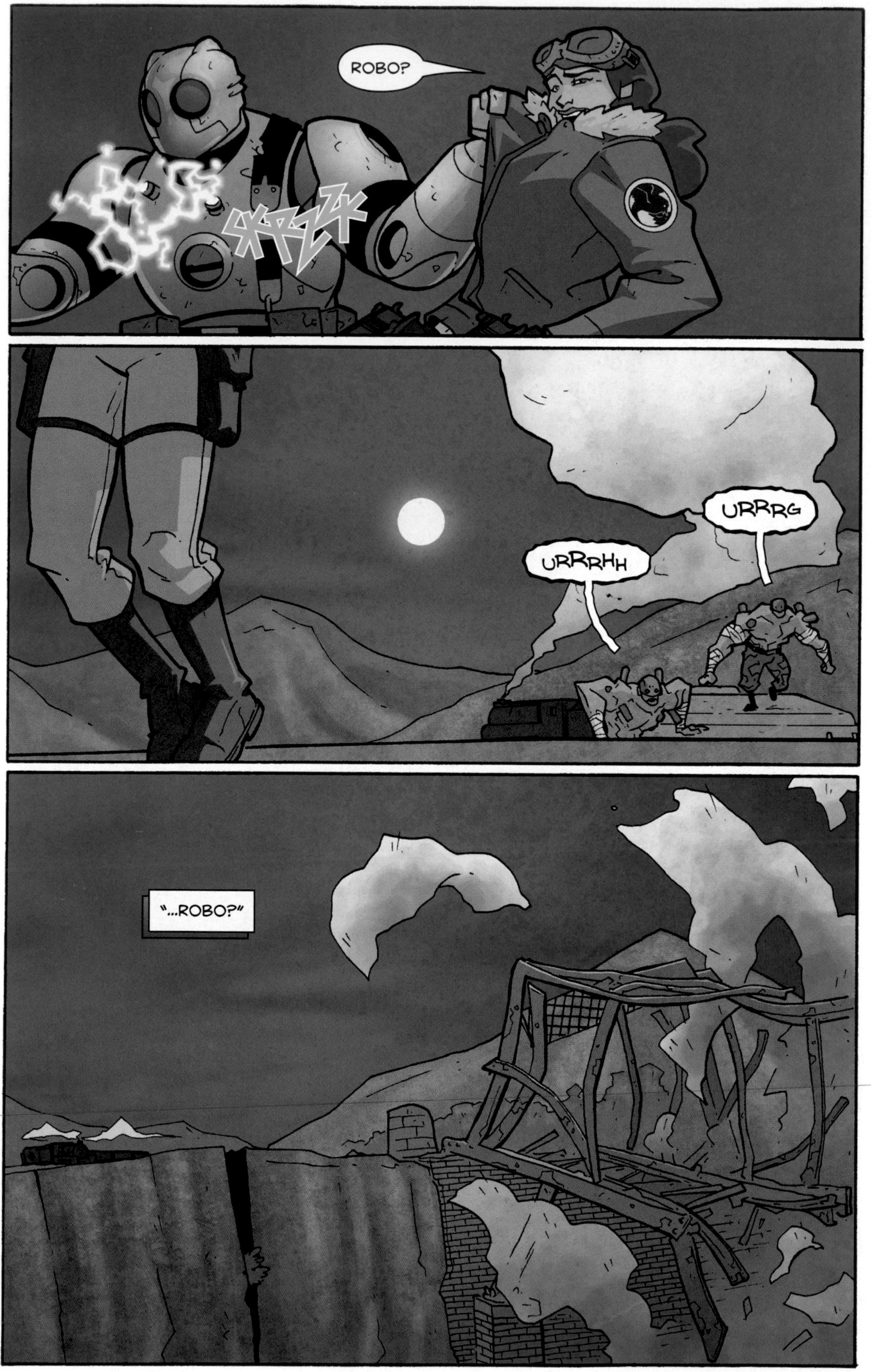
ROBO?
SKRZZK
URRRG
URRRHH
"...ROBO?"

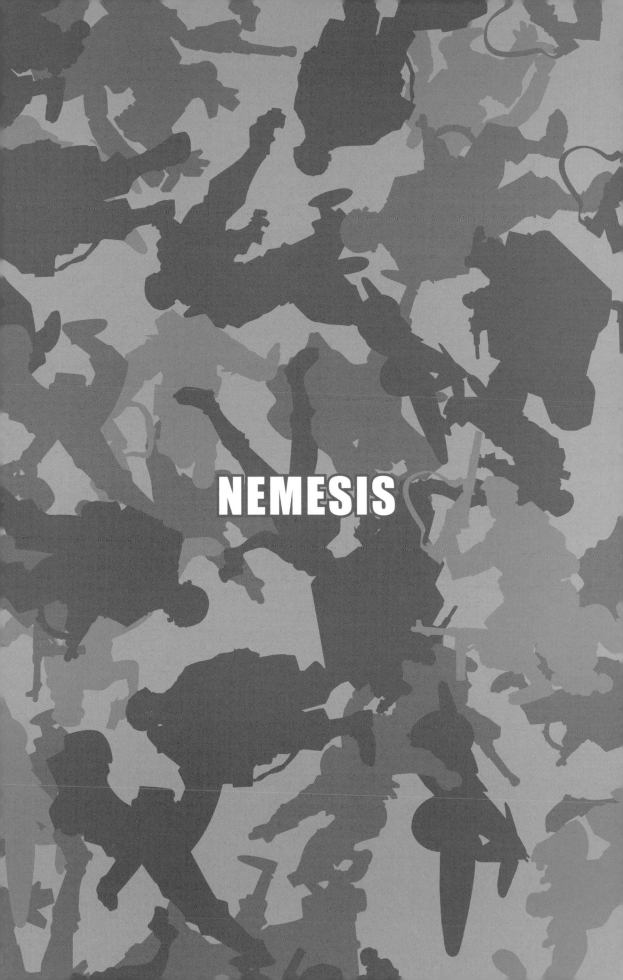

# NEMESIS

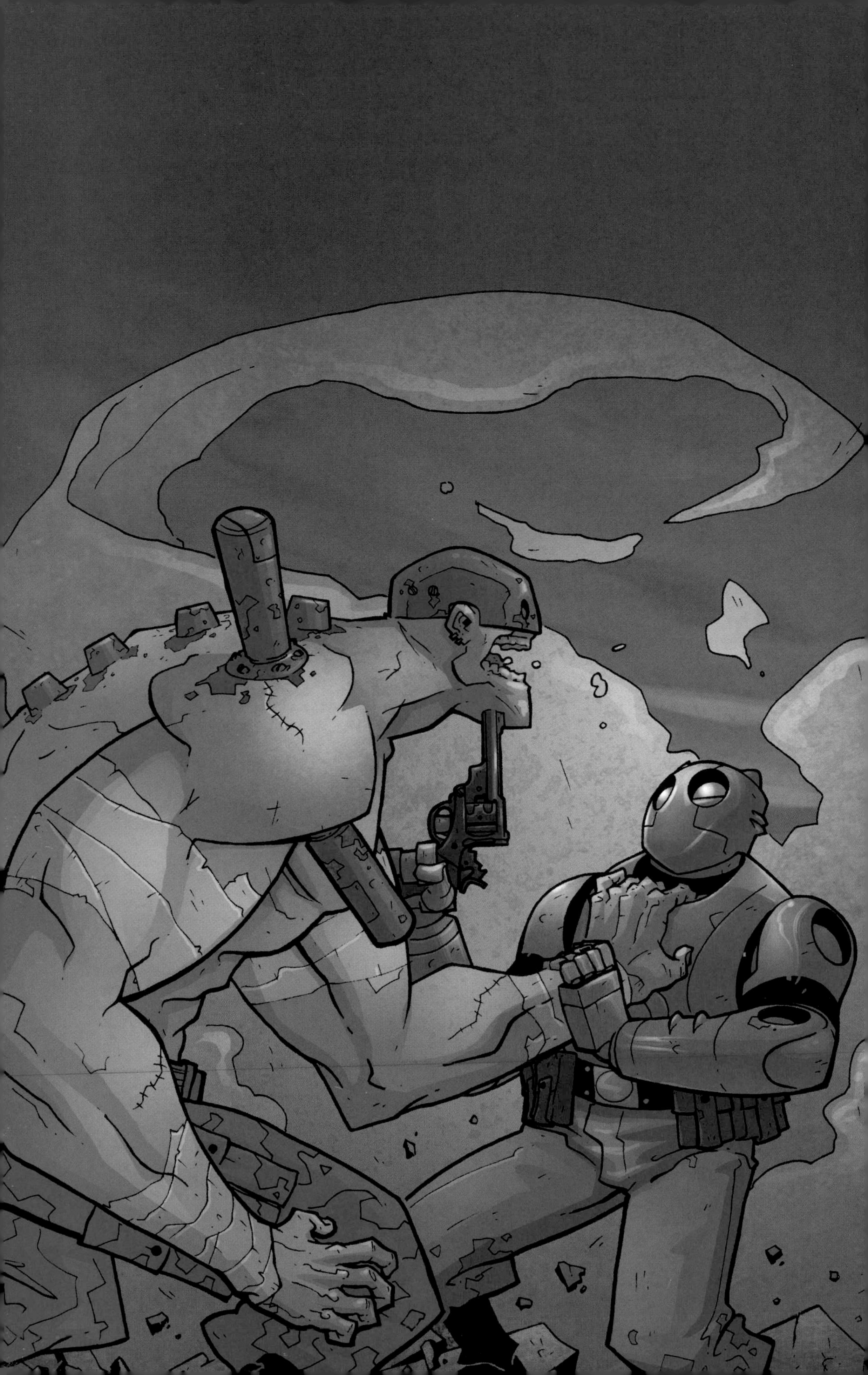

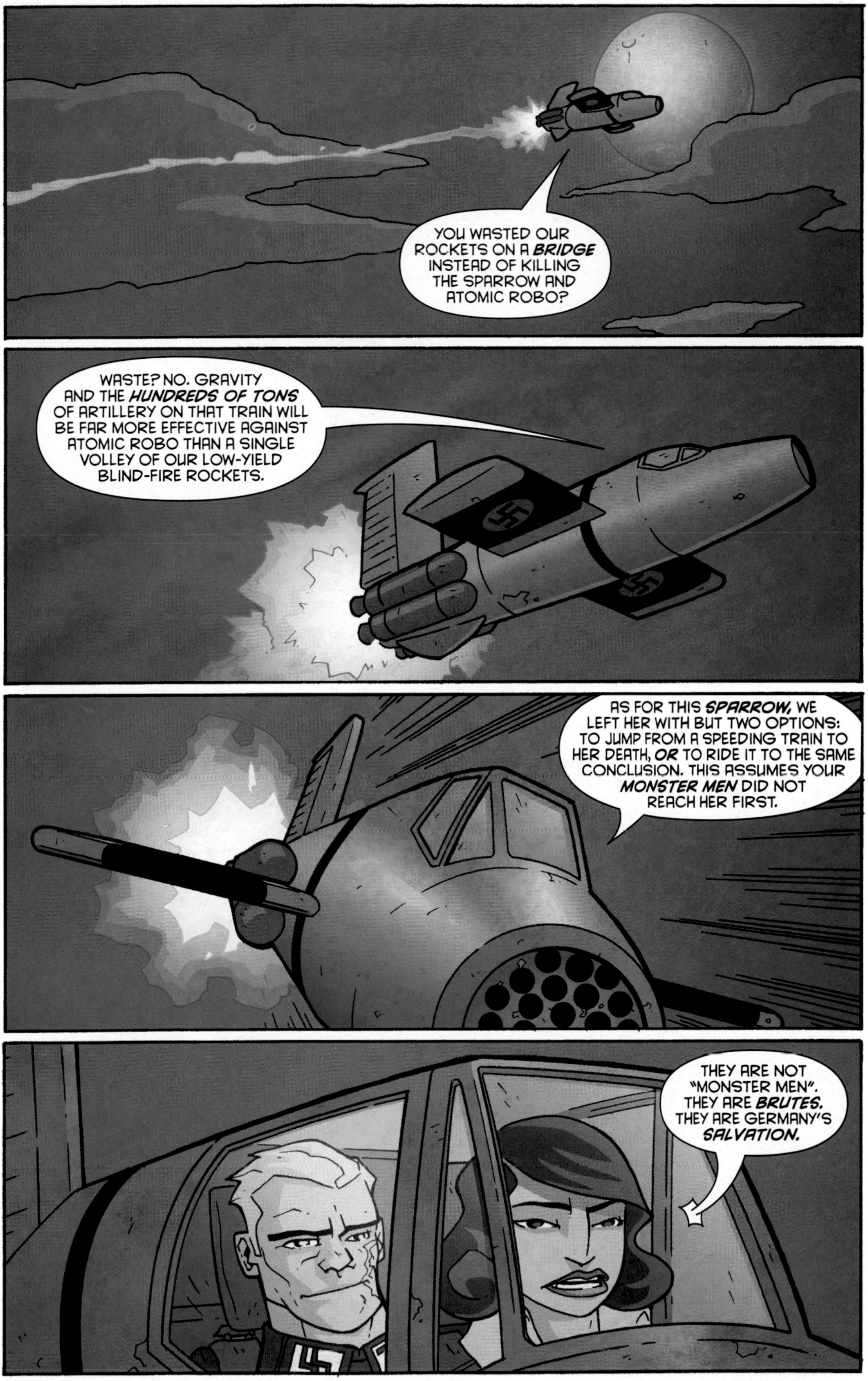

YOU WASTED OUR ROCKETS ON A *BRIDGE* INSTEAD OF KILLING THE SPARROW AND ATOMIC ROBO?
WASTE? NO. GRAVITY AND THE *HUNDREDS OF TONS* OF ARTILLERY ON THAT TRAIN WILL BE FAR MORE EFFECTIVE AGAINST ATOMIC ROBO THAN A SINGLE VOLLEY OF OUR LOW-YIELD BLIND-FIRE ROCKETS.
AS FOR THIS *SPARROW,* WE LEFT HER WITH BUT TWO OPTIONS: TO JUMP FROM A SPEEDING TRAIN TO HER DEATH, *OR* TO RIDE IT TO THE SAME CONCLUSION. THIS ASSUMES YOUR *MONSTER MEN* DID NOT REACH HER FIRST.
THEY ARE NOT "MONSTER MEN". THEY ARE *BRUTES.* THEY ARE GERMANY'S *SALVATION.*

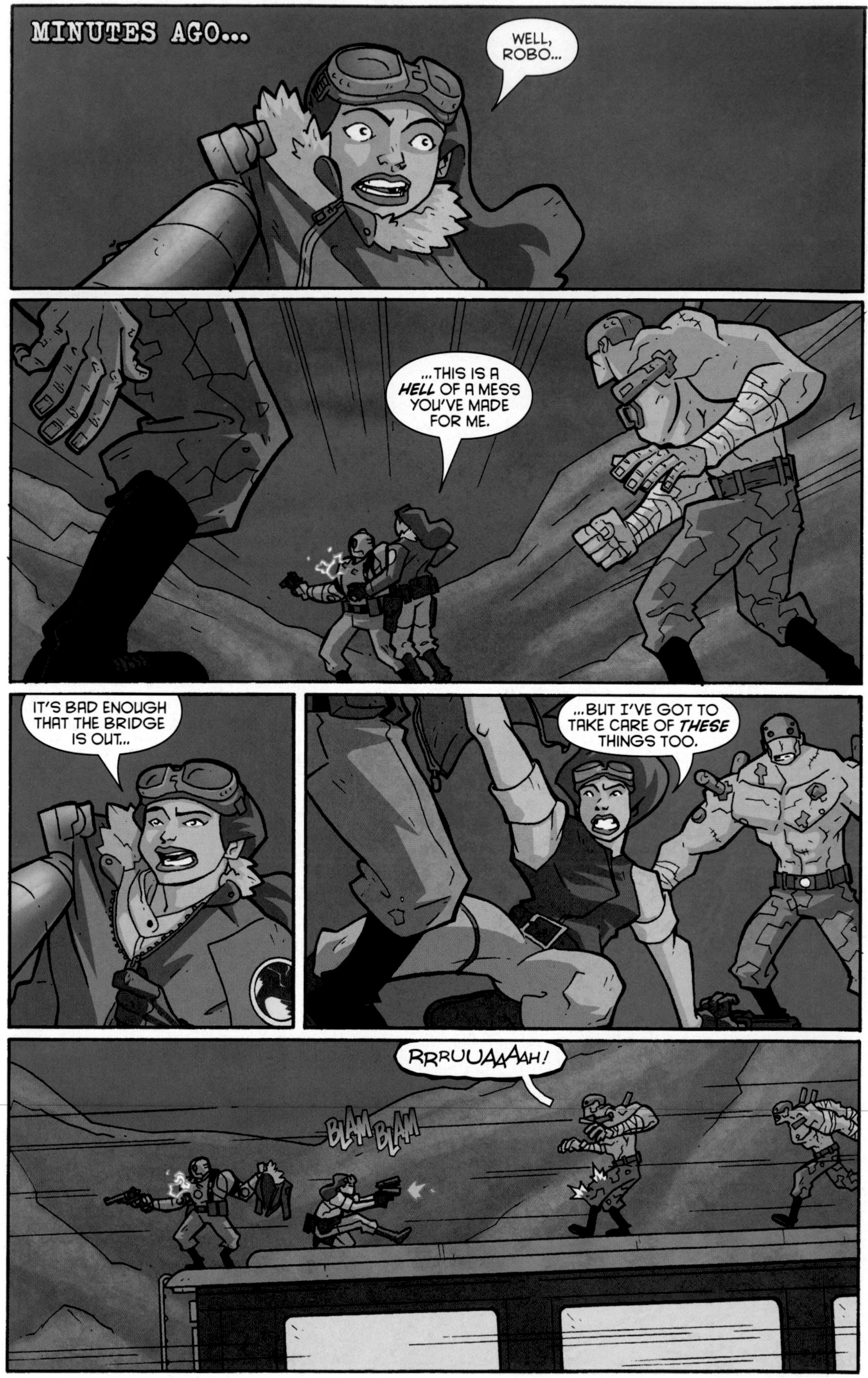
MINUTES AGO...
WELL, ROBO...
...THIS IS A HELL OF A MESS YOU'VE MADE FOR ME.
IT'S BAD ENOUGH THAT THE BRIDGE IS OUT...
...BUT I'VE GOT TO TAKE CARE OF THESE THINGS TOO.
RRRUUAAAAH!
BLAM BLAM

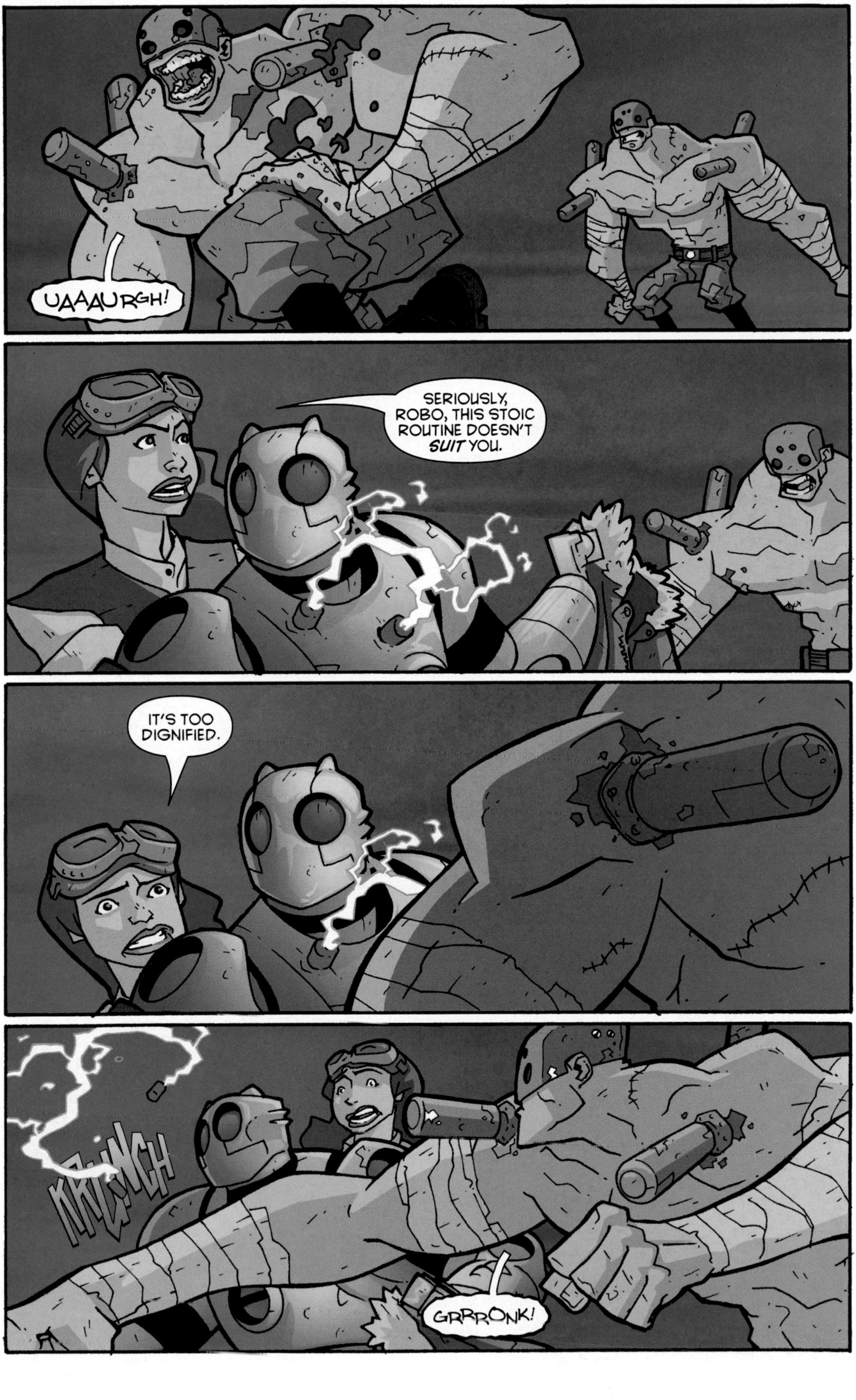
UAAAURGH!
SERIOUSLY, ROBO, THIS STOIC ROUTINE DOESN'T *SUIT* YOU.
IT'S TOO DIGNIFIED.
KRUNCH
GRRRONK!

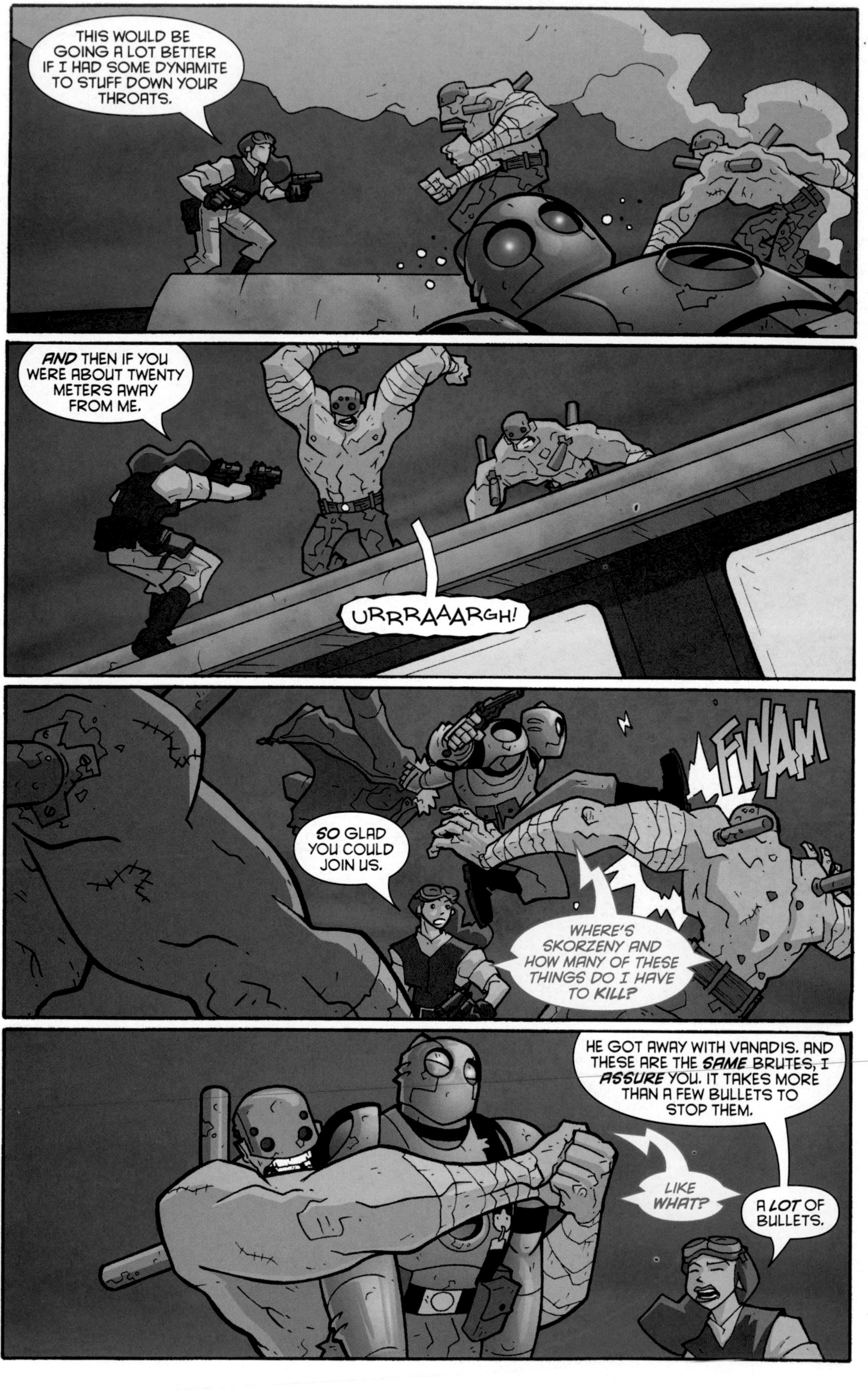
THIS WOULD BE GOING A LOT BETTER IF I HAD SOME DYNAMITE TO STUFF DOWN YOUR THROATS.
**AND** THEN IF YOU WERE ABOUT TWENTY METERS AWAY FROM ME.
URRRAAARGH!
FWAM
**SO** GLAD YOU COULD JOIN US.
WHERE'S SKORZENY AND HOW MANY OF THESE THINGS DO I HAVE TO **KILL?**
HE GOT AWAY WITH VANADIS. AND THESE ARE THE **SAME** BRUTES, I **ASSURE** YOU. IT TAKES MORE THAN A FEW BULLETS TO STOP THEM.
LIKE **WHAT?**
A **LOT** OF BULLETS.

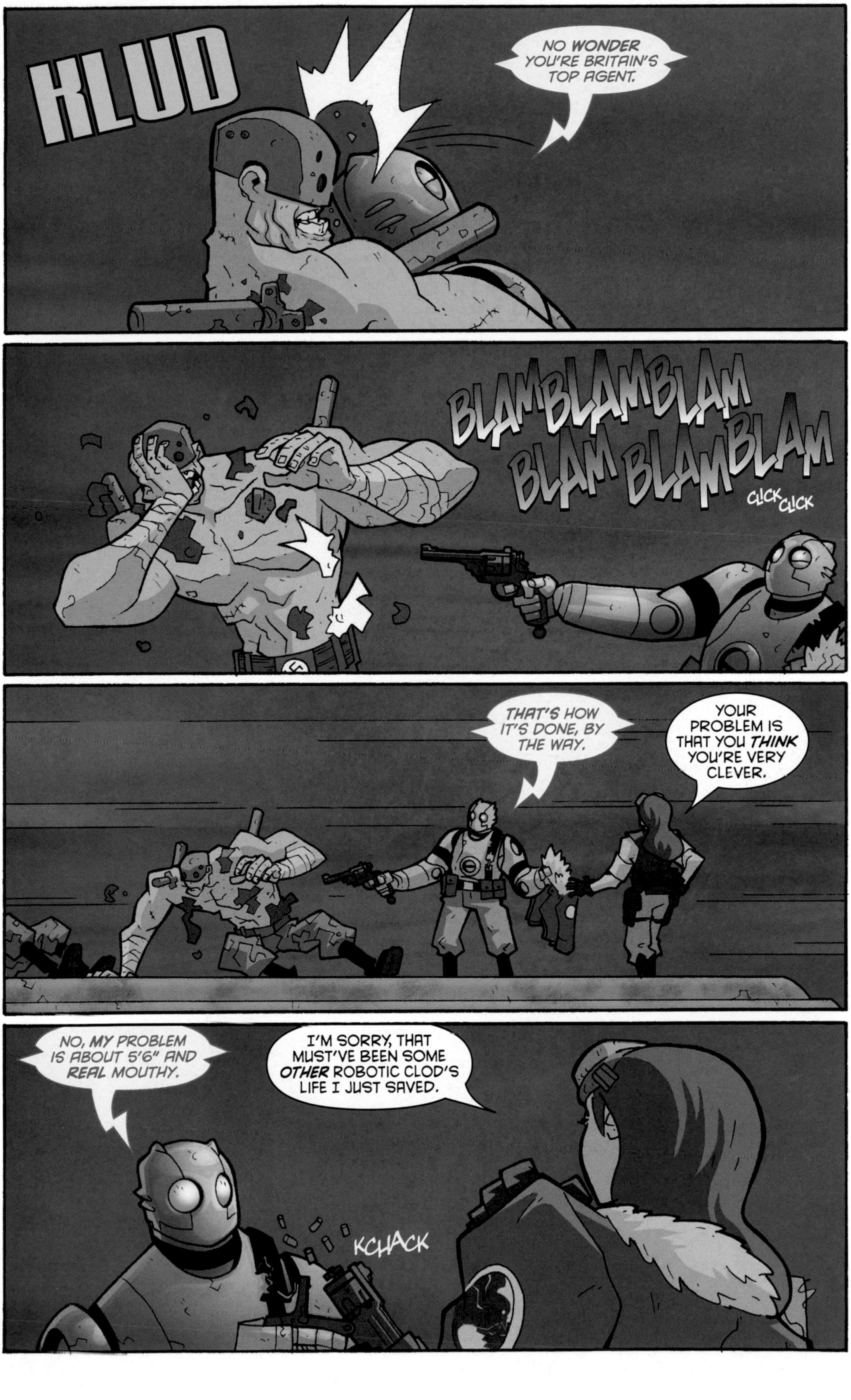
KLUD
NO WONDER YOU'RE BRITAIN'S TOP AGENT.
BLAMBLAMBLAM BLAM BLAMBLAM
CLICK CLICK
THAT'S HOW IT'S DONE, BY THE WAY.
YOUR PROBLEM IS THAT YOU THINK YOU'RE VERY CLEVER.
NO, MY PROBLEM IS ABOUT 5'6" AND REAL MOUTHY.
I'M SORRY, THAT MUST'VE BEEN SOME OTHER ROBOTIC CLOD'S LIFE I JUST SAVED.
KCHACK

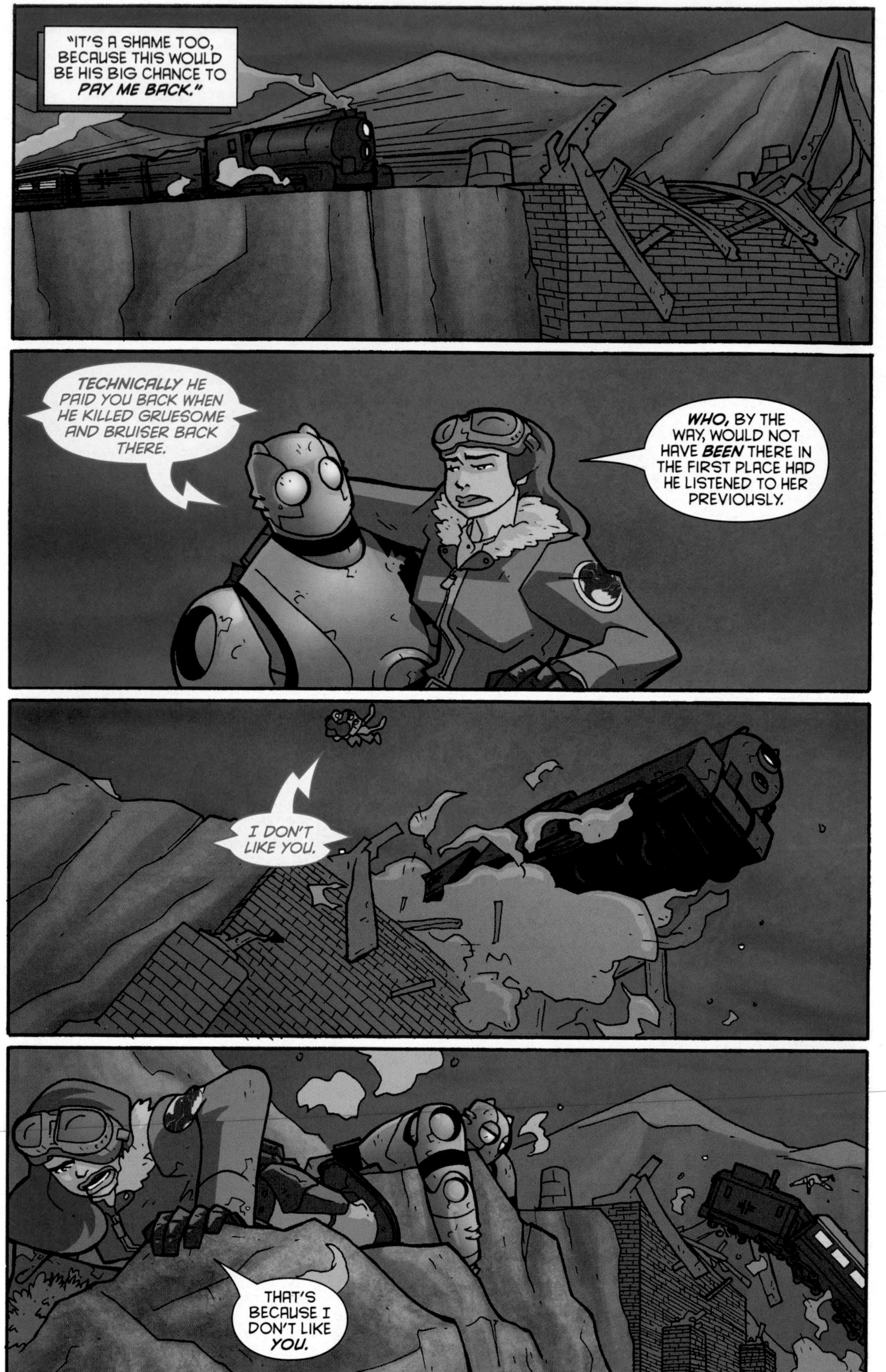
"IT'S A SHAME TOO, BECAUSE THIS WOULD BE HIS BIG CHANCE TO PAY ME BACK."
TECHNICALLY HE PAID YOU BACK WHEN HE KILLED GRUESOME AND BRUISER BACK THERE.
WHO, BY THE WAY, WOULD NOT HAVE BEEN THERE IN THE FIRST PLACE HAD HE LISTENED TO HER PREVIOUSLY.
I DON'T LIKE YOU.
THAT'S BECAUSE I DON'T LIKE YOU.

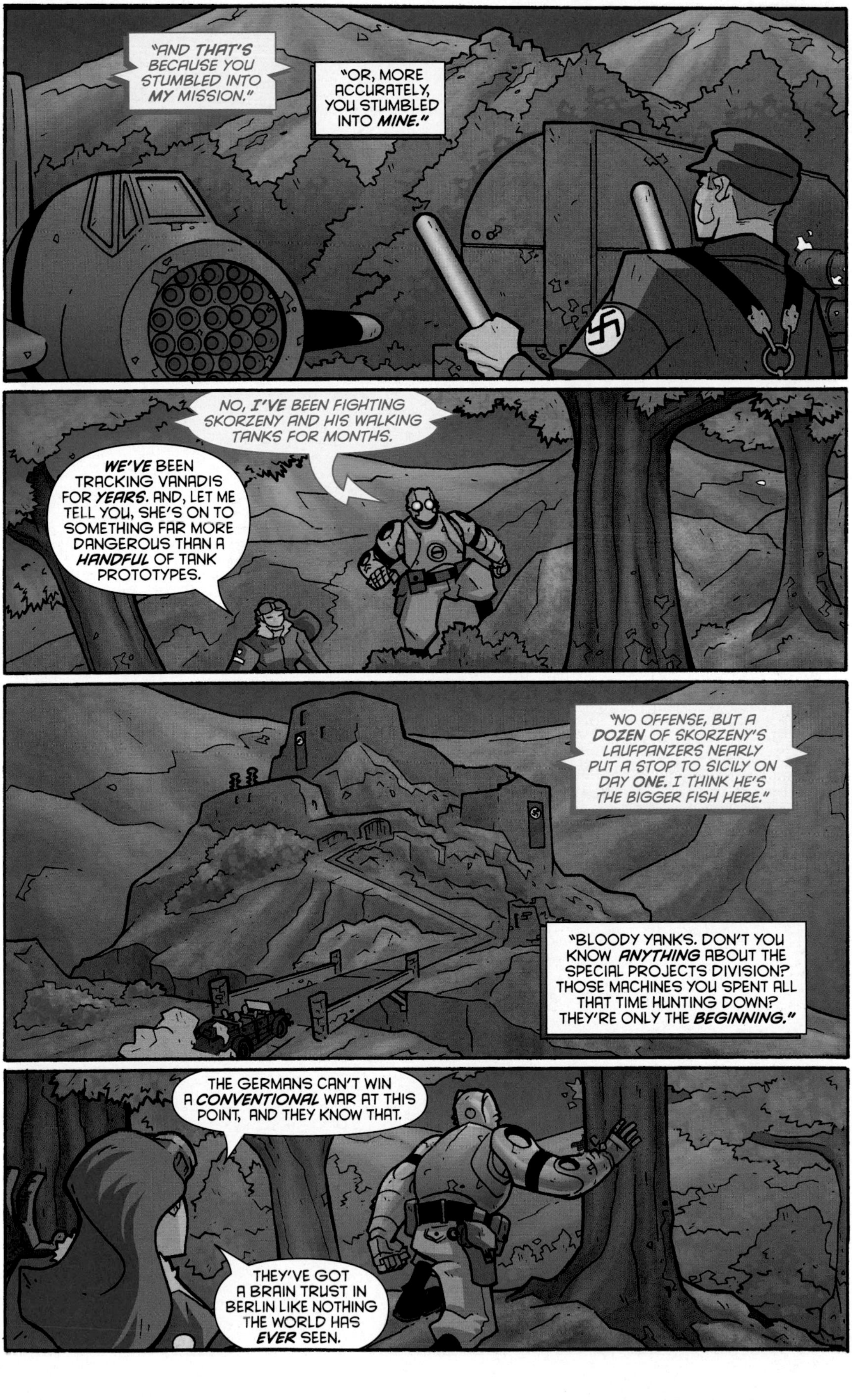
"AND THAT'S BECAUSE YOU STUMBLED INTO MY MISSION."
"OR, MORE ACCURATELY, YOU STUMBLED INTO MINE."
NO, I'VE BEEN FIGHTING SKORZENY AND HIS WALKING TANKS FOR MONTHS.
WE'VE BEEN TRACKING VANADIS FOR YEARS. AND, LET ME TELL YOU, SHE'S ON TO SOMETHING FAR MORE DANGEROUS THAN A HANDFUL OF TANK PROTOTYPES.
"NO OFFENSE, BUT A DOZEN OF SKORZENY'S LAUFPANZERS NEARLY PUT A STOP TO SICILY ON DAY ONE. I THINK HE'S THE BIGGER FISH HERE."
"BLOODY YANKS. DON'T YOU KNOW ANYTHING ABOUT THE SPECIAL PROJECTS DIVISION? THOSE MACHINES YOU SPENT ALL THAT TIME HUNTING DOWN? THEY'RE ONLY THE BEGINNING."
THE GERMANS CAN'T WIN A CONVENTIONAL WAR AT THIS POINT, AND THEY KNOW THAT.
THEY'VE GOT A BRAIN TRUST IN BERLIN LIKE NOTHING THE WORLD HAS EVER SEEN.

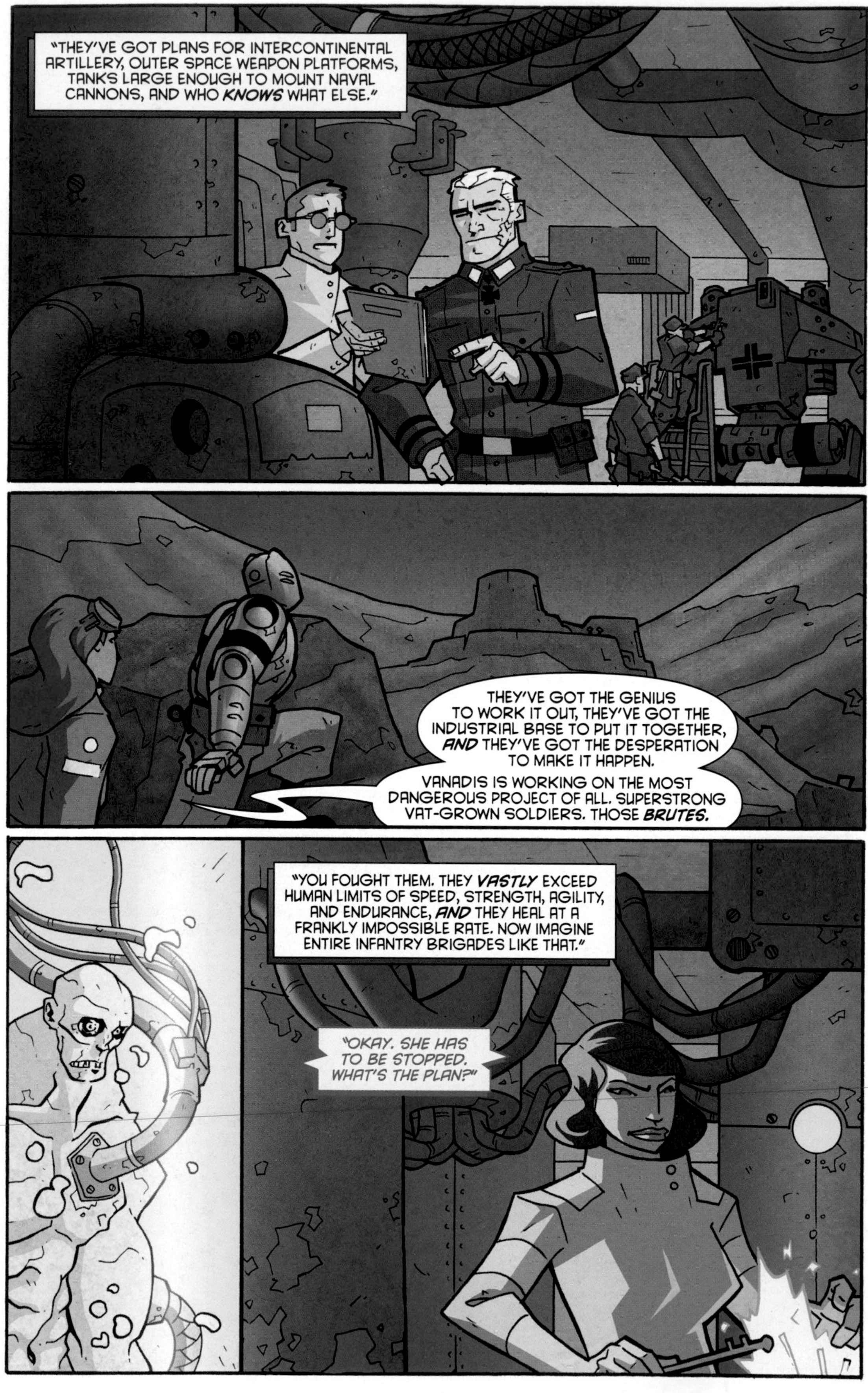
"THEY'VE GOT PLANS FOR INTERCONTINENTAL ARTILLERY, OUTER SPACE WEAPON PLATFORMS, TANKS LARGE ENOUGH TO MOUNT NAVAL CANNONS, AND WHO *KNOWS* WHAT ELSE."
THEY'VE GOT THE GENIUS TO WORK IT OUT, THEY'VE GOT THE INDUSTRIAL BASE TO PUT IT TOGETHER, *AND* THEY'VE GOT THE DESPERATION TO MAKE IT HAPPEN.
VANADIS IS WORKING ON THE MOST DANGEROUS PROJECT OF ALL. SUPERSTRONG VAT-GROWN SOLDIERS. THOSE *BRUTES.*
"YOU FOUGHT THEM. THEY *VASTLY* EXCEED HUMAN LIMITS OF SPEED, STRENGTH, AGILITY, AND ENDURANCE, *AND* THEY HEAL AT A FRANKLY IMPOSSIBLE RATE. NOW IMAGINE ENTIRE INFANTRY BRIGADES LIKE THAT."
*"OKAY. SHE HAS TO BE STOPPED. WHAT'S THE PLAN?"*

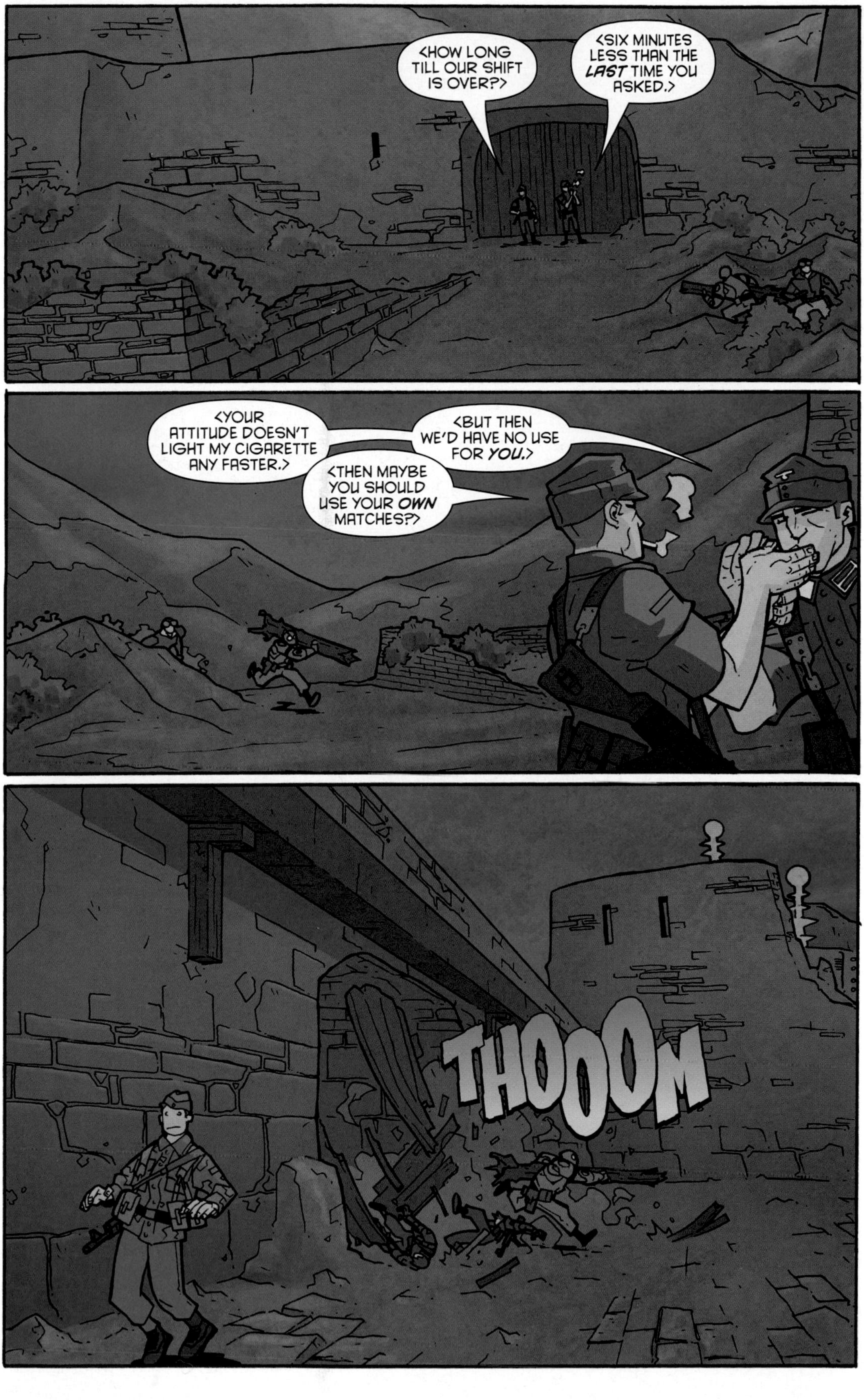
<HOW LONG TILL OUR SHIFT IS OVER?>
<SIX MINUTES LESS THAN THE LAST TIME YOU ASKED.>
<YOUR ATTITUDE DOESN'T LIGHT MY CIGARETTE ANY FASTER.>
<THEN MAYBE YOU SHOULD USE YOUR OWN MATCHES?>
<BUT THEN WE'D HAVE NO USE FOR YOU.>
THOOOM

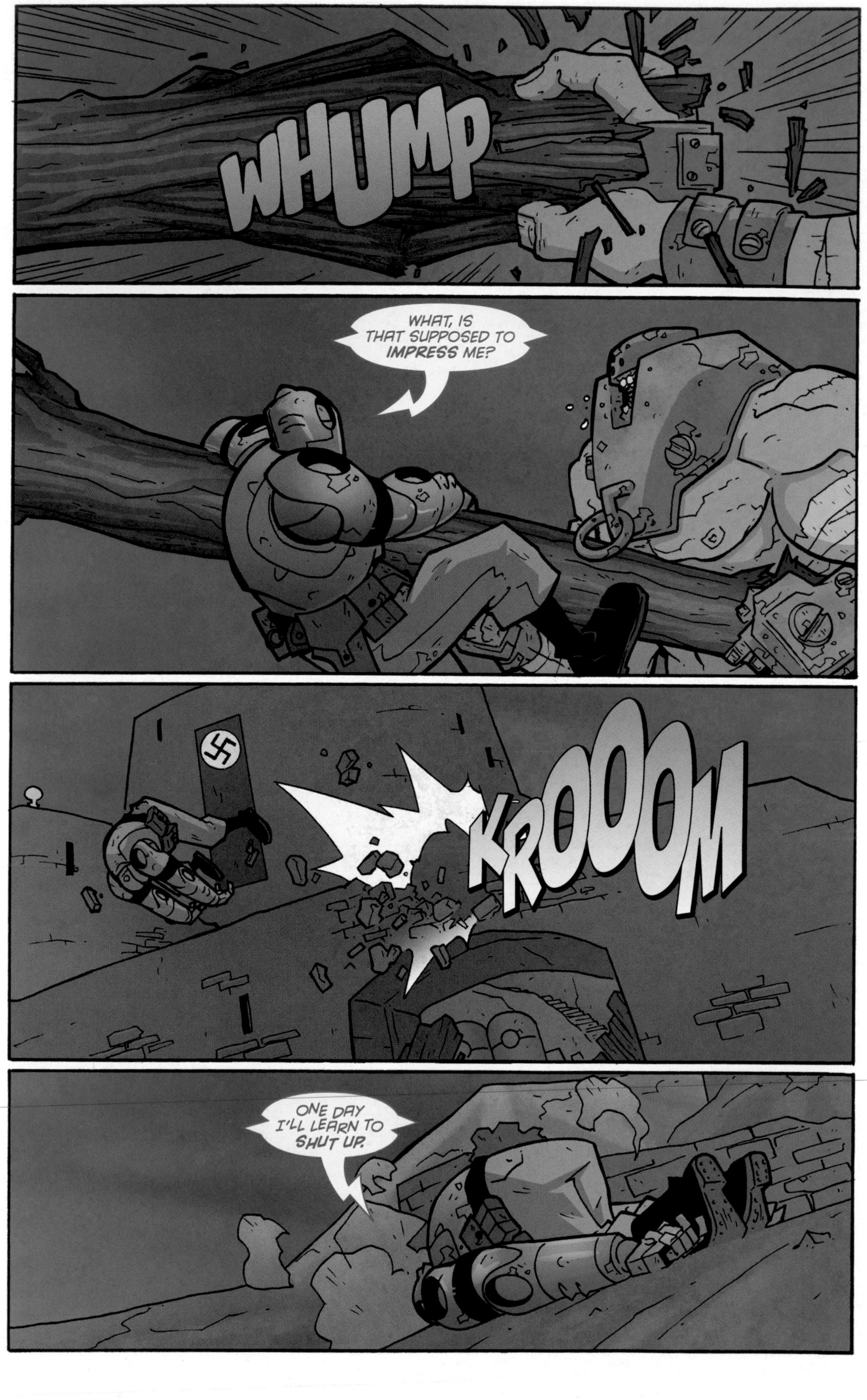
WHUMP
WHAT, IS THAT SUPPOSED TO IMPRESS ME?
KROOOM
ONE DAY I'LL LEARN TO SHUT UP.

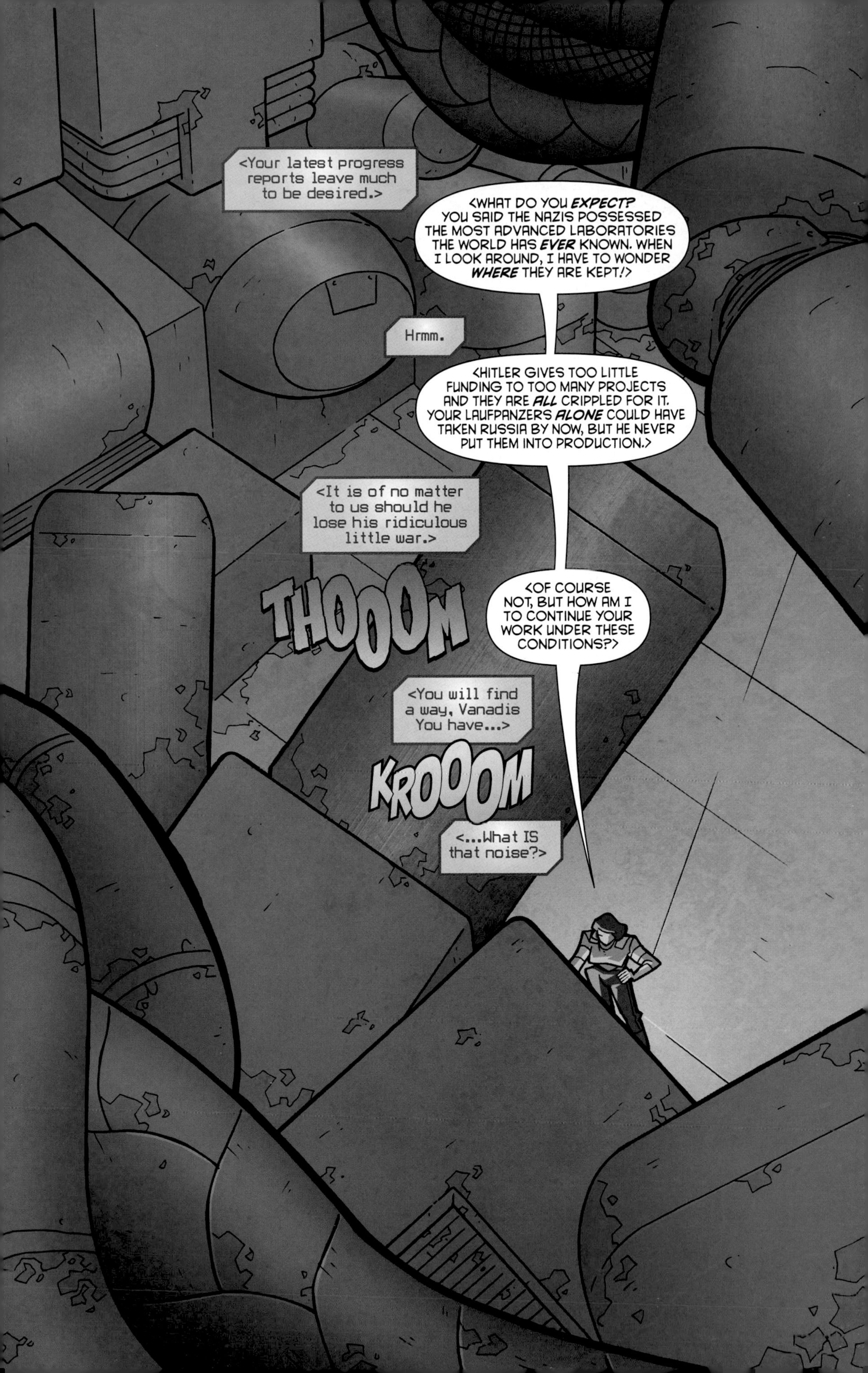
<Your latest progress reports leave much to be desired.>
<WHAT DO YOU EXPECT? YOU SAID THE NAZIS POSSESSED THE MOST ADVANCED LABORATORIES THE WORLD HAS EVER KNOWN. WHEN I LOOK AROUND, I HAVE TO WONDER WHERE THEY ARE KEPT!>
Hrmm.
<HITLER GIVES TOO LITTLE FUNDING TO TOO MANY PROJECTS AND THEY ARE ALL CRIPPLED FOR IT. YOUR LAUFPANZERS ALONE COULD HAVE TAKEN RUSSIA BY NOW, BUT HE NEVER PUT THEM INTO PRODUCTION.>
<It is of no matter to us should he lose his ridiculous little war.>
THOOOM
<OF COURSE NOT, BUT HOW AM I TO CONTINUE YOUR WORK UNDER THESE CONDITIONS?>
<You will find a way, Vanadis You have...>
KROOOM
<...What IS that noise?>

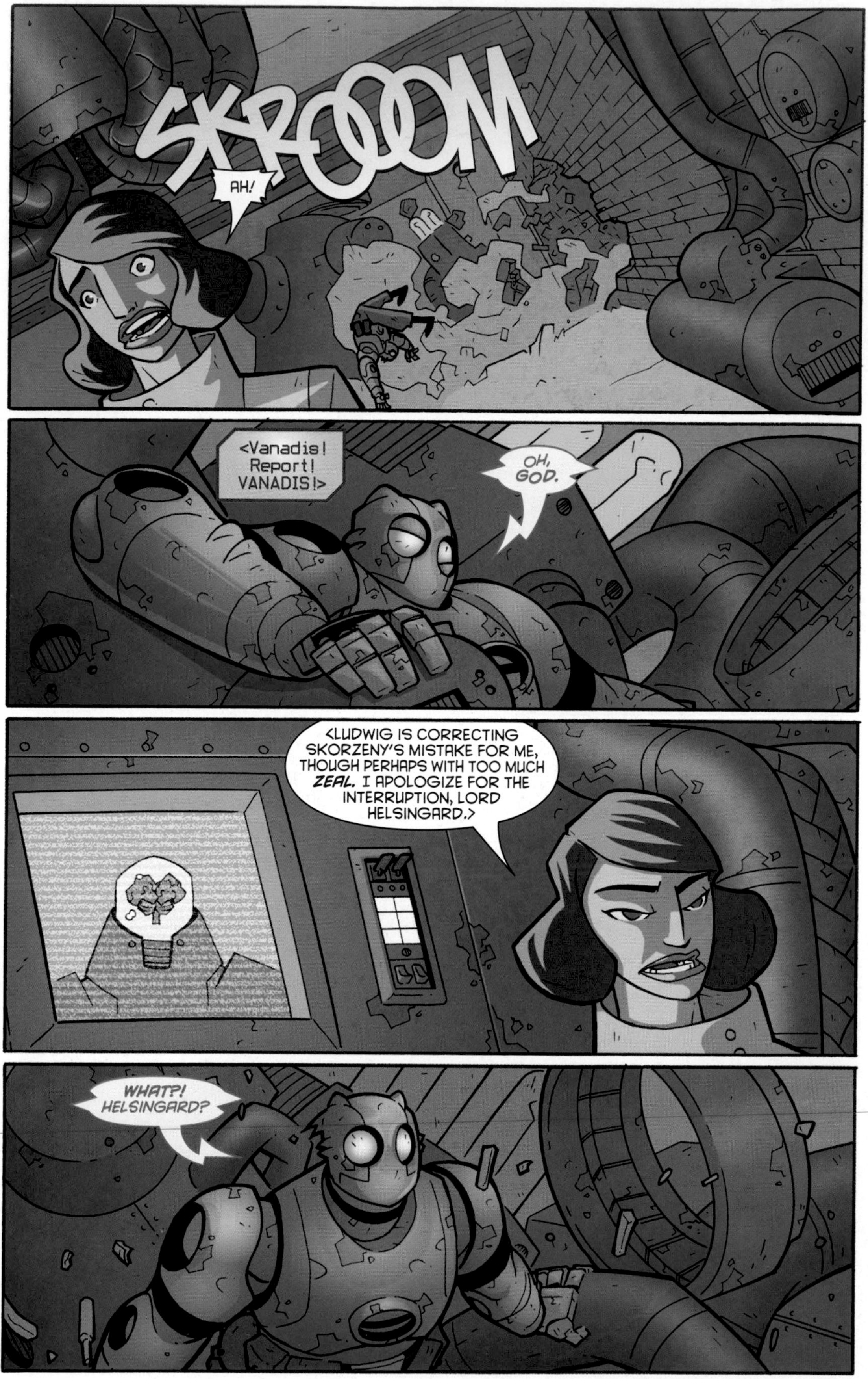
SKROOOM
AH!
<Vanadis! Report! VANADIS!>
OH, GOD.
<LUDWIG IS CORRECTING SKORZENY'S MISTAKE FOR ME, THOUGH PERHAPS WITH TOO MUCH ZEAL. I APOLOGIZE FOR THE INTERRUPTION, LORD HELSINGARD.>
WHAT?! HELSINGARD?

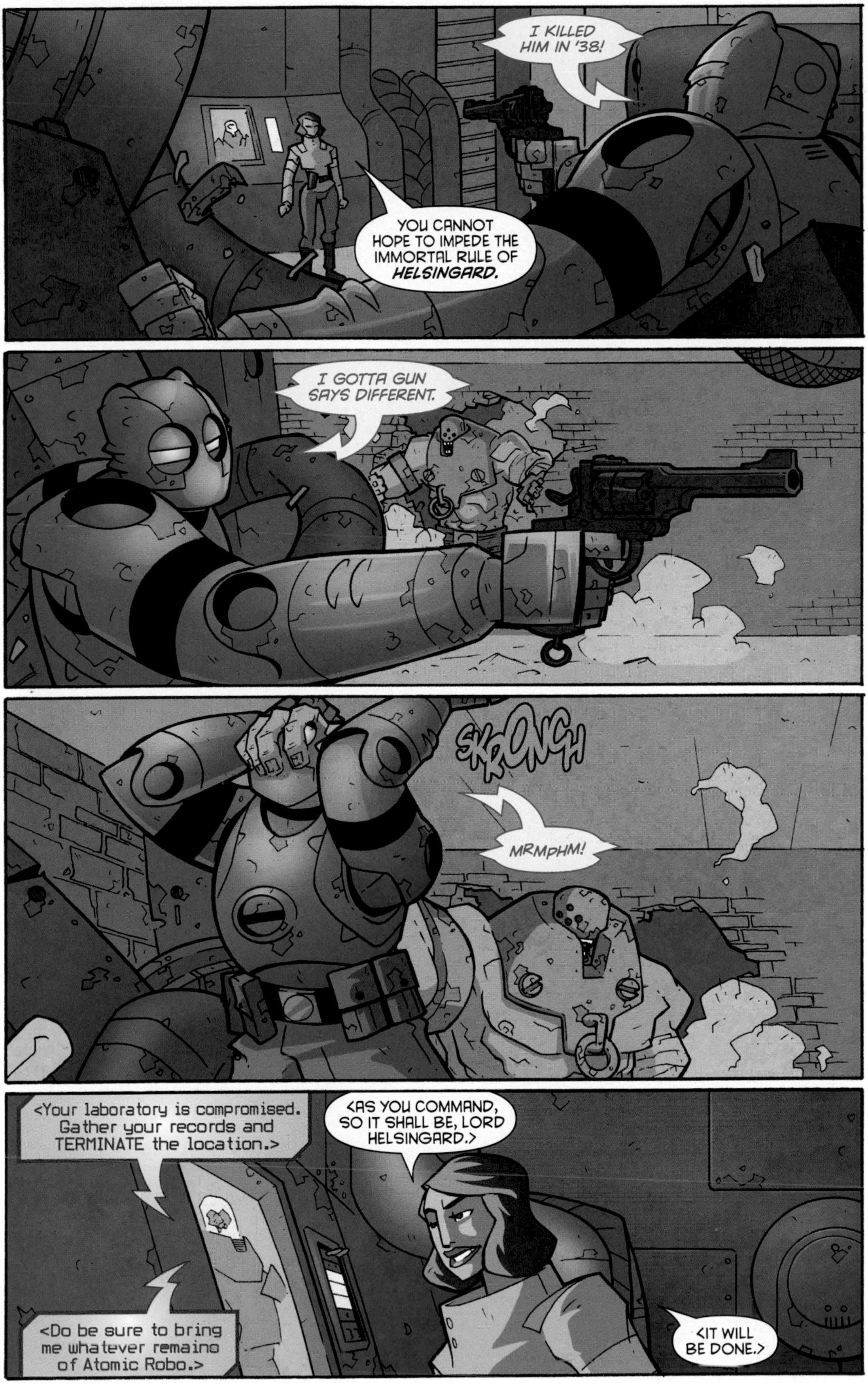
I KILLED HIM IN '38!
YOU CANNOT HOPE TO IMPEDE THE IMMORTAL RULE OF HELSINGARD.
I GOTTA GUN SAYS DIFFERENT.
SKRONCH
MRMPHM!
<Your laboratory is compromised. Gather your records and TERMINATE the location.>
<AS YOU COMMAND, SO IT SHALL BE, LORD HELSINGARD.>
<Do be sure to bring me whatever remains of Atomic Robo.>
<IT WILL BE DONE.>

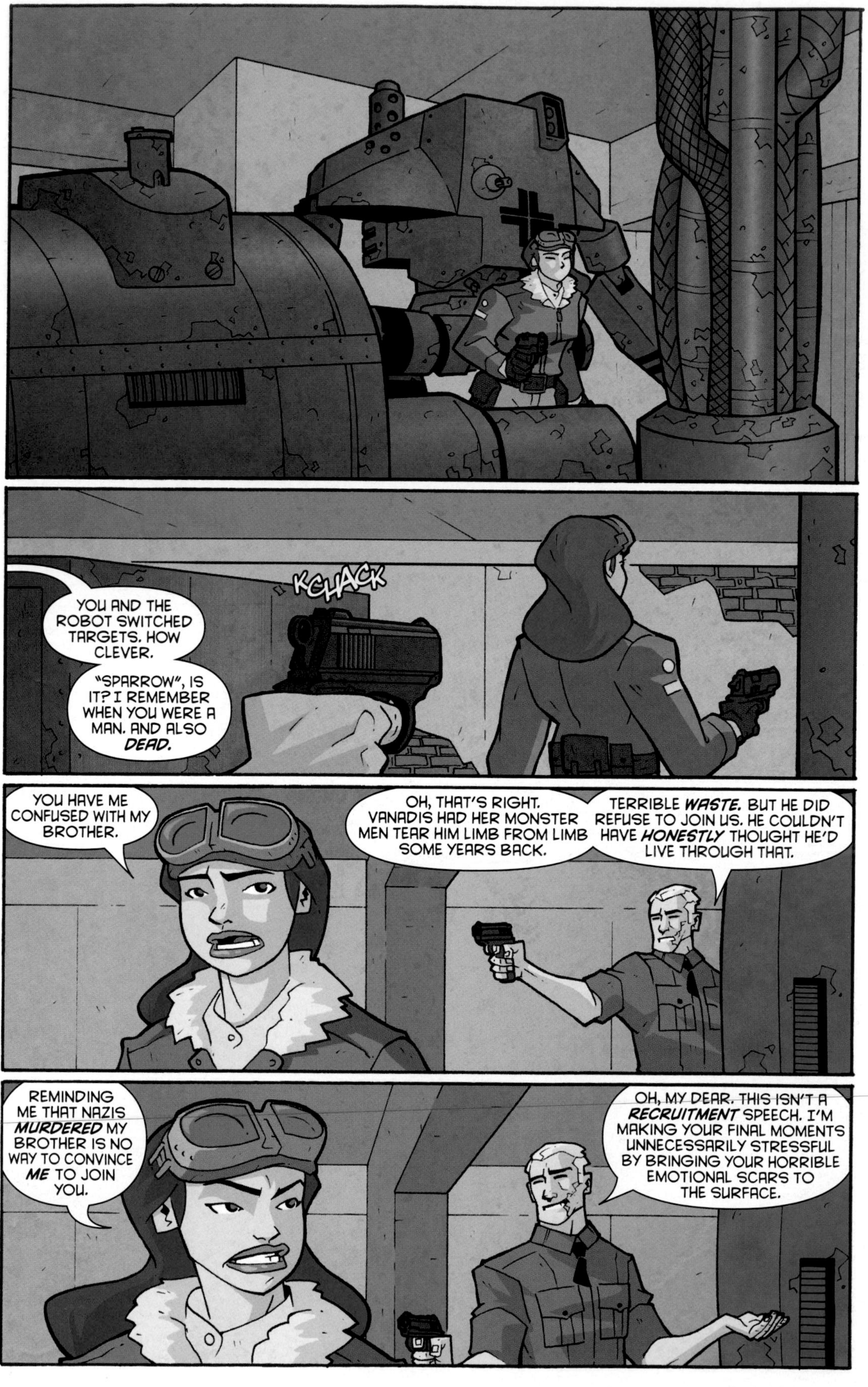
KCHACK
YOU AND THE ROBOT SWITCHED TARGETS. HOW CLEVER.
"SPARROW", IS IT? I REMEMBER WHEN YOU WERE A MAN. AND ALSO *DEAD.*
YOU HAVE ME CONFUSED WITH MY BROTHER.
OH, THAT'S RIGHT. VANADIS HAD HER MONSTER MEN TEAR HIM LIMB FROM LIMB SOME YEARS BACK.
TERRIBLE *WASTE.* BUT HE DID REFUSE TO JOIN US. HE COULDN'T HAVE *HONESTLY* THOUGHT HE'D LIVE THROUGH THAT.
REMINDING ME THAT NAZIS *MURDERED* MY BROTHER IS NO WAY TO CONVINCE *ME* TO JOIN YOU.
OH, MY DEAR. THIS ISN'T A *RECRUITMENT* SPEECH. I'M MAKING YOUR FINAL MOMENTS UNNECESSARILY STRESSFUL BY BRINGING YOUR HORRIBLE EMOTIONAL SCARS TO THE SURFACE.

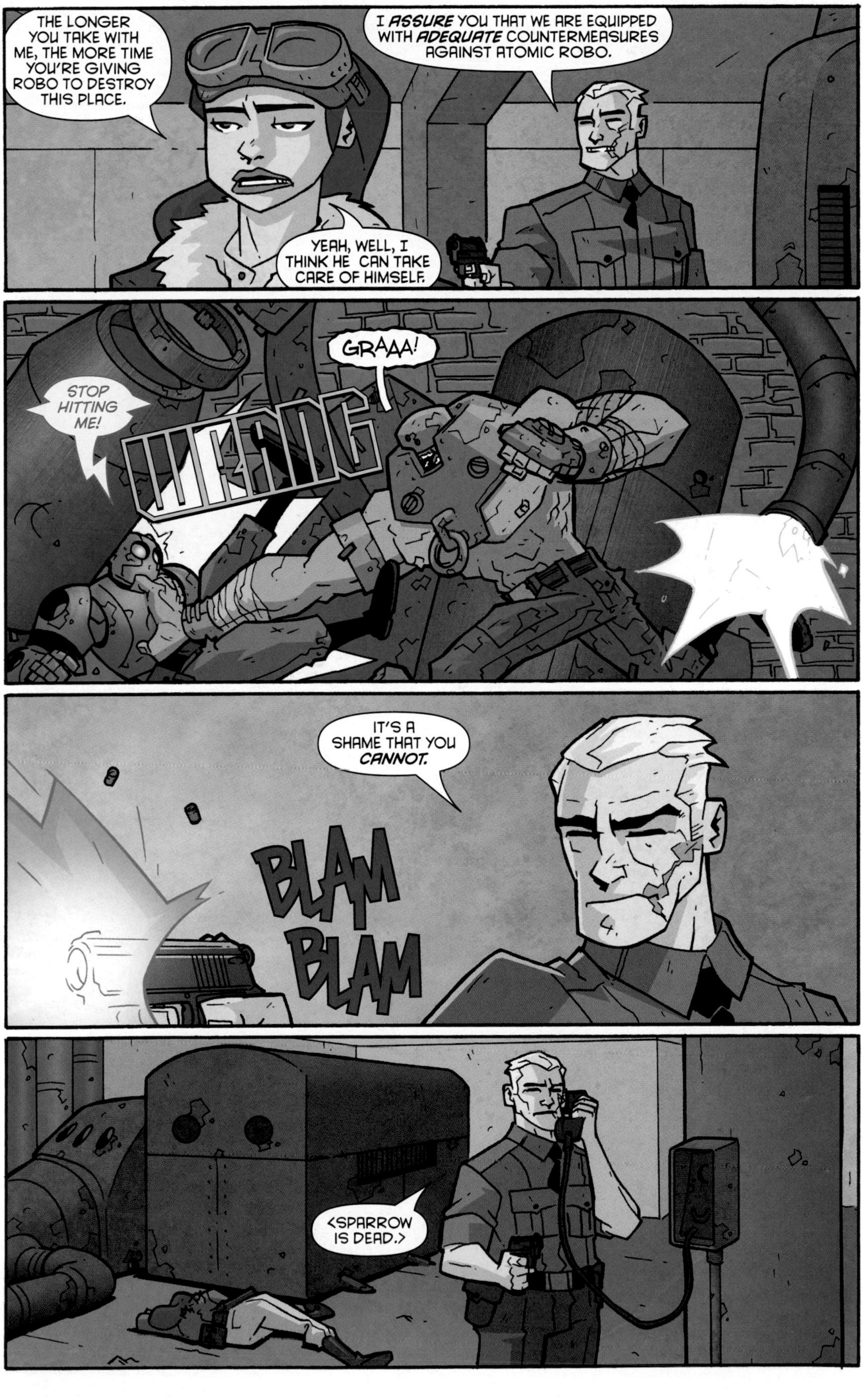
THE LONGER YOU TAKE WITH ME, THE MORE TIME YOU'RE GIVING ROBO TO DESTROY THIS PLACE.
I ASSURE YOU THAT WE ARE EQUIPPED WITH ADEQUATE COUNTERMEASURES AGAINST ATOMIC ROBO.
YEAH, WELL, I THINK HE CAN TAKE CARE OF HIMSELF.
STOP HITTING ME!
WCRNG
GRAAA!
IT'S A SHAME THAT YOU CANNOT.
BLAM
BLAM
<SPARROW IS DEAD.>

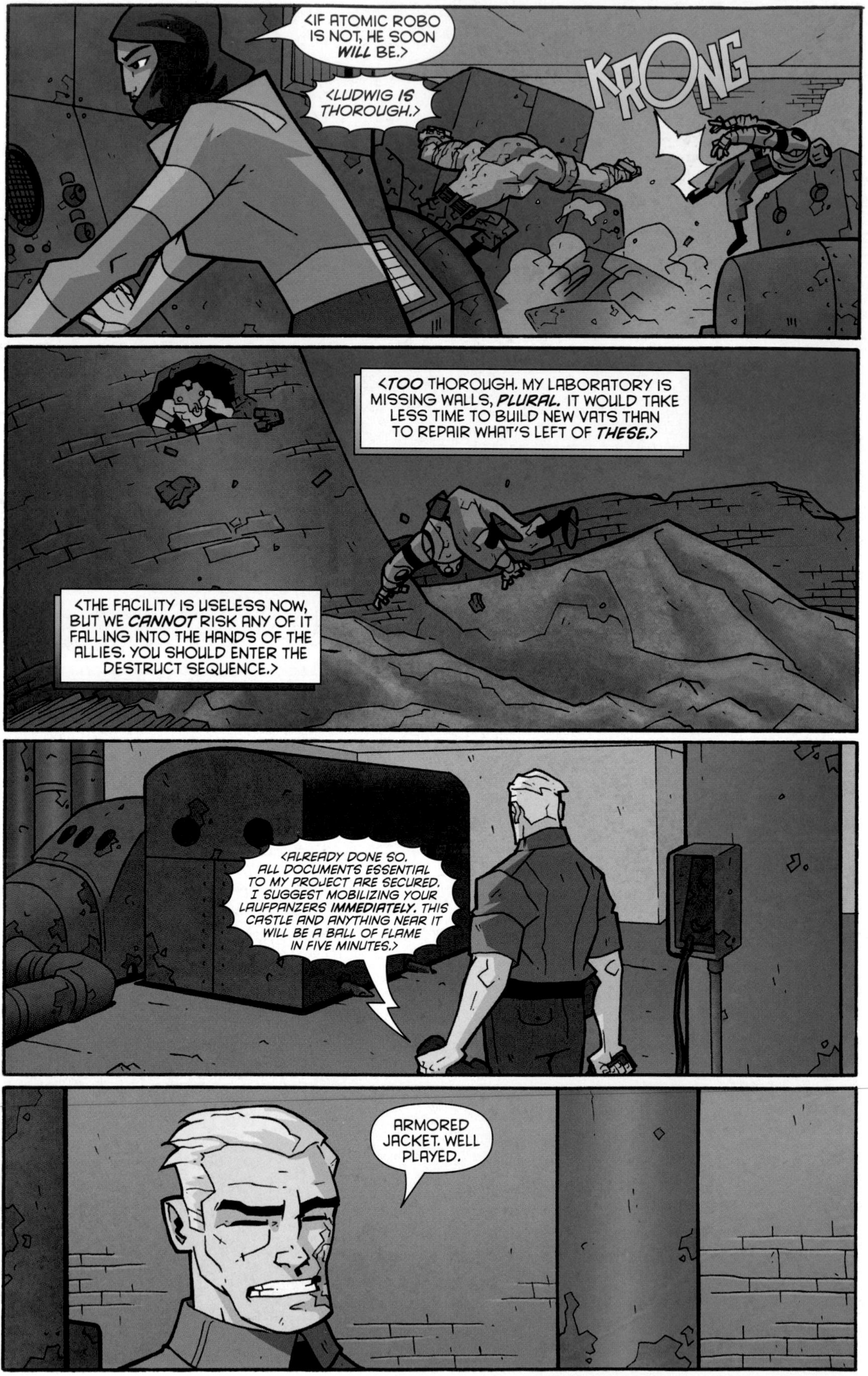

<IF ATOMIC ROBO IS NOT, HE SOON WILL BE.>
<LUDWIG IS THOROUGH.>
KRONG
<TOO THOROUGH. MY LABORATORY IS MISSING WALLS, PLURAL. IT WOULD TAKE LESS TIME TO BUILD NEW VATS THAN TO REPAIR WHAT'S LEFT OF THESE.>
<THE FACILITY IS USELESS NOW, BUT WE CANNOT RISK ANY OF IT FALLING INTO THE HANDS OF THE ALLIES. YOU SHOULD ENTER THE DESTRUCT SEQUENCE.>
<ALREADY DONE SO. ALL DOCUMENTS ESSENTIAL TO MY PROJECT ARE SECURED. I SUGGEST MOBILIZING YOUR LAUFPANZERS IMMEDIATELY. THIS CASTLE AND ANYTHING NEAR IT WILL BE A BALL OF FLAME IN FIVE MINUTES.>
ARMORED JACKET. WELL PLAYED.

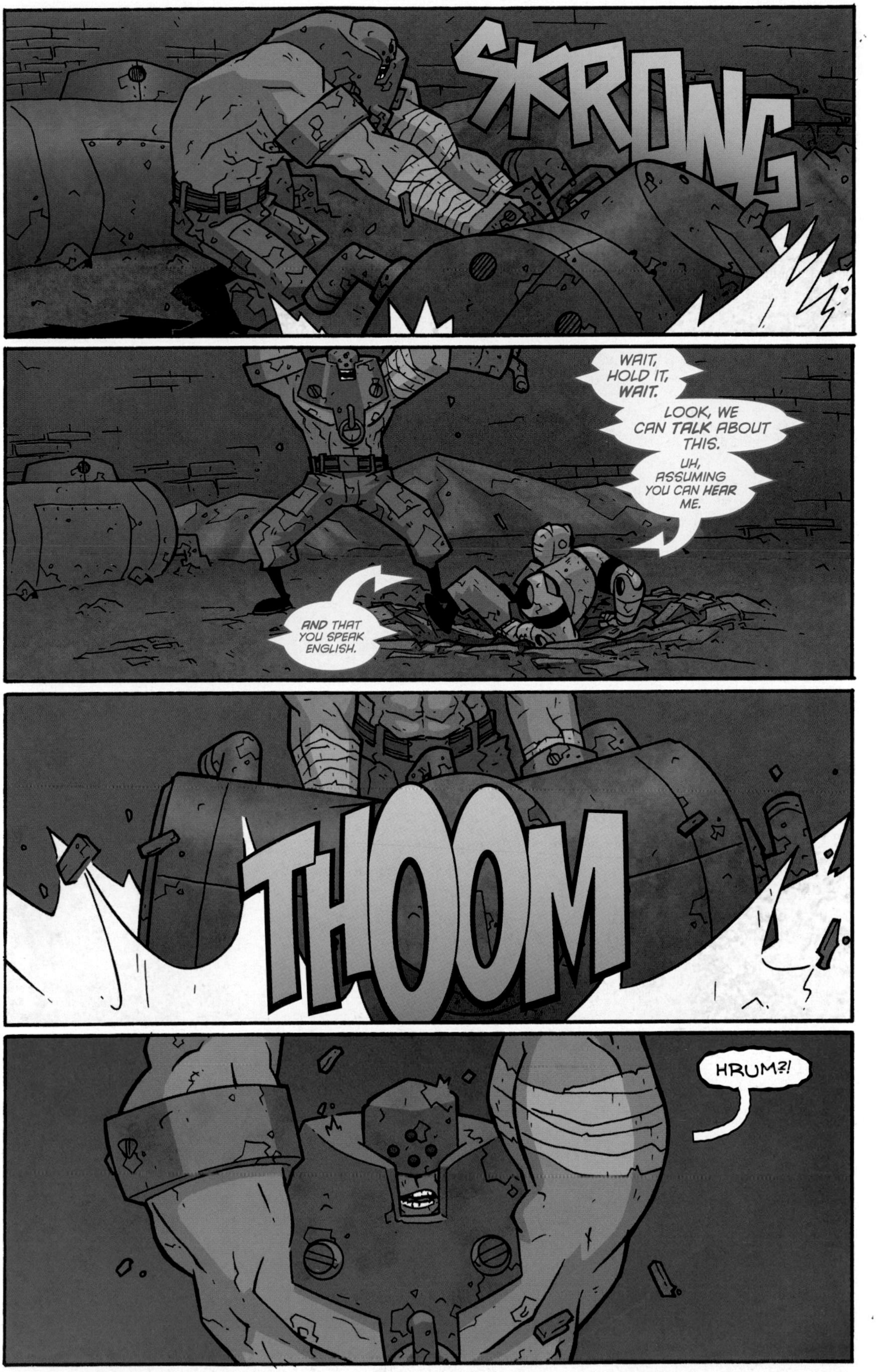
SKRONG
WAIT, HOLD IT, WAIT.
LOOK, WE CAN TALK ABOUT THIS.
UH, ASSUMING YOU CAN HEAR ME.
AND THAT YOU SPEAK ENGLISH.
THOOM
HRUM?!

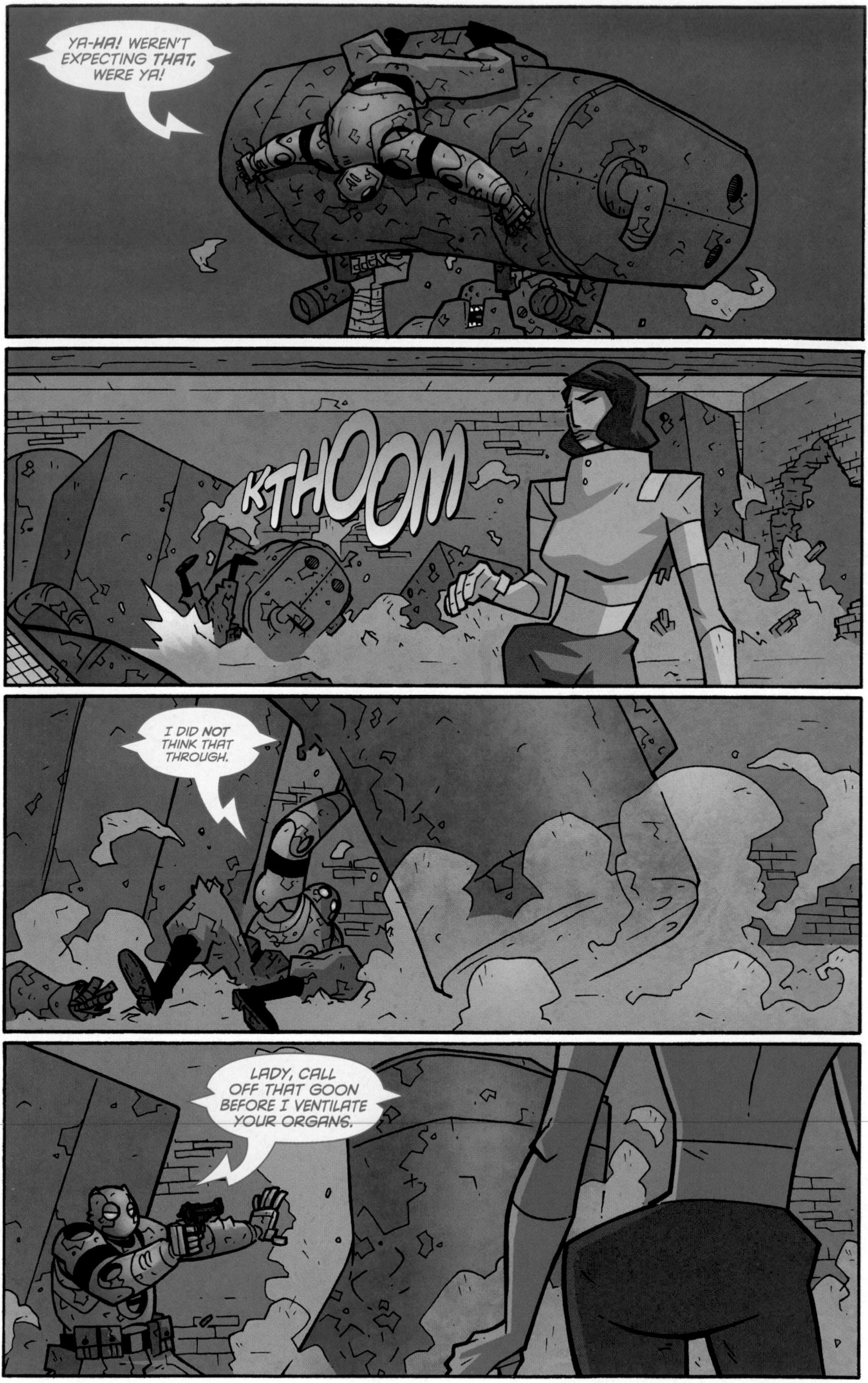
YA-HA! WEREN'T EXPECTING THAT, WERE YA!
KTHOOM
I DID NOT THINK THAT THROUGH.
LADY, CALL OFF THAT GOON BEFORE I VENTILATE YOUR ORGANS.

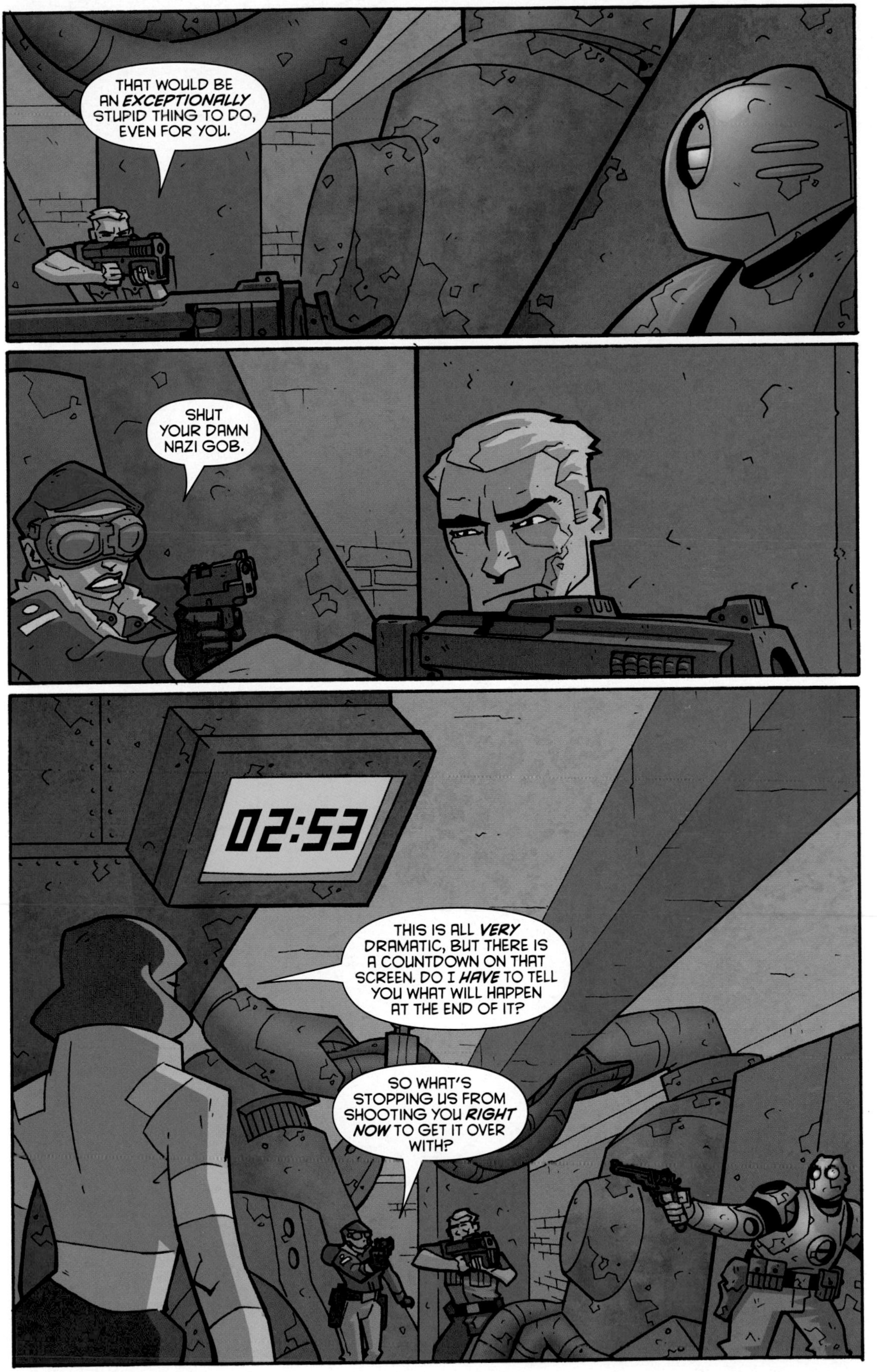
THAT WOULD BE AN EXCEPTIONALLY STUPID THING TO DO, EVEN FOR YOU.
SHUT YOUR DAMN NAZI GOB.
02:53
THIS IS ALL VERY DRAMATIC, BUT THERE IS A COUNTDOWN ON THAT SCREEN. DO I HAVE TO TELL YOU WHAT WILL HAPPEN AT THE END OF IT?
SO WHAT'S STOPPING US FROM SHOOTING YOU RIGHT NOW TO GET IT OVER WITH?

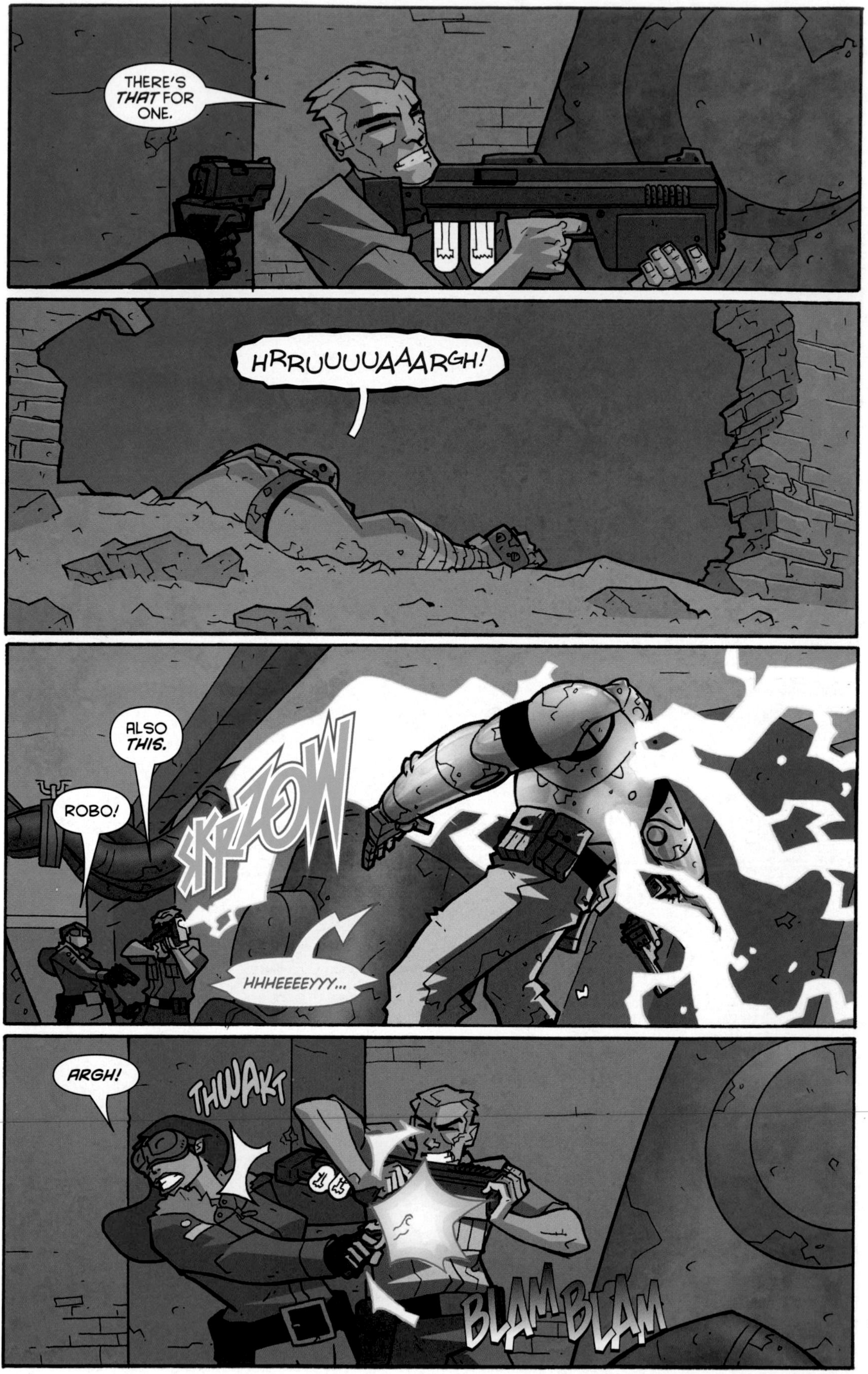
THERE'S *THAT* FOR ONE.
HRRUUUUAAARGH!
ALSO *THIS.*
ROBO!
SKRZOW
HHHEEEEYYY...
ARGH!
THWAKT
BLAM BLAM

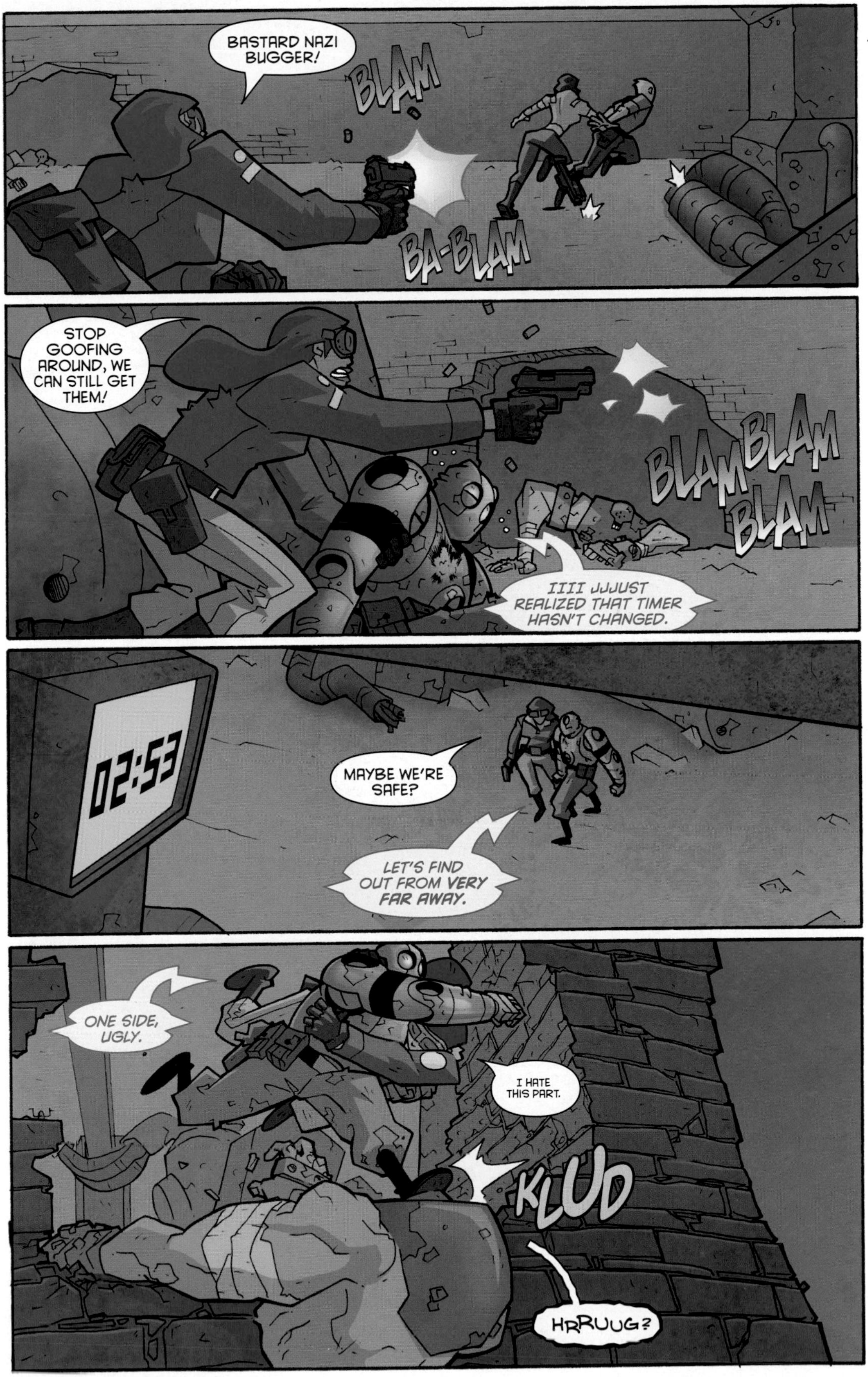
BASTARD NAZI BUGGER!
BLAM
BA-BLAM
STOP GOOFING AROUND, WE CAN STILL GET THEM!
BLAMBLAM BLAM
IIII JJJJUST REALIZED THAT TIMER HASN'T CHANGED.
02:53
MAYBE WE'RE SAFE?
LET'S FIND OUT FROM VERY FAR AWAY.
ONE SIDE, UGLY.
I HATE THIS PART.
KLUD
HRRUUG?

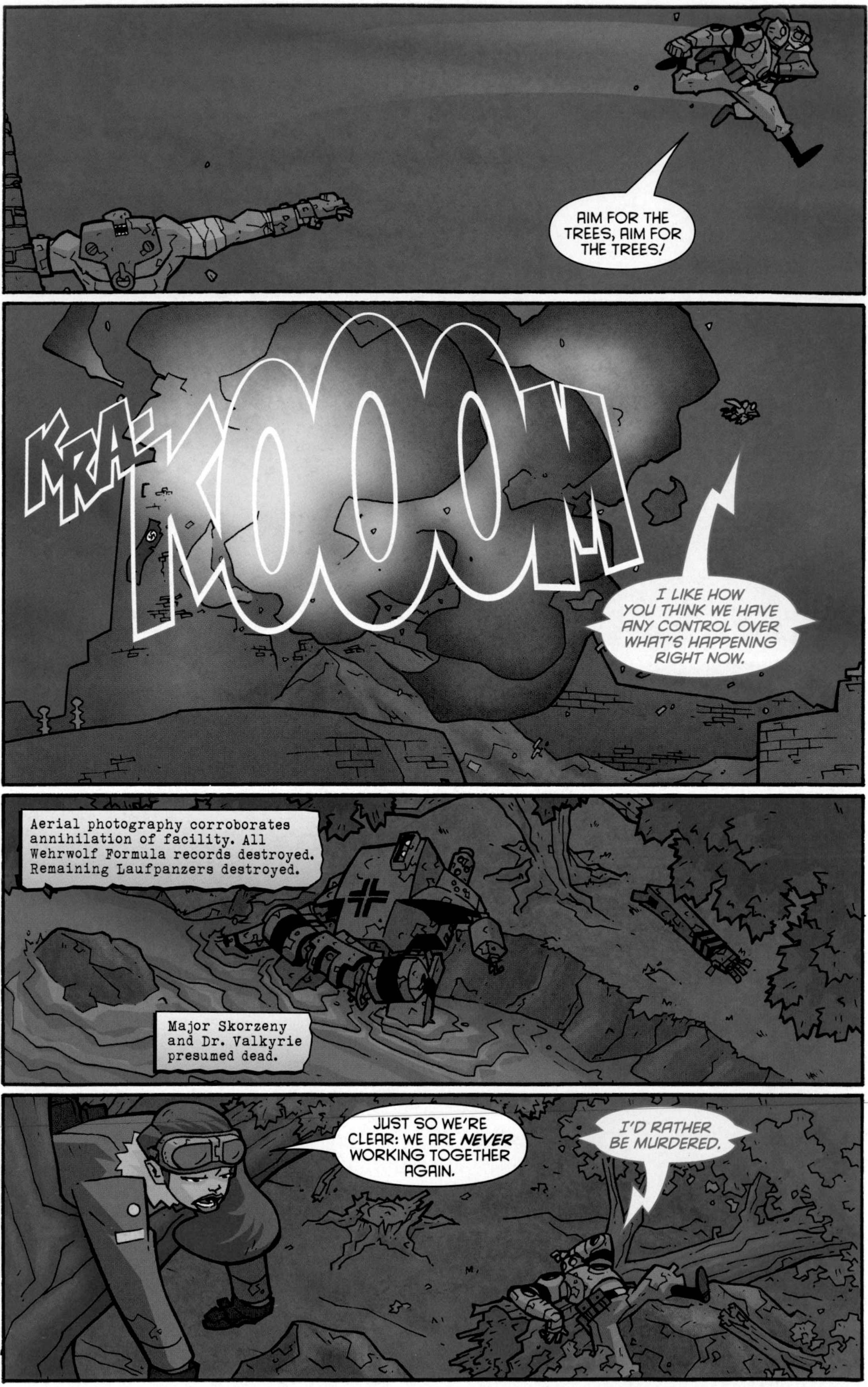
AIM FOR THE TREES, AIM FOR THE TREES!
KRA-KOOOM
I LIKE HOW YOU THINK WE HAVE ANY CONTROL OVER WHAT'S HAPPENING RIGHT NOW.
Aerial photography corroborates annihilation of facility. All Wehrwolf Formula records destroyed. Remaining Laufpanzers destroyed.
Major Skorzeny and Dr. Valkyrie presumed dead.
JUST SO WE'RE CLEAR: WE ARE *NEVER* WORKING TOGETHER AGAIN.
I'D RATHER BE MURDERED.

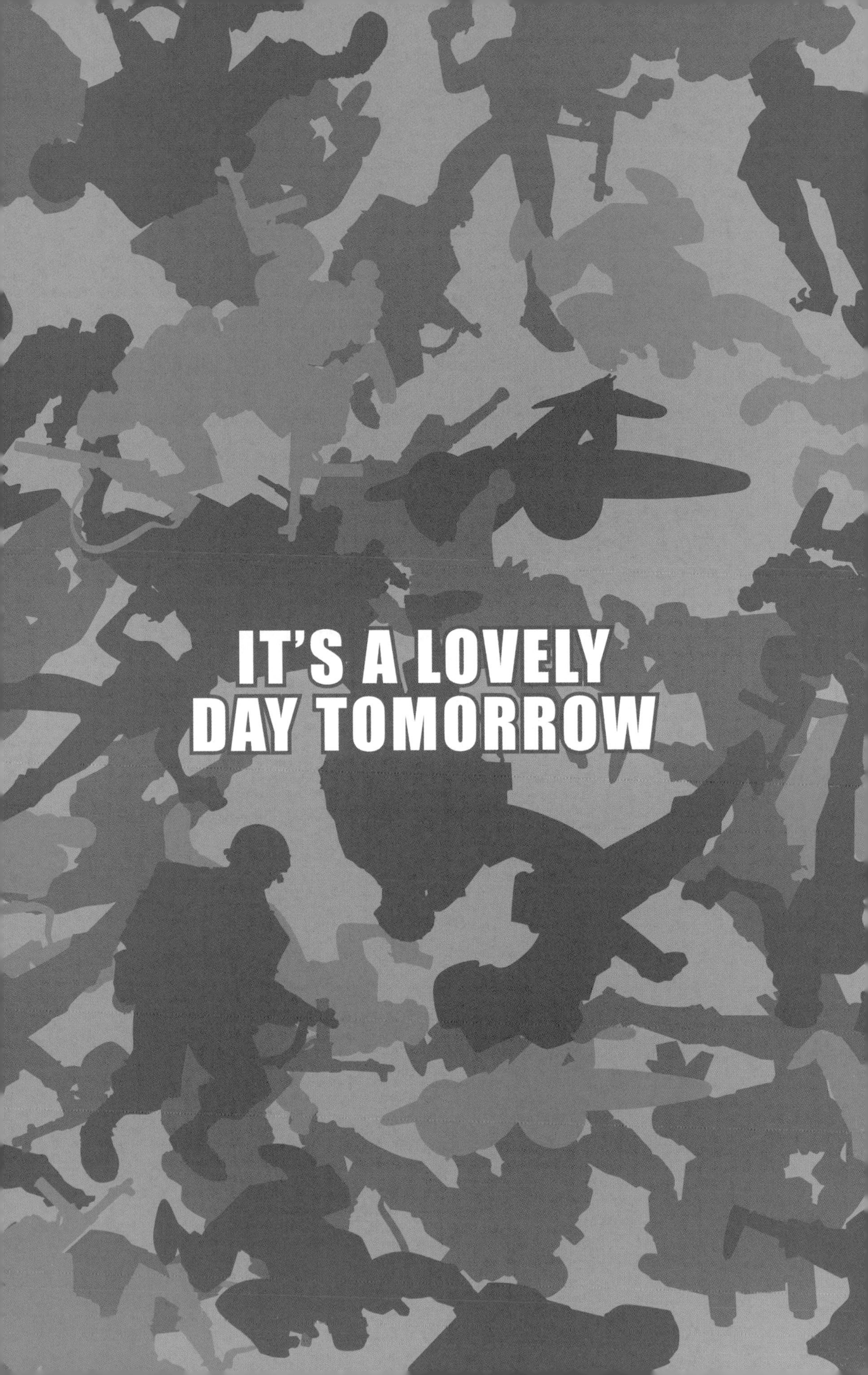

# IT'S A LOVELY DAY TOMORROW

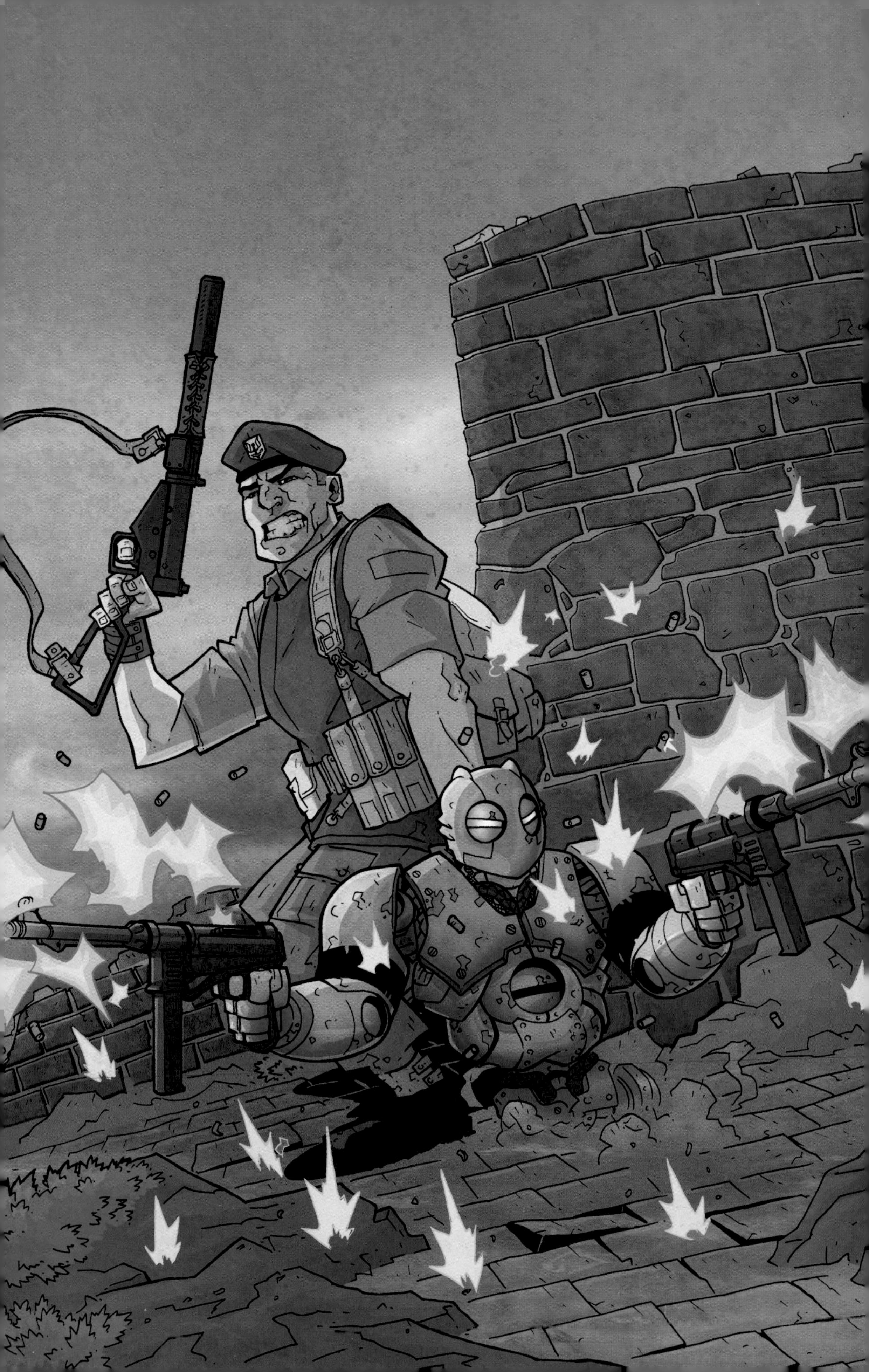

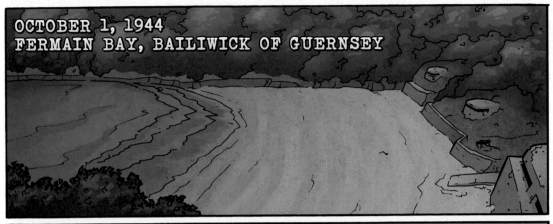

**OCTOBER 1, 1944**
**FERMAIN BAY, BAILIWICK OF GUERNSEY**

ENGINES OFF.

LET'S KEEP THIS QUIET AND QUICK.

BOOM

WHAT THE--?!

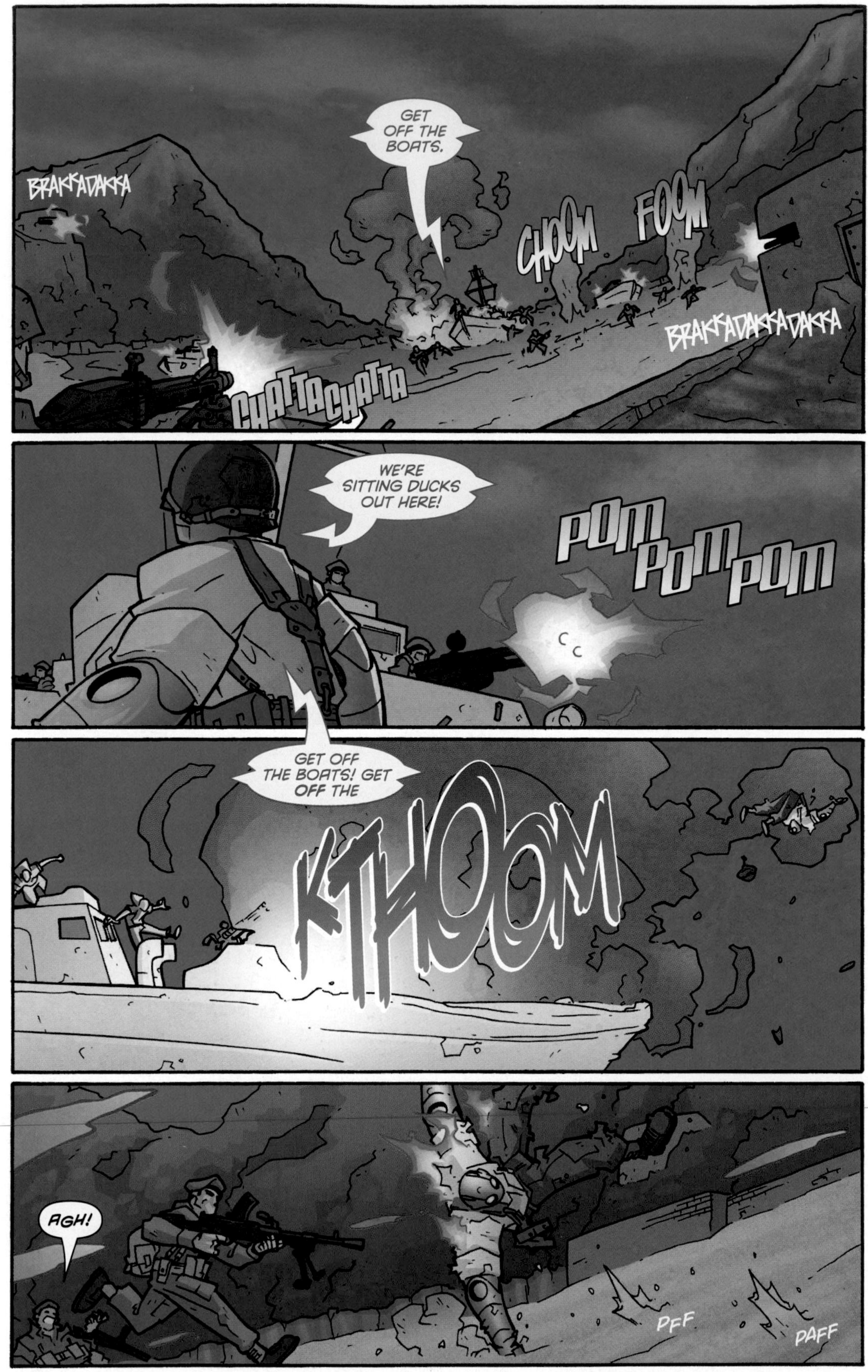
GET OFF THE BOATS.
BRAKKADAKKA
CHOOM
FOOM
BRAKKADAKKADAKKA
CHATTACHATTA
WE'RE SITTING DUCKS OUT HERE!
POM POM POM
GET OFF THE BOATS! GET OFF THE
KTHOOM
AGH!
PFF
PAFF

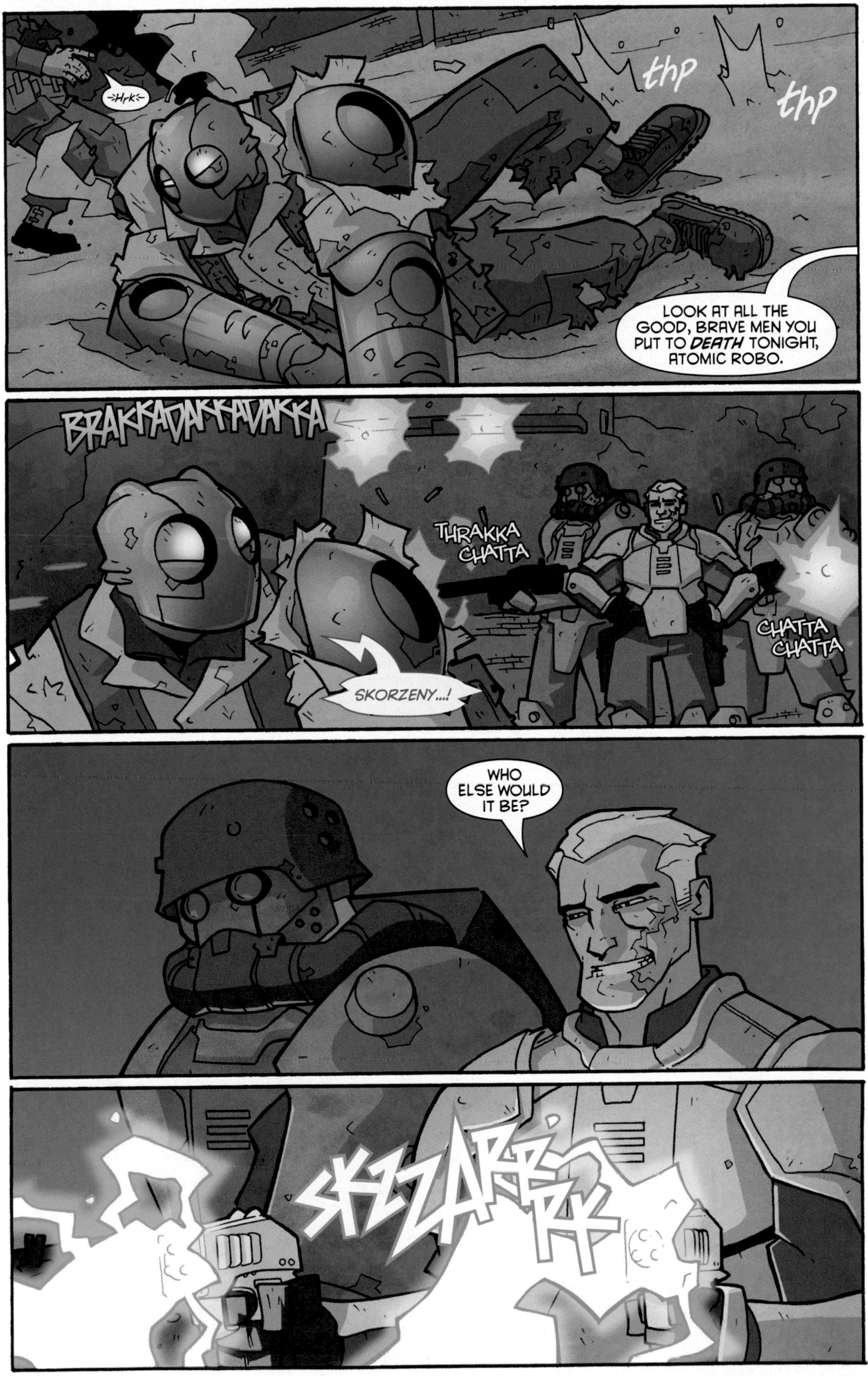
Hrk
thp
thp
LOOK AT ALL THE GOOD, BRAVE MEN YOU PUT TO DEATH TONIGHT, ATOMIC ROBO.
BRAKKADAKKADAKKA
THRAKKA CHATTA
CHATTA CHATTA
SKORZENY...!
WHO ELSE WOULD IT BE?
SKZZARRRK

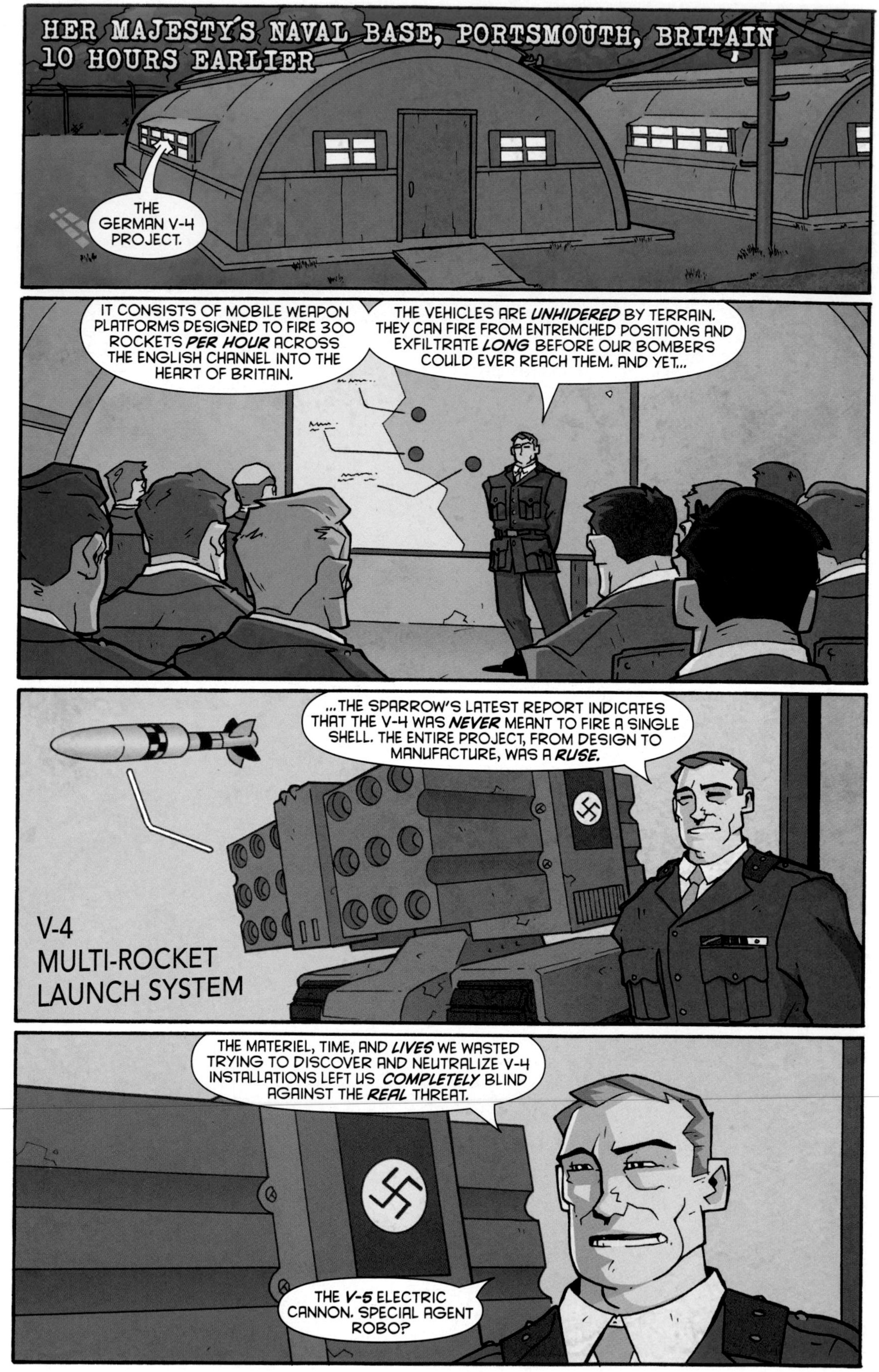
HER MAJESTY'S NAVAL BASE, PORTSMOUTH, BRITAIN
10 HOURS EARLIER
THE GERMAN V-4 PROJECT.
IT CONSISTS OF MOBILE WEAPON PLATFORMS DESIGNED TO FIRE 300 ROCKETS PER HOUR ACROSS THE ENGLISH CHANNEL INTO THE HEART OF BRITAIN.
THE VEHICLES ARE UNHIDERED BY TERRAIN. THEY CAN FIRE FROM ENTRENCHED POSITIONS AND EXFILTRATE LONG BEFORE OUR BOMBERS COULD EVER REACH THEM. AND YET...
...THE SPARROW'S LATEST REPORT INDICATES THAT THE V-4 WAS NEVER MEANT TO FIRE A SINGLE SHELL. THE ENTIRE PROJECT, FROM DESIGN TO MANUFACTURE, WAS A RUSE.
V-4
MULTI-ROCKET
LAUNCH SYSTEM
THE MATERIEL, TIME, AND LIVES WE WASTED TRYING TO DISCOVER AND NEUTRALIZE V-4 INSTALLATIONS LEFT US COMPLETELY BLIND AGAINST THE REAL THREAT.
THE V-5 ELECTRIC CANNON. SPECIAL AGENT ROBO?

GUERNSEY ISLAND

THANK YOU, GENERAL. THE THEORY BEHIND THE V-4 WAS AT THE CUTTING EDGE OF WEAPONS TECHNOLOGY. THE V-5 IS SOMETHING OUT OF SCIENCE FICTION.

YES, I RECOGNIZE THE IRONY.

BASED ON MY EXPERIENCE WITH ALTERNATIVE WEAPONS RESEARCH UNDER MR. TESLA, MY GUESS IS THAT THIS V-5 PROPELS *ENORMOUS* EXPLOSIVE SLUGS USING PRECISELY TIMED ELECTROMAGNETIC ARRAYS.

IMAGINE A BULLET FIRED WITH ALL THE FORCE OF A *HUNDRED* SEPARATE CHARGES. NOW APPLY THAT TO NAVAL ARTILLERY SHELLS.

GUERNSE

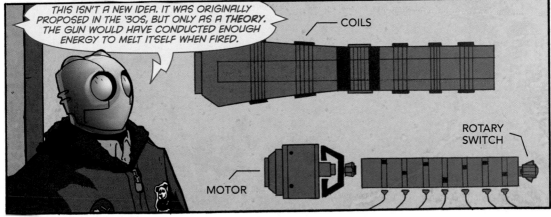

THIS ISN'T A NEW IDEA. IT WAS ORIGINALLY PROPOSED IN THE '30S, BUT ONLY AS A *THEORY*. THE GUN WOULD HAVE CONDUCTED ENOUGH ENERGY TO MELT ITSELF WHEN FIRED.

COILS

ROTARY SWITCH

MOTOR

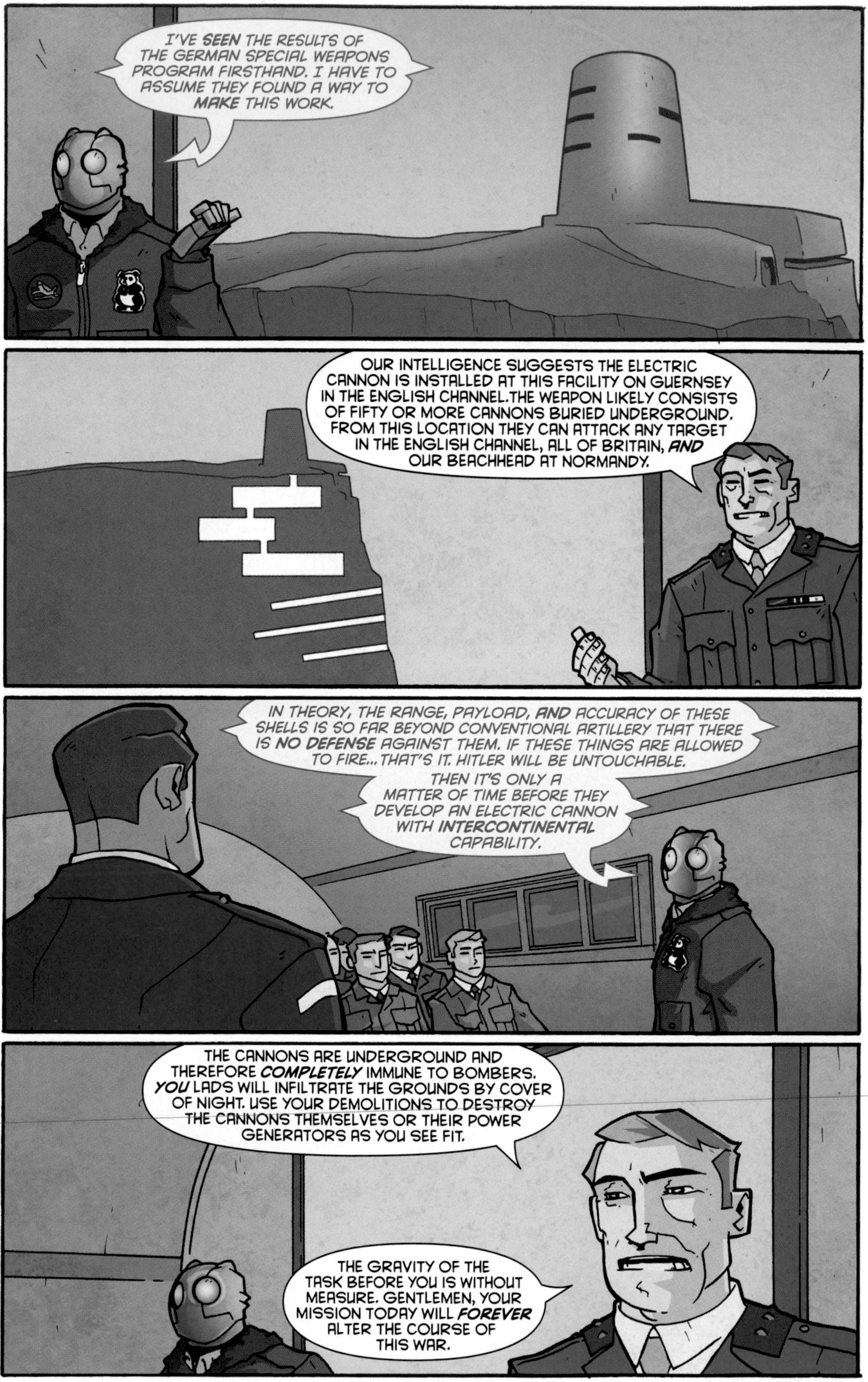
I'VE SEEN THE RESULTS OF THE GERMAN SPECIAL WEAPONS PROGRAM FIRSTHAND. I HAVE TO ASSUME THEY FOUND A WAY TO MAKE THIS WORK.
OUR INTELLIGENCE SUGGESTS THE ELECTRIC CANNON IS INSTALLED AT THIS FACILITY ON GUERNSEY IN THE ENGLISH CHANNEL.THE WEAPON LIKELY CONSISTS OF FIFTY OR MORE CANNONS BURIED UNDERGROUND. FROM THIS LOCATION THEY CAN ATTACK ANY TARGET IN THE ENGLISH CHANNEL, ALL OF BRITAIN, AND OUR BEACHHEAD AT NORMANDY.
IN THEORY, THE RANGE, PAYLOAD, AND ACCURACY OF THESE SHELLS IS SO FAR BEYOND CONVENTIONAL ARTILLERY THAT THERE IS NO DEFENSE AGAINST THEM. IF THESE THINGS ARE ALLOWED TO FIRE...THAT'S IT. HITLER WILL BE UNTOUCHABLE.
THEN IT'S ONLY A MATTER OF TIME BEFORE THEY DEVELOP AN ELECTRIC CANNON WITH INTERCONTINENTAL CAPABILITY.
THE CANNONS ARE UNDERGROUND AND THEREFORE COMPLETELY IMMUNE TO BOMBERS. YOU LADS WILL INFILTRATE THE GROUNDS BY COVER OF NIGHT. USE YOUR DEMOLITIONS TO DESTROY THE CANNONS THEMSELVES OR THEIR POWER GENERATORS AS YOU SEE FIT.
THE GRAVITY OF THE TASK BEFORE YOU IS WITHOUT MEASURE. GENTLEMEN, YOUR MISSION TODAY WILL FOREVER ALTER THE COURSE OF THIS WAR.

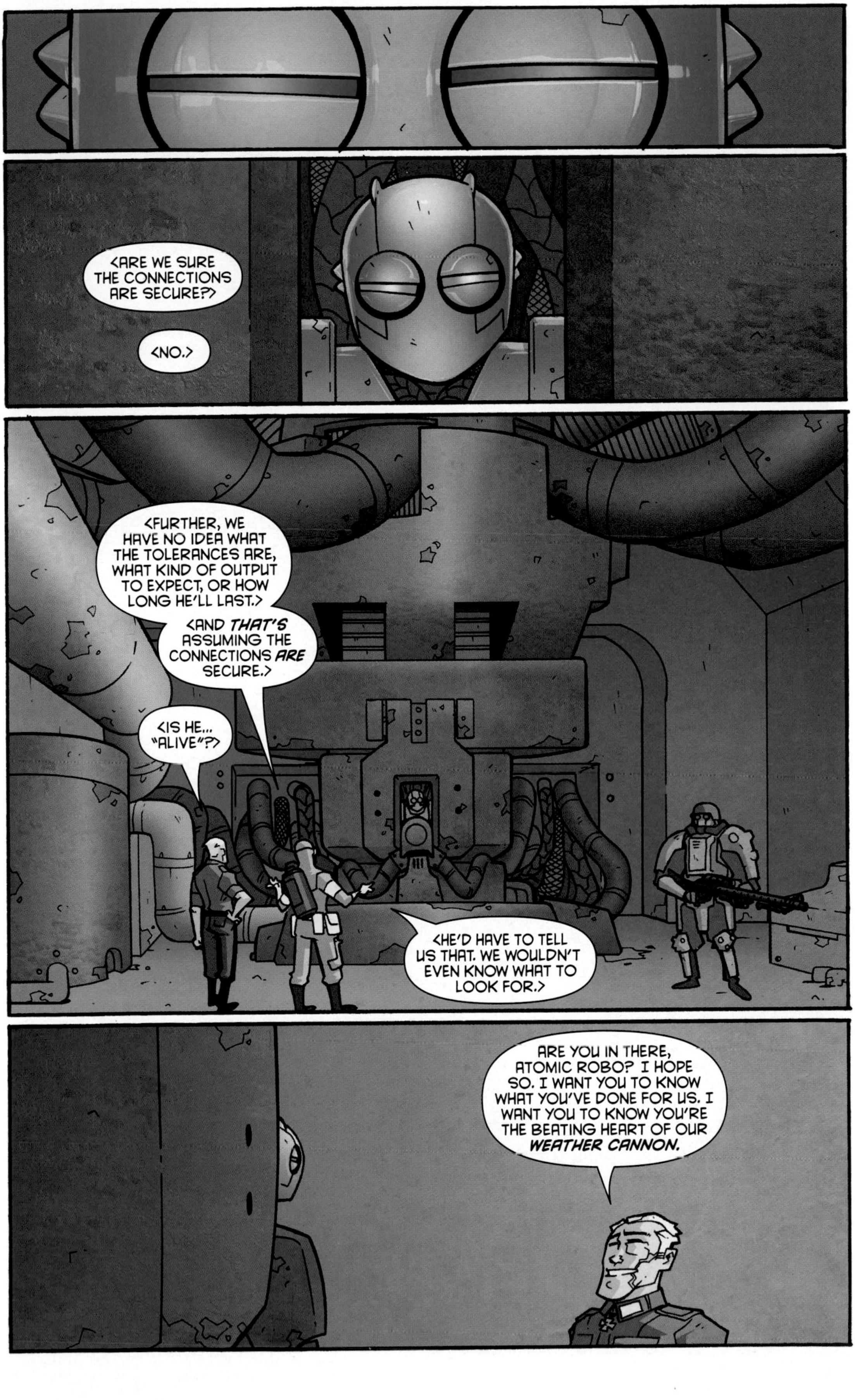
<ARE WE SURE THE CONNECTIONS ARE SECURE?>
<NO.>
<FURTHER, WE HAVE NO IDEA WHAT THE TOLERANCES ARE, WHAT KIND OF OUTPUT TO EXPECT, OR HOW LONG HE'LL LAST.>
<AND *THAT'S* ASSUMING THE CONNECTIONS *ARE* SECURE.>
<IS HE... "ALIVE"?>
<HE'D HAVE TO TELL US THAT. WE WOULDN'T EVEN KNOW WHAT TO LOOK FOR.>
ARE YOU IN THERE, ATOMIC ROBO? I HOPE SO. I WANT YOU TO KNOW WHAT YOU'VE DONE FOR US. I WANT YOU TO KNOW YOU'RE THE BEATING HEART OF OUR *WEATHER CANNON.*

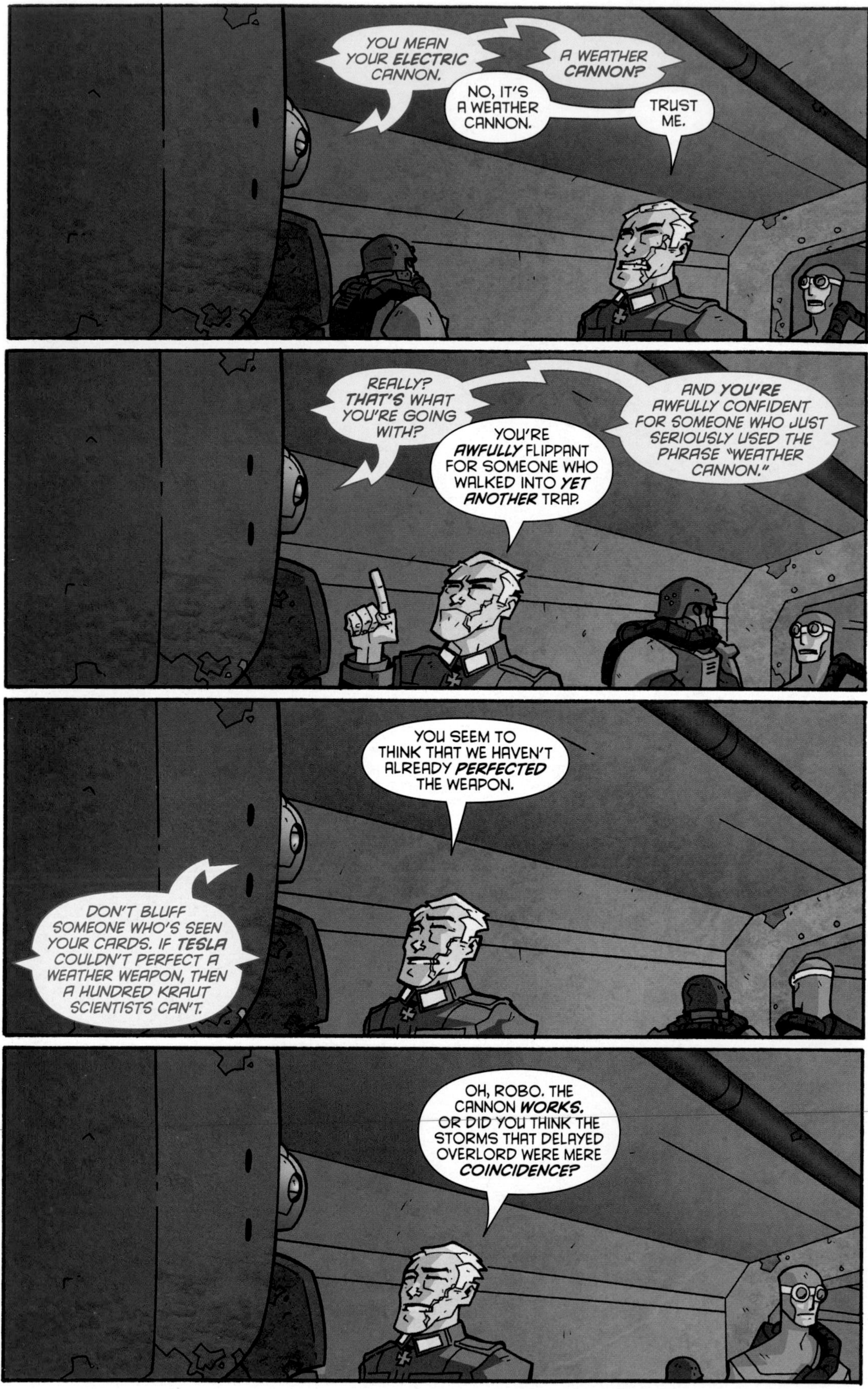
YOU MEAN YOUR ELECTRIC CANNON.
A WEATHER CANNON?
NO, IT'S A WEATHER CANNON.
TRUST ME.
REALLY? THAT'S WHAT YOU'RE GOING WITH?
YOU'RE AWFULLY FLIPPANT FOR SOMEONE WHO WALKED INTO YET ANOTHER TRAP.
AND YOU'RE AWFULLY CONFIDENT FOR SOMEONE WHO JUST SERIOUSLY USED THE PHRASE "WEATHER CANNON."
YOU SEEM TO THINK THAT WE HAVEN'T ALREADY PERFECTED THE WEAPON.
DON'T BLUFF SOMEONE WHO'S SEEN YOUR CARDS. IF TESLA COULDN'T PERFECT A WEATHER WEAPON, THEN A HUNDRED KRAUT SCIENTISTS CAN'T.
OH, ROBO. THE CANNON WORKS. OR DID YOU THINK THE STORMS THAT DELAYED OVERLORD WERE MERE COINCIDENCE?

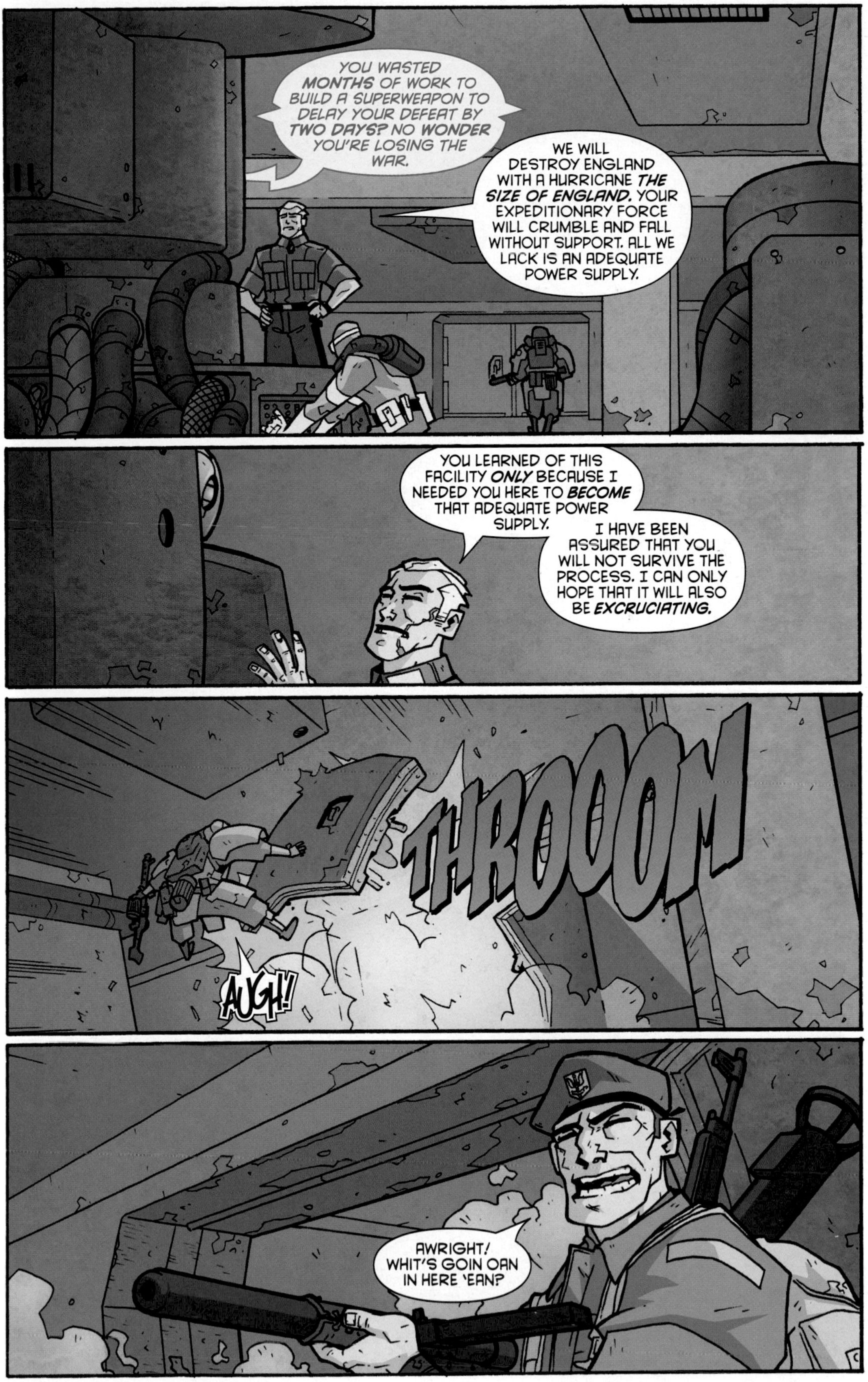
YOU WASTED MONTHS OF WORK TO BUILD A SUPERWEAPON TO DELAY YOUR DEFEAT BY TWO DAYS? NO WONDER YOU'RE LOSING THE WAR.
WE WILL DESTROY ENGLAND WITH A HURRICANE THE SIZE OF ENGLAND. YOUR EXPEDITIONARY FORCE WILL CRUMBLE AND FALL WITHOUT SUPPORT. ALL WE LACK IS AN ADEQUATE POWER SUPPLY.
YOU LEARNED OF THIS FACILITY ONLY BECAUSE I NEEDED YOU HERE TO BECOME THAT ADEQUATE POWER SUPPLY.
I HAVE BEEN ASSURED THAT YOU WILL NOT SURVIVE THE PROCESS. I CAN ONLY HOPE THAT IT WILL ALSO BE EXCRUCIATING.
THROOOM
AUGH!
AWRIGHT! WHIT'S GOIN OAN IN HERE 'EAN?

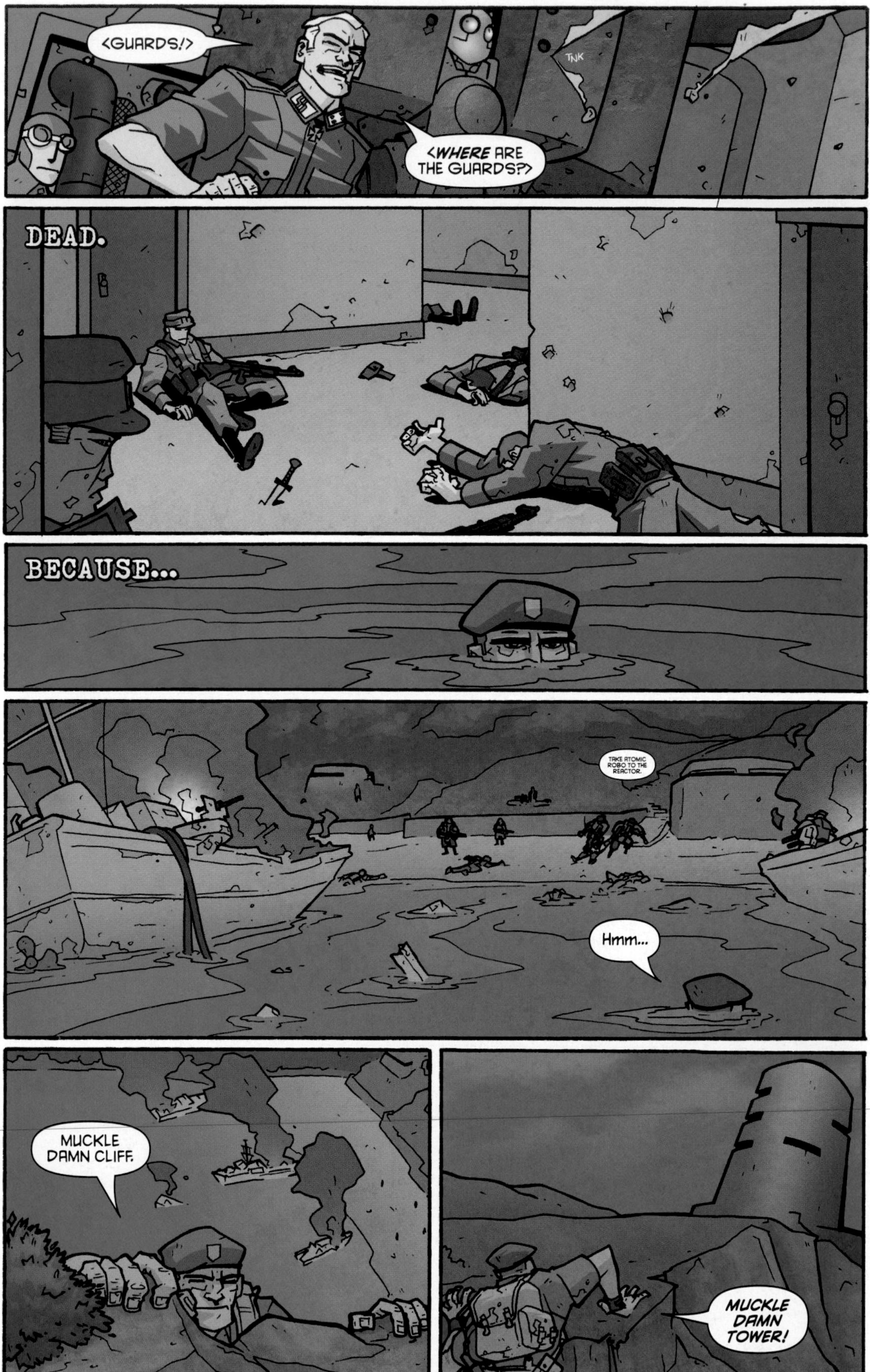
<GUARDS!>
TNK
<*WHERE* ARE THE GUARDS?>
DEAD.
BECAUSE...
TAKE ATOMIC ROBO TO THE REACTOR.
Hmm...
MUCKLE DAMN CLIFF.
*MUCKLE DAMN TOWER!*

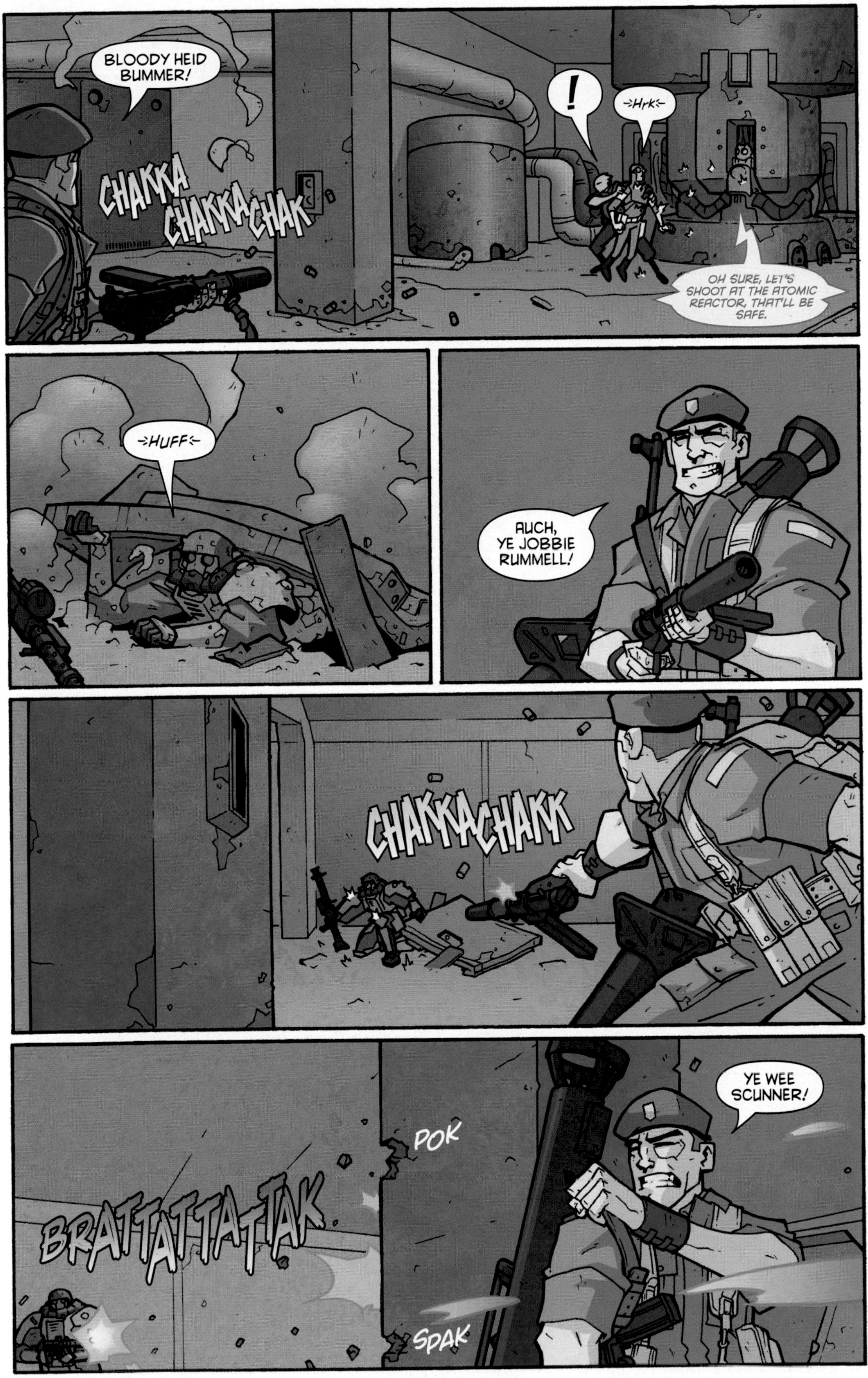
BLOODY HEID BUMMER!
CHAKKA CHAKKACHAK
!
Hrk
OH SURE, LET'S SHOOT AT THE ATOMIC REACTOR, THAT'LL BE SAFE.
HUFF
AUCH, YE JOBBIE RUMMELL!
CHAKKACHAKK
YE WEE SCUNNER!
POK
BRATTATTATTAK
SPAK

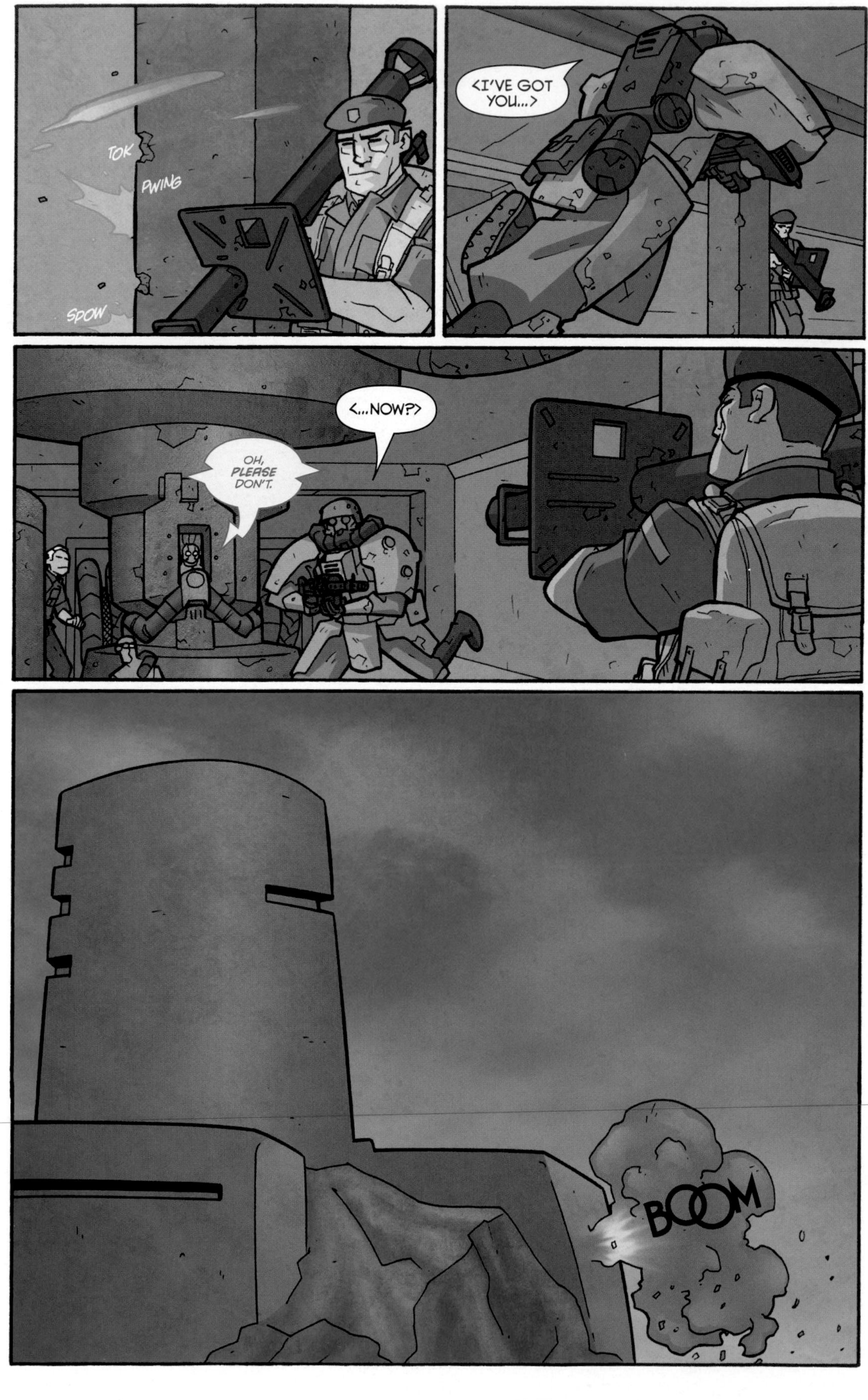
TOK
PWING
SPOW
<I'VE GOT YOU...>
<...NOW?>
OH, PLEASE DON'T.
BOOM

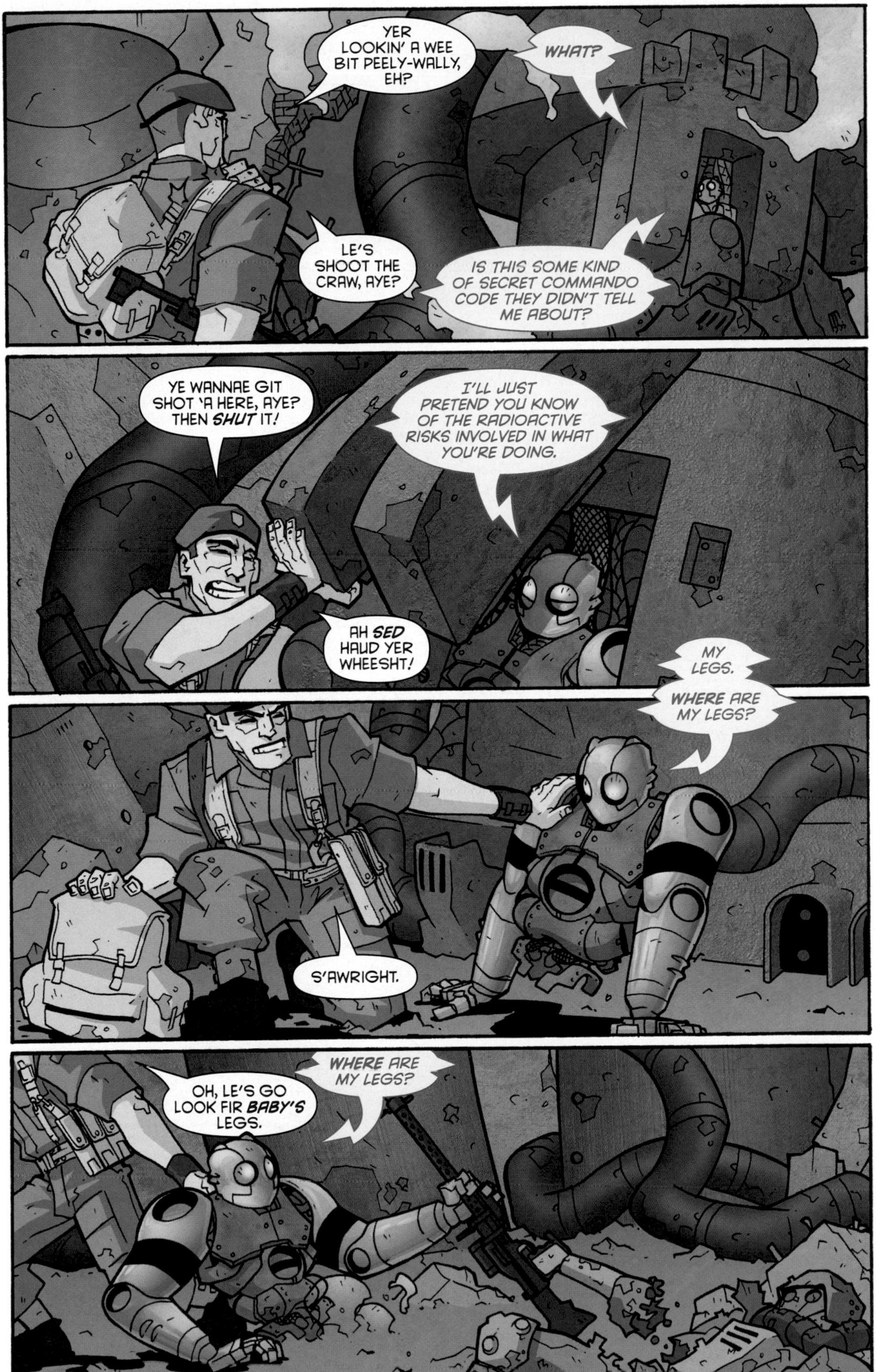
YER LOOKIN' A WEE BIT PEELY-WALLY, EH?
WHAT?
LE'S SHOOT THE CRAW, AYE?
IS THIS SOME KIND OF SECRET COMMANDO CODE THEY DIDN'T TELL ME ABOUT?
YE WANNAE GIT SHOT 'A HERE, AYE? THEN SHUT IT!
I'LL JUST PRETEND YOU KNOW OF THE RADIOACTIVE RISKS INVOLVED IN WHAT YOU'RE DOING.
AH SED HAUD YER WHEESHT!
MY LEGS.
WHERE ARE MY LEGS?
S'AWRIGHT.
WHERE ARE MY LEGS?
OH, LE'S GO LOOK FIR BABY'S LEGS.

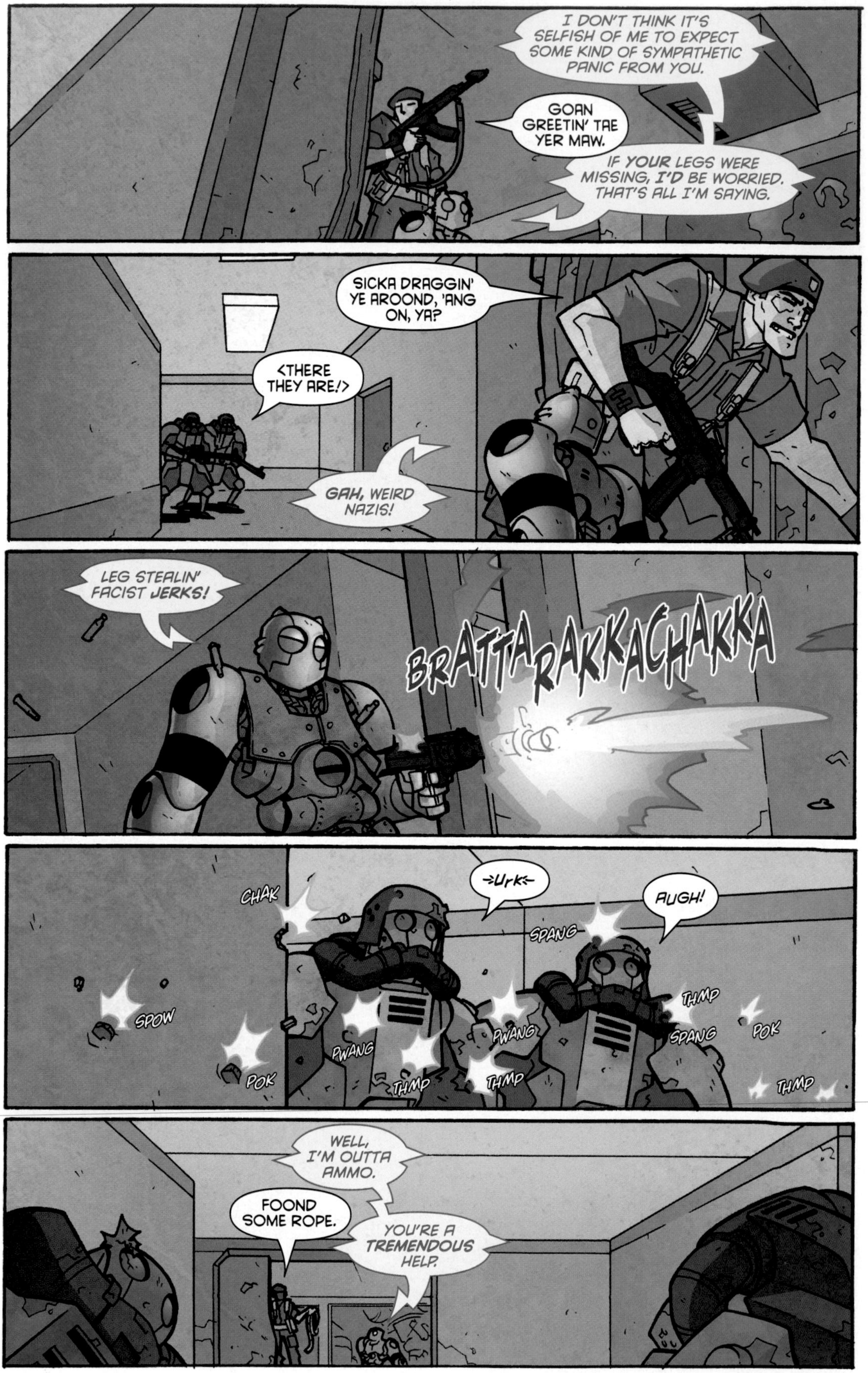
I DON'T THINK IT'S SELFISH OF ME TO EXPECT SOME KIND OF SYMPATHETIC PANIC FROM YOU.
GOAN GREETIN' TAE YER MAW.
IF YOUR LEGS WERE MISSING, I'D BE WORRIED. THAT'S ALL I'M SAYING.
SICKA DRAGGIN' YE AROOND, 'ANG ON, YA?
<THERE THEY ARE!>
GAH, WEIRD NAZIS!
LEG STEALIN' FACIST JERKS!
BRATTARAKKACHAKKA
CHAK
Urk
AUGH!
SPANG
SPOW
THMP
PWANG
PWANG
SPANG
POK
POK
THMP
THMP
THMP
WELL, I'M OUTTA AMMO.
FOOND SOME ROPE.
YOU'RE A TREMENDOUS HELP.

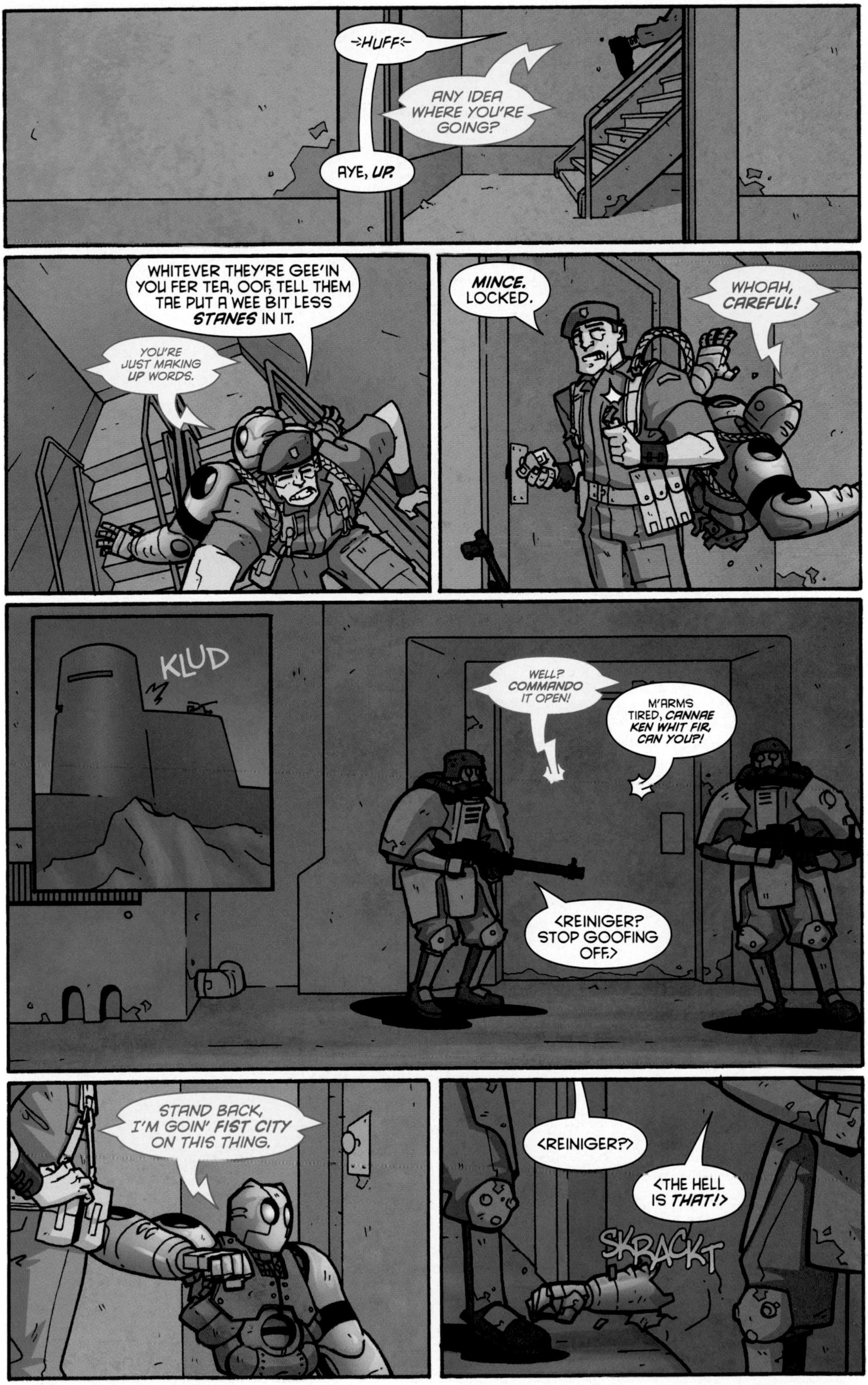

HUFF
ANY IDEA WHERE YOU'RE GOING?
AYE, UP.
WHITEVER THEY'RE GEE'IN YOU FER TEA, OOF, TELL THEM TAE PUT A WEE BIT LESS STANES IN IT.
YOU'RE JUST MAKING UP WORDS.
MINCE. LOCKED.
WHOAH, CAREFUL!
KLUD
WELL? COMMANDO IT OPEN!
M'ARMS TIRED, CANNAE KEN WHIT FIR, CAN YOU?!
<REINIGER? STOP GOOFING OFF.>
STAND BACK, I'M GOIN' FIST CITY ON THIS THING.
<REINIGER?>
<THE HELL IS THAT!>
SKRACKT

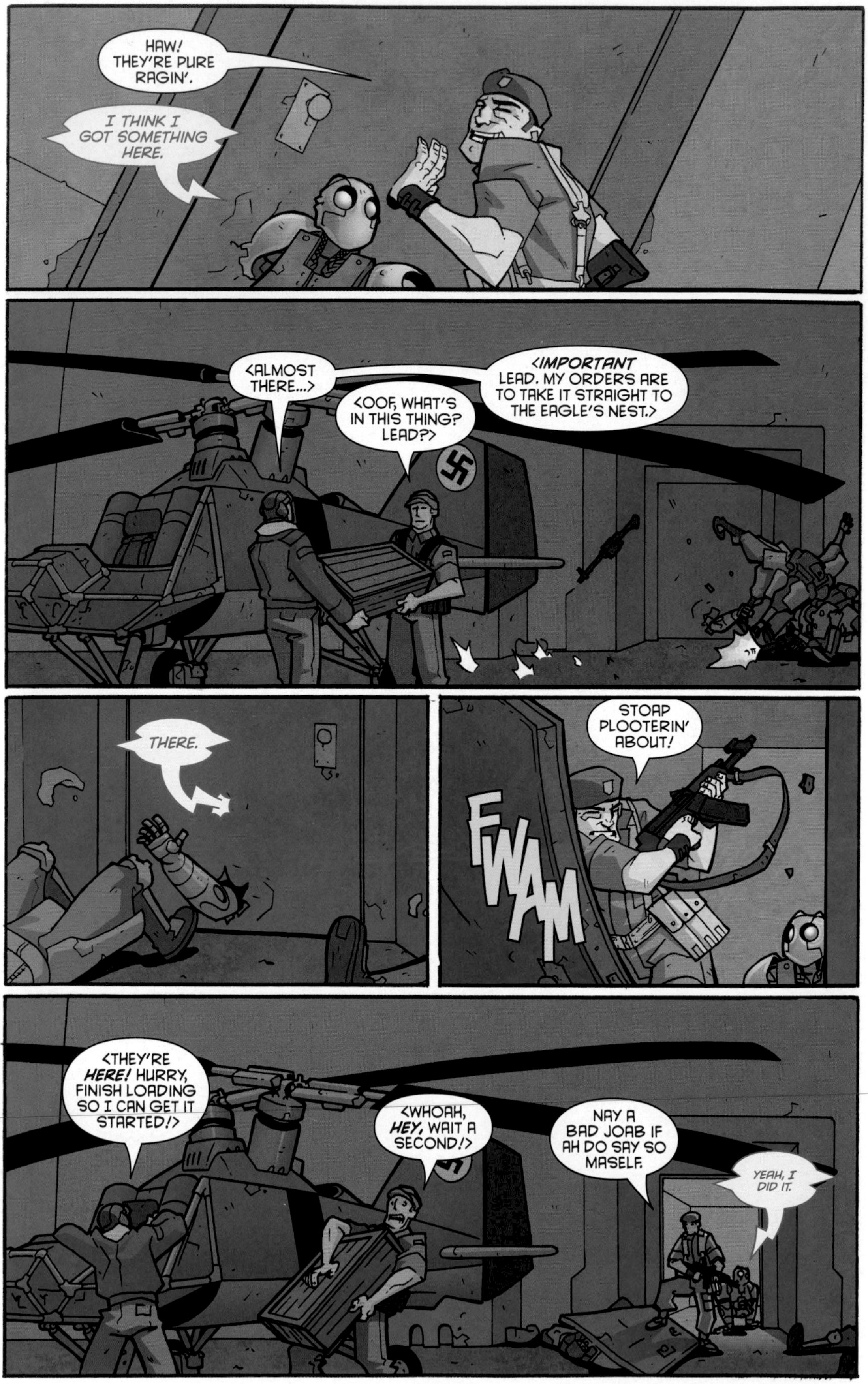

HAW! THEY'RE PURE RAGIN'.
I THINK I GOT SOMETHING HERE.
<ALMOST THERE...>
<OOF, WHAT'S IN THIS THING? LEAD?>
<IMPORTANT LEAD. MY ORDERS ARE TO TAKE IT STRAIGHT TO THE EAGLE'S NEST.>
THERE.
STOAP PLOOTERIN' ABOUT!
FWAM
<THEY'RE HERE! HURRY, FINISH LOADING SO I CAN GET IT STARTED!>
<WHOAH, HEY, WAIT A SECOND!>
NAY A BAD JOAB IF AH DO SAY SO MASELF.
YEAH, I DID IT.

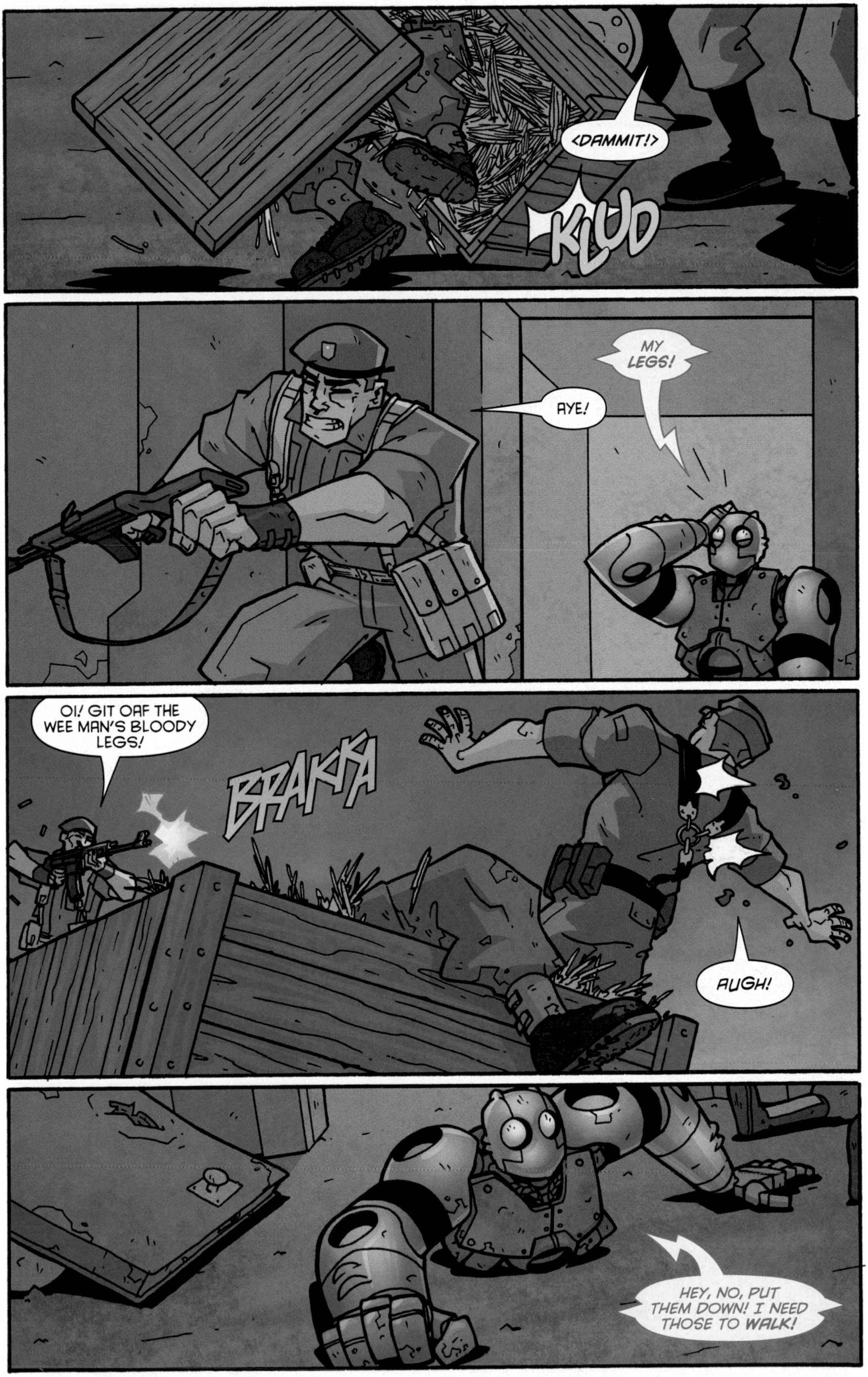
<DAMMIT!>
KLUD
AYE!
MY LEGS!
OI! GIT OAF THE WEE MAN'S BLOODY LEGS!
BRAKKA
AUGH!
HEY, NO, PUT THEM DOWN! I NEED THOSE TO WALK!

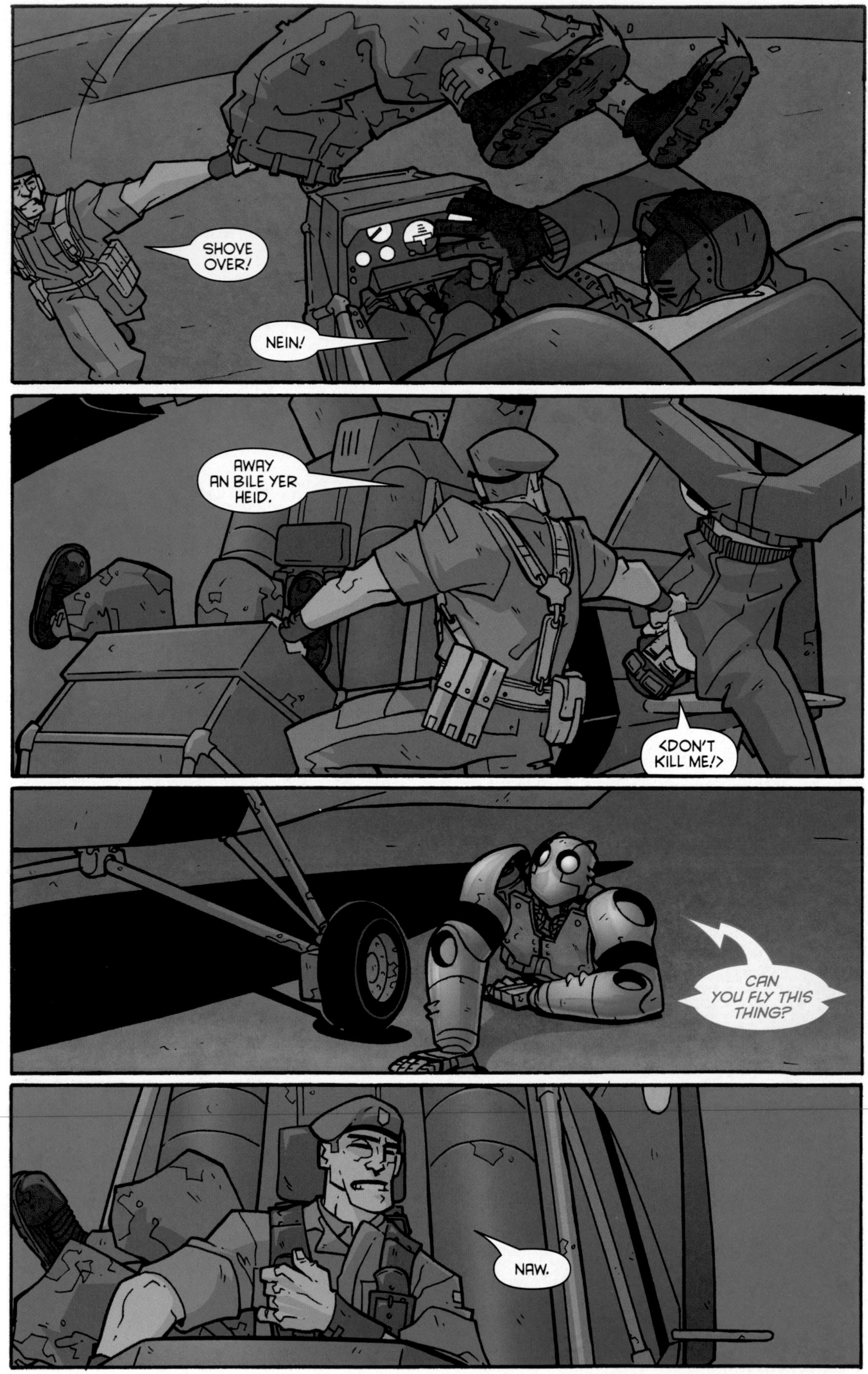
SHOVE OVER!
NEIN!
AWAY AN BILE YER HEID.
<DON'T KILL ME!>
CAN YOU FLY THIS THING?
NAW.

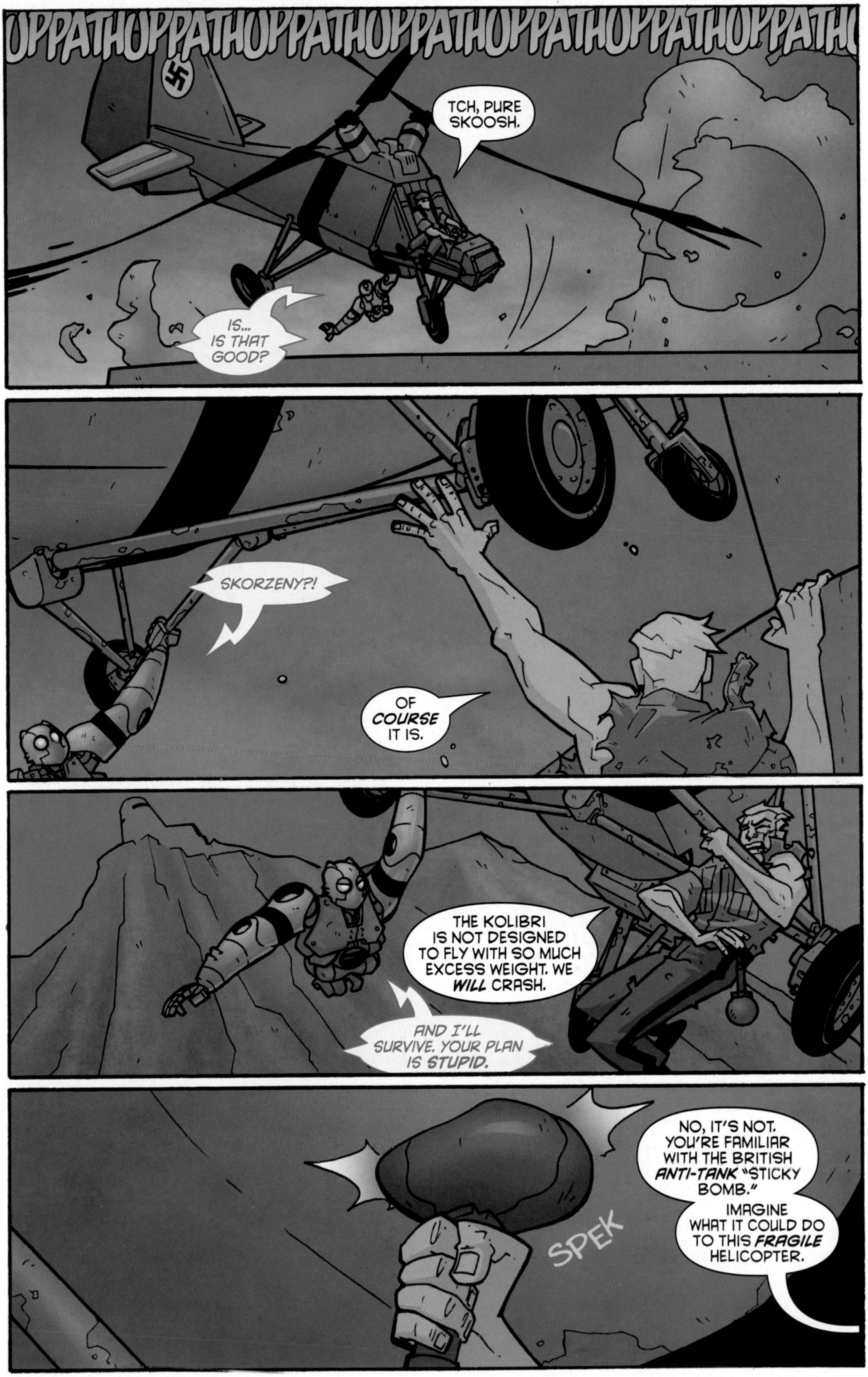
UPPATHUPPATHUPPATHUPPATHUPPATHUPPATHUPPATHUPPATH
TCH, PURE SKOOSH.
IS... IS THAT GOOD?
SKORZENY?!
OF COURSE IT IS.
THE KOLIBRI IS NOT DESIGNED TO FLY WITH SO MUCH EXCESS WEIGHT. WE WILL CRASH.
AND I'LL SURVIVE. YOUR PLAN IS STUPID.
SPEK
NO, IT'S NOT. YOU'RE FAMILIAR WITH THE BRITISH ANTI-TANK "STICKY BOMB."
IMAGINE WHAT IT COULD DO TO THIS FRAGILE HELICOPTER.

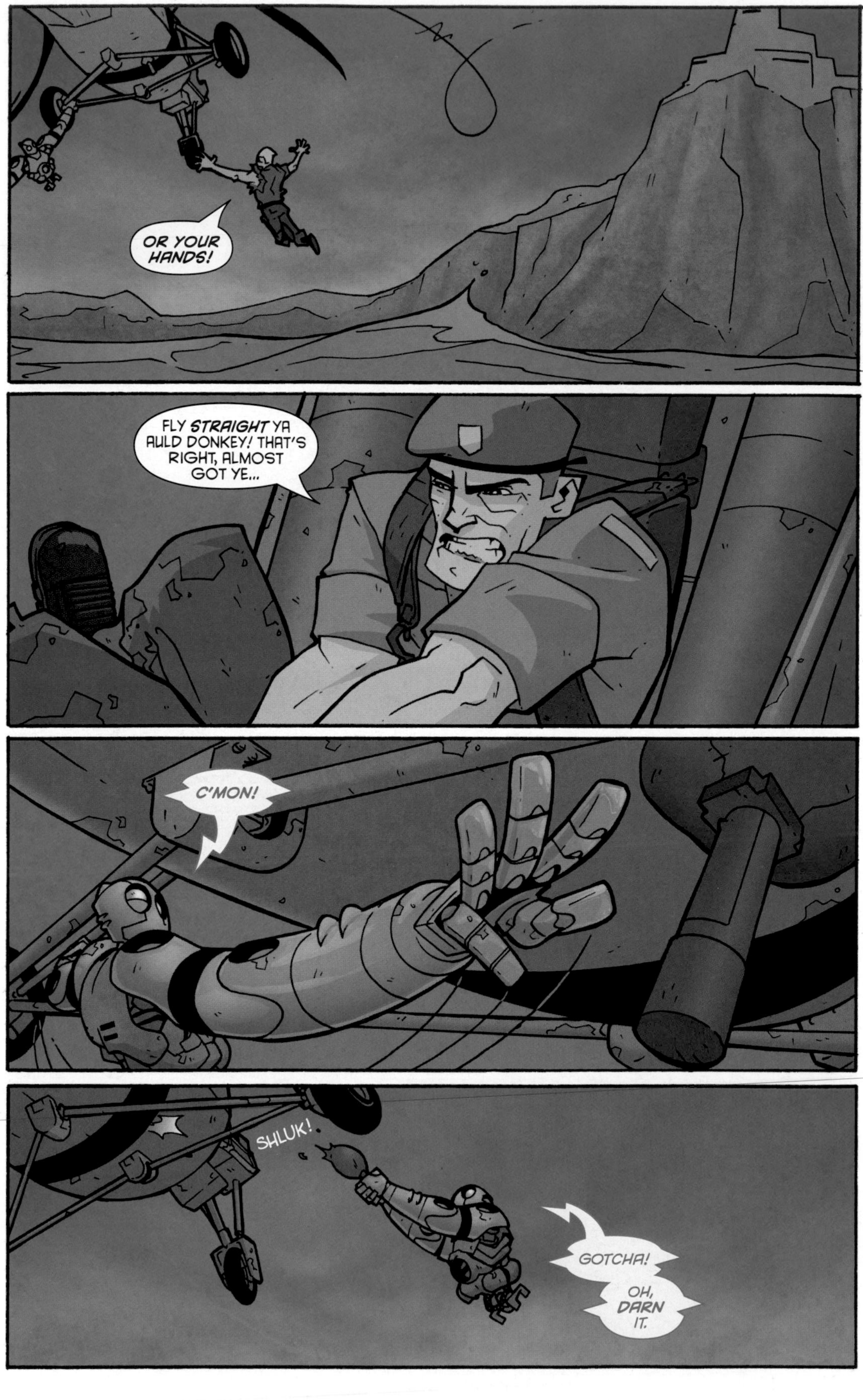
OR YOUR HANDS!
FLY STRAIGHT YA AULD DONKEY! THAT'S RIGHT, ALMOST GOT YE...
C'MON!
SHLUK!
GOTCHA!
OH, DARN IT.

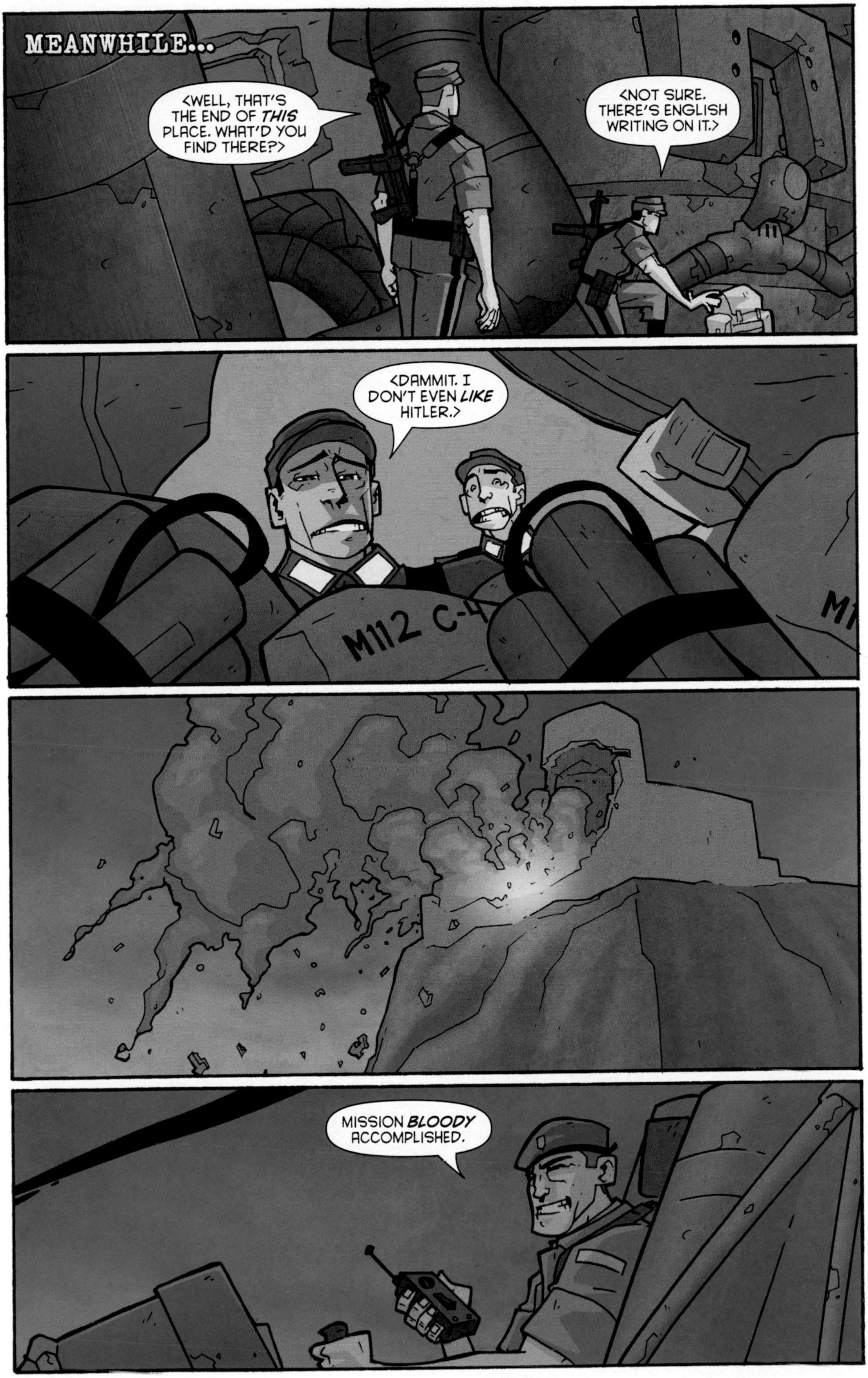
MEANWHILE...
<WELL, THAT'S THE END OF THIS PLACE. WHAT'D YOU FIND THERE?>
<NOT SURE. THERE'S ENGLISH WRITING ON IT.>
<DAMMIT. I DON'T EVEN LIKE HITLER.>
M112 C-4
MISSION BLOODY ACCOMPLISHED.

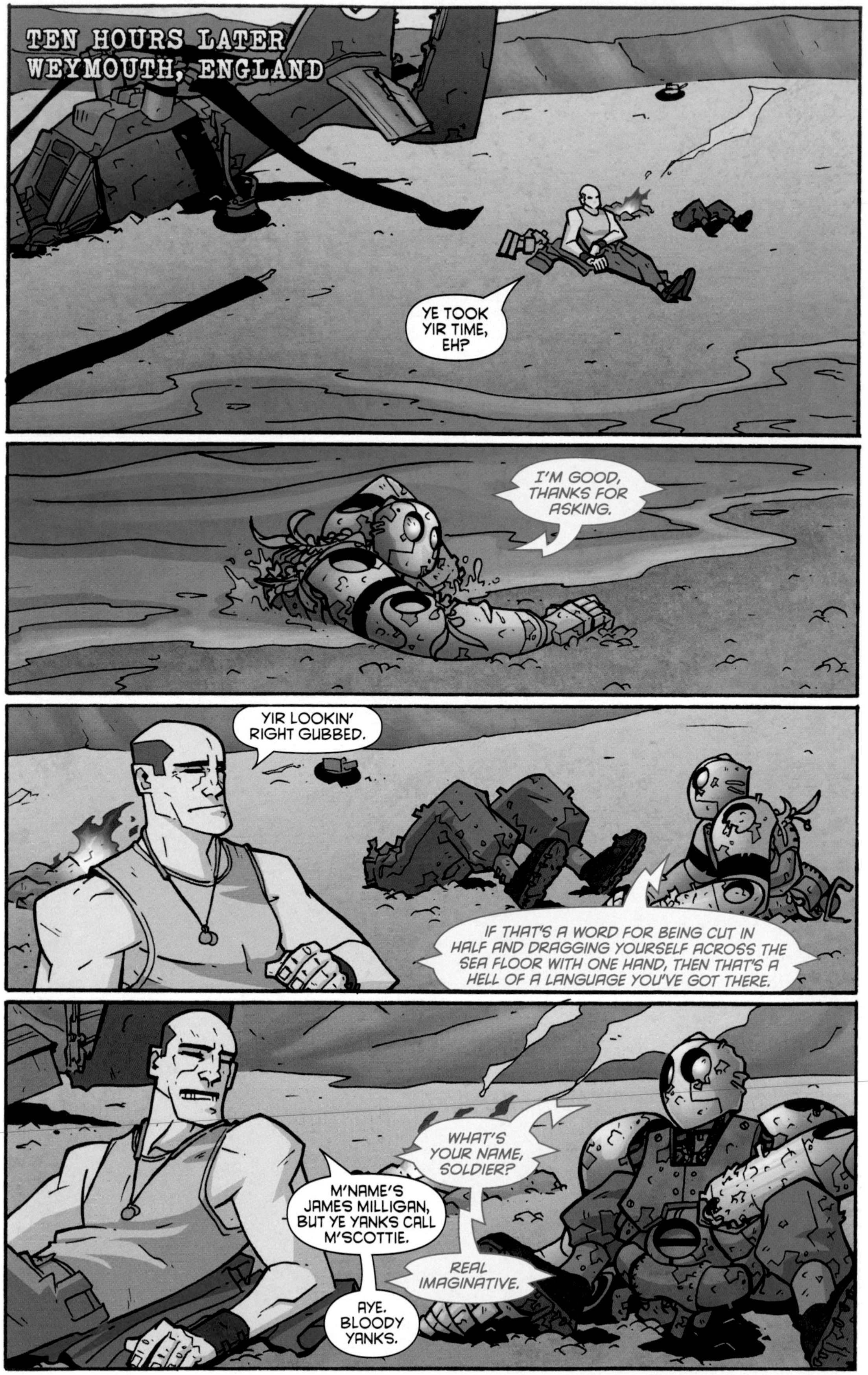
TEN HOURS LATER
WEYMOUTH, ENGLAND
YE TOOK YIR TIME, EH?
I'M GOOD, THANKS FOR ASKING.
YIR LOOKIN' RIGHT GUBBED.
IF THAT'S A WORD FOR BEING CUT IN HALF AND DRAGGING YOURSELF ACROSS THE SEA FLOOR WITH ONE HAND, THEN THAT'S A HELL OF A LANGUAGE YOU'VE GOT THERE.
WHAT'S YOUR NAME, SOLDIER?
M'NAME'S JAMES MILLIGAN, BUT YE YANKS CALL M'SCOTTIE.
REAL IMAGINATIVE.
AYE. BLOODY YANKS.

"B" STORIES

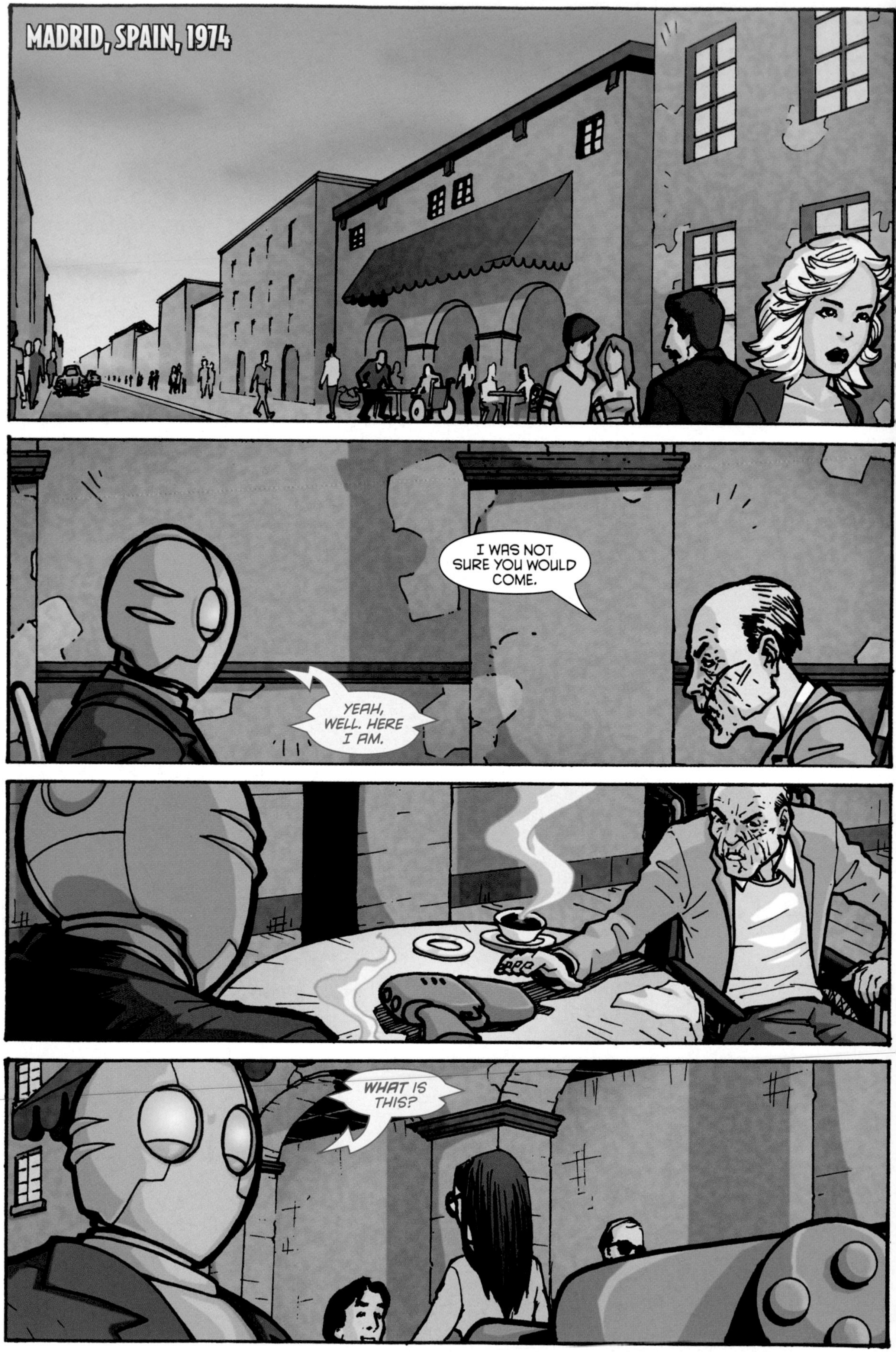
MADRID, SPAIN, 1974
I WAS NOT SURE YOU WOULD COME.
YEAH, WELL. HERE I AM.
WHAT IS THIS?

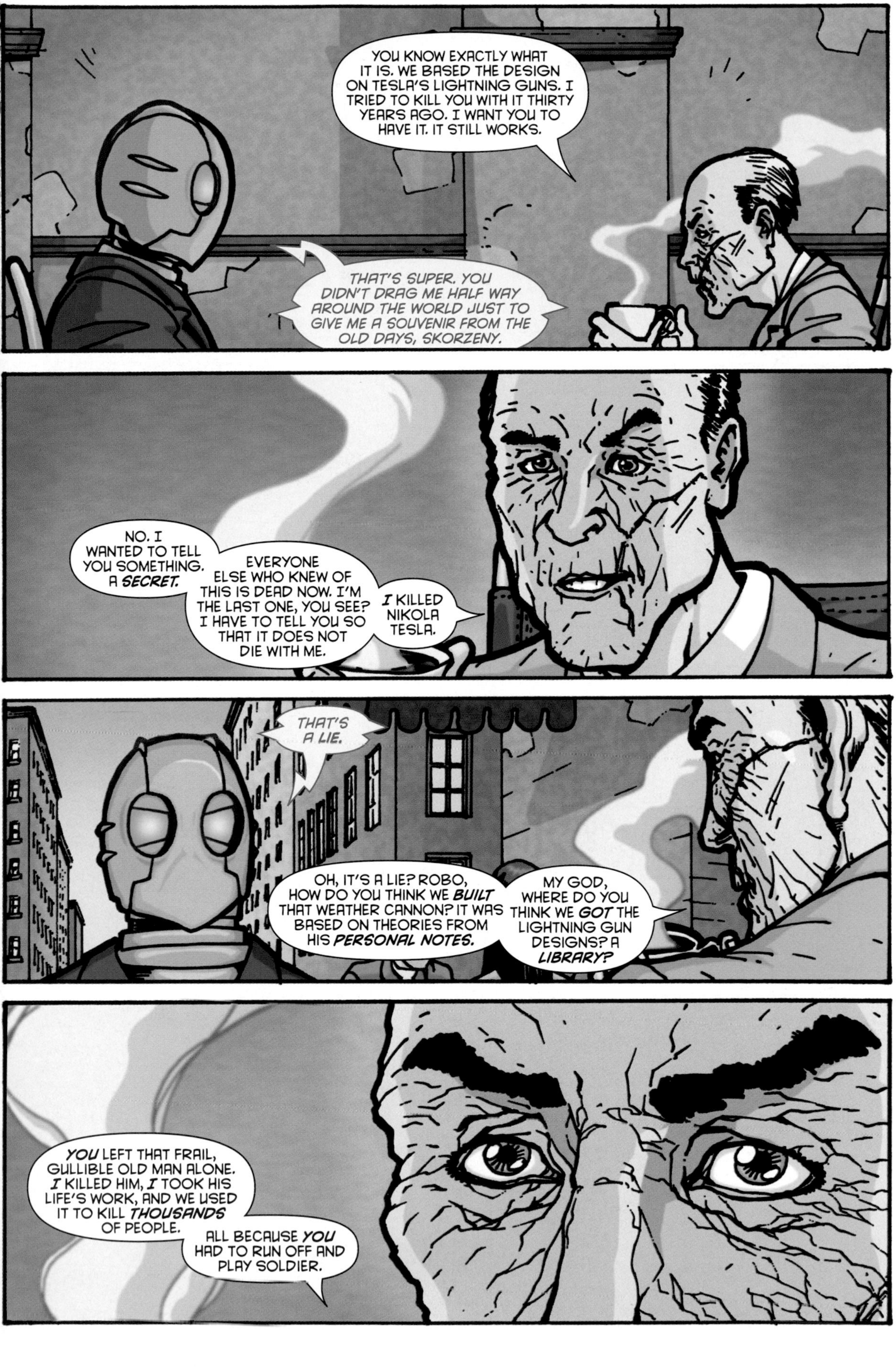
YOU KNOW EXACTLY WHAT IT IS. WE BASED THE DESIGN ON TESLA'S LIGHTNING GUNS. I TRIED TO KILL YOU WITH IT THIRTY YEARS AGO. I WANT YOU TO HAVE IT. IT STILL WORKS.
THAT'S SUPER. YOU DIDN'T DRAG ME HALF WAY AROUND THE WORLD JUST TO GIVE ME A SOUVENIR FROM THE OLD DAYS, SKORZENY.
NO. I WANTED TO TELL YOU SOMETHING. A SECRET.
EVERYONE ELSE WHO KNEW OF THIS IS DEAD NOW. I'M THE LAST ONE, YOU SEE? I HAVE TO TELL YOU SO THAT IT DOES NOT DIE WITH ME.
I KILLED NIKOLA TESLA.
THAT'S A LIE.
OH, IT'S A LIE? ROBO, HOW DO YOU THINK WE BUILT THAT WEATHER CANNON? IT WAS BASED ON THEORIES FROM HIS PERSONAL NOTES.
MY GOD, WHERE DO YOU THINK WE GOT THE LIGHTNING GUN DESIGNS? A LIBRARY?
YOU LEFT THAT FRAIL, GULLIBLE OLD MAN ALONE. I KILLED HIM, I TOOK HIS LIFE'S WORK, AND WE USED IT TO KILL THOUSANDS OF PEOPLE.
ALL BECAUSE YOU HAD TO RUN OFF AND PLAY SOLDIER.

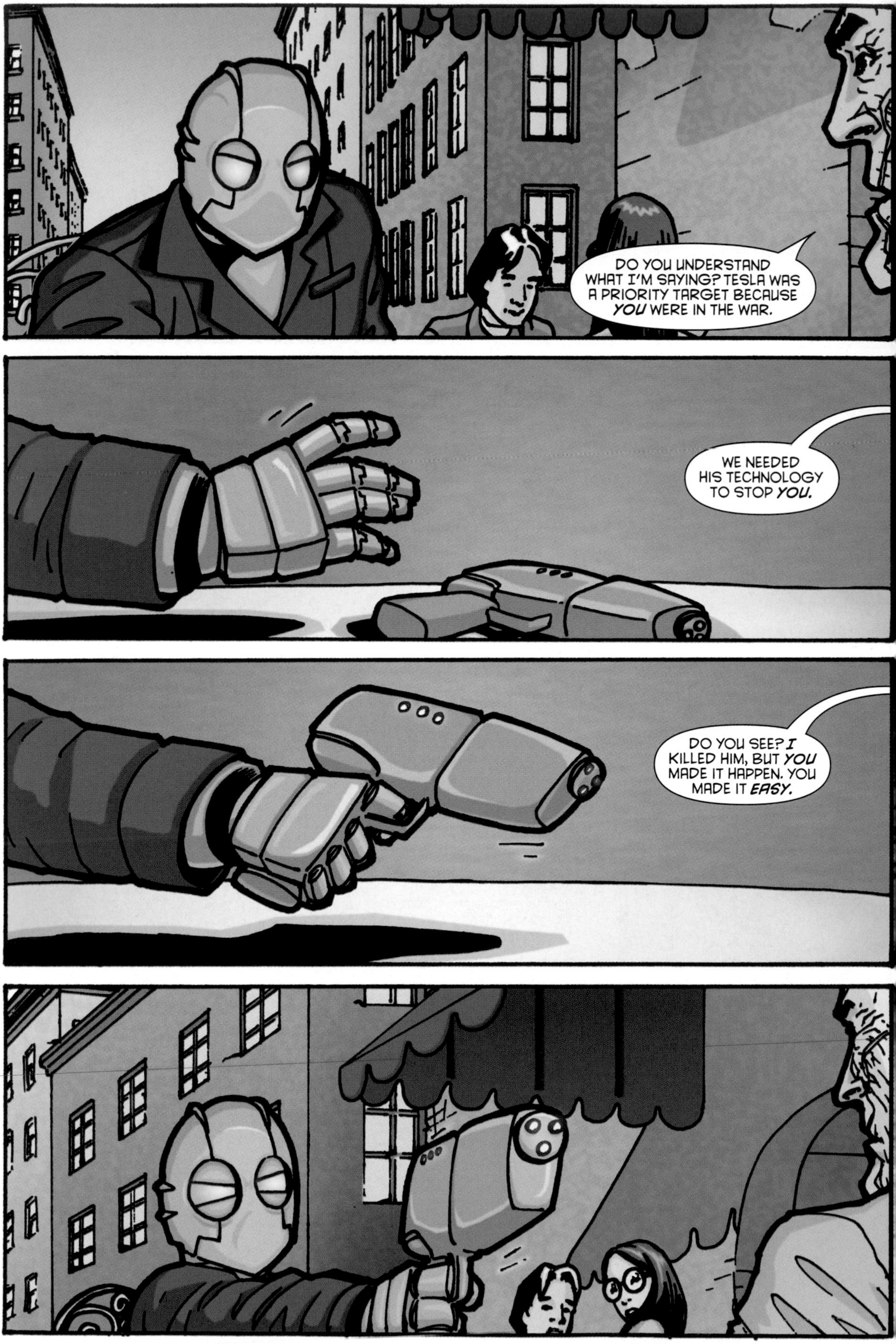
DO YOU UNDERSTAND WHAT I'M SAYING? TESLA WAS A PRIORITY TARGET BECAUSE *YOU* WERE IN THE WAR.
WE NEEDED HIS TECHNOLOGY TO STOP *YOU.*
DO YOU SEE? *I* KILLED HIM, BUT *YOU* MADE IT HAPPEN. YOU MADE IT *EASY.*

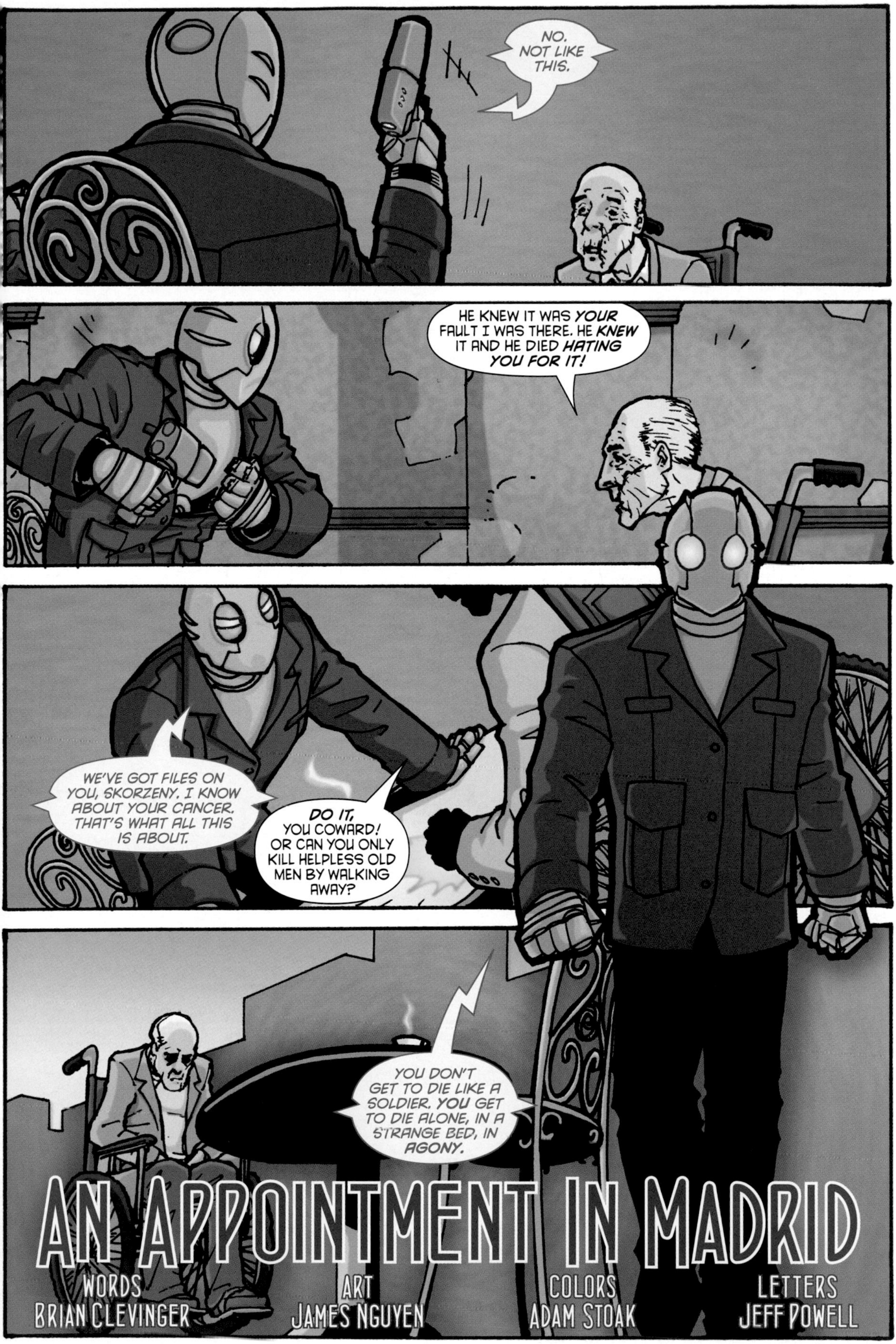
NO. NOT LIKE THIS.
HE KNEW IT WAS YOUR FAULT I WAS THERE. HE KNEW IT AND HE DIED HATING YOU FOR IT!
WE'VE GOT FILES ON YOU, SKORZENY. I KNOW ABOUT YOUR CANCER. THAT'S WHAT ALL THIS IS ABOUT.
DO IT, YOU COWARD! OR CAN YOU ONLY KILL HELPLESS OLD MEN BY WALKING AWAY?
YOU DON'T GET TO DIE LIKE A SOLDIER. YOU GET TO DIE ALONE, IN A STRANGE BED, IN AGONY.
AN APPOINTMENT IN MADRID
WORDS BRIAN CLEVINGER
ART JAMES NGUYEN
COLORS ADAM STOAK
LETTERS JEFF POWELL

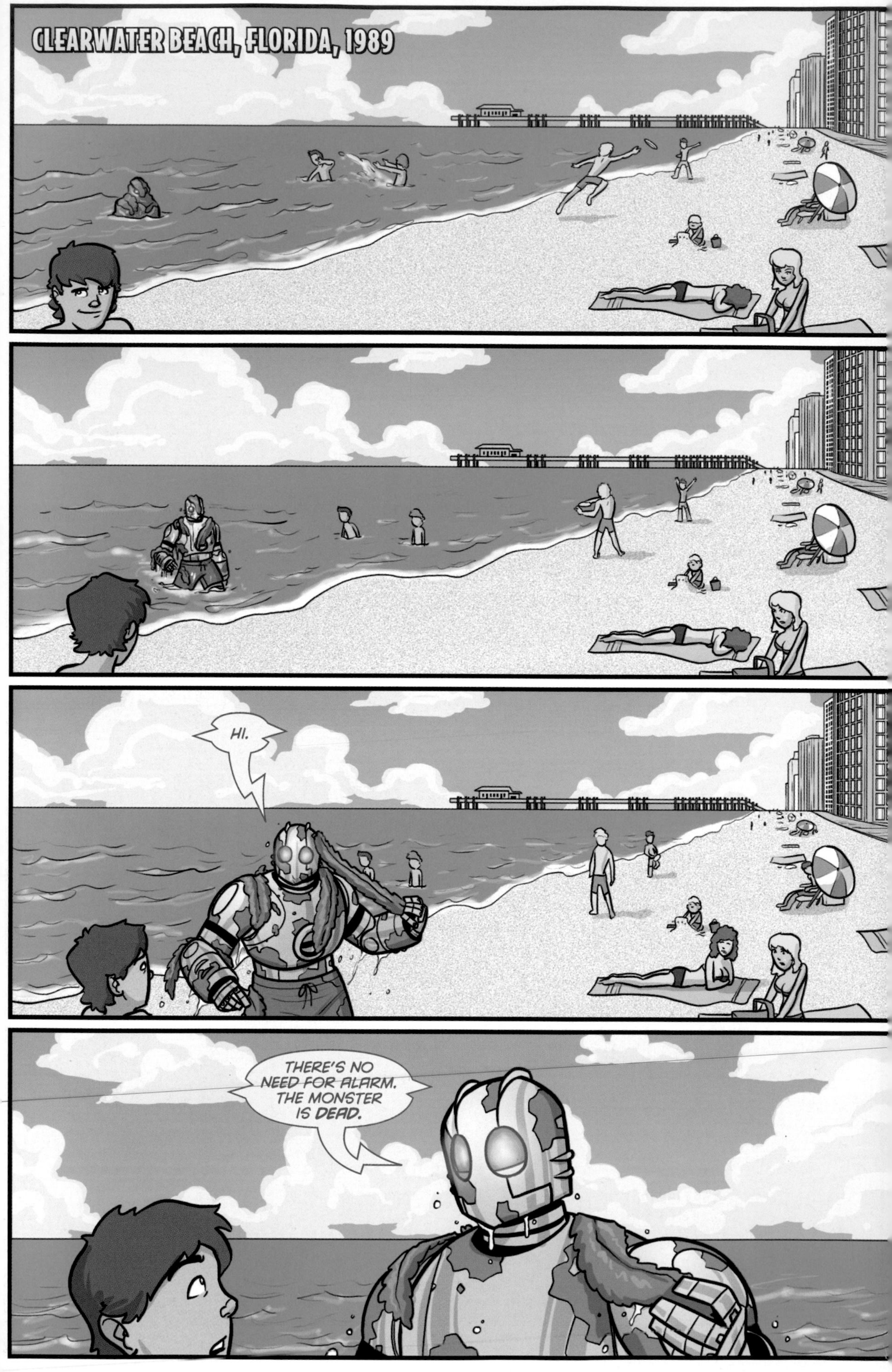
CLEARWATER BEACH, FLORIDA, 1989
HI.
THERE'S NO NEED FOR ALARM. THE MONSTER IS *DEAD.*

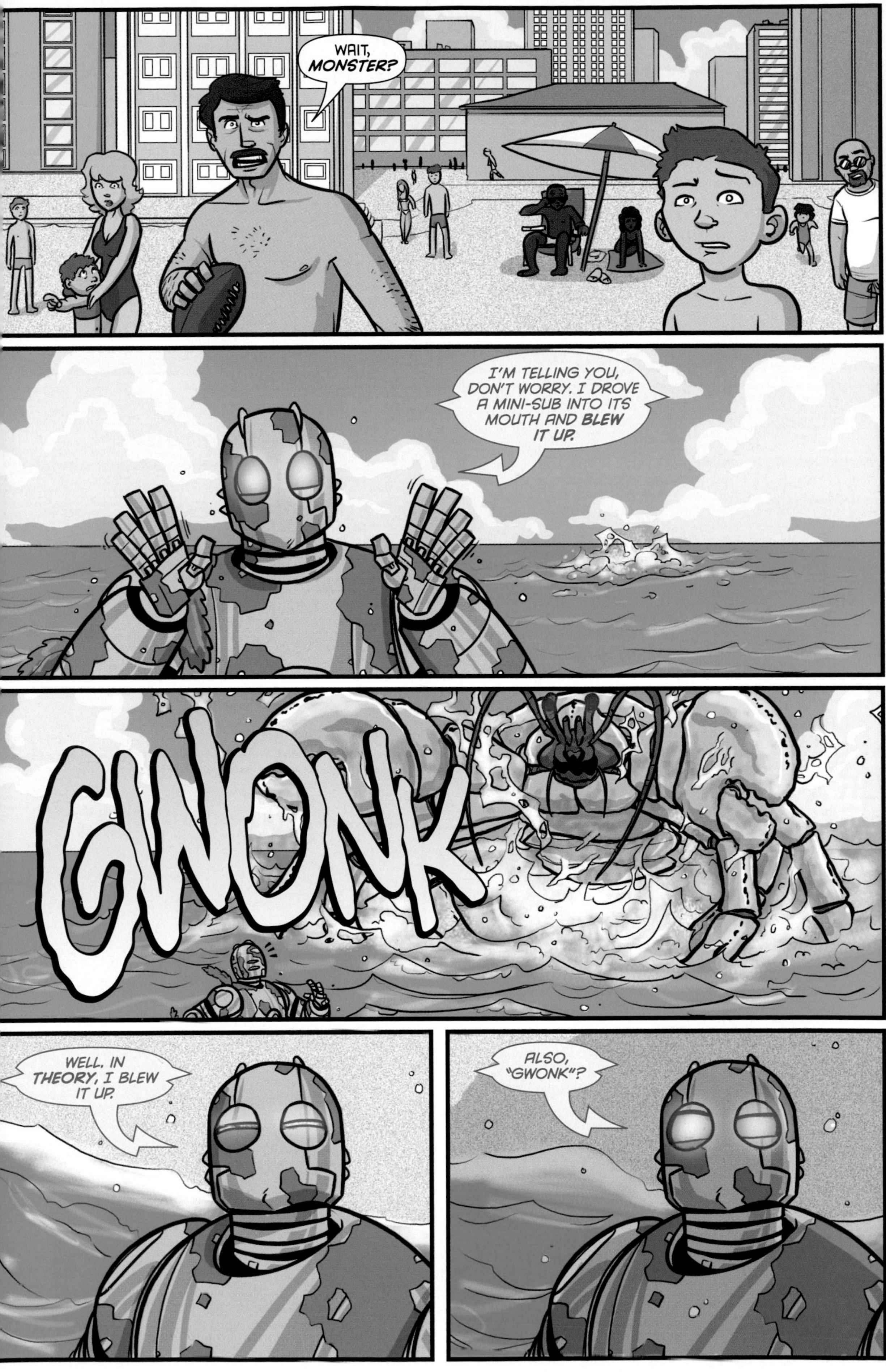
WAIT, MONSTER?
I'M TELLING YOU, DON'T WORRY. I DROVE A MINI-SUB INTO ITS MOUTH AND BLEW IT UP.
GWONK
WELL. IN THEORY, I BLEW IT UP.
ALSO, "GWONK"?

H'OKAY.
LET'S DO THIS
AGAIN.

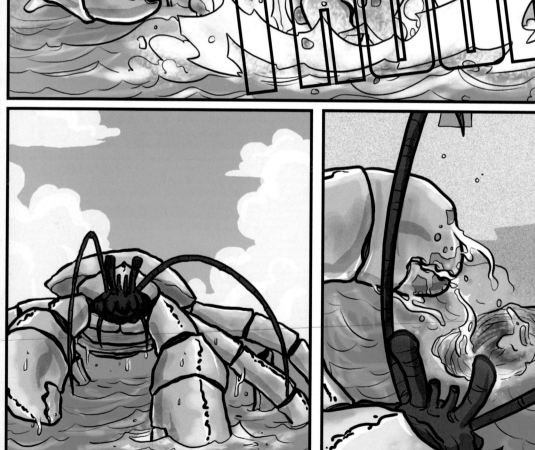

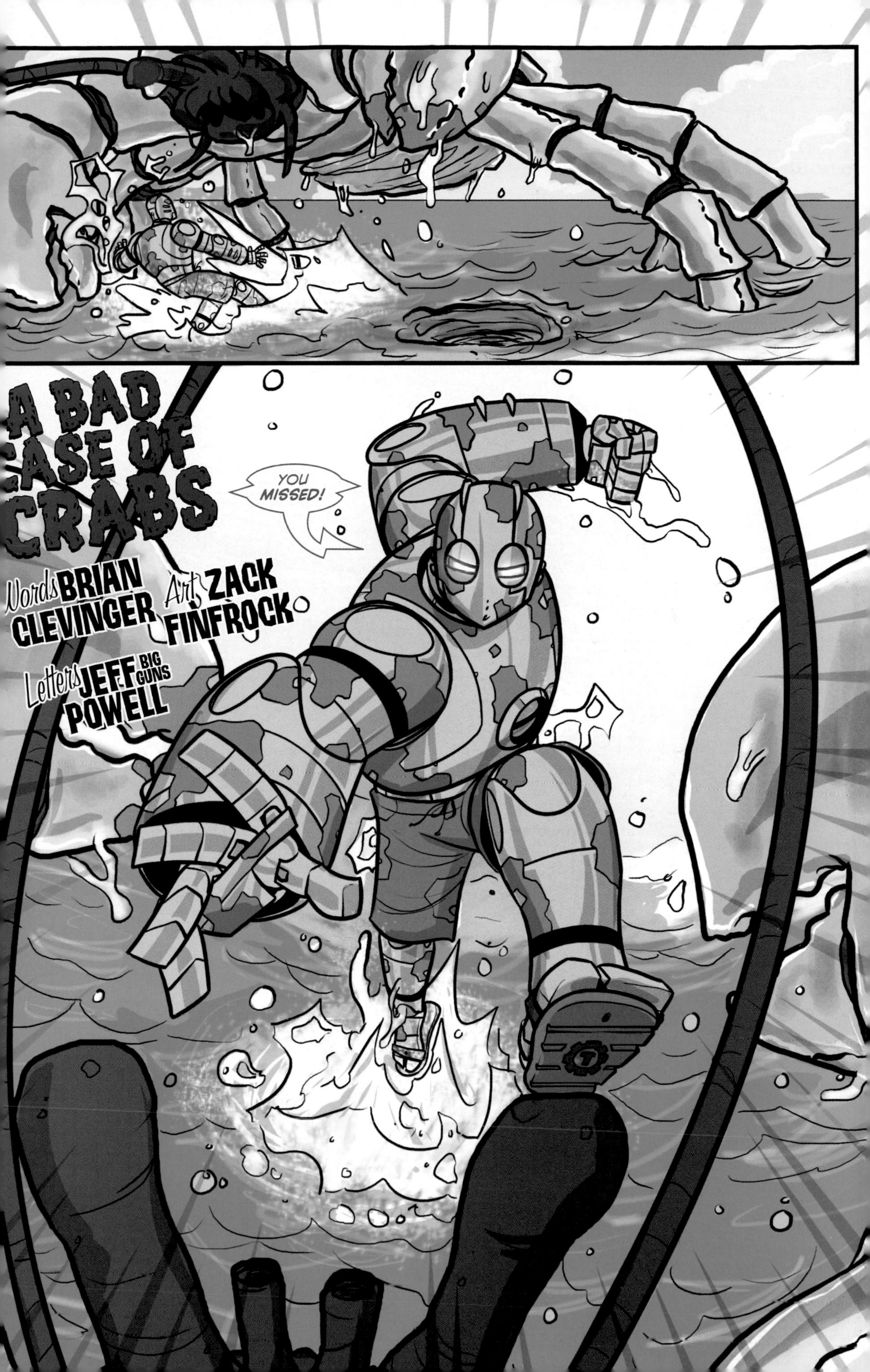
A BAD CASE OF CRABS
Words BRIAN CLEVINGER
Art ZACK FINFROCK
Letters JEFF BIG GUNS POWELL
YOU MISSED!

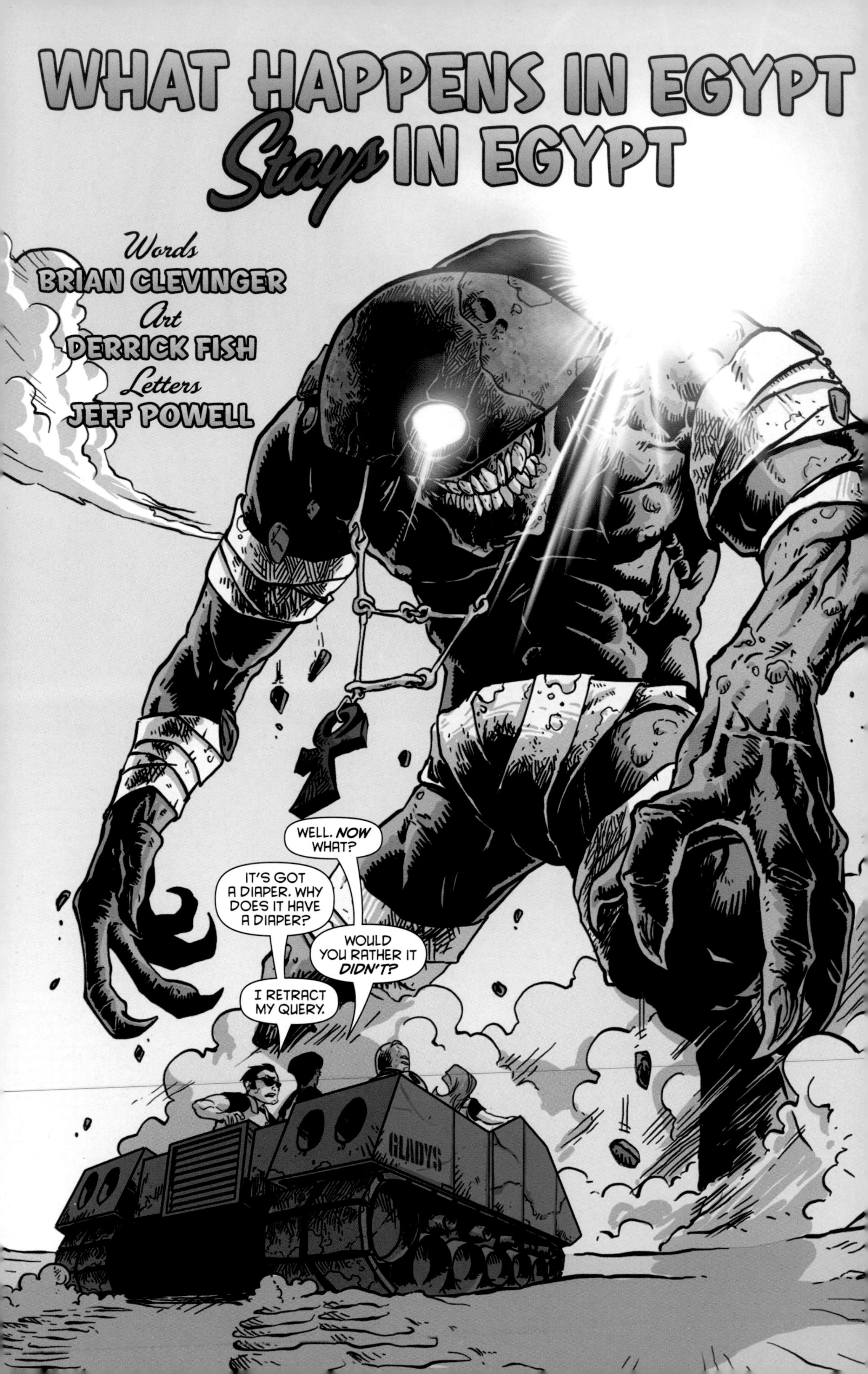
WHAT HAPPENS IN EGYPT Stays IN EGYPT
Words BRIAN CLEVINGER
Art DERRICK FISH
Letters JEFF POWELL
WELL. NOW WHAT?
IT'S GOT A DIAPER. WHY DOES IT HAVE A DIAPER?
WOULD YOU RATHER IT DIDN'T?
I RETRACT MY QUERY.
GLADYS

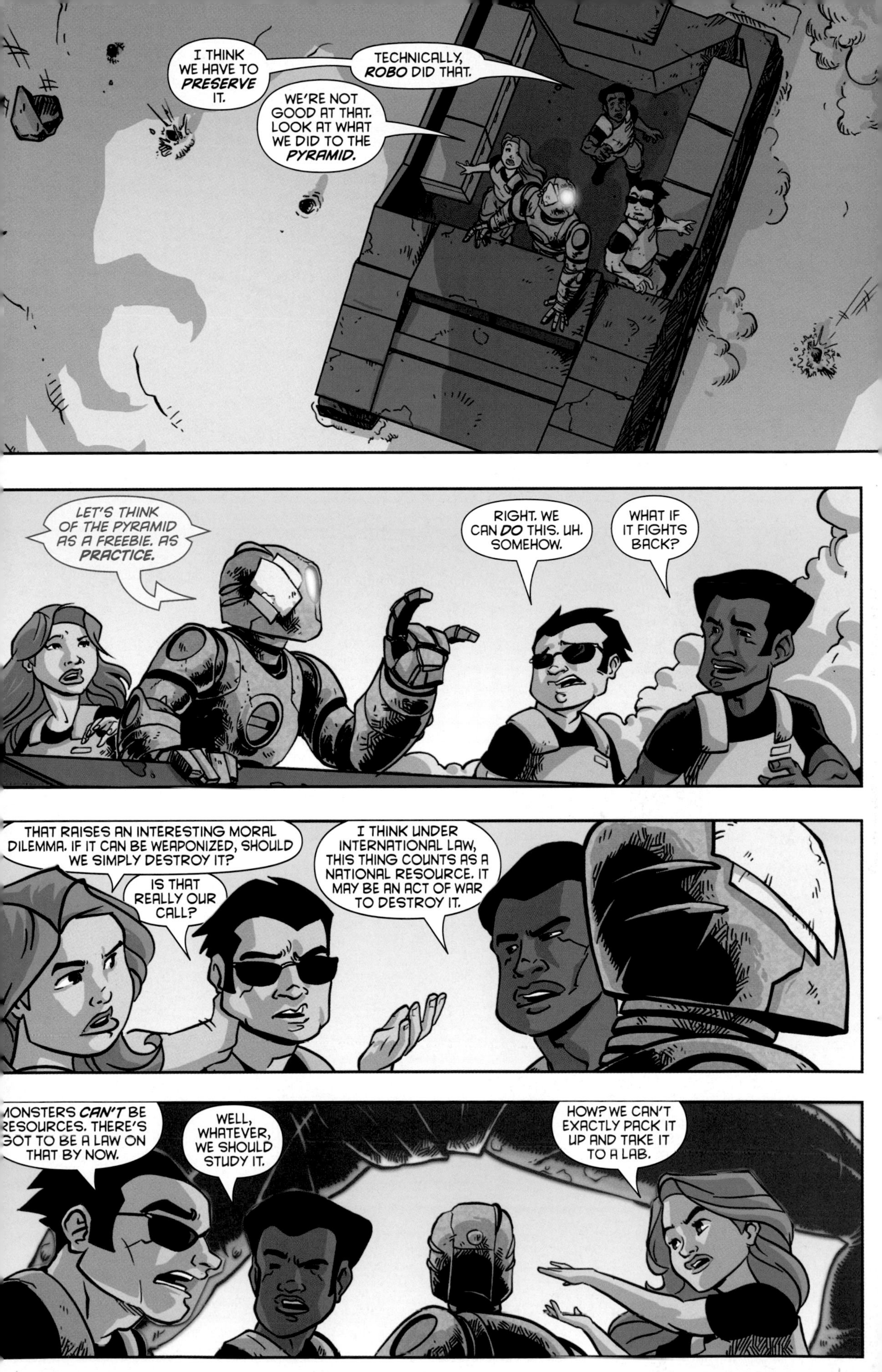
I THINK WE HAVE TO PRESERVE IT.
TECHNICALLY, ROBO DID THAT.
WE'RE NOT GOOD AT THAT. LOOK AT WHAT WE DID TO THE PYRAMID.
LET'S THINK OF THE PYRAMID AS A FREEBIE. AS PRACTICE.
RIGHT. WE CAN DO THIS. UH. SOMEHOW.
WHAT IF IT FIGHTS BACK?
THAT RAISES AN INTERESTING MORAL DILEMMA. IF IT CAN BE WEAPONIZED, SHOULD WE SIMPLY DESTROY IT?
IS THAT REALLY OUR CALL?
I THINK UNDER INTERNATIONAL LAW, THIS THING COUNTS AS A NATIONAL RESOURCE. IT MAY BE AN ACT OF WAR TO DESTROY IT.
MONSTERS CAN'T BE RESOURCES. THERE'S GOT TO BE A LAW ON THAT BY NOW.
WELL, WHATEVER, WE SHOULD STUDY IT.
HOW? WE CAN'T EXACTLY PACK IT UP AND TAKE IT TO A LAB.

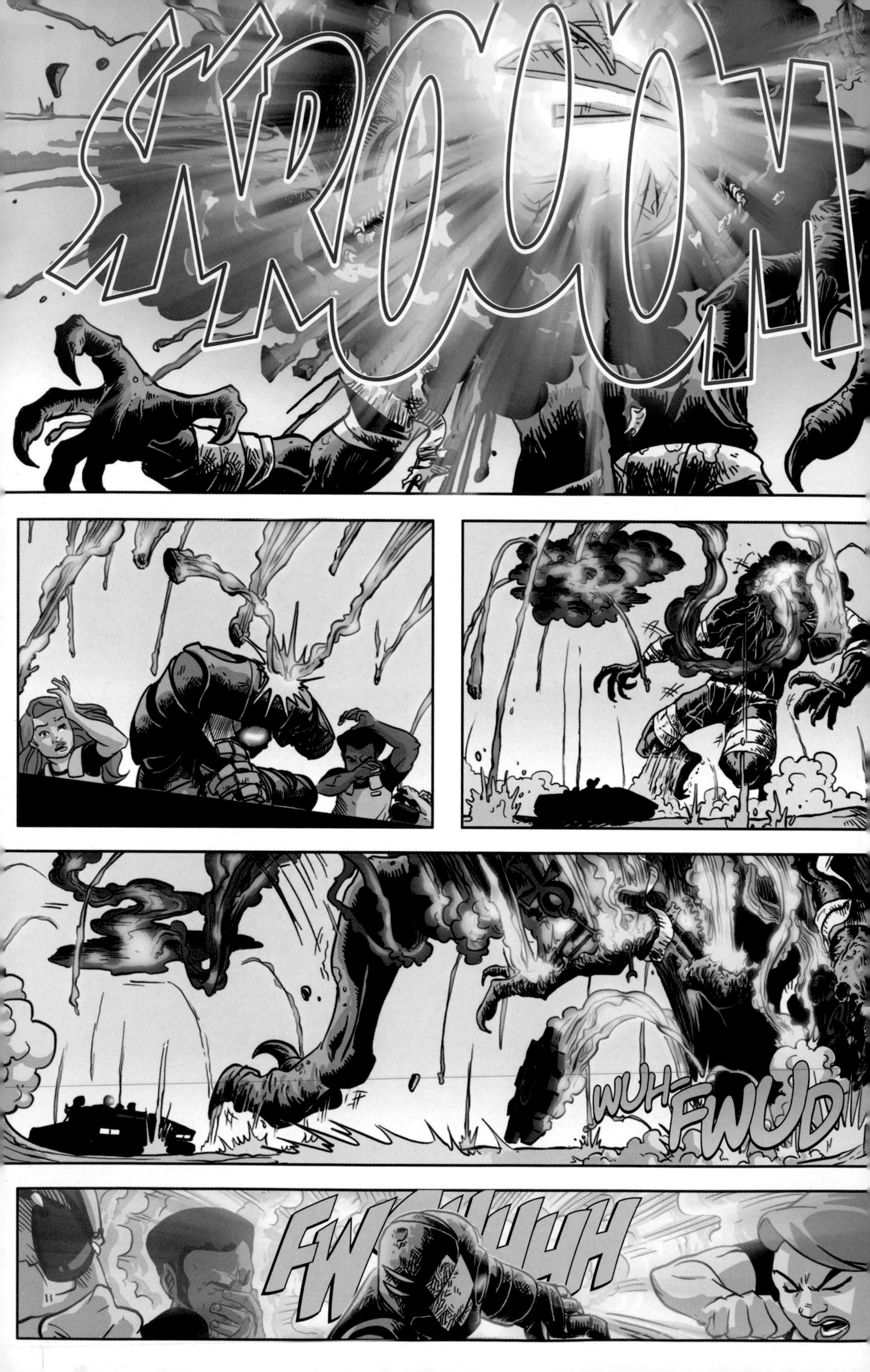
SKROOOM
WUH-FWUD

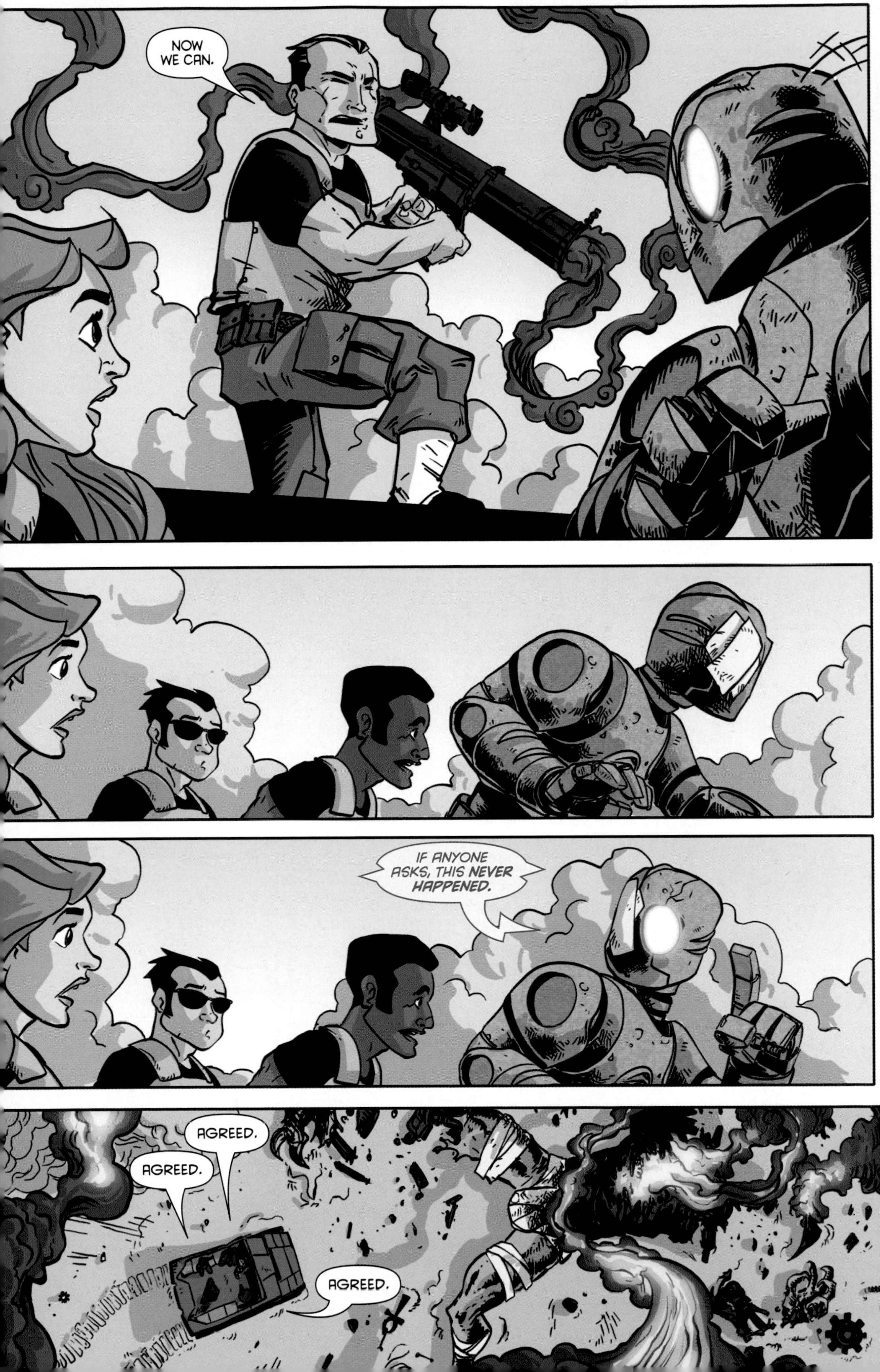
NOW WE CAN.
IF ANYONE ASKS, THIS **NEVER HAPPENED.**
AGREED.
AGREED.
AGREED.

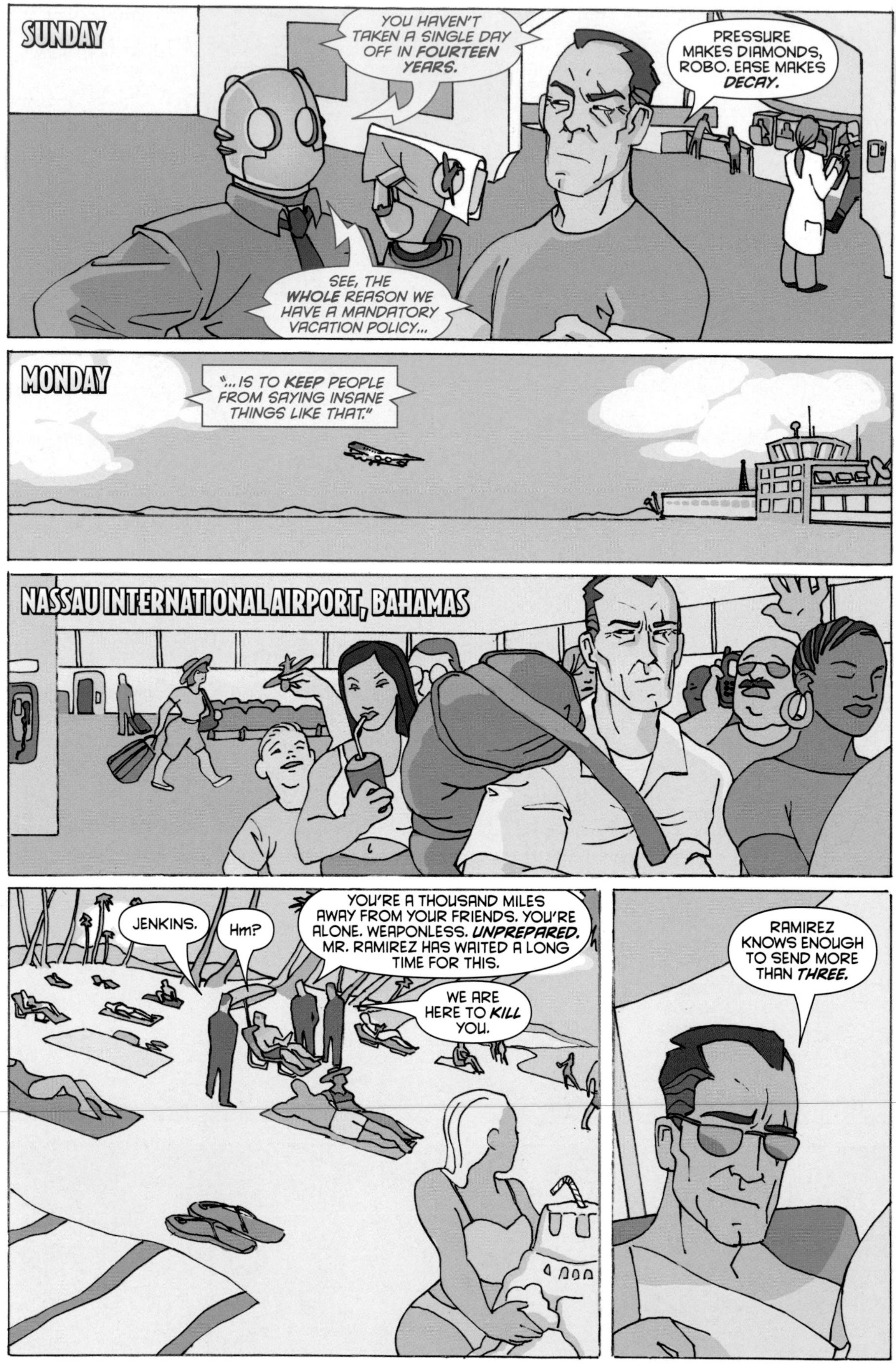
SUNDAY
YOU HAVEN'T TAKEN A SINGLE DAY OFF IN FOURTEEN YEARS.
PRESSURE MAKES DIAMONDS, ROBO. EASE MAKES DECAY.
SEE, THE WHOLE REASON WE HAVE A MANDATORY VACATION POLICY...
MONDAY
"...IS TO KEEP PEOPLE FROM SAYING INSANE THINGS LIKE THAT."
NASSAU INTERNATIONAL AIRPORT, BAHAMAS
JENKINS.
Hm?
YOU'RE A THOUSAND MILES AWAY FROM YOUR FRIENDS. YOU'RE ALONE. WEAPONLESS. UNPREPARED. MR. RAMIREZ HAS WAITED A LONG TIME FOR THIS.
WE ARE HERE TO KILL YOU.
RAMIREZ KNOWS ENOUGH TO SEND MORE THAN THREE.

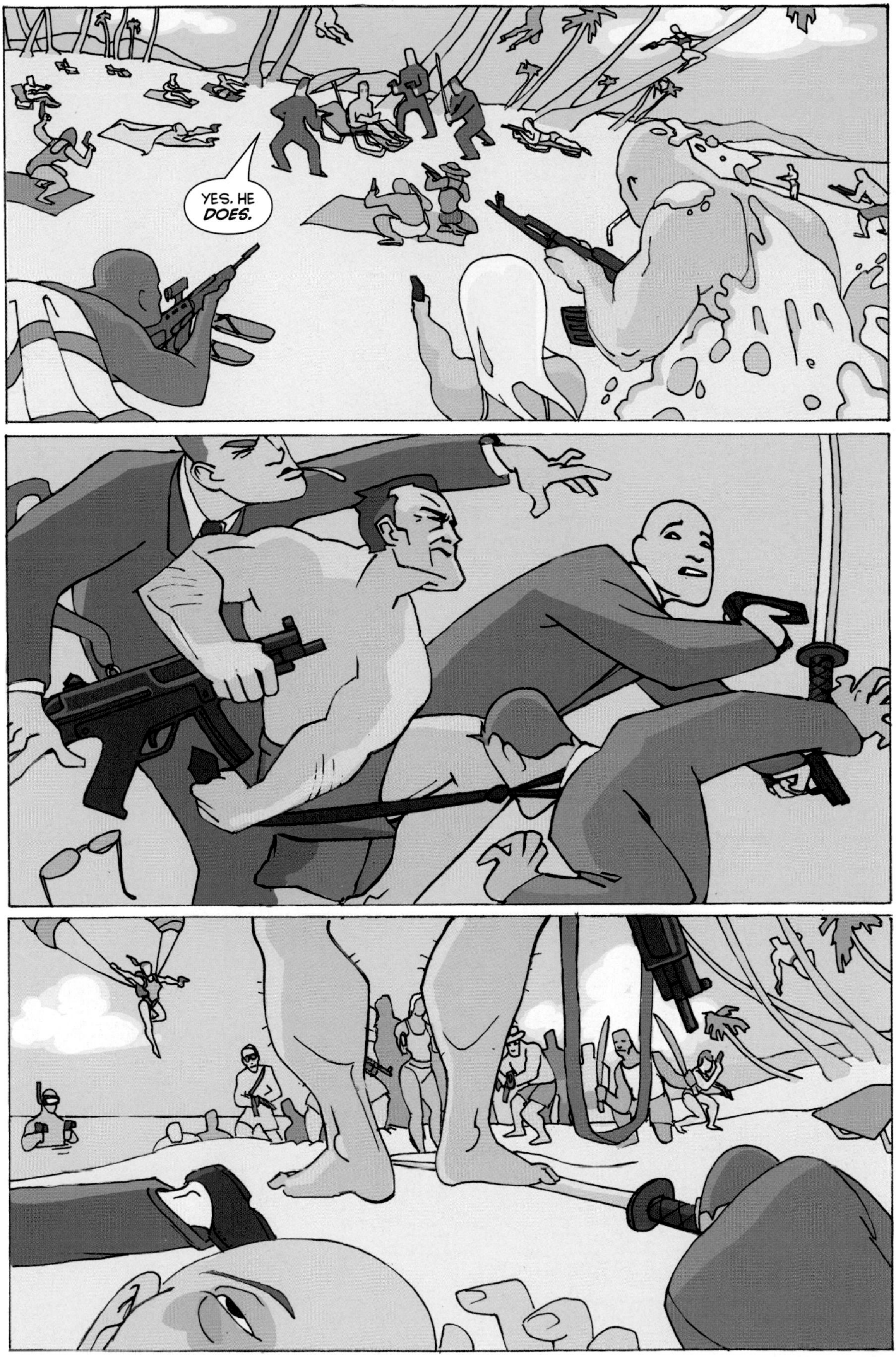
YES. HE DOES.

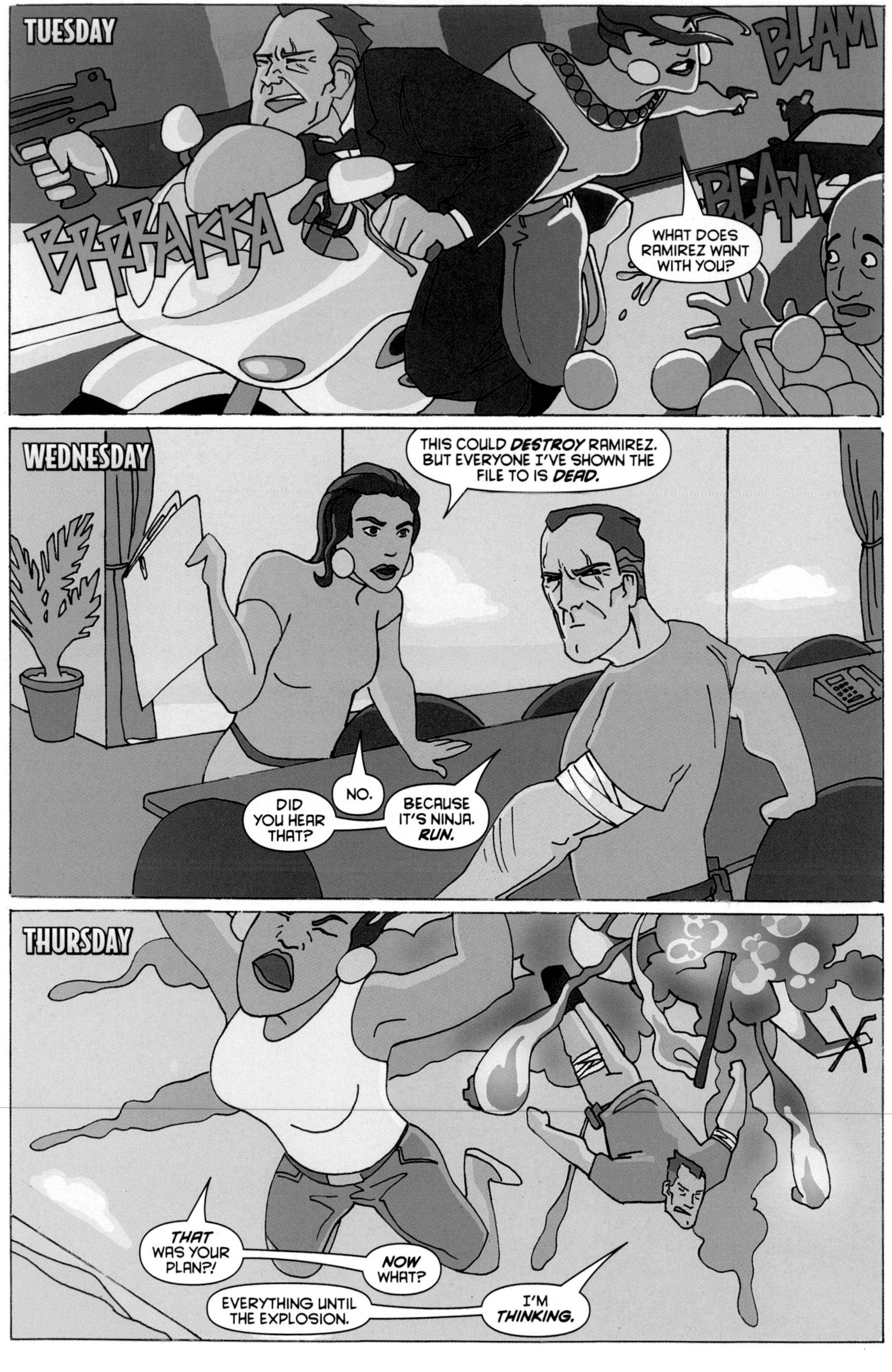
TUESDAY
BRRRAKKA
BLAM
BLAM
WHAT DOES RAMIREZ WANT WITH YOU?
WEDNESDAY
THIS COULD DESTROY RAMIREZ. BUT EVERYONE I'VE SHOWN THE FILE TO IS DEAD.
DID YOU HEAR THAT?
NO.
BECAUSE IT'S NINJA. RUN.
THURSDAY
THAT WAS YOUR PLAN?!
NOW WHAT?
EVERYTHING UNTIL THE EXPLOSION.
I'M THINKING.

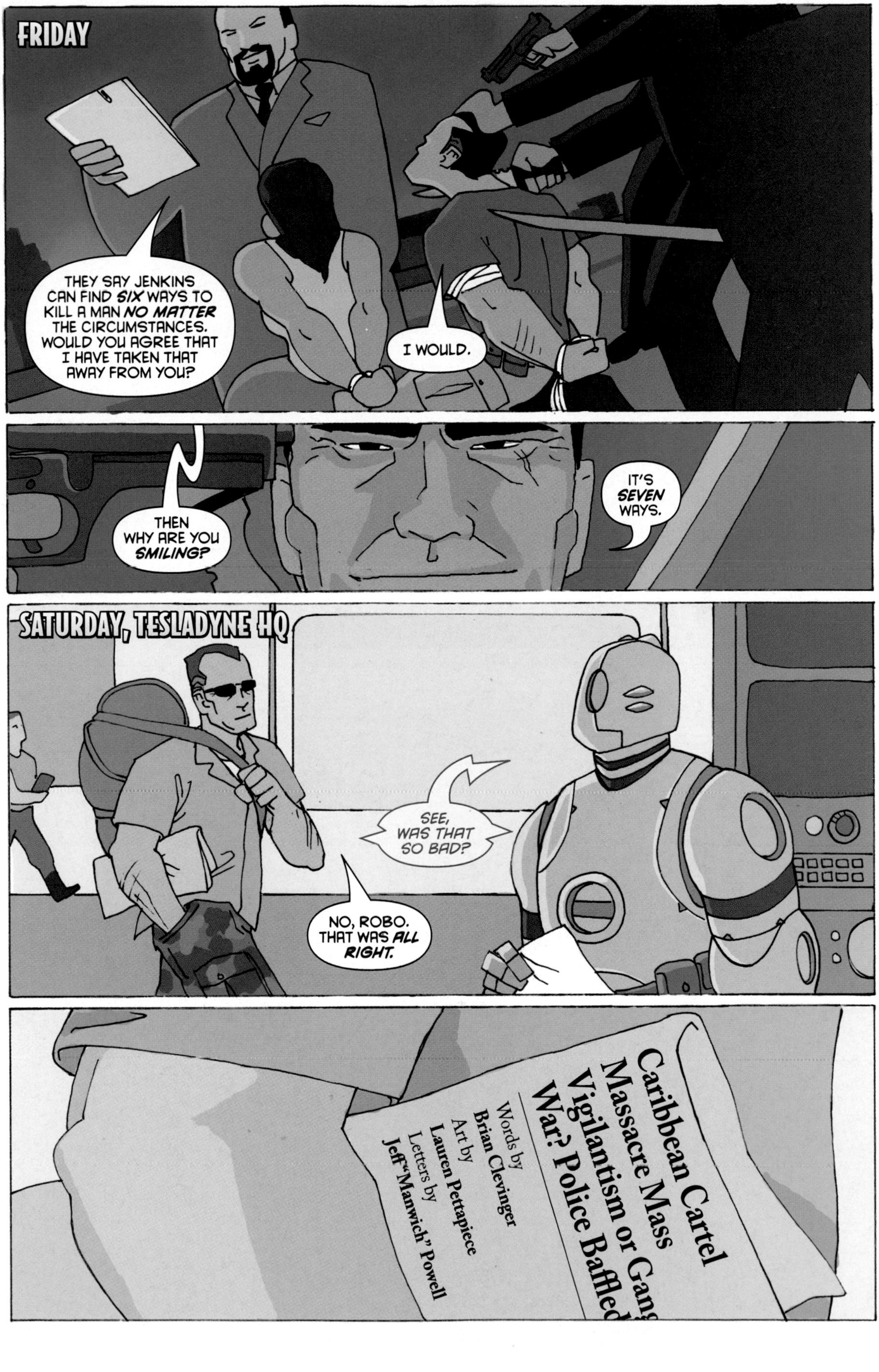
FRIDAY
THEY SAY JENKINS CAN FIND SIX WAYS TO KILL A MAN NO MATTER THE CIRCUMSTANCES. WOULD YOU AGREE THAT I HAVE TAKEN THAT AWAY FROM YOU?
I WOULD.
THEN WHY ARE YOU SMILING?
IT'S SEVEN WAYS.
SATURDAY, TESLADYNE HQ
SEE, WAS THAT SO BAD?
NO, ROBO. THAT WAS ALL RIGHT.
Caribbean Cartel Massacre Mass Vigilantism or Gang War? Police Baffled
Words by Brian Clevinger
Art by Lauren Pettapiece
Letters by Jeff "Manwich" Powell

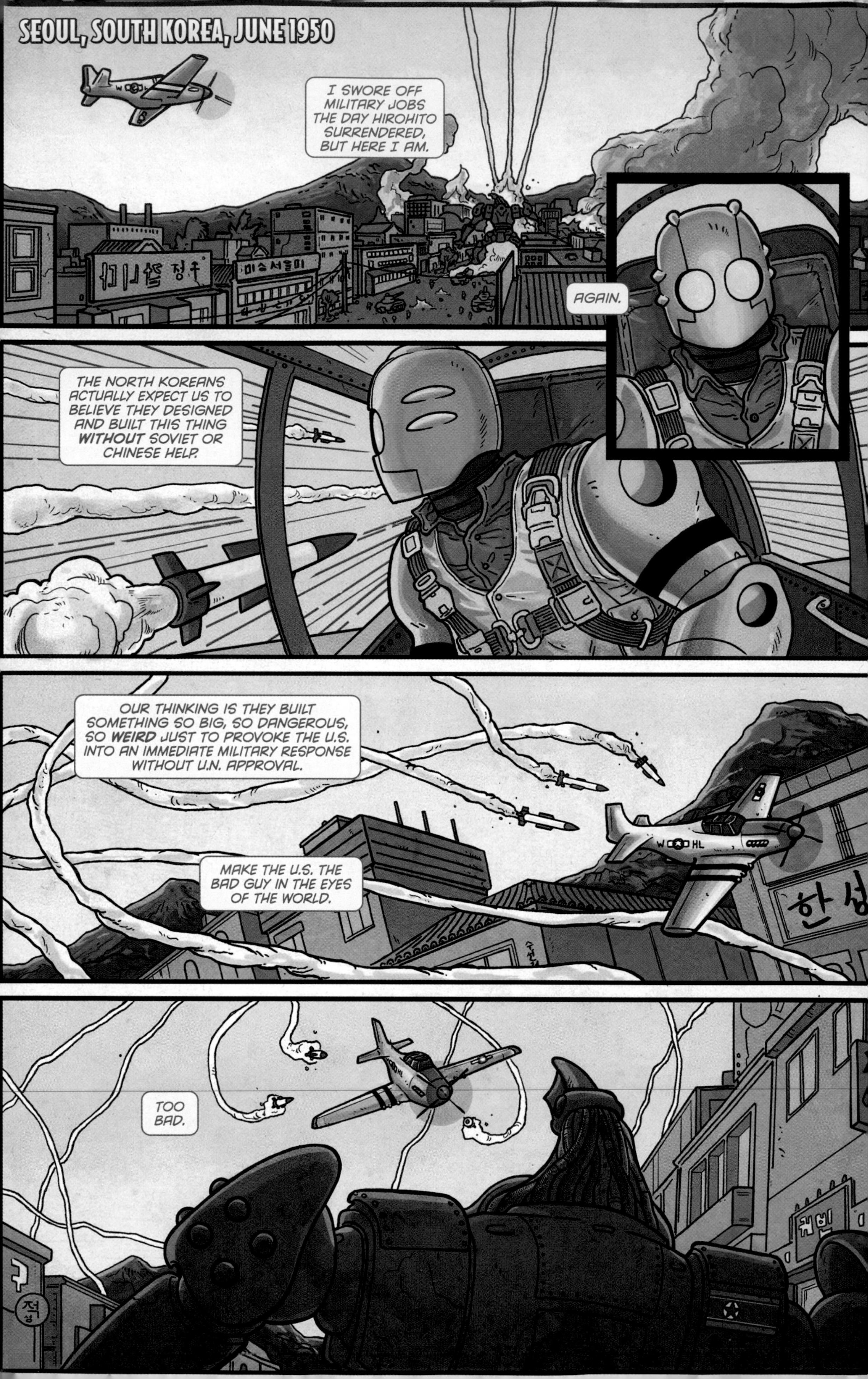
SEOUL, SOUTH KOREA, JUNE 1950
I SWORE OFF MILITARY JOBS THE DAY HIROHITO SURRENDERED, BUT HERE I AM.
AGAIN.
THE NORTH KOREANS ACTUALLY EXPECT US TO BELIEVE THEY DESIGNED AND BUILT THIS THING **WITHOUT** SOVIET OR CHINESE HELP.
OUR THINKING IS THEY BUILT SOMETHING SO BIG, SO DANGEROUS, SO **WEIRD** JUST TO PROVOKE THE U.S. INTO AN IMMEDIATE MILITARY RESPONSE WITHOUT U.N. APPROVAL.
MAKE THE U.S. THE BAD GUY IN THE EYES OF THE WORLD.
TOO BAD.

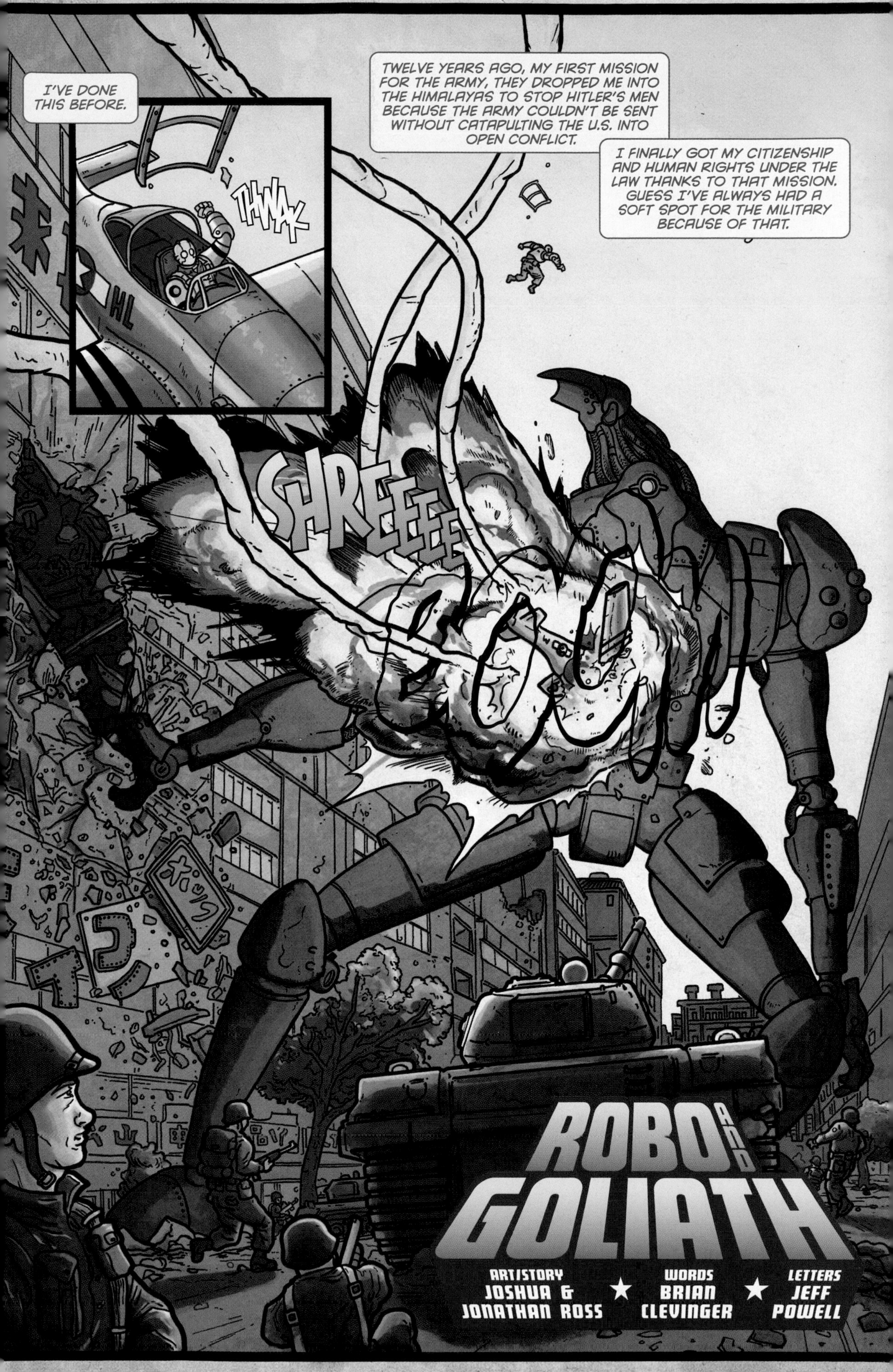
I'VE DONE THIS BEFORE.
THWAK
TWELVE YEARS AGO, MY FIRST MISSION FOR THE ARMY, THEY DROPPED ME INTO THE HIMALAYAS TO STOP HITLER'S MEN BECAUSE THE ARMY COULDN'T BE SENT WITHOUT CATAPULTING THE U.S. INTO OPEN CONFLICT.
I FINALLY GOT MY CITIZENSHIP AND HUMAN RIGHTS UNDER THE LAW THANKS TO THAT MISSION. GUESS I'VE ALWAYS HAD A SOFT SPOT FOR THE MILITARY BECAUSE OF THAT.
SHREEEEE
ROBO AND GOLIATH
ART/STORY JOSHUA & JONATHAN ROSS
WORDS BRIAN CLEVINGER
LETTERS JEFF POWELL

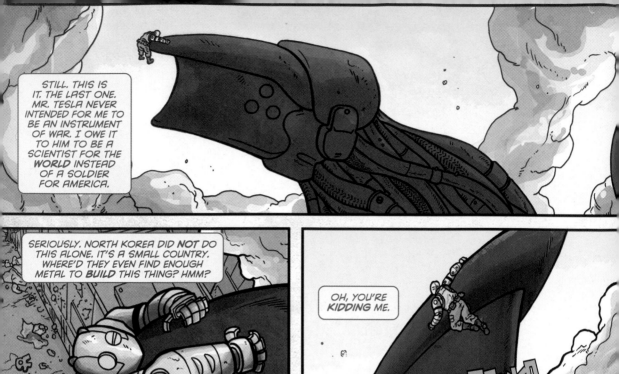

STILL. THIS IS IT. THE LAST ONE. MR. TESLA NEVER INTENDED FOR ME TO BE AN INSTRUMENT OF WAR. I OWE IT TO HIM TO BE A SCIENTIST FOR THE **WORLD** INSTEAD OF A SOLDIER FOR AMERICA.

SERIOUSLY. NORTH KOREA DID **NOT** DO THIS ALONE. IT'S A SMALL COUNTRY. WHERE'D THEY EVEN FIND ENOUGH METAL TO **BUILD** THIS THING? HMM?

OH, YOU'RE KIDDING ME.

BRAKKA DAKKA

YOU DO **NOT** OPEN UP YOUR HUGE WAR MACHINE TO SHOOT AT THE BULLETPROOF ROBOT.

BLAM BLAMBLAM

AMATEURS.

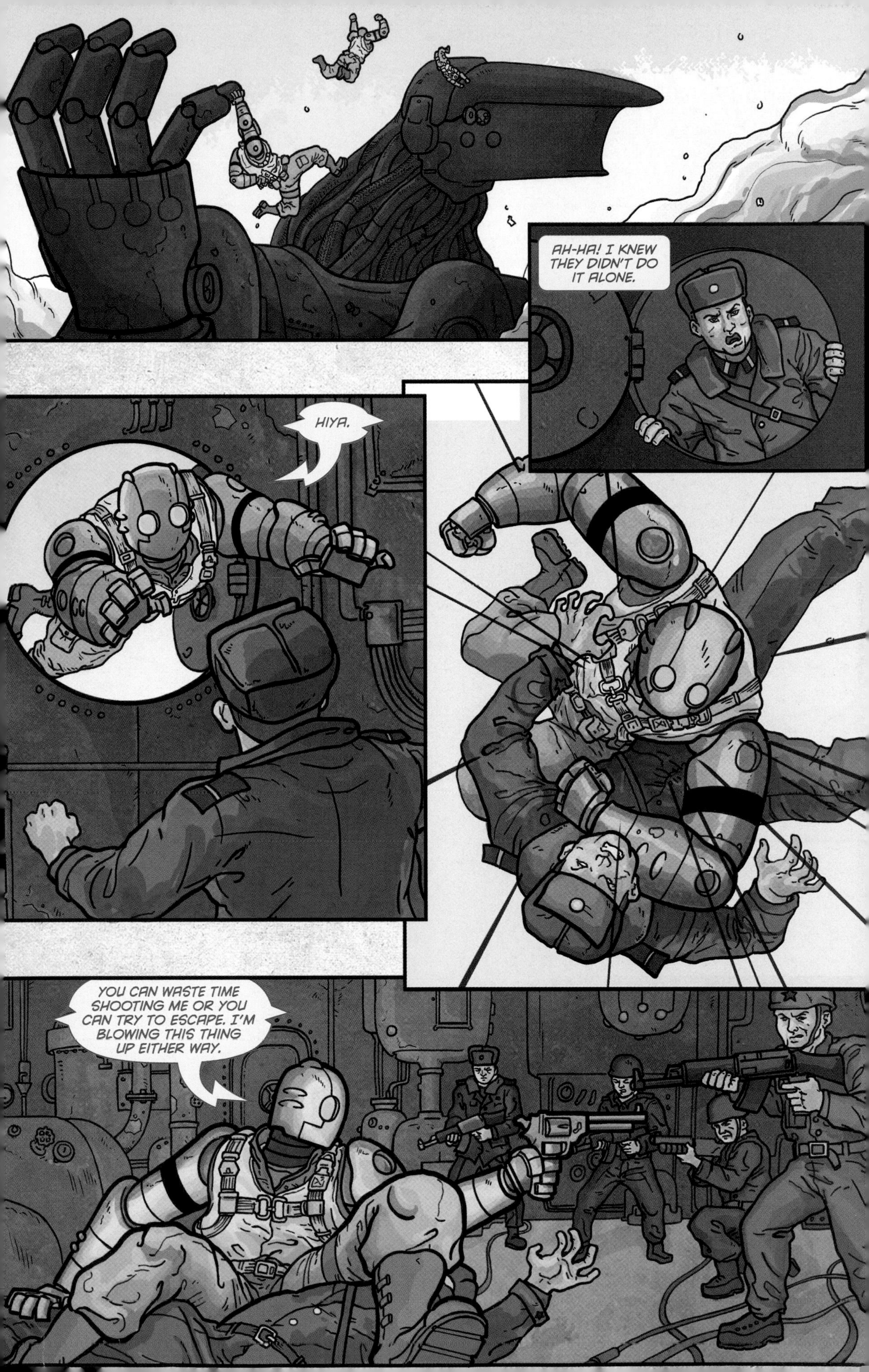
AH-HA! I KNEW THEY DIDN'T DO IT ALONE.
HIYA.
YOU CAN WASTE TIME SHOOTING ME OR YOU CAN TRY TO ESCAPE. I'M BLOWING THIS THING UP EITHER WAY.

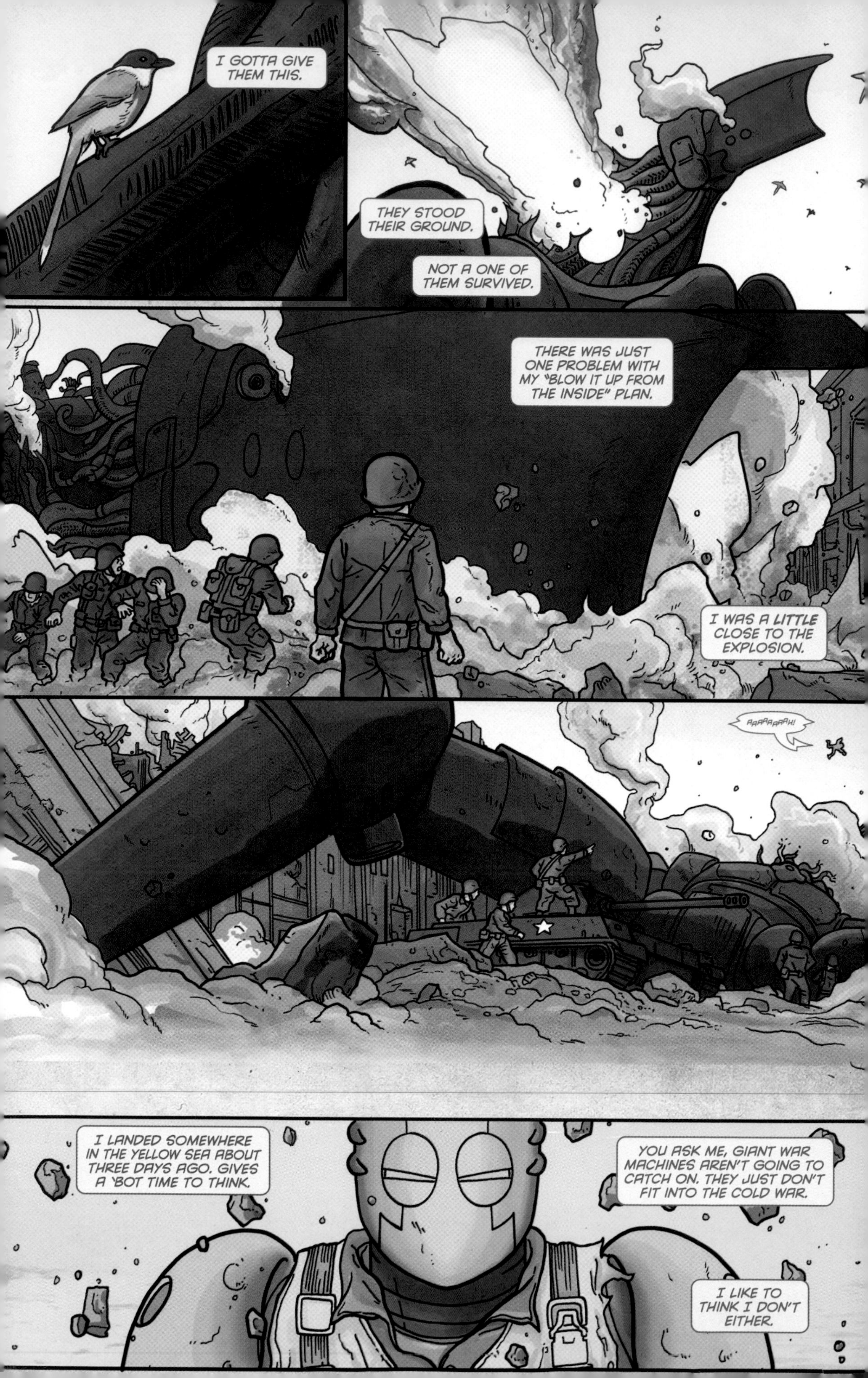
I GOTTA GIVE THEM THIS.
THEY STOOD THEIR GROUND.
NOT A ONE OF THEM SURVIVED.
THERE WAS JUST ONE PROBLEM WITH MY "BLOW IT UP FROM THE INSIDE" PLAN.
I WAS A LITTLE CLOSE TO THE EXPLOSION.
AAAAAAAAH!
I LANDED SOMEWHERE IN THE YELLOW SEA ABOUT THREE DAYS AGO. GIVES A 'BOT TIME TO THINK.
YOU ASK ME, GIANT WAR MACHINES AREN'T GOING TO CATCH ON. THEY JUST DON'T FIT INTO THE COLD WAR.
I LIKE TO THINK I DON'T EITHER.

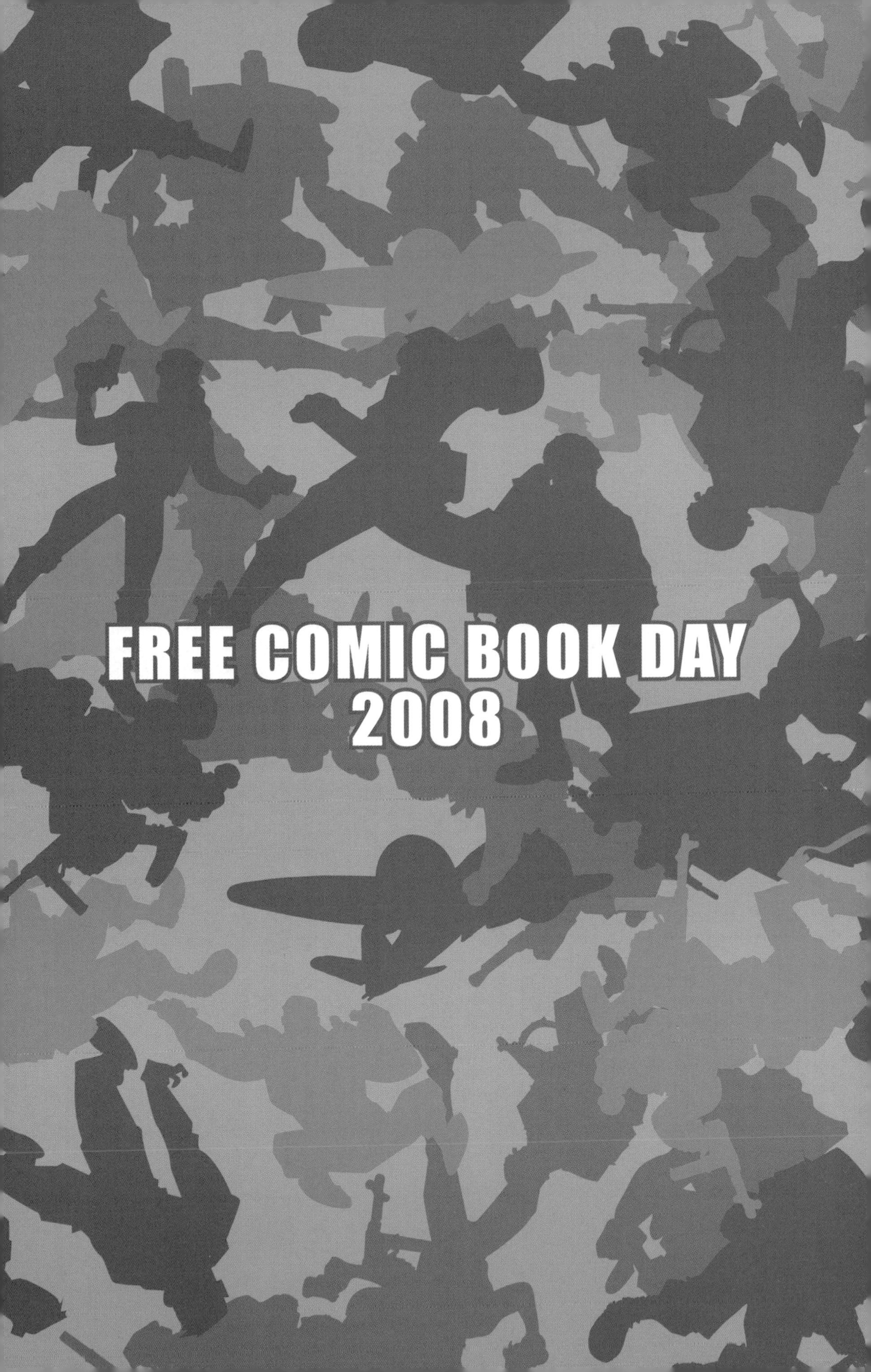
FREE COMIC BOOK DAY
2008

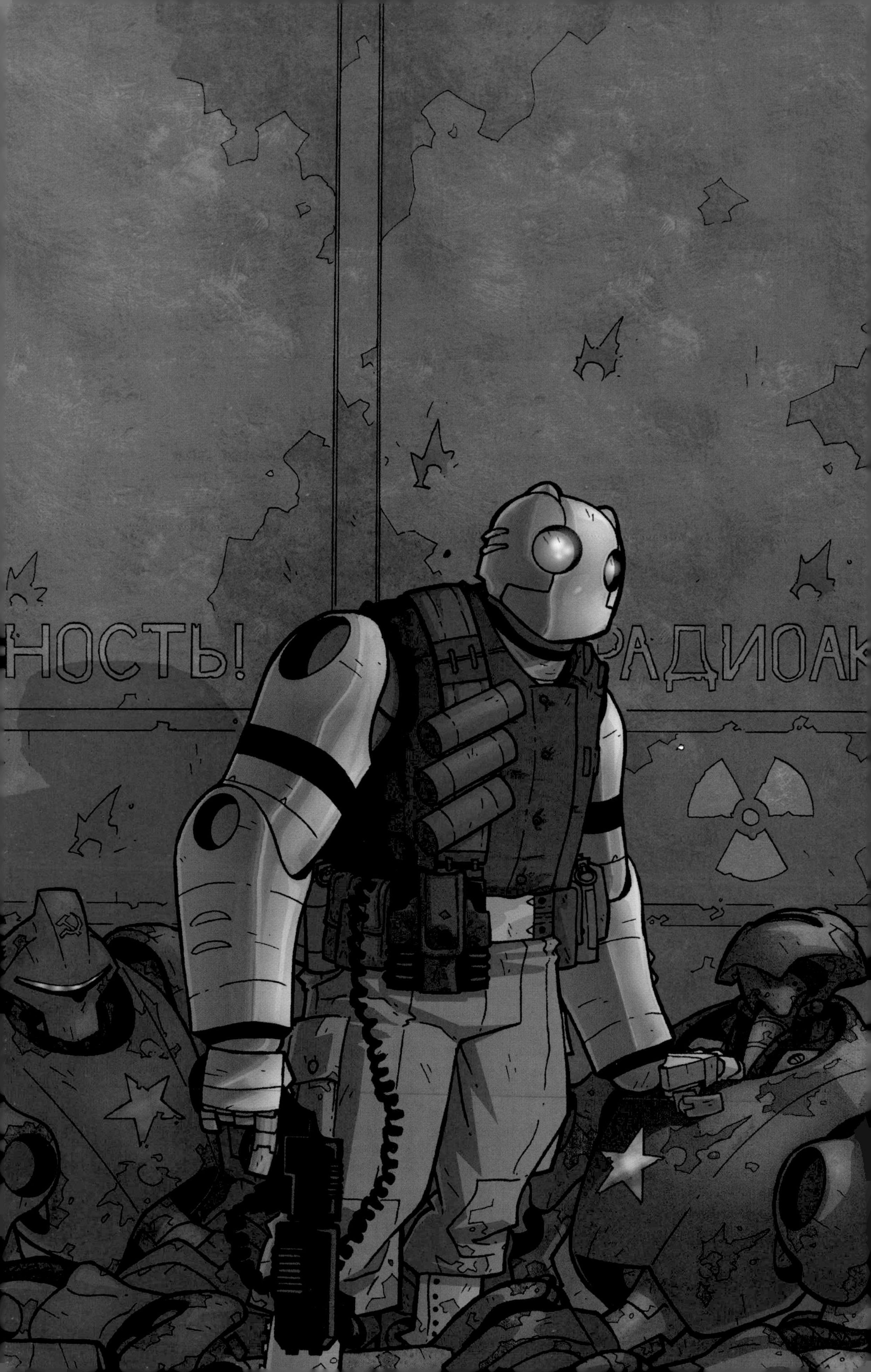
НОСТЬ!
РАДИОАК

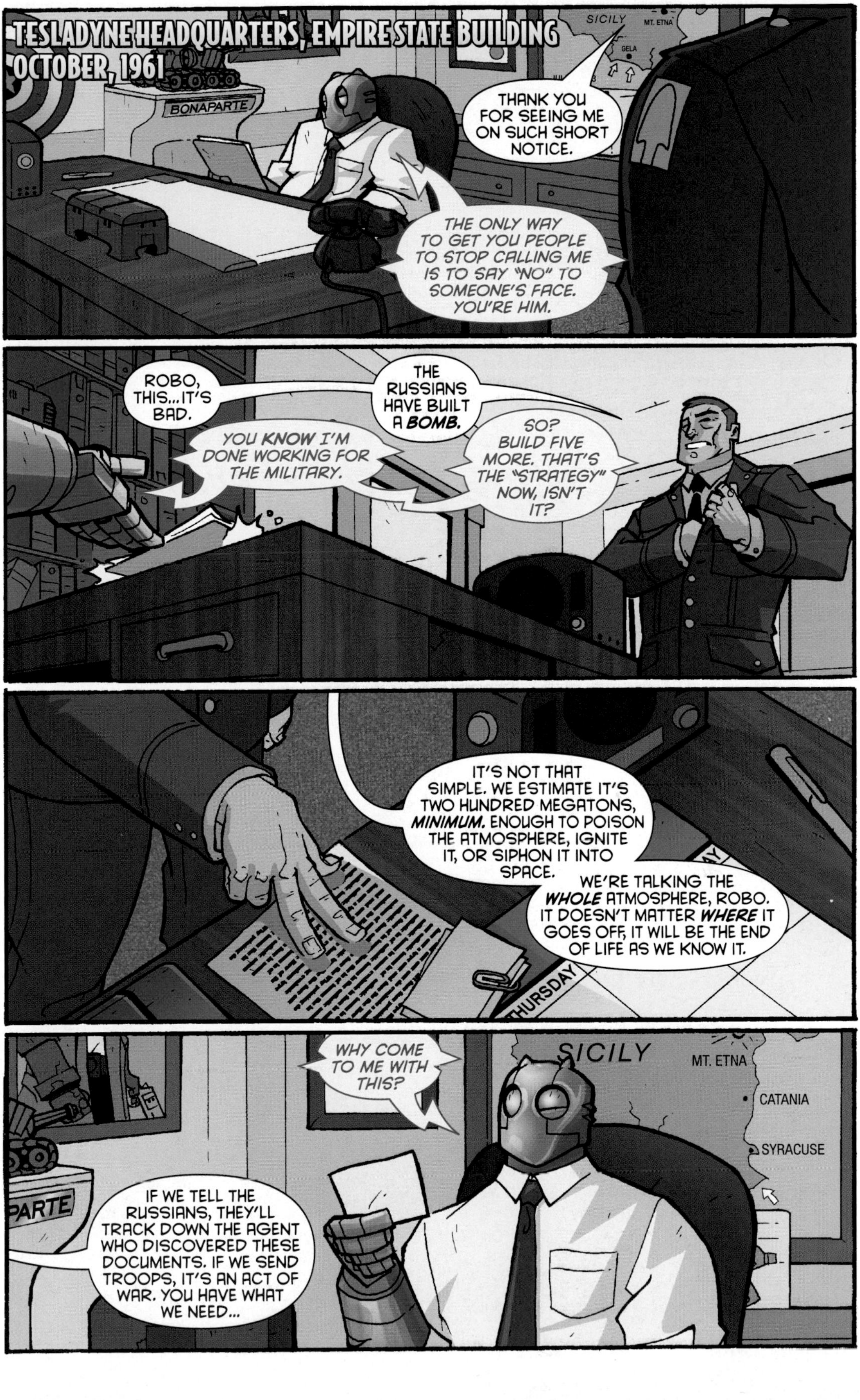
TESLADYNE HEADQUARTERS, EMPIRE STATE BUILDING
OCTOBER, 1961
SICILY
MT. ETNA
GELA
BONAPARTE
THANK YOU FOR SEEING ME ON SUCH SHORT NOTICE.
THE ONLY WAY TO GET YOU PEOPLE TO STOP CALLING ME IS TO SAY "NO" TO SOMEONE'S FACE. YOU'RE HIM.
ROBO, THIS...IT'S BAD.
THE RUSSIANS HAVE BUILT A BOMB.
YOU KNOW I'M DONE WORKING FOR THE MILITARY.
SO? BUILD FIVE MORE. THAT'S THE "STRATEGY" NOW, ISN'T IT?
IT'S NOT THAT SIMPLE. WE ESTIMATE IT'S TWO HUNDRED MEGATONS, MINIMUM. ENOUGH TO POISON THE ATMOSPHERE, IGNITE IT, OR SIPHON IT INTO SPACE.
WE'RE TALKING THE WHOLE ATMOSPHERE, ROBO. IT DOESN'T MATTER WHERE IT GOES OFF, IT WILL BE THE END OF LIFE AS WE KNOW IT.
THURSDAY
WHY COME TO ME WITH THIS?
SICILY
MT. ETNA
CATANIA
SYRACUSE
PARTE
IF WE TELL THE RUSSIANS, THEY'LL TRACK DOWN THE AGENT WHO DISCOVERED THESE DOCUMENTS. IF WE SEND TROOPS, IT'S AN ACT OF WAR. YOU HAVE WHAT WE NEED...

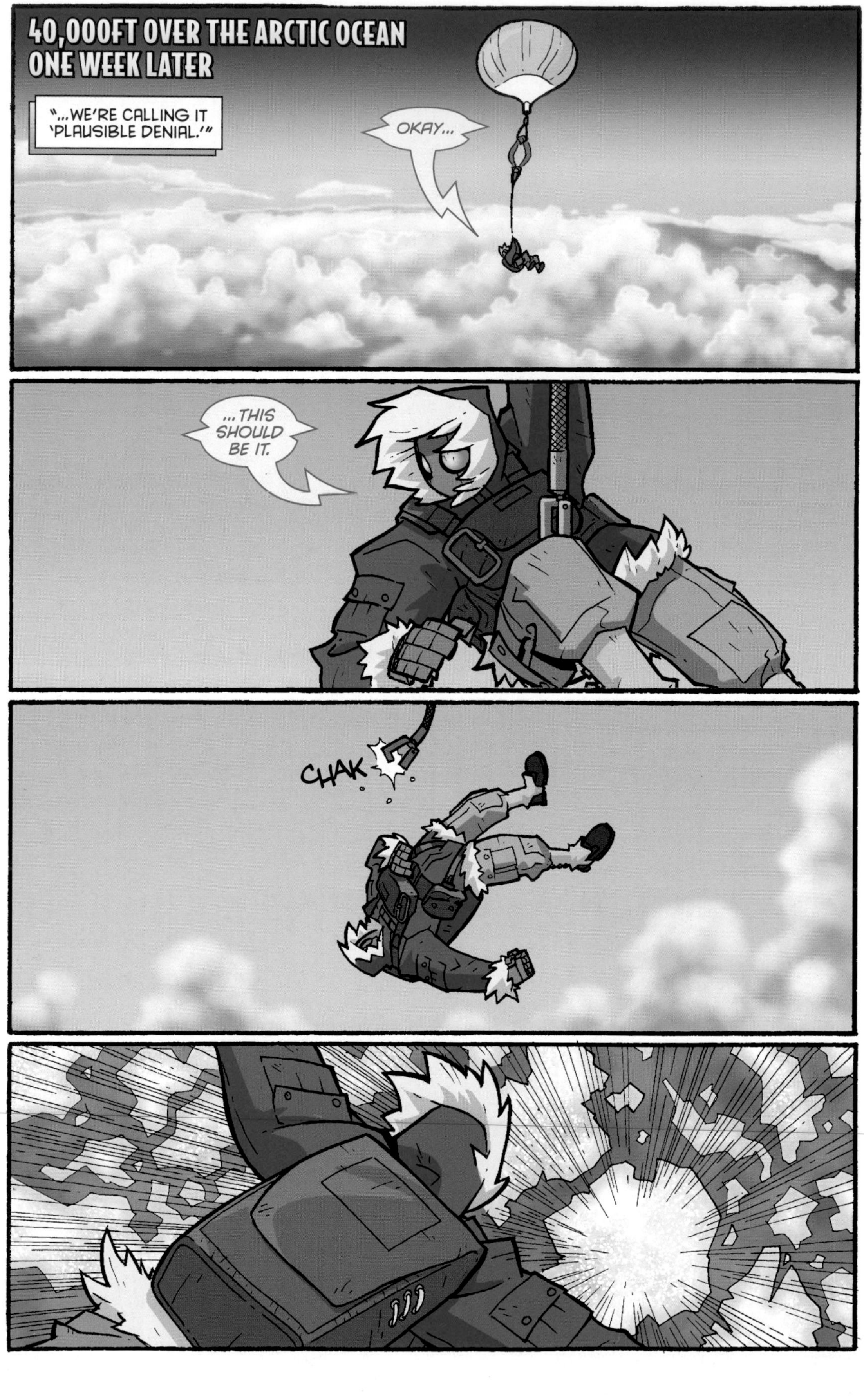
40,000FT OVER THE ARCTIC OCEAN
ONE WEEK LATER
"...WE'RE CALLING IT 'PLAUSIBLE DENIAL.'"
OKAY...
...THIS SHOULD BE IT.
CHAK

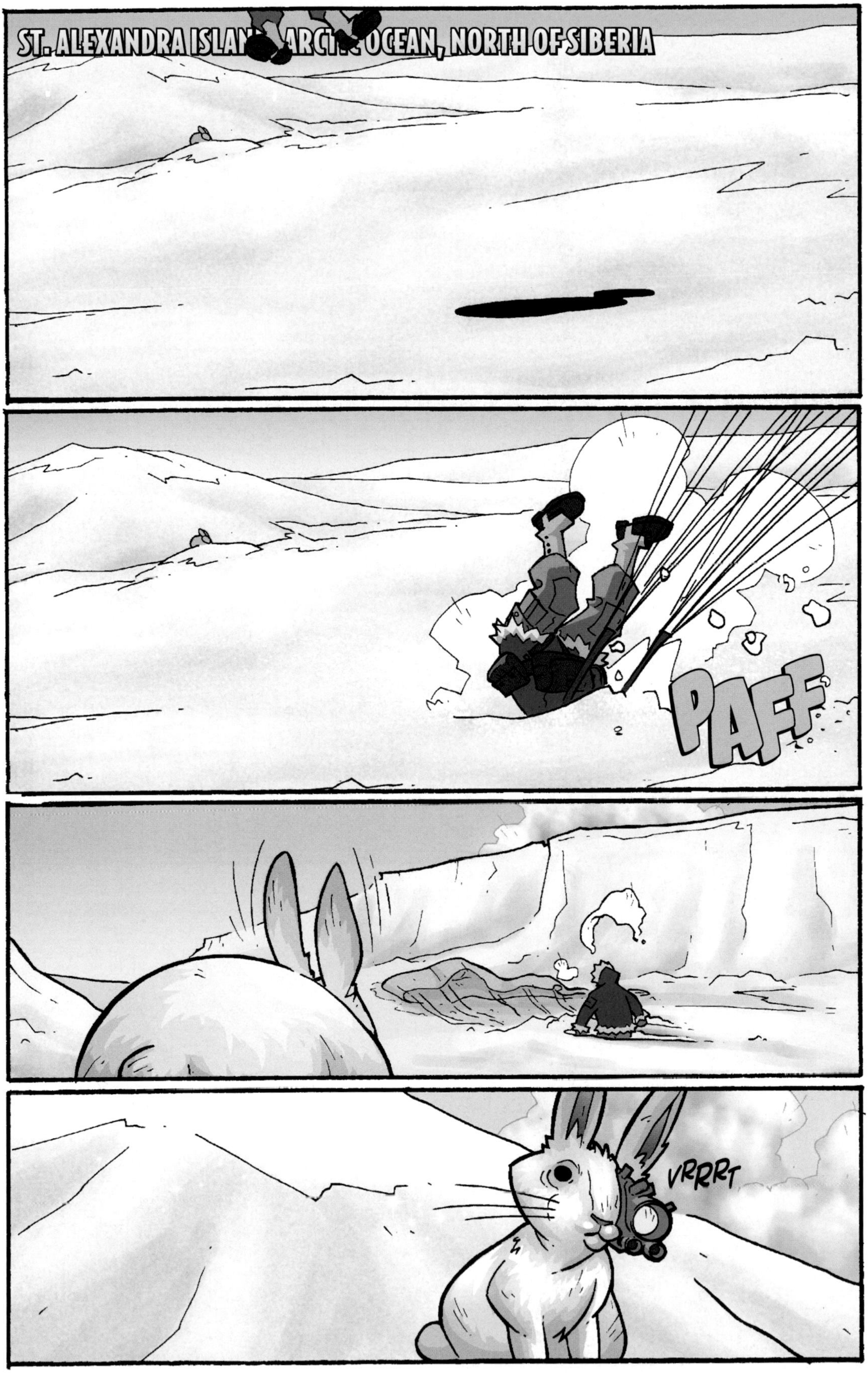
ST. ALEXANDRA ISLAN ARCTI OCEAN, NORTH OF SIBERIA
PAFF
VRRRT

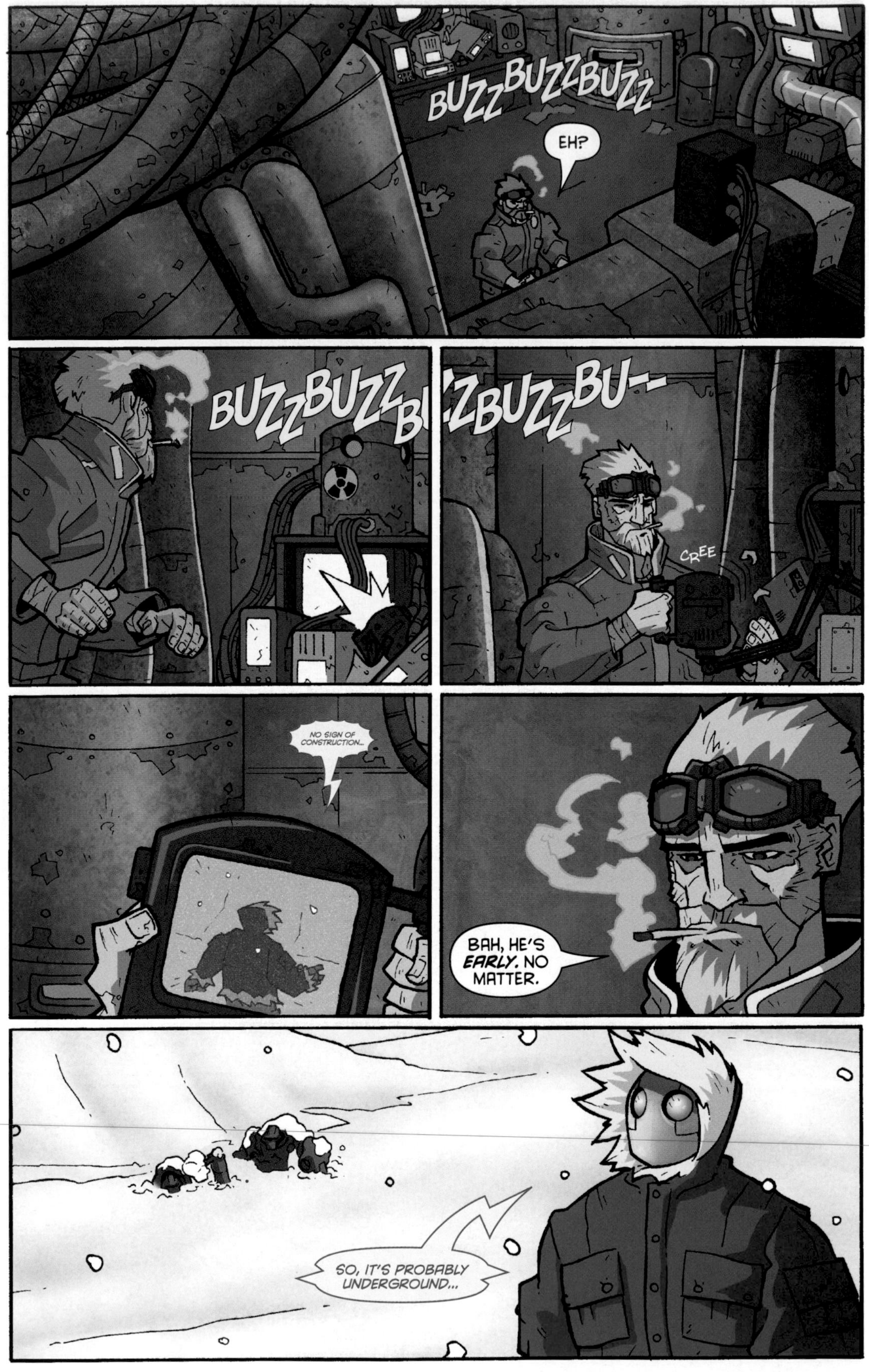
BUZZBUZZBUZZ
EH?
BUZZBUZZBUZZBUZZBU--
CREE
NO SIGN OF CONSTRUCTION...
BAH, HE'S *EARLY.* NO MATTER.
SO, IT'S PROBABLY UNDERGROUND...

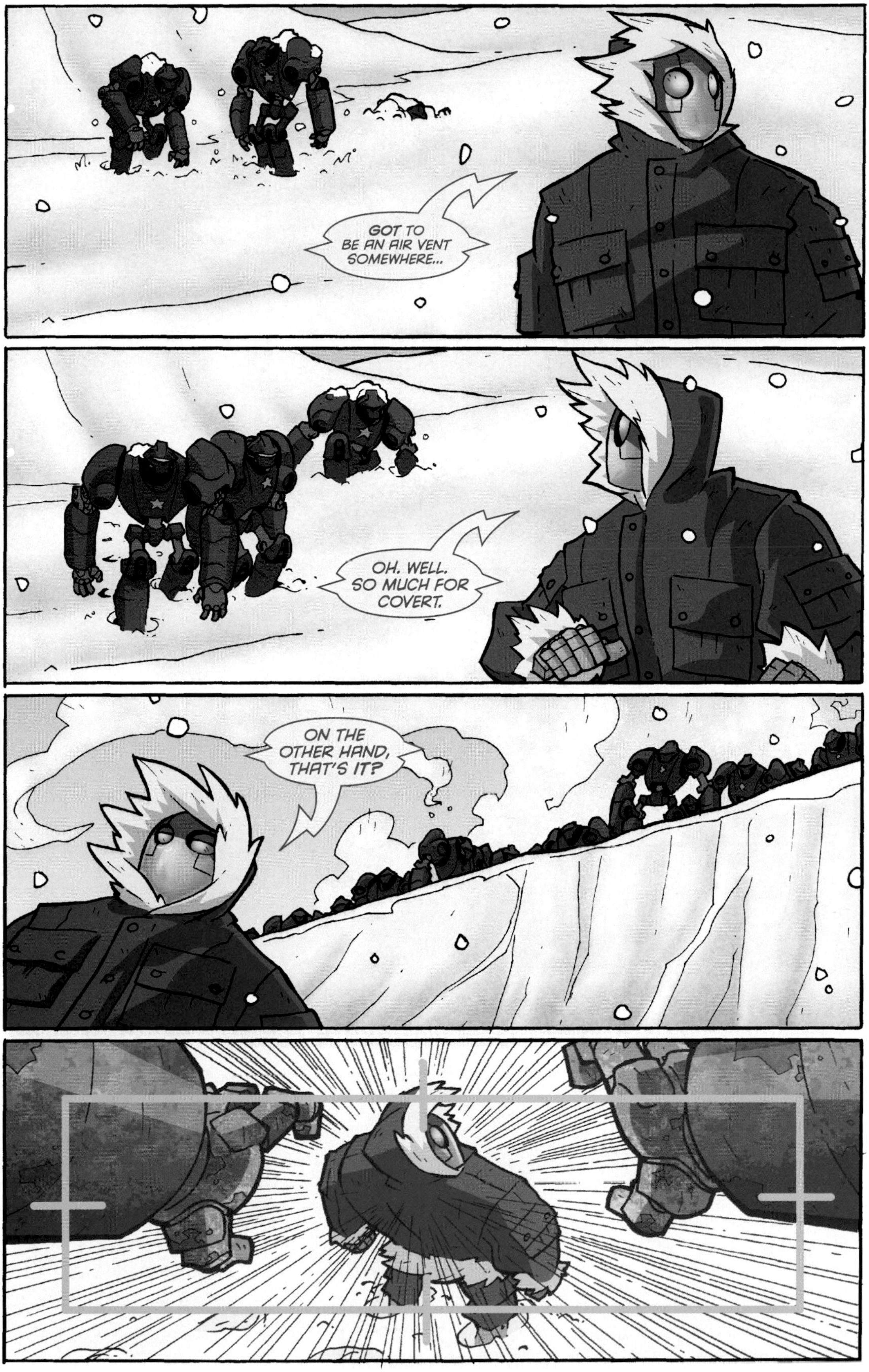
GOT TO BE AN AIR VENT SOMEWHERE...
OH. WELL. SO MUCH FOR COVERT.
ON THE OTHER HAND, THAT'S IT?

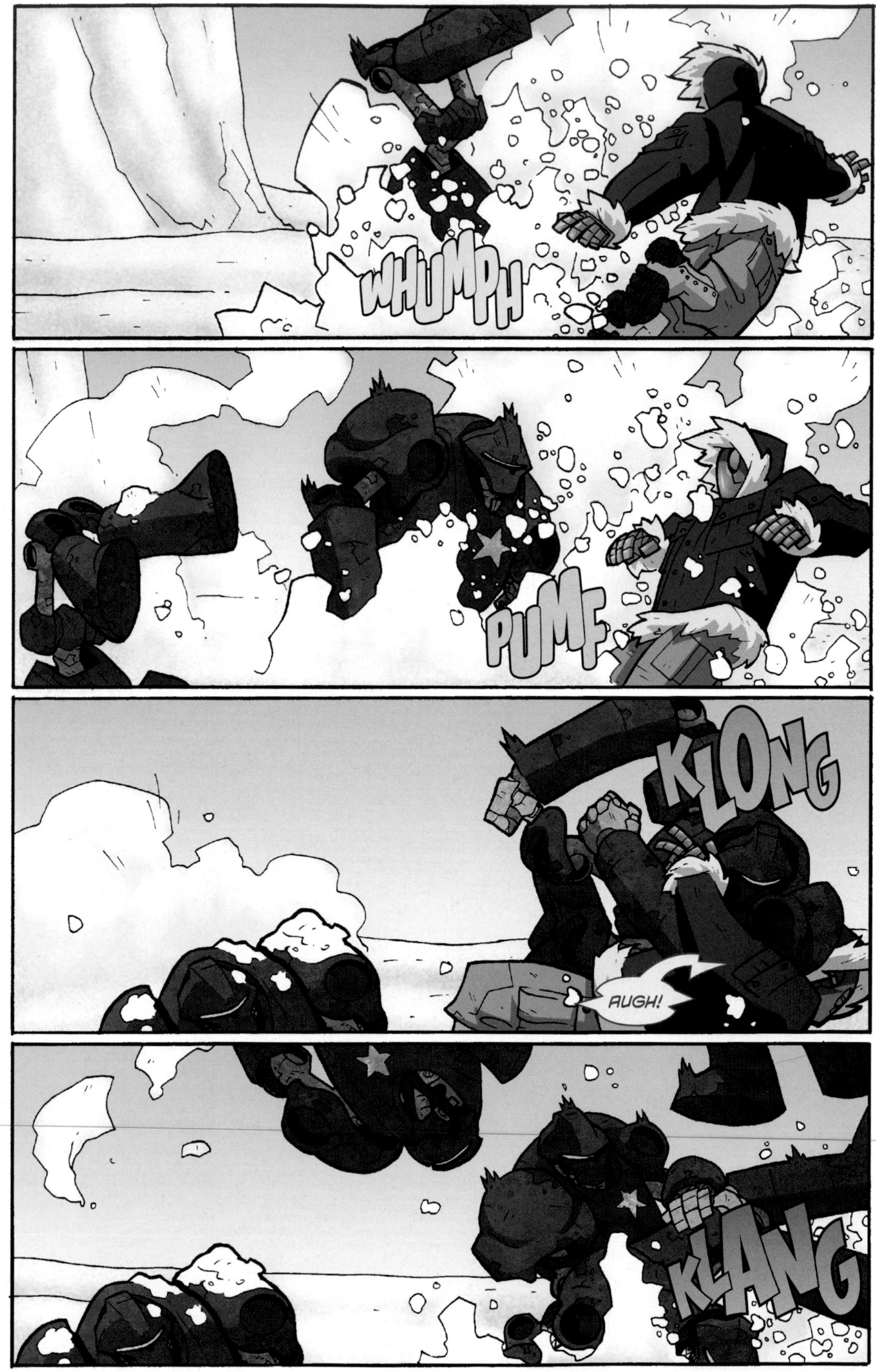
WHUMPH
PUMF
KLONG
AUGH!
KLANG

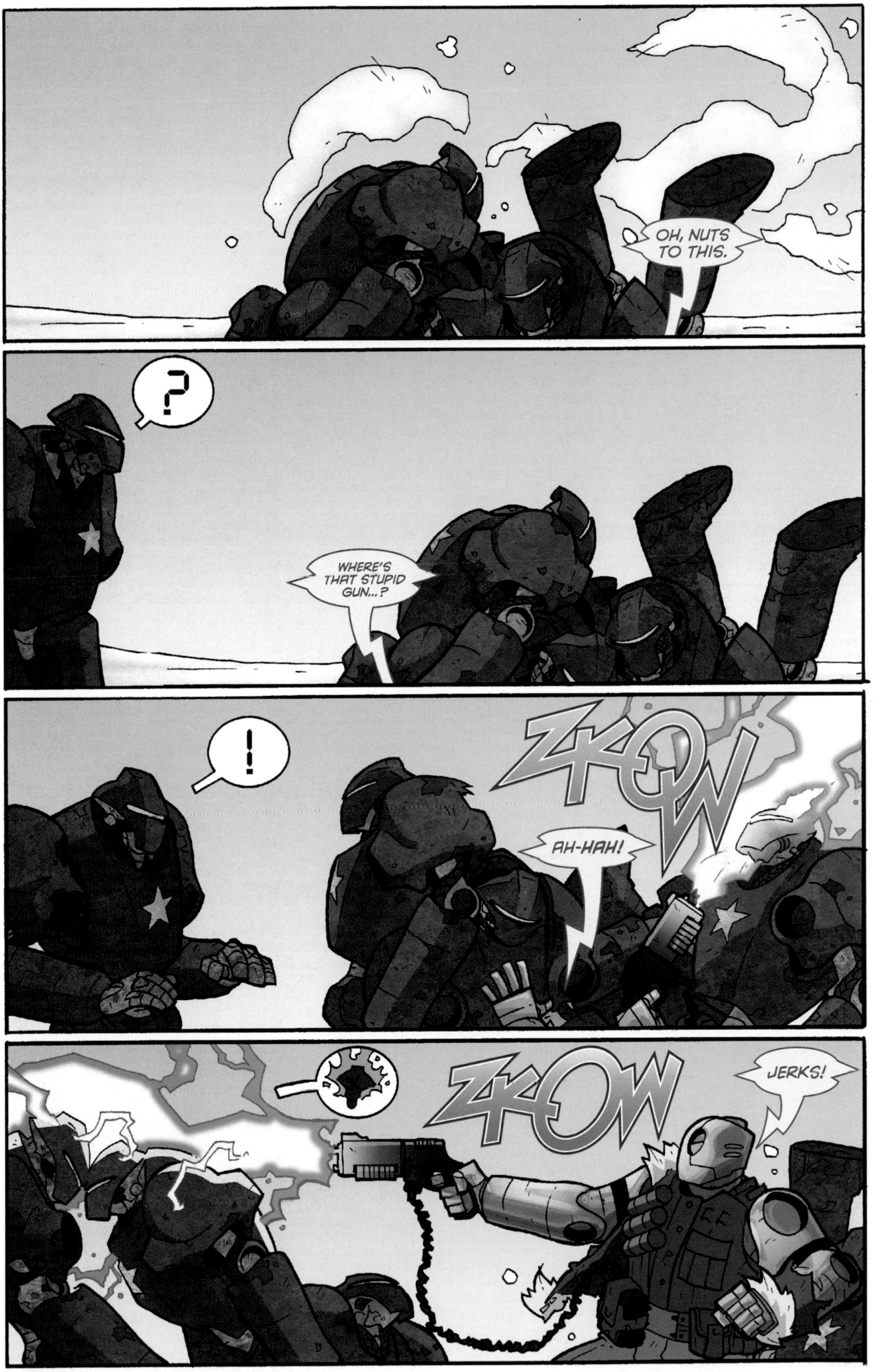
OH, NUTS TO THIS.
?
WHERE'S THAT STUPID GUN...?
!
ZKOW
AH-HAH!
ZKOW
JERKS!

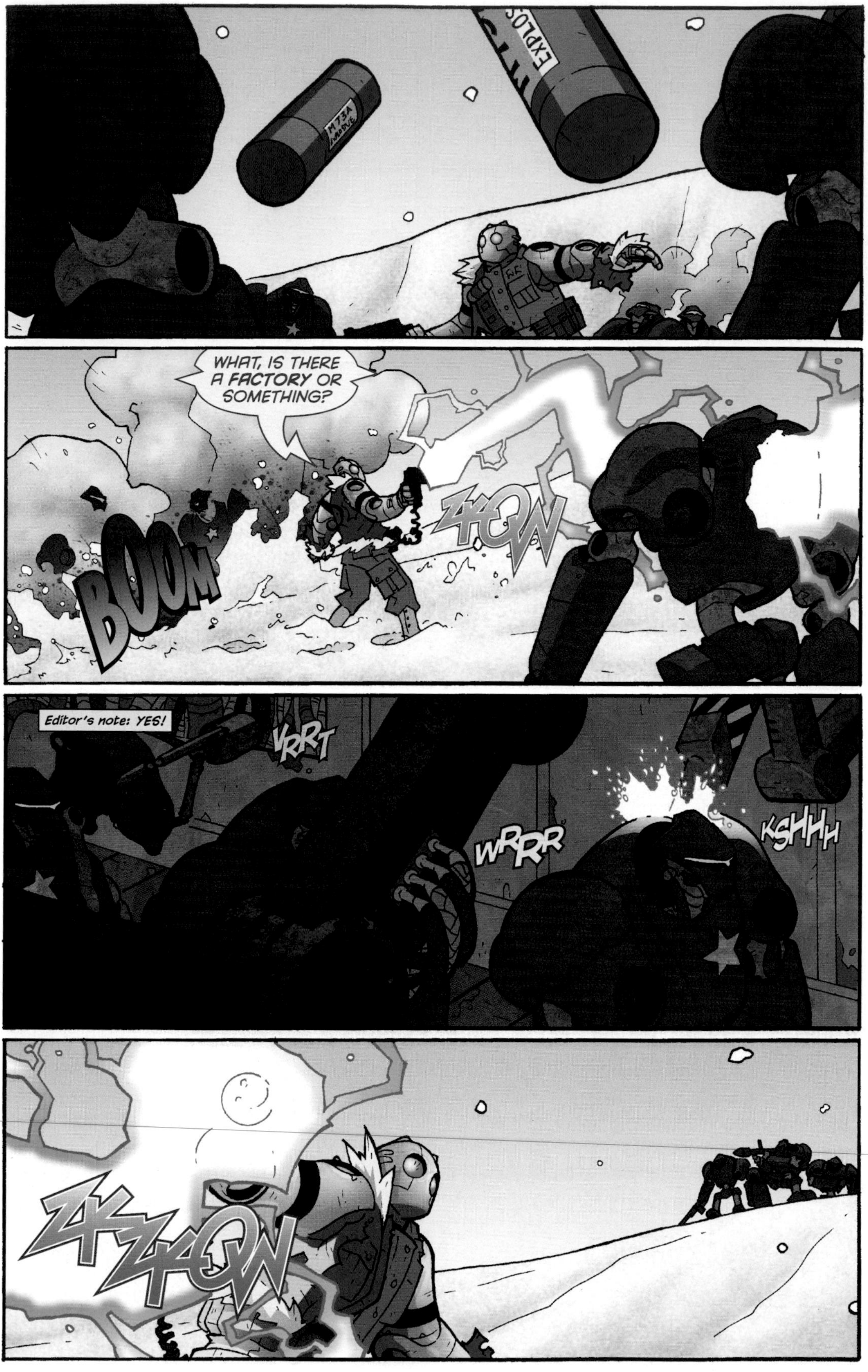
M73A
EXPLOS
WHAT, IS THERE A FACTORY OR SOMETHING?
BOOM
ZZOW
Editor's note: YES!
VRRT
WRRR
KSHHH
ZKZKOW

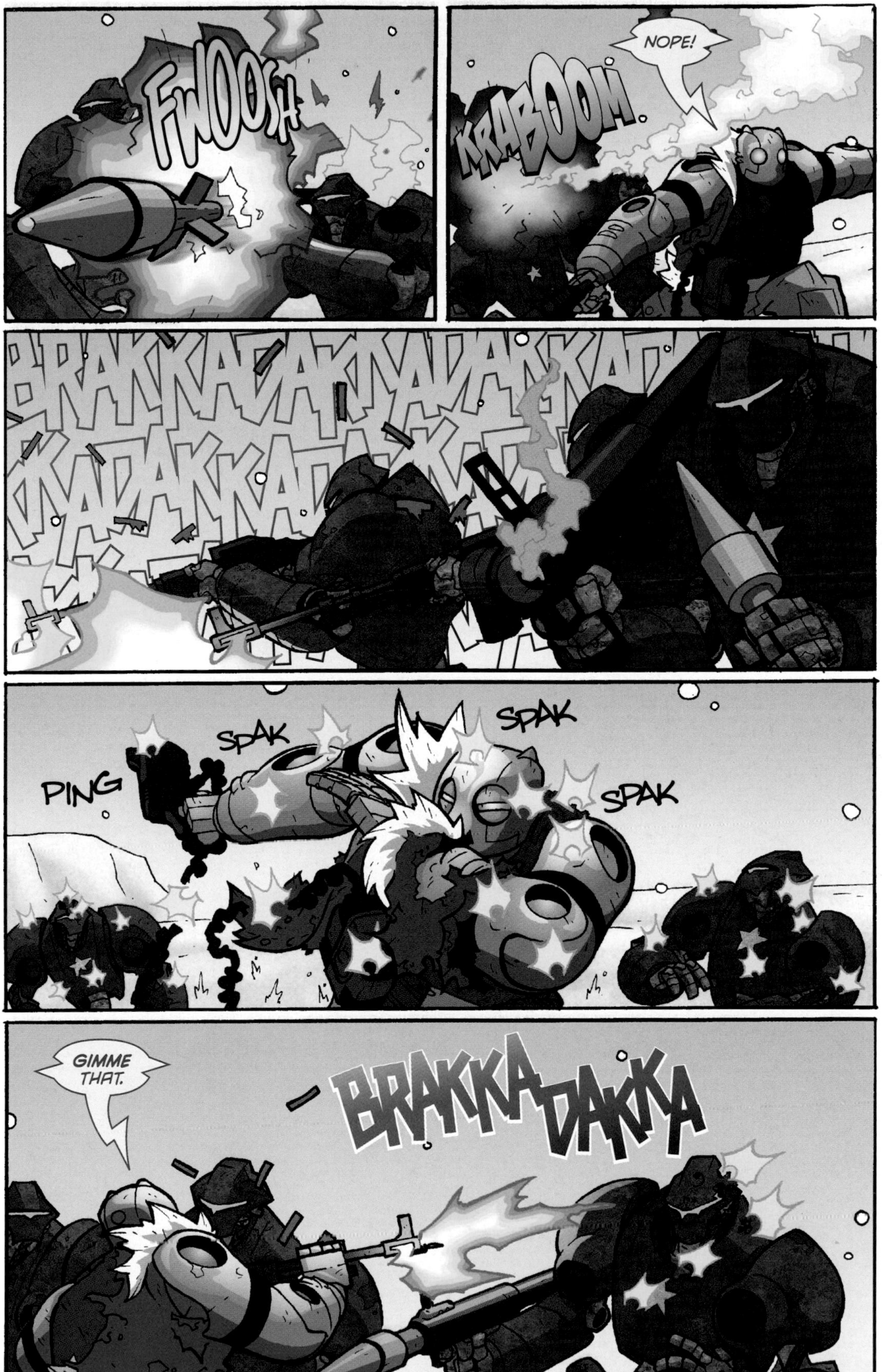
FWOOSH
NOPE!
KRABOOM
BRAKKADAKKADAKKADAKKA
SPAK
PING
SPAK
SPAK
GIMME THAT.
BRAKKA DAKKA

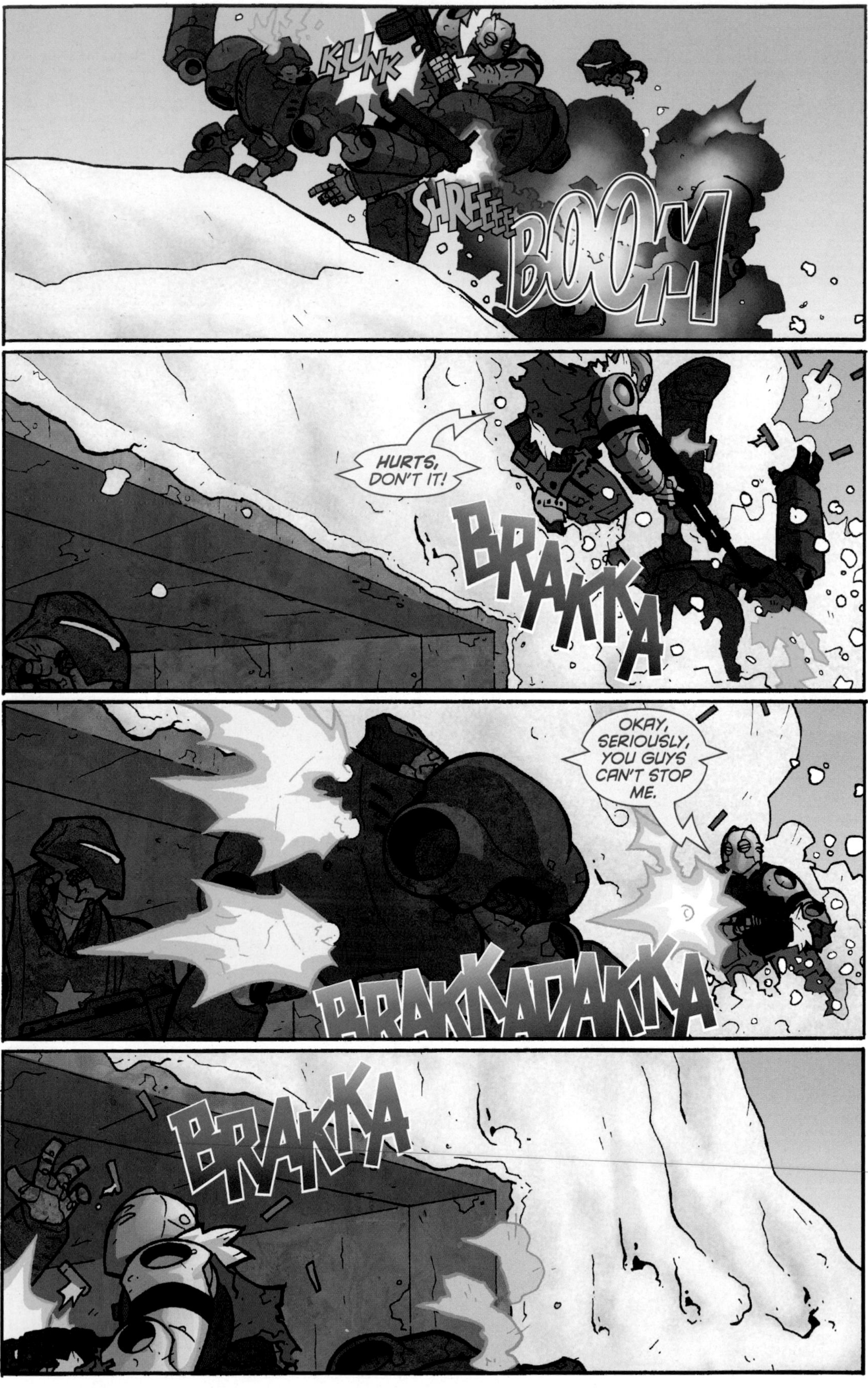
KLUNK
SHREEEE
BOOM
HURTS, DON'T IT!
BRAKKA
OKAY, SERIOUSLY, YOU GUYS CAN'T STOP ME.
BRAKKADAKKA
BRAKKA

I WAS DOING PRETTY GOOD UNTIL THE END THERE...

YOU DO NOT KNOW WHO I AM, DO YOU?

I KNOW YOU'VE GOT THE BEST CLUB HOUSE ON THE BLOCK.

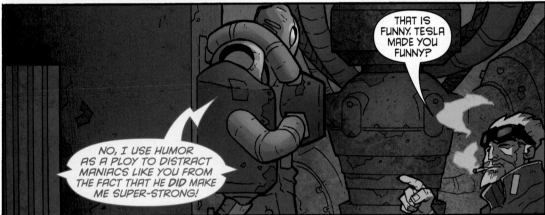

THAT IS FUNNY. TESLA MADE YOU FUNNY?

NO, I USE HUMOR AS A PLOY TO DISTRACT MANIACS LIKE YOU FROM THE FACT THAT HE *DID* MAKE ME SUPER-STRONG!

YEEARGH!

YES, VERY STRONG. THAT IS WHY WE USED THE *INCREDIBLY* STRONG ELECTROMAGNETIC RESTRAINTS.

OH.

THEY DID NOT TELL YOU MY NAME BECAUSE *I DO NOT EXIST.*

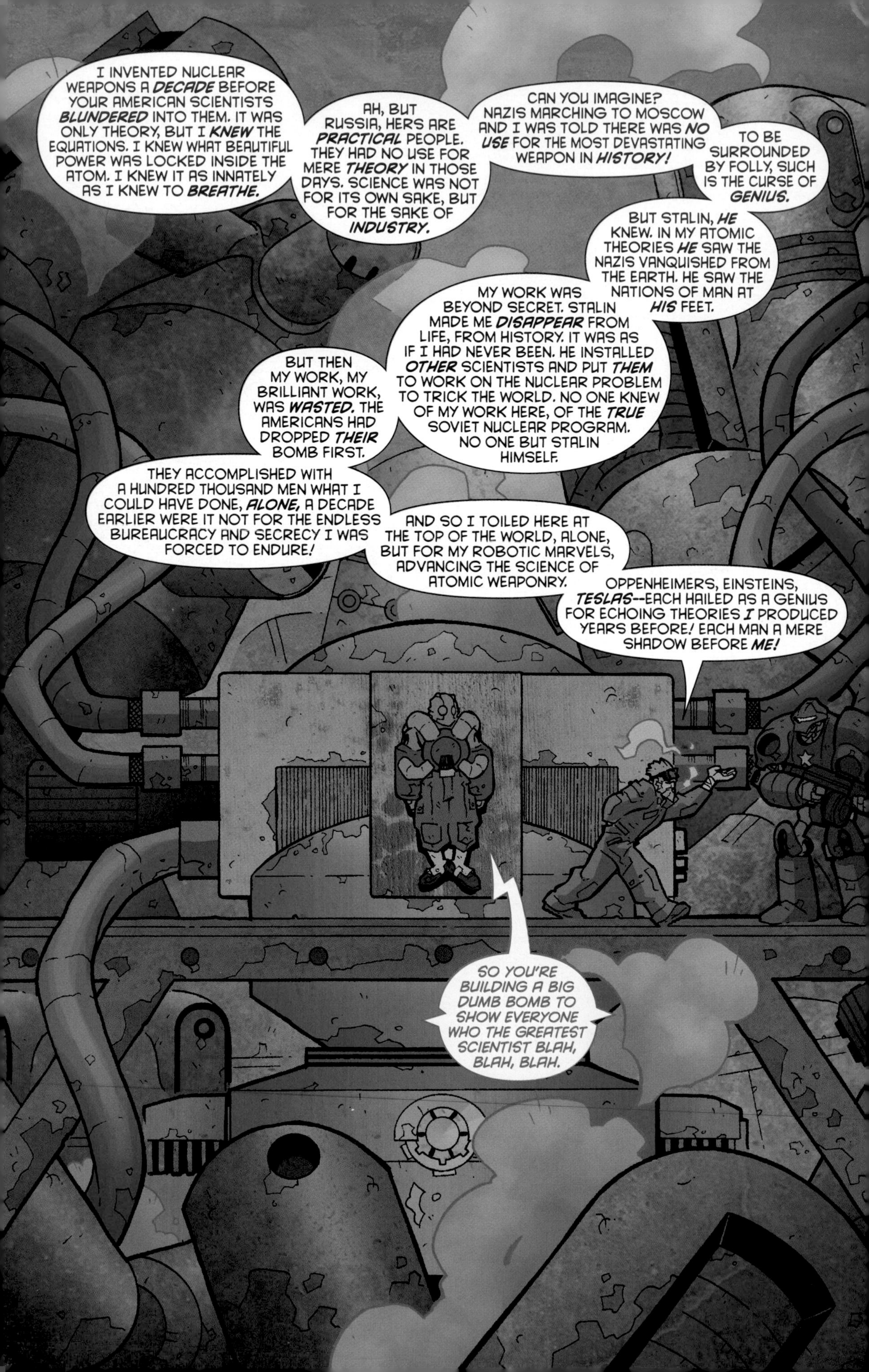
I INVENTED NUCLEAR WEAPONS A *DECADE* BEFORE YOUR AMERICAN SCIENTISTS *BLUNDERED* INTO THEM. IT WAS ONLY THEORY, BUT I *KNEW* THE EQUATIONS. I KNEW WHAT BEAUTIFUL POWER WAS LOCKED INSIDE THE ATOM. I KNEW IT AS INNATELY AS I KNEW TO *BREATHE.*
AH, BUT RUSSIA, HERS ARE *PRACTICAL* PEOPLE. THEY HAD NO USE FOR MERE *THEORY* IN THOSE DAYS. SCIENCE WAS NOT FOR ITS OWN SAKE, BUT FOR THE SAKE OF *INDUSTRY.*
CAN YOU IMAGINE? NAZIS MARCHING TO MOSCOW AND I WAS TOLD THERE WAS *NO USE* FOR THE MOST DEVASTATING WEAPON IN *HISTORY!*
TO BE SURROUNDED BY FOLLY, SUCH IS THE CURSE OF *GENIUS.*
BUT STALIN, *HE* KNEW. IN MY ATOMIC THEORIES *HE* SAW THE NAZIS VANQUISHED FROM THE EARTH. HE SAW THE NATIONS OF MAN AT *HIS* FEET.
MY WORK WAS BEYOND SECRET. STALIN MADE ME *DISAPPEAR* FROM LIFE, FROM HISTORY. IT WAS AS IF I HAD NEVER BEEN. HE INSTALLED *OTHER* SCIENTISTS AND PUT *THEM* TO WORK ON THE NUCLEAR PROBLEM TO TRICK THE WORLD. NO ONE KNEW OF MY WORK HERE, OF THE *TRUE* SOVIET NUCLEAR PROGRAM. NO ONE BUT STALIN HIMSELF.
BUT THEN MY WORK, MY BRILLIANT WORK, WAS *WASTED.* THE AMERICANS HAD DROPPED *THEIR* BOMB FIRST.
THEY ACCOMPLISHED WITH A HUNDRED THOUSAND MEN WHAT I COULD HAVE DONE, *ALONE,* A DECADE EARLIER WERE IT NOT FOR THE ENDLESS BUREAUCRACY AND SECRECY I WAS FORCED TO ENDURE!
AND SO I TOILED HERE AT THE TOP OF THE WORLD, ALONE, BUT FOR MY ROBOTIC MARVELS, ADVANCING THE SCIENCE OF ATOMIC WEAPONRY.
OPPENHEIMERS, EINSTEINS, *TESLAS*--EACH HAILED AS A GENIUS FOR ECHOING THEORIES *I* PRODUCED YEARS BEFORE! EACH MAN A MERE SHADOW BEFORE *ME!*
*SO YOU'RE BUILDING A BIG DUMB BOMB TO SHOW EVERYONE WHO THE GREATEST SCIENTIST BLAH, BLAH, BLAH.*

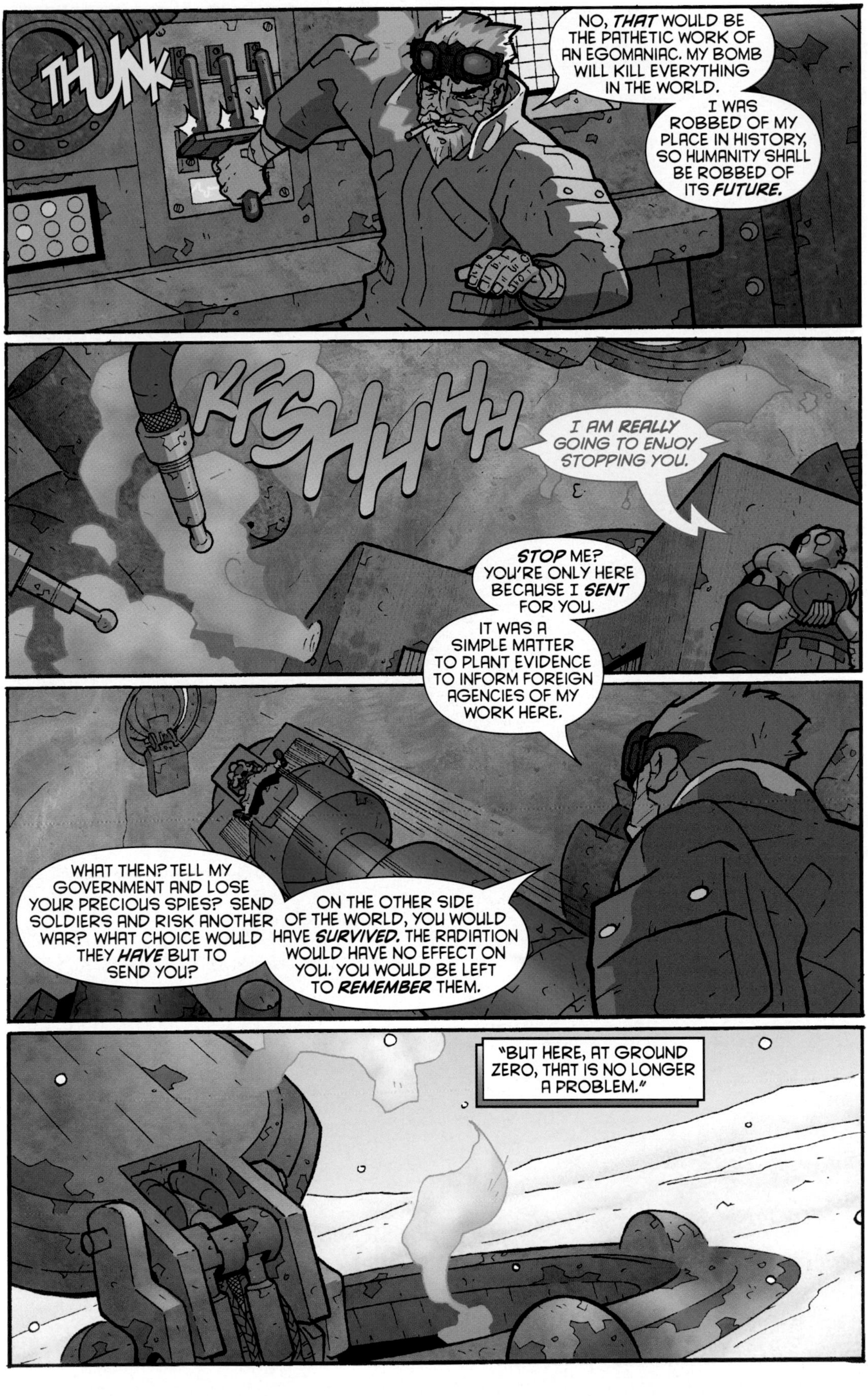
THUNK
NO, THAT WOULD BE THE PATHETIC WORK OF AN EGOMANIAC. MY BOMB WILL KILL EVERYTHING IN THE WORLD.
I WAS ROBBED OF MY PLACE IN HISTORY, SO HUMANITY SHALL BE ROBBED OF ITS FUTURE.
KFSHHHHH
I AM REALLY GOING TO ENJOY STOPPING YOU.
STOP ME? YOU'RE ONLY HERE BECAUSE I SENT FOR YOU.
IT WAS A SIMPLE MATTER TO PLANT EVIDENCE TO INFORM FOREIGN AGENCIES OF MY WORK HERE.
WHAT THEN? TELL MY GOVERNMENT AND LOSE YOUR PRECIOUS SPIES? SEND SOLDIERS AND RISK ANOTHER WAR? WHAT CHOICE WOULD THEY HAVE BUT TO SEND YOU?
ON THE OTHER SIDE OF THE WORLD, YOU WOULD HAVE SURVIVED. THE RADIATION WOULD HAVE NO EFFECT ON YOU. YOU WOULD BE LEFT TO REMEMBER THEM.
"BUT HERE, AT GROUND ZERO, THAT IS NO LONGER A PROBLEM."

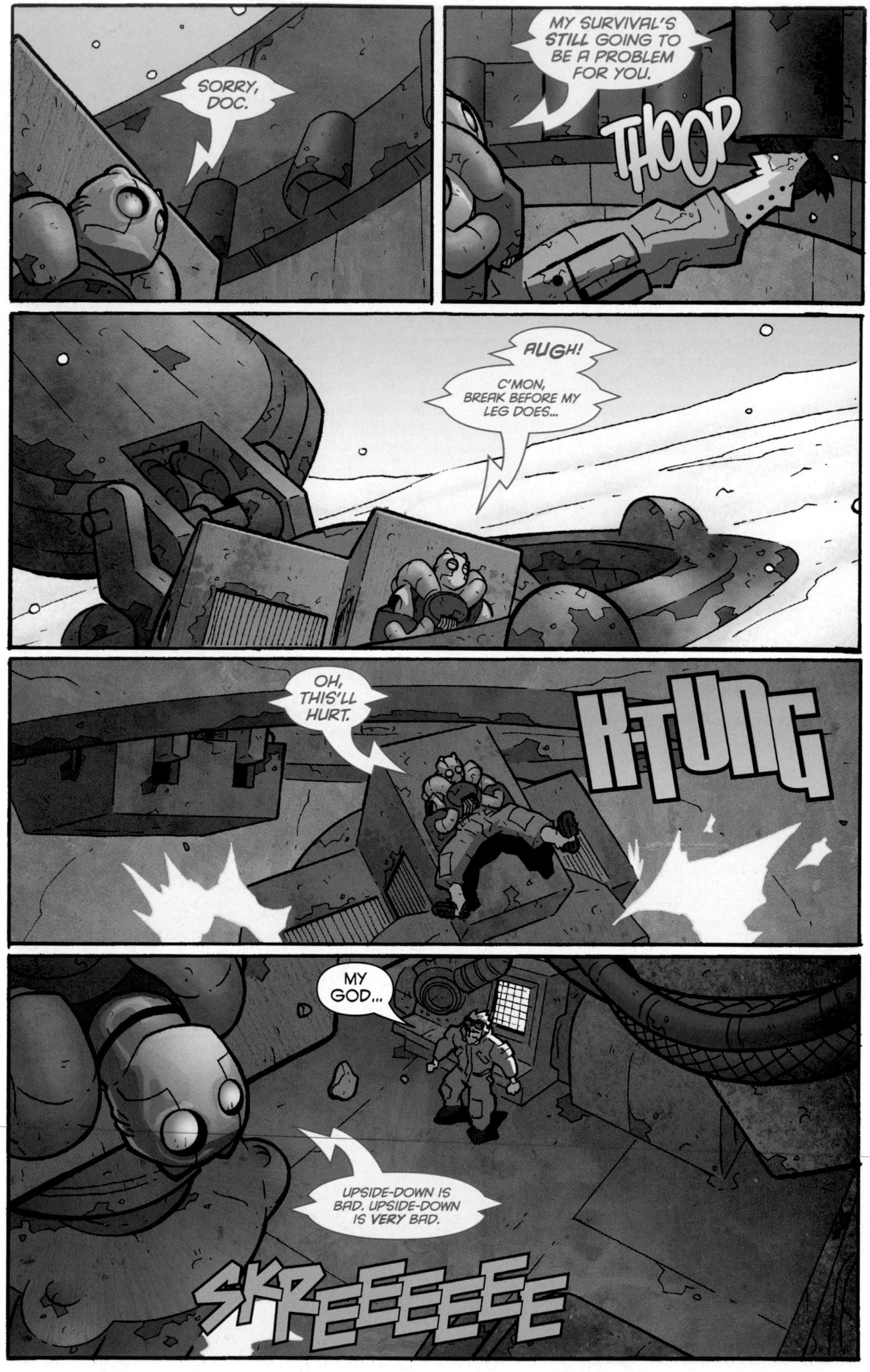
SORRY, DOC.
MY SURVIVAL'S STILL GOING TO BE A PROBLEM FOR YOU.
THOOP
AUGH!
C'MON, BREAK BEFORE MY LEG DOES...
OH, THIS'LL HURT.
K-TUNG
MY GOD...
UPSIDE-DOWN IS BAD. UPSIDE-DOWN IS VERY BAD.
SKREEEEEEE

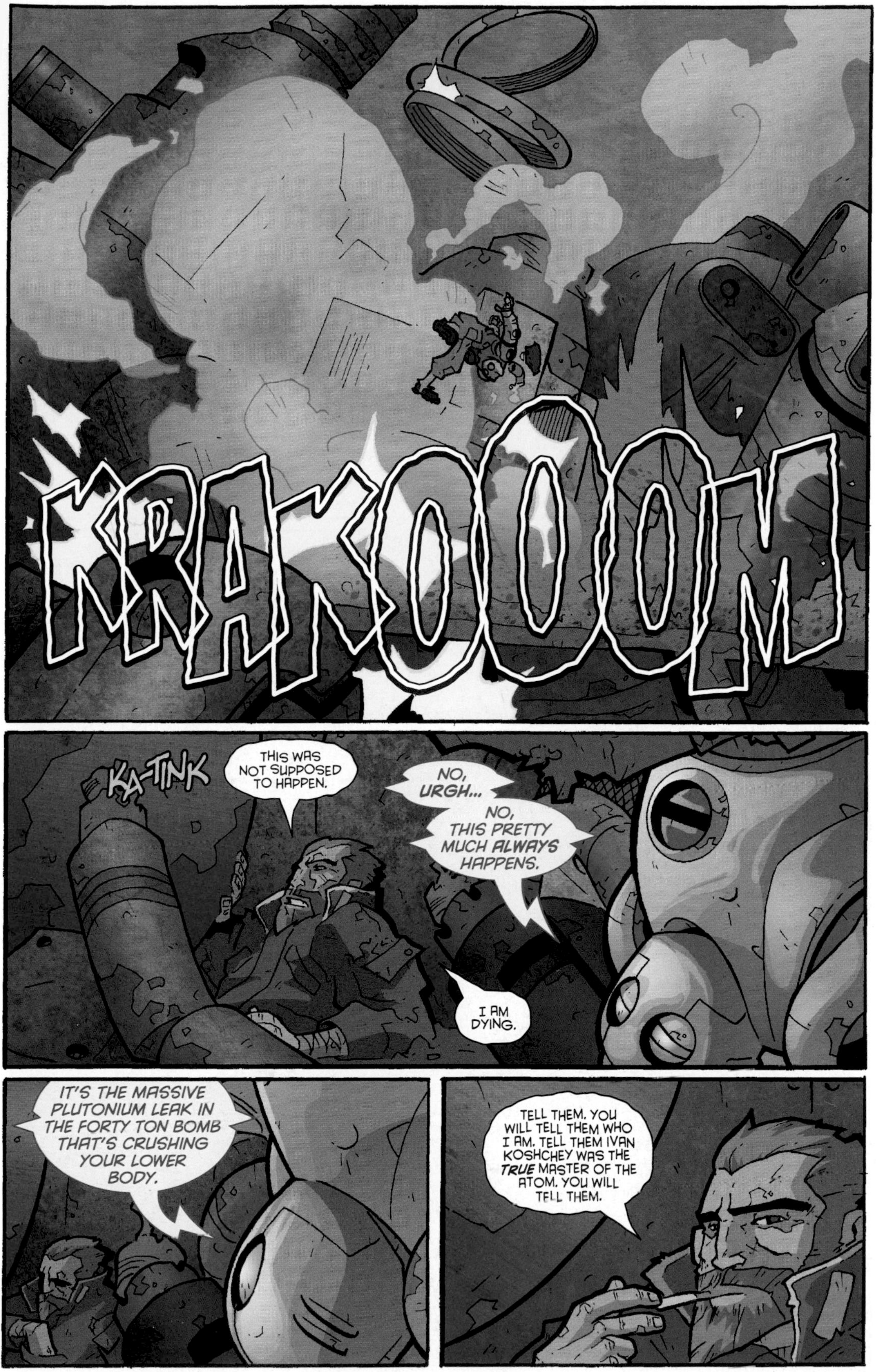
KRAKOOOOM
KA-TINK
THIS WAS NOT SUPPOSED TO HAPPEN.
NO, URGH...
NO, THIS PRETTY MUCH ALWAYS HAPPENS.
I AM DYING.
IT'S THE MASSIVE PLUTONIUM LEAK IN THE FORTY TON BOMB THAT'S CRUSHING YOUR LOWER BODY.
TELL THEM. YOU WILL TELL THEM WHO I AM. TELL THEM IVAN KOSHCHEY WAS THE TRUE MASTER OF THE ATOM. YOU WILL TELL THEM.

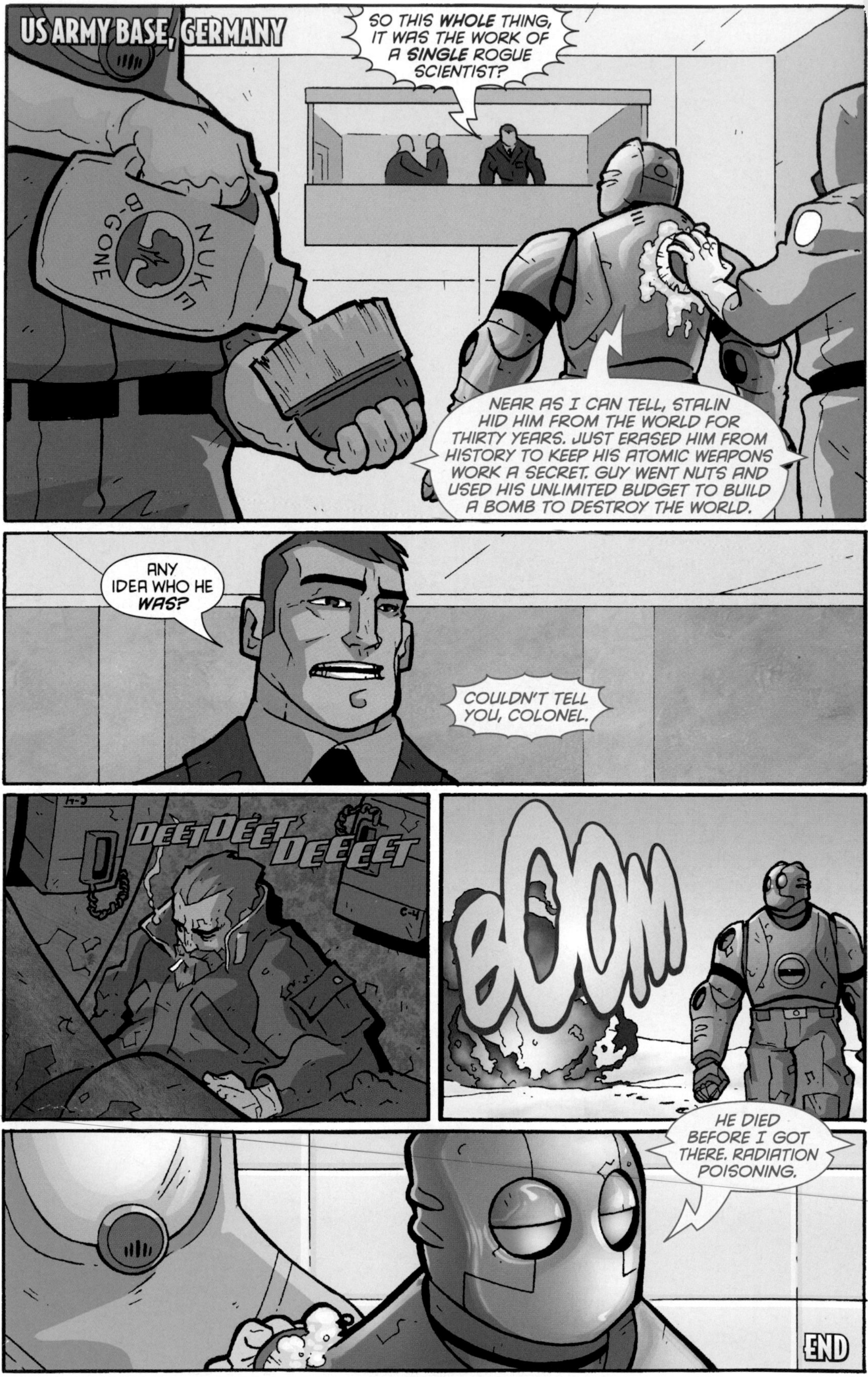
US ARMY BASE, GERMANY
SO THIS WHOLE THING, IT WAS THE WORK OF A SINGLE ROGUE SCIENTIST?
NUKE B-GONE
NEAR AS I CAN TELL, STALIN HID HIM FROM THE WORLD FOR THIRTY YEARS. JUST ERASED HIM FROM HISTORY TO KEEP HIS ATOMIC WEAPONS WORK A SECRET. GUY WENT NUTS AND USED HIS UNLIMITED BUDGET TO BUILD A BOMB TO DESTROY THE WORLD.
ANY IDEA WHO HE WAS?
COULDN'T TELL YOU, COLONEL.
DEETDEET DEEEEET
BOOM
HE DIED BEFORE I GOT THERE. RADIATION POISONING.
END